BURNING ISSUES

By
Allan Wright

A Fire Officer's memoirs

of

Belfast's Firefighters baptism of terrorism

during the troubled years

1968-1988.

September 1999

Published by Rosepark Publishing
40 Rosepark, Donaghadee,
Co. Down BT21 0BN.
Tel/Fax: (01247) 888192
E-mail: allwright@rosepark.softnet.co.uk

Copyright Allan Wright 1999

Printed by Shanway/Creative Graphics
Antrim Road, Belfast

Edited by P.P. Burns

Cartoons by R. Pollock

Cover by Michael McKernon

ISBN 0 9536493 O X
Publisher Prefix 0 9536493

About the Author...

When I was a young child my beloved Mother told me how she stood on the hills at dusk overlooking Belfast in the Spring of 1941 while the German Luftwaffe carried out their Blitz on the city during the Second World War. When they were finally finished and their Mercedes-Benz engines droned away into the night two of our Firefighter Martyrs lay in their final sleep in the ruins of York Street, a principal thoroughfare near the city centre. My Mother used to describe in graphic detail how the city glowed in the dark as it burned for days. Firefighters came from as far away as Dublin to help. This reflects that comradely bond forged in war. There are no words for Border, Nationality, Race, nor Creed, in a Firefighter's lexicon.

So Firefighters had spilled their drops of blood before on the streets of Belfast during conflict. It was not to be their last drop.

Belfast city was to have another similar visitation in the late sixties and early seventies. Only this time the witches cauldron was brewed in the city itself. When that era flickered to extinguishment another of our Firefighter Martyrs lay dead of gunshot wounds in the gutter as the firestorms and gunfire raged around his earthly remains.

Little could I envisage as a child that later, as a young man, while in the Belfast Fire Brigade myself, I would see the first flickering flames of this second maelstrom or that a close personal friend and colleague Allan Wright would in concert with my old Brigade struggle through another nightmare of firestorms and in the process pay such a heavy price for dispensing common humanity and compassion to the Public they joined the Brigade to so unreservedly serve.

Allan was born in April 1943 into a working class family, in an area of South Belfast close to the Queen's University in the very heartland of the City.

iii

Immediately prior to joining the Fire Brigade he was employed as a sewing machine mechanic. The job had many points to it but none which he could see which would challenge him for the rest of his life.

He joined, or as he puts it, was press-ganged into the Belfast Fire Brigade on the 29th July 1963, aged 20. His parents had, without his knowledge, requested and obtained an application form from the Brigade following a job advertisement in the local press.

Clearly at that time, and Allan would agree, he did not have any particular penchant to be a Firefighter; save that which most youngsters have in their youthful dreams-those who dreamt of being a Firefighter-a Train Driver-or a Policeman. However, once having joined, it was not too long before he became totally enthused and became deeply immersed in his profession-a profession which was to grow into a deep vocation-and as all true Firefighters see it, a special calling.

By 1969, although still a Firefighter, he had studied for, taken, and passed, all the three legally necessary Statutory examinations, which qualified him to hold the rank of Station Officer. Promotions followed quickly and by 1970 he had held the ranks of Leading Firefighter, Sub Officer, and thence up to Temporary Station Officer rank. A rapidity of advance which was unparalleled in the history of the Belfast Fire Brigade.

The rapidity of this rise from the ranks-unprepared as he was for it-left him a little bemused and surprised. It was his perception that he had studied and taken the examinations for the sheer satisfaction of the knowledge that was to be acquired, knowledge which was essential for his newly chosen profession. He also had little insight what the promotional implications might have for the direction of his young life as the social order began to rapidly deteriorate within Belfast city and the Province.

He was the youngest Firefighter to hold the rank of Station Officer in the United Kingdom and at that time the first Station Officer to be promoted to this position by statutory qualification alone, within the Belfast Fire Brigade. Promotion by statutory qualification was introduced and encouraged within Belfast by the then Chief Fire Officer Mr. Robert Mitchell M.C., Q.F.S.M., M.I.Fire.E., a forward looking English import, newly appointed in 1962. Before that, promotion was often by political patronage or Lodge. This development changed little.

He was to be the first of a new young breed and generation of Fire Officer in an old institutionalised Brigade. He was substantiated in his rank in 1972, having served in the interim period 1970-1972 in all of Belfast's Stations as either a Leading Firefighter, Sub Officer, or Temporary Station Officer. Those were critical years in the history of Belfast's Fire Brigade and were to prove a sound training ground for him and my former colleagues in the ensuing holocaust that is all too often inaccurately and poetically described as the 'Troubles'.

He remained a front line operational Watch Commander until 1987 when he transferred to Brigade Headquarters. Allan retired from the Service in 1989 on medical grounds.

It was on the Recruits Course in the summer of '63 that Allan and I were to meet for the first time. A deep friendship rapidly developed between the city slicker and the country farm boy. A friendship I am glad to say which endures until this very day. A strange alliance this. We were in Northern Ireland tribal terms communities apart but we had more in common than divided us even given this diversity of backgrounds. We both liked a physical and intellectual challenge and if that encompassed a good deep discussion all the better. We were children of the universe and there to conquer the world.

What, after all, were these silly metaphorical windmills sitting there for if it was not for the likes of us. We needed no second invitation to climb up on our mighty steeds and Don Quixote like charge at them-and if this was not sport enough-we would fall exhausted from our chargers into the nearest she-been where there was always the opportunity over a few mere drops of nectar to plot and scheme how we would assault the virtuous in their Fire Service ivory towers which were liberally sprinkled among these very windmills.

We just loved the Fire Service operational life. We did not mind where the fire was spreading to-when the next incoming assisting crew was due-if the water was going to last out or not-whether the grand and aggrandisers were making the correct Command decisions or not. Who cared. We were the men in the Big Picture-sledge hammering the doors in-spraying water to the left and right-spluttering, coughing, and retching onto the front of our tunics on our way up the stairs. Breathing apparatus, well that was for mere mortals wasn't it, ardently into the inferno until either we had rescued the buxom blonde of our dreams, or perished in the attempt. Ah!... impetuous youth. Yes, that was us.

So what is this person called Allan Wright really like, this Quixotic like upstart, this protester, or should that be protestant?

Allan, as his writing exemplifies, is a political animal but then any Irishman worth his salt is. The Irish are born to fight and Allan is no exception. Given a just cause, and they all are, are they not? We will just about fight anything to a standstill for the sheer hell of it. At an exceptional time in the history of the Belfast Fire Brigade, Allan, a fair minded man, regularly climbed out of his trench over his years of service and strode off alone into No Man's Land with his shillelagh to take on the Brigade Establishment over their institutionalised policies of discrimination and corruption. As part of the 'ruling tribe' he did not have to do that. It is even more courageous, if, like Allan, you knew the price to pay before you put your head over the parapet. Let me tell you dear reader, these were, and remain, meritorious deeds, but they did not come without their final price in promotional terms.

The North of Ireland people are a particularly tenacious breed of folk and Allan is clearly a proud torchbearer of his cultural heritage and as such is quite demonstrably an unapologetic Ulsterman. He has been known to speak with pride of his forebears in the 36th Ulster Division who fought alongside the Catholics from the 16th Irish during the Battle of the Somme in the Great War in 1916. This Division, consisting of men recruited from the entire island of Ireland, was the only Division in the British Army to advance and hold the ground on the opening day of the renewed offensive of the 1st of July 1916 and to die together later at Messines Ridge in 1917. On other occasions he speaks with equally thoughtful passion on his vision for a peaceful Ulster and Ireland and of the future he perceives for his children and his neighbours of all 'persuasions'.

Allan was in accord with millions of Firefighters around the world an astute, compassionate, and at times, humorous observer of human nature in all its kaleidoscopic colours and moods. This is reflected in this **work** where not only did he observe, but he observed while he worked, covered in the grime, blood, sweat and the ceaseless tears of many of his beloved Ulster people. He captures the mood and ennobles the spirit of the 'Ordinary' people in Belfast and the Province during the nadir of their darkest hours; a warm complex people of ready smile and cheery industrious disposition; of deep decency and compassion; and yet capable of the darkest passions. Nevertheless, he remains full of optimism for his fellow Ulster men and women and for the Province as a whole. Those very citizens who can with some justification describe their Firefighters in their warm northern brogue as 'dacent people'.

Although Allan has now retired from the Fire Service he still carries with him many of the emotional and physical gunshot scars of his work in the hostile streets of Belfast. He lives with a sense of relief and gratitude for having made it in off the battlefield, mostly in one piece. Others, whether it be in their body or emotionally, did not. They were honourable casualties also.

In telling his story he seeks like many another Firefighter no special anthem of acclaim. He simply says that any Firefighter anywhere in the world when called upon to do their duty will always respond like he and his colleagues did. That after all is why Firefighters have a special vocation and why they join. He was, and is, proud to have been a Firefighter. It is a noble calling.

As Allan is wont to muse on occasions-in a classical understatement-'Well, that was an interesting time....it was all bells, bombs...and bloody bullets'.

Pax Vobiscum.

Paul P. Burns.

Firefighter.

THIS BOOK IS DEDICATED TO THE GOOD GUYS

THOSE WHO SERVED THE TITANIC CITY
OF
BELFAST

AND DID NOT LIVE TO READ THEIR STORY...

AND TO

THE FIREFIGHTERS OF THE WORLD

WITH THE PRAYER

THAT THEY WILL...

BURNING ISSUES

CONTENTS.

Introduction . . . .

The Prelude... Although this is essentially a work describing some of the incidents attended by, and exploits of, Belfast Firefighters during the troubled years of 1968 to 1988, the dangers that we were exposed to, including the ever present threat posed by street violence, was no different to that which the other emergency services endured during this period. Though I am bound to add that while engaged in the task of alleviating the sufferings of fellow human beings at incidents it was rather fascinating to see yet other, so called, Homo Sapiens, trying to kill one another. Funny old sub species humans, and whether or not it was clear to me, no doubt the universe was unfolding as it should.

Because these events have been acted out within the complex tapestry of a continuous and continuing campaigns of violence and political instability, I have allowed myself the luxury from time to time as a native Ulsterman, of inter-weaving some of these events. This has been done in an effort to describe in a sensitive way the poignancy of the treatment the people of Ulster as a whole have had to endure and to show the futility, and for some, the finality of violence.

During this period in 1973 The Belfast Fire Brigade and the Northern Ireland Fire Authority amalgamated to become the Fire Authority for Northern Ireland and latterly the Northern Ireland Fire Brigade. It was not a happy marriage. Arranged marriages rarely are.

The fact that this book crosses this time span, a period-when Belfast's own city Brigade lost its identity-does not detract it in any way from the work being a tribute to the 'boys of the B.F.B.' as the lyrics of the old unofficial Brigade song said. These Firefighters continued loyally and conscientiously to serve two masters during their collective illustrious careers.

The stories related are true accounts of incidents that the Brigade attended since the re-commencement of the present 'Troubles' in 1966. Yes, indeed, from 1966. Civil disturbance calls were being attended by the Brigade and other emergency services from that summer of '66. This was long before they were considered prominent enough to warrant column space or air time by the world news media and prior to government of the day giving official recognition to a burgeoning problem.

Even at that time sectarian burnings of people's homes and property, civil rights marches, and riots following 'peaceful' processions, were the order of the day. This Wagnerian prelude was taking place in what we now know was the unorchestrated build up to the major civil disturbances of 1969-'70. Unfortunately no official Brigade records exist for that time. The records themselves having fallen prey to the petrol bombers. Published press reports and unpublished private written records and memories retained by myself and colleagues are the sole sources for the information contained in my *work.*

During this, what we now whimsically call the 'working up' period, lessons had to be learned in a hurry from scratch and new fire-fighting techniques developed quite literally on the hoof and on the spur of the moment, as we dealt with incidents and situations completely alien to our previous experiences. In these early days it was only through vigilance and a large slice of good luck that we achieved any measure of success without serious injury or mishap to the personnel involved. Sadly this was not always to remain the case.

There is no Manual of Firemanship published, that I know of, that teaches Firefighters self preservation techniques, or how to deal with incidents such as a bombings where mutilation and dismemberment of human beings is the order of the day. Now that world terrorism has become a well established and practised black art and the malaise of the twentieth century-when violence is used to achieve political ends-it is perhaps time that some government or Fire Service related organisation published the fruits of our bitterly harvested experience in the hope that those lessons will not be lost to the next generation of Firefighters. A generation I am glad to say which now includes female Firefighters. Heroism is indivisible and genderless. In a job where smoke blackened faces are the order of the day there are apparently still some folk who will do just about *anything* to cut down on their mascara bill!

The terrorist blitz of Belfast was, and still remains, a unique situation for a peacetime civilian Fire Brigade to find itself in. The Fire Service in the Province has had to sustain a state of readiness now for some thirty years not, not just in relation to its Statutory obligation to protect life and property from fire but also from terrorist attack in whichever mutating form it presents itself. Extraordinarily some personnel have served the full duration of their entire careers on a war footing.

In putting these lessons to good use, and as often as not employing them for self preservation on the job, never let anyone mislead you that the personal instinct for survival is not the strongest of the senses, it is in actuality the sixth sense. Anyone who has stared death in the face, as I have, will testify to this. Each incident whether it be a bombing, fire, killing, or maiming was another personal milestone of survival along the road to where the Province is politically today, some thirty years on. It can be succinctly put as 'on the road from Purgatory-final destination-unknown'.

A question often mused over in a so called democratic Christian society is, do the politicians who purport to represent the electorate's views do so, or do they foster and further their own ideologies? I fear that throughout the history of Ireland the latter has always been the case. I can still recall a quote given me by my father in which he gives his definition of a politician. *'A politician is a person who will send your son to fight his war.'* A simple quote yet with a depth of meaning which for me, if applied in a global context throughout history, transcends the test of time and an interpretation which is equally applicable to the Irish question and its politicians today.

This is not my story alone but that of all those valiant Belfast Firefighters, even the rogues, and we had those too. They were valiant also. At the time they had very little other choice in the matter. So 'any similarity to any person either living or dead is not purely coincidental'.

It was they who served through this sad and traumatic period of our Province's history in the 100 square miles of a compact city of three quarters of a million souls. It was they who worked on the darkened wet mean streets in the wee small hours shivering in their pitifully inadequate Glasgow serge tunics when any reasonably sane person was in a warm bed behind locked and barred doors.

This **work** can of necessity only reflect a small cross section of the incidents which we had to deal with. The actions of the Belfast Firefighters were and shall, we hope, remain unique in the annals of Fire Service history and should be recorded for posterity, lest the people of Ulster and others, forget the continuing debt of gratitude which can never be repaid to this collection of individuals know as the civilian emergency services. Some, as they say, achieve greatness, yet others have greatness thrust upon them, in so saying, this was to be the case in respect of Belfast's Firefighters.

The majority of incidents that I focus on are those which I attended or was personally involved with in one way or another while serving as the Watch Commander of Blue Watch in Ardoyne's Station area between 1972 and 1973. Prior to this period there had been a unparalleled upsurge in terrorist activities.

These covert actions eventually metamorphasised into such a huge number of concentrated civil disturbances or terrorist related incidents that the Brigade was almost overwhelmed. Never again, even during the continuing paramilitary campaigns in the decades that were to follow, did the Brigade receive such an onslaught of incidents of mass destruction and death than it experienced during this relatively brief period. Before this period was over the Brigade and its Firefighters were quite literally reeling from this offensive.

Were we ever offered help from our colleagues in the rest of the Service? Yes, of course we were, but they knew when they offered that we, like them in similar circumstances, would politely refuse. It was our City and our people, and we would handle it.

Some of these incidents have little significance within the wider sphere of the overall scheme of things, as if this ferocious madness had any rhyme, reason, or scheme to it in any event. However, prominence is given to a number of the more disastrous tragedies. The one thing that they all have in common-be they major or minor-is that someone's life was touched, affected, indelibly and irreversibly marked in one way or another by each and every one of them. The material used which describes incidents and events is unexpurgated. Not only does it describe incidents as they actually occurred but also encompasses other events, warts and all, which are not necessarily terrorist or Fire Brigade operationally related but which nevertheless affected Brigade personnel.

The final outcome and the overall picture painted of any occurrence whatever it may have been is not solely confined to either the perpetrators or the traumatised recipients. All who participated in these dramas following the initiation of an incident whether it be a fire or a bombing became part of and party to how successful, or not, the final resolution of events became. It was the collective community's effort and the high degree of expertise shown by the Fire Brigade in dealing with it that determined the collage of news which the gathered media portrayed to the world and how it will be recorded in the annals of history for future generations to reflect on and to learn from. The images portrayed and individual stories told are only small glimpses of the violence that has gone on in Ulster for generations. The whole truth with its many facets will never be known to any single person. Least of all to its population.

Events recorded here are fact not fiction they may shock, sadden, or sicken, therefore by their very nature they may also at times hurt. All the operational events described are not wholly morbid, nor of a serious nature. Some are tinged with a degree of humour best perhaps appreciated by the participants in retrospect, most certainly not at the time of the event. Humour is as diverse as the people who perceive it. It can be subtle, morbid, black, satirical, twisted, or cynical. Each of us interpreting it as one or other of these qualities depending on the makeup our individual personality. Without it one could not on occasions cope with these visions on a dark side that each one of us has from time to time to face in the course of our own individual daily toils. So, it is just the same in the Fire Service.

Too often, it has been the case in the Province that when the truth was not admitted, or it was distorted at the time, it came back eventually to haunt and ensnare the perpetrator and sometimes the innocent alike. Abhorrent acts and actions repugnant to all decent minded people have and will continue to happen here. Perhaps, at the expense of shocking those folk, if the real truth had been told at the time and they had been made more fully aware of things that had been done supposedly in their name it might well have served in some small way to prevent them happening again in the future. The truth is after all supposed to make you free.

To ask you, dear reader, to enjoy the stories contained within would be a contradiction in terms. Suffice it to say, read and mentally digest how a peace time Fire Brigade had to rapidly readjust and adopt its fire-fighting techniques to carrying out its duties in an urban guerrilla warfare nightmare scenario as the marauding bands fought their way back and forth across the city, and learn how its personnel coped within the working environment of a divided so called civilised society. A society with plenty of religion but damned little Christianity which despite the best efforts of many of the well intentioned to avert a disaster was predestined by historical decisions and events enacted by our forefathers decades, if not generations before, to partially self destruct. This was in reality Titanic Town.
Let the sins of the fathers be visited on the children..........

My Lagan Love ....

Waxing lyrical... Once upon a time, there was a tranquil valley- a tranquil river-and a tranquil City. The source of the river, the Lagan, rises on Slieve Croob in the heart of the granite Mourne mountains in the County of Down. Its actual life begins way out to the west near the town of Newport, not however the Newport of County Mayo...God bless us all.... but that upstart parish called Newport in the new colonies of Massachusetts. From here the warm westerly winds drift eastwards quaffing deeply from the spindrift of the wild Atlantic ocean. A spindrift which, in its own sweet time, falls as genial rain on a dark soft Ulster morn. The sun eager as ever to chase away these nimble cumulous and the spooky shadows from the boreens sweeps up over the Mournes changing its purple dormant repose into the ceaseless mantle of forty shades of green. As it smiles, its children the sunbeams, light each dew laden cobweb into a tiara of crystal diamonds.

In her early morning eagerness the corncrake sweeps by in all her majesty momentarily dislodging these crystal dew drops as they splash to the sward below. In their eagerness to gossip the dewdrops rush to greet and hug each other as they drift gently twirling and dancing in a trickle of joy down the mountain bogland to the fairy glen. These bee laden glades of curtseying bluebells filled with mystery and delight; of mischievous fables and toadstool lolling leprechauns.

Onward-onward, bubbling, chuckling, kissing the stones, waving to the big black and white Friesian girls as they munch their way belly deep through the succulent grass in the riverside pastures, down past the whitewashed cottages with their lazy plumes of sweet scented turf. Onward-following the undulations and contours, swelled now by many small anonymous streams to become my Lagan Love. A mature river this Lagan, comfortable with itself no longer a sheugh nor a stream, a river that meanders leisurely along, eastwards through the Lagan valley, with its mountains to the North, and hills to the South.

The river, in no particular hurry to greet the sea at Belfast Lough some fifty miles away, is now and then disturbed by a fussy mother moor hen. There was a time when her brood was disturbed by the cresting waves of the passing barges that carried cargoes as varied as animal feeds and bulk coal up-river to some of the towns and villages situated along its lower reaches. The townlands and hamlets of Lisburn, Lambeg, and Dunmurry, eventually returning City bound with home produced goods such as flax for linen and potatoes to the port of Belfast. Converging with goods and produce from other areas of the Province either for local consumption or to be loaded onto ocean going vessels for export all over the world.

Leaning indolently over the parapet of the old stone arched Shaw's Bridge on the outskirts of the City, the setting for that evocative song 'My Lagan Love' many a resting Sash bedecked Protestant Orangeman 'taking a spell' from his triumphal march on the annual Twelfth of July parade on the pilgrim's way to 'The Field' to reaffirm his Loyalty has been able to glance down on the river flow as it narrows where it passes under the bridge, its pace quickening and cascading over the hidden boulders beneath its surface.

If the Orangeman's fervour was a touch jaded on a pleasant lazy sunny day he could always be minded to swop his pleasantries by joining the regular host of walkers leisurely strolling on the old towpath along its scenic route into Titanic town's heartland disturbing the erratic cabbage butterflies beside the river as he strolled by. The self same towpath that the once mighty Clydesdale horses trod. Grunting gently as they clip clopped along puffing great sweet clouds of steam out of their distended nostrils on a soft autumnal morning as they hauled their laden barges through the cauldrons of mist, deep in thought on many a misty morn in the pursuit of their destiny and a bucket of warm Guinness laden bran.

Some hundred yards further downstream from Shaw's Bridge the Lagan gathers its composure once again to continue gently towards Stranmillis a few miles away downstream. It was here many years ago as a child that I used to fish for sticklebacks with my little muslin and wire net stuck into the end of a Bamboo cane or maybe tadpoles-now there is one of life's great mysteries at work-to fetch them home in jam jars supported by a string carrying handle and watch their metamorphosis into frogs. Sadly many a tadpole did not survive long enough to become a frog, their very fate dependent on the expertise and the skill of the fumbled fingered string tier.

The river is finally halted here at Stranmillis by one of the many locks where the barges used to lock-in to enable them to make the transition from a higher level to a lower one. I used to help the lockkeeper, in between puffs on his silver capped pipe, he let me have a green gilled puff once as we heaved on the timber booms in order to close the gates and gazed in wonderment as the heavily laden barge with its gunwales almost awash slowly disappeared from view whenever the gurgling water poured out of the paddles to equalise the level with the river downstream. The river divides here to create the Lagan canal which was excavated in the eighteen hundreds. In the middle of the fork is a little island created by this division, on it stands the old Belfast Tennis Club, the refuge of the privileged. The bushes in its vicinity were the lurking habitat for the lost ball scavenging profiteers for resale to the landed gentry of the Club-a few of these scallywags went on to become politicians the rest of the mob just became successful.

Between the Stranmillis locks and Kings Bridge on the left hand side stand the pompous gates of Ulster's world renowned seat of learning, Stranmillis College, beckoning beacons for those masochistic scholars who aspire to teach. It is at this junction that Stranmillis Road after its descent from the Ulster Museum some half a mile up the hill makes a hairpin turn to join the embankment. It is here on what was previously a small triangle of waste ground that a dozen or so asbestos pre-fabricated buildings, know locally as 'the prefabs', were constructed in the late 40's. They still endured until recently. These pre-fabs were a 'temporary' post World War II legacy built to house an expanding population in a society unable to afford permanent dwellings. Other such sites existed throughout the City, but it was not until the 1980s that they were to totally disappear. The river now widens and its banks become more manicured as it passes under the Kings Bridge and on through suburbia.

It has become tidal by now embraced by the refreshing Irish Sea, its level noticeably interdependent on the phases of the moon and state of the tide at its mouth. Low tide exposes the black glar, the glutinous mud that is its bed, out of which yesterdays half buried waste rears its ugly head. Their grotesque shapes mummified as if half finished sculptures coated in black plaster. Man's sophistication greets the river with banks which, by now, have the luxury of footpaths and tarmacadam roads to accompany it on its way to the sea. On past the Annadale embankment where allotments once supplemented the diet of many City folk during and after the Second World War years, blocks of flats now grow there instead.

Under the Ormeau Bridge now and on past the rear of the old brick built Victorian Gasworks, surrounded by its rows of 'one up one down' high density terrace houses, its gas holders and belching retorts dominating the skyline. The coal cooked in its retorts produced not only gas but by-products ranging from coke, tar, and creosote to disease and pollution. Each of these consumables could be bought direct from the gasworks. The disease and pollution came gratis to the local householders, although every city ratepayer was entitled to a free gallon of disinfectant every year. Must keep the servants sterile and ensure the asphyxiated corpse is clean!

On a bad day downwind from the Gasworks, one could be forgiven for thinking that the mythological giant Finn MacCoole had had a bad dose of flatulence such were the noxious sulphurous fumes wafting by to assault the nasal membranes. Coal barges could be seen tied up at the Gasworks jetty. Cranes busily bobbing and weaving as they unloaded their black diamond cargo. Rising plumes of coal dust were carried on the breeze to coat the surrounding streets and houses, the gutters running black whenever it rained.

Many's the time my Mum would send me down the Donegall Pass the few hundred yards to the Gasworks to fetch a bag of coke or a bucket of tar to splash on around the base of the yard wall, just freshly painted and gleaming white with whitewash. We might have been poor but by God and the Gasworks we were clean!

On summer evenings along this stretch of the river the skullers and rowing eights from Queen's University and Methodist College could be seen straining into their oars in between clearing their throats, hawking, and spitting over the side into the, by now, weary river.

Only two more bridges to navigate now, the Queens and the Albert. The Lagan mingles now with the brackish water of the docklands and gently laps around the slipways of Harland and Wolff's giant shipyard -the birthplace of the Titan sisters-its journey from source to mouth by now complete as it embraces Belfast Lough. A Lough which points its broad blue finger due east, the short distance, to the western Scottish shore of the Rhynns of Galloway, which smile a greeting on a clear day....ah!... the sheer poetry of it all.

It is here in the basin of the Lagan at its confluence with the Belfast Lough and the all but forgotten Farset stream that the City grew and prospered. A casual visitor could be mistaken for assuming that this, by now, fully grown Lagan was the river that gave birth to the City, but in the perversity that is an Ulsterman's trade mark-what has logic got to do with it-it did not.

The Gaelic name for the City is Beal Feirste which has been generally accepted in its loose translation in Angrish-Irish/English-as the 'mouth' of the Farset (sandbank). Though Gaelic academic purists are prone to argue that it may mean an 'approach to a ford'. Either way the locals pronounce Belfast phonetically as Bell-faast thus reflecting its Gaelic roots and they should know. Belfast's Coat-of-Arms reflects the city's historical beginnings by depicting a bell and a blue stylised river with a sail trading vessel on it. The bell was to warn vessels away from the sandbanks along the shoreline of the trading settlement which was ultimately to grow into Belfast. This stylised river represents the river Farset not the Lagan. The Farset stream also flows into Belfast Lough a short distance from where the Lagan disgorges its waters. The Farset is no longer visible for most of its course. It has become a subterranean sewer that runs, albeit in tranquillity, under the City centre near High Street, built over as the City developed and grew.

Although an industrial and commercial City of historical repute its scenic location and panoramic views can easily compare with many of the world's more renowned major cities such as Hong Kong, San Francisco, Capetown and Rio de Janeiro. The overall visual aspects of Belfast can best be appreciated by an observer from the hills north and south of Belfast Lough. Divis, Black Mountain, and Cavehill to the north which tumble down gently to its shores from the County Antrim plateau. The Castlereagh Hills on the south shores which also give a commanding view of the City westwards to those lush pastures of the Lagan valley and eastwards along the Belfast Lough as its ten mile long ribbon of water points easterly to the Irish Sea, the North Channel, and Scotland.

As a youth growing up in the fifties, some of my friends and I would often make our way at weekends and holidays up onto the Cavehill a promontory reputed to look like the Emperor Napoleon asleep on his back and on whose 'Nose' I was later on to carry out the rescues of inept climbers. On the Cavehill we would explore its secrets, collect fossils, and gaze down on the beautiful, and silent spectacle of the Lough and City. A City whose population worked, slept and played safely within its boundaries. A City that was temporarily at peace with itself.

The ride into 'town' for the new visitor in the mid sixties would usually commence at the recently renamed International Airport at Aldergrove located on the Antrim plateau near Lough Neagh the largest inland lake in Europe. This airport had originally been an RAF base both during and since the second

World War, and was to rapidly expand on its new war footing. Visitors had previously landed at the nearby aptly named Nutt's Corner aerodrome but this was regarded by the aviation authorities as hardly an inspiring name so we became 'Belfast International'. Maybe on reflection, they should not have changed the name at all. In any event any journey into the City would no doubt be filled with some trepidation and expectation for 'foreigners'.

The old route into the City from the north over the plateau was via Ligoniel along quiet uncluttered country roads. Cresting the intervening ridges, as one approached the city outskirts, would reveal momentary tantalising glimpses of the vista of the City sprawled out far below in the Lagan valley. Down now, over the crest of Wolf Hill with its massive jute mill, twisting and turning at the hairpin bends, and then the swooping political cresta run straight down past the affluent suburbs of the Upper Crumlin Road to the beginning of 'Indian' country at the 'Y' junction-with its sentinel of Ardoyne Fire Station-and the choice whether to take passage down the lower Crumlin or Woodvale Roads. Onwards-worthy coachman-for your very life may rest upon the choice-the unwitting passengers unaware that they were about to run their first gauntlet. What would they know about tribal areas or sectarianism.

Flashing past the fidelus defenderii of Ardoyne Fire Station, like the Beatles Penney Lane where the 'Firemen keep their fire engines clean'. This well ordered life taken in with a casual glance through the open engine room doors. The Firefighters all in a line swilling out their engine room with their bass brooms and galvanised buckets of 'sugee' carbolic making it sterile for their already gleaming brass bell 'clean machines'. Into 'political pawn lands' now by whichever sectarian route. The side streets as they hurtle by on the switch backed ride down into the city's heart would reveal to the keen eyed visitor the monotonous rows of one up one down sub standard kitchen houses that both communities of a politically and religiously divided society shared. They were united on only three issues poverty, deprivation, and political exploitation.

On every day in the week unemployed cloth capped men-segregated into groups according to age and intent-would stand at the street corners. Pensioners and yesteryear war veterans smoking pipes filled with locally produced brands of tobacco from Gallaher's or Murray's enormous tobacco factories. Brand names such as Condor or Warhorse blended for the hardened native connoisseur. The sweet scented smoke drifting up over street corner signs like Berlin and Cambrai, Dover, and North Howard, reflecting the past glories of the Empire-quietly reminiscing about today's news or the bygone days-the future hardly ever discussed-what future?

The unemployed younger men bantering about the latest win or defeat of the local Blues or Glens football teams and which pub they were up against in the next round of the darts league. The eternally hopeful seeking work-information exchanged from last night's job section of the Belfast Telegraph or this mornings Newsletter and Irish News. The unemployable artful dodgers scurrying in and out of the local bookies betting on this 'sure thing' or that-busily plotting from where or whom they could purloin the next few bob for a bet and a pint of the 'black stuff', Guinness.

The industrious and thrifty housewives ploughing their imperious way hither and thither along the steep inclines of crowded footpaths in endless pursuit of the bargain-back and forth from the little grocers shops owned and run by friendly people from the area where the 'slate' was an essential cornerstone of trade or survival-gathering in the basic essentials such as locally grown Comber spuds-scallions-and the cheap cuts of meat for the evenings plate of stew and champ, or that extra treat, a little oval tin of meat in gravy-all to keep a hungry family well but simply nourished. There must be a Heaven for such dear departed blessed heroines.....there simply has to be.

The arterial routes of Dover and North Howard Streets were two of the umbilicals that linked the Shankill and Falls. It was only one third of a mile from one end to the other, just a belligerents' stone's throw. Here at street corners in similar slum surroundings, under street names such as Sevastopol, Balkan, and Serbia, the Fall's natives lived out the same daily routine and discussed the same domestic issues that united them with their Shankill counterparts. This no man's land was to become, before the end of the sixties, the arena where many of these fundamentally decent folk were to confront one another not only verbally but physically as well on the burning issues that divided them. The final obscenity-the poor fighting the poor-whilst the delighted manipulators watched from splendiferous settings.

This curiosity seekers dalliance over-its off now on down the gentler slopes-the short distance to the sophistication of the city centre where poverty rubs shoulders with sloth. Nevertheless for three quarter of a million citizens to walk around the Belfast City centre in the mid sixties and sample the atmosphere was still a pleasant experience. To browse around the growing number of large chain stores or to wander into the old established ale houses named after shipbuilding successes for a drink or snack where an infectious air of friendliness existed was still a heart warming experience. People were relaxed and friendly eager to impress and please both stranger and local alike. Directions given to the stranger were comprehensive and enthusiastic sometimes ending with the words…'perhaps you might be better not starting from here'…

The stranger, wandering past Bells Coffee shop with its romantic smells of far off lands, or idling on the street corner watching in the evening gloom the trolley buses negotiating their electronic junctions as the conductors wrestled with their long bamboo poles standing 'neath great showers of sparks, would not have been aware of the cultural or religious differences of the populace with whom they were rubbing shoulders or having a bit of craic, nor should they. In the distance they might hear the departing ferry for the 'mainland' sounding its forlorn three blasts of the horn as it bade farewell to the place of the Black Velvet band and the sounds of the tin whistle as a youthful Jimmy Galway practised dextrously with the Orange flute band over in the York street district.

Belfast, a Victorian lady with grubby petticoats, could not however be compared with its southern counterpart Dublin which was and still is considered to be the cultural and cosmopolitan capital of Ireland. However its nightlife was continuing to flourish and expand with any number of new fangled nightclubs opening their doors for Joan Biaz and her-'we shall overcome generation'-in spite of haughty disapproval by the Opera lovers at the Opera House. Although all was not well with the world and opera fans might have to pick their way around the horse doovers of a passing coal cart it was tolerable for all that.

By the end of the sixties most of this ambience was to change.

The cancerous change was almost imperceptible at first. Foreign visitors, with the exception of journalists, were becoming fewer. Tension was replacing relaxation in an expectant, jittery, and uneasy City. Shops, pubs, and nightclubs were beginning to close early. A ring of steel fencing started to encircle the City Centre with its vehicular and pedestrian entrances and exits controlled by security guards manning gates and turnstiles in a vain attempt to control the flow of car bomb attacks. Only emergency vehicles, buses and delivery vehicles were permitted in but still 'they' got through. Private security companies blossomed. This was the era of the genderless fire bomber. All customers entering the stores were searched. It was not unusual for the out of town female to return to find that hubbies car had been blown to pieces by an enthusiastic Ammunitions Technical Officer while parked in a restricted zone. The ultimate excuse for being late!

Eventually the City centre simply became a ghost town by night and sometimes by day as the 'shopping' jungle drums beat out the message that 'it is bad down town today'. Titanic Town was on collision course with her iceberg The tribal boundaries of the twenties and fifties were being redefined and the uncaged Beasts of Fear and Intimidation began stalking friend and foe alike as gunmen began to shoot out the street lights on the by now deserted nocturnal streets of my sad Lagan Love.

A Sling Shot History Of The Fire Service ... A little fact, a little fancy. The trail blazer of all the Fire Brigades in the world was established in Rome, although snooty Greek scholars may try tell you otherwise, indeed the Great Emperor Chin might challenge this also. However for sake of progress let us agree that the progenitors of the modern world-wide Fire Service is the Italian Fire Service. It was quite simply the oldest Fire Service in the first millennium and a few hundred years after its inception it was to provide the Fire Service with its very own patron Saint, St.Florian also born out of early Roman history.

History records that St.Florian-in Latin-Marcus Annius Florianus born 19th August 232ad-died 9th September, 276ad became Roman Emperor from June to September 276ad. The brother, by a different father, of the emperor Tacitus, he seized power on the death of his brother. Although his action was tolerated by the Senate and the armies of the West, the Legions in Syria promoted their own general, Probus. A civil war broke out which resulted in the sudden death of Florian, either at the hands of his own soldiers or by suicide, thus ending his brief reign of 4 months. Florian apparently, was a former pagan whose compassion for the Roman Christian people later earned him Sainthood. For Christian Firefighters world-wide, especially in predominantly Catholic Europe, St.Florian still remains the Patron Saint of Firefighters.

As well as having its historical origins within the Roman Empire the Fire Service is also inextricably linked with the city of Rome and its politics. Since its inception the city had provided its rulers with constant organisational and administrative problems. Rome's political and Fire Service history is surprisingly closely interwoven starting around the time of Julius Caesar who first attempted to deal with the city's development in a systematic manner.

However, after old Brutus quite literally stabbed him in the back, he did not live long enough to carry out his plans.

His adopted son and successor Augustus-the First Roman Emperor, after what had been, politically speaking, a Republic-grappled with the problems and although he lays claim to the fact that he found Rome as a brick city and left it as marble his claim is rather disingenuous. Nevertheless he did provide many fine public buildings baths, theatres, temples, and warehouses. However, many of the 'masses' employed in these projects still lived in unsafe and unsanitary tenements amid the narrow, winding streets and alleys of old Rome. In concert with his city redevelopment plan-Emperor Augustus-moved ahead to reorganise the city's administration creating necessary institutions and public services including the fire brigade.

In response to an obvious need, Augustus organised the fire brigade in 21bc BC, placing a number of public slaves under the command of aediles-officials in charge of streets and markets but all under the ultimate charge of the Urban Prefect. The office of Urban Prefect-which Augustus revived in 26bc-covered a huge range of duties. This appointment did not become per-manent until much later in the expanded Empire when the post became the most important in Rome. In effect the Prefect was the first Fire Chief in histo-ry.

This Prefect was recruited from the Equestrian Order which in time became the Imperial Civil Service. This rather elitist group-created by Augustus-was open to membership by Roman citizens of means and reputa-tion but not necessarily of good birth. Ultimately, there were thousands of equites throughout the empire. Although this was a lower aristocracy, a good career was available to them. After tours of duty as an army officer-the so-called Militiae Equestres-an aspiring Eques might serve as the Emperor's agent-procurator-in various capacities and eventually become one of the pow-erful Prefects-of the Fleet-of the Vigiles, or Fire Brigade-of the grain supply-of Egypt-or of the Praetorian Guard.

In a further development of the Rome's Fire Brigade Augustus divided Rome into 14 regiones-wards, each divided into vici-precincts, overseen by vicomagistri responsible for fire protection, among other administrative and religious duties.

In the year 6ad, after a particularly bad fire, Augustus expanded and for-malised the city's Fire Brigade into a Corps of Vigiles-these progenitors of today's Italian Fire Service who still bear the historical name Vigili del Fuoco-

to cover a population of over one million people, a statistic which is hardly surprising, when one considers that all roads led to Rome. The Corps consisted of seven squads, or Cohorts of 1,000 freedmen or Vigilium. Each Cohort was responsible for fire in two regiones and-especially at night-police protection duties. Ironically the police-cohortes urbanae-did not come along formally for another 7 years when they were created to supplement the duties of the Brigade which sounds about right for their proper position in the 'pecking' order and is consistent with their speed of 'turnout' throughout the succeeding centuries.

It was not until the time of the reign of the Emperor Nero that the Vigiles were to be put fully to the test in the Great Fire of Rome 64ad.

Nero Claudius Caesar Drusus Germanicus, original name Lucius Domitius Ahenobarbus, born December 15th 37ad, Antium, Latium. Died by his own hand 9th June 68ad, Rome. The fifth Roman Emperor (54-68ad) was stepson and heir of the Emperor Claudius. He was infamous for his personal debaucheries and extravagances.

Nero came to power in 54ad as a mere youth of 16. He started well enough and was happy to leave the administration to capable advisers. He devoted himself mostly to artistic works and rather fancied himself as a thespian, lyre player, and all round court jester. A few years later in 62ad he appointed Tigellinus Ofonius as his chief adviser a gentleman who became notorious for his bad influence on the young Emperor.

A Sicilian by birth, Tigellinus was Prefect of the Vigiles before becoming Prefect of the Praetorian Guard in 62ad. Early sources maintain that he rose to power by encouraging Nero in his vices and excesses. Tigellinus was suspected of incendiarism in the Great Fire of Rome. Probably Tigellinus would only have acted as an arsonist at the behest of his master who had great and grand notions for the redevelopment of Rome. The great fire that ravaged Rome in 64ad illustrates how low Nero's reputation had sunk by this time. Taking 'advantage' of the fire's destruction, Nero had the city reconstructed in the Greek style and began building a prodigious palace aptly named the Golden House which, had it ever have been finished, would have covered an area one third the size of Rome.

During the fire Nero was conveniently at his villa at Antium 35 miles from Rome and therefore cannot be held responsible for the burning of the city, or so he said, he was too busy having an orgy. But the Roman populace believed that he himself had organised the fire in Rome in order to indulge his aesthetic tastes in the city's subsequent reconstruction. According to the Annals of the Roman historian Tacitus Nero's response was to try and shift responsibility for the fire on to the Christians-probably after sacking the incumbent unfortunate Fire Chief-Christians who were popularly thought to engage in many wicked practices. So right from the outset Fire Chiefs were proven to have their political and practical uses as we all know.

After this debacle Nero's empire started to come apart at the seams in spite of him establishing a School of Applause, a sycophantic clique, numbering 5000 soldiers who followed him on his concert tours ensuring his success. Gets to sound more like Fire Brigade HQ everyday!

Suffice it to say things were none too happy in the Fire Brigade either what with routine regular infernos and the odd grand slam or two as Nero re-arranged the city and a crack down on efficiency by the new Chief.

Historians tell us these routine infernos were caused by howling dogs and trumpeting elephants dashing about overturning cooking fires in their ever vain attempt to match every nuance of the sound drifting out of the imperial palace as Nero strummed on his old instrument, during one of his many cathartic exercises, loosely described by his drunken toadies as music, but it was not so.

Rome had been regularly rearranging itself by inferno ever since he started taking music lessons.

Nero, normally a bright lad, had an intense dislike of dole queues, layabouts, and wastrels cluttering the street corners. So, on one of his weekly stride-abouts through the still smouldering ruins he had another neurological cascade, why not, he mused, solve both these tiresome problems by putting these ne'er do wells to work in the Corps of Vigiles....Oh! what a wonderful idea cried the sycophants-they could patrol the streets during his musical endeavours soothing the menageries and spotting the odd overturned brassiere, sorry brazier, before it could do any harm, the brazier I mean, and even now and again throwing in the odd rescue or three of a comely slave girl, just in sheer bon vivant. Hardly seems to have changed at all over the years!

So there you have it in a nutshell. The complete history of the world girdling organisation now known as the Fire Brigade. Simple..eh? There was however one trifling oversight...These press ganged members of the Vigiles were newly 'freed' slaves from all over the Roman Empire and they did not necessarily see things in such a bounteous light and there was as a consequence a few slight, picky, teething problems...

The Spanish Vigiles for example had the unpleasant and disconcerting habit of whipping the jump sheet away to a chorus of 'olea' just as the Roman nobility were about to land safely in their arms. Now on the other hand the Irish Vigiles on their rapid response donkeys-well you just had to watch them-they were intelligent-though masters of the devious. During one of Nero's practice sessions on one traumatic occasion in a Roman courtyard-with a central water well-a Roman Senator had become trapped by an inferno on an upper floor just out of reach of the ladders. The Irish Vigilium in charge-an honest chap from Donegall Pass-trying as usual to do his best, thought it would be a good idea if he placed his donkey beneath the portly Senator and persuaded him to jump on to it in the hope it would break his fall.

In the event the Senator was persuaded to jump and the discriminating donkey perceived as the Senator hurtled down towards him that he was not wearing the correct Orange Lodge Sash and at the last moment the ass sidestepped the onrush. As a consequence the politician fell into the well and was drowned-which just goes to prove that in politics-as in rescues-you really do have to know the difference between your ass and a hole in the ground...

A **Brief History Of Belfast Fire Brigade...** and so, many centuries later it was thought by the 'powers that be' that it might be a good idea to pay Firefighters some form of emoluments if only to reduce the 'risk from rescue'. An insurance policy so to speak.

Have you noticed by now how many people down through the centuries have had bright ideas about the Fire Brigade. It continues today. The British Fire Service have had more departmental inquiries than there were cease fires in Lebanon.

Then along came the insurance companies, the 'Fear' Brigade.....they thought it would be a another grand idea to reduce their insurance losses by sticking a badge, a Fire Mark, on the front of 'their' properties and setting up a Fire Brigade just for their customers. Each company had its own lead seal with the company's coat of arms emblazoned on it. No seal-no water. Well as you can imagine these modern day collectibles became rather fluid in an emergency and generally just before the horse drawn steamers would arrive pandemonium would ensue. The first priority for the victim after throwing themselves from the windows would be to 'borrow' a firemark from a convenient building and then lean nonchalantly against the well alight premises casually pointing at their firemark.

So that did not work too well either. This was clearly an inequitable state of affairs in that commerce and industry could be afford protection from the ravages of fire, albeit at a price, but the general population were being left to fend for themselves in an emergency. Some parishes had hand pumping appliances with ladders available and supplies of water situated at strategic locations within their locality, but fire and rescue cover was not uniform and was at it very best, threadbare. So in the mid-eighteen hundreds Local Authority Fire Brigades were formed, after the usual disaster or two, in order to eliminate these inequities. It was ever thus. Even today the 'necessary evil', as some local authorities refer to the Fire Brigade, only advances technologically and financially after the disaster horse has bolted yet again.

... the dobbins came two by two!

These fledgling Brigades, sometimes amalgamated with the Police as Police Fire Brigades, were financed from the coffers of the Borough exchequers and were properly equipped and housed in custom built fire stations. Firefighter's fire fighting garb in those days consisted of a heavy Melton fire tunic and trousers supported by a wide leather belt, their feet and lower legs protected by leather knee boots. Their heads were crowned with a magnificent brass helmet. This latter piece of equipment was indeed a work of art and engineering. Individual parts being designed to be replaced as they were damaged. It was quite simply the 'tin bashers' piece de resistance.

The Helmet, the crowning glory of Firefighters around the world and still the centre piece of their 'suit of lights' was the granddaddy of all helmets. It was thoughtfully designed to protect the head from all the hazards the wearer was ever likely to experience in his working life. Hazards which have changed little today. The design featured the mighty and artistic comb to deflect falling debris, the peak to save the wearer's face and eyes as they fell face down, right through to the tail board to protect the vulnerable neck from melted lead, hot tar, sparks, and scalding water. This particular design endured for almost two centuries. It was probably not conceived by a Brigade Public Watch Committee.

Initially hours of duty for the personnel of these Brigades were a full week on and one day off. Over the decades working conditions gradually improved and the duty rotas worked evolved to a full twenty four hour day on and twenty four off. However pay right up until the Firefighters Strike of 1977/78 remained a festering sore. Because of the long working hours of these shifts, Firefighters and their families, were housed in flats within the precincts of the station. On stand down periods they were still on call. Single men were billeted in dormitories and fed from the 'galley' on station. Stations even had their own communal laundry. A gathering place for the women of the station who could, for those who wished, freely exchange all the latest gossip. All a very cosy arrangement, however, the personnel in this landlord/servant relationship had to keep their noses clean or they would rapidly find themselves with their family in the middle of the street with all their belongings-next stop the Poor House.

A brief little anecdote serves to illustrate the point that this autocratic, 'landord' owning body and soul relationship with power vested in the hands of the old BFB chiefs was still being exercised in the nineteen fifties era, be it for good, or ill. Little changes over the years. These old fiefs were even able to determine if a Firefighter got a pension or not and how much it would be. An old colleague of mine called Johnty whose father's Christian name was also Leslie was an old BFB man who reared his small family while residing on Fire Stations, mostly Ardoyne, in the fifties alongside the likes of a young George Morrision (more of whom later). Mr Smith, the then Chief, must have taken a sudden dislike to Leslie senior for on Xmas eve he transferred him lock, stock, and barrel, to the top floor barrack flat in Whitla Station just vacated by a not so house proud family who shall be nameless. On arrival Leslie senior booked on duty at his new Station and before they were able to get their bits and pieces in situ he got a fire call to the old Plaza ballroom. His young family did not see him for two days over Xmas. Johnty remembers going to bed on Xmas Eve in a bare cold flat with the turkey hanging on the end of his bed.

By the late 1950's a fifty six hour week was introduced on a three Watch duty system and today the standard length of duty system of whole time Brigades in the United Kingdom is a forty two hour week on a four Watch system.

Although Belfast Fire Brigade was formally created in 1845 ad, fire-fighting plans for Belfast had existed 214 years before. In the year 1686 a levy was imposed on all citizens with over £69 per annum income 'to buy leather buckets, ladders, poles, hooks and chains for fire-fighting in the town'. All but 10 of the 500 houses then had thatched roofs although Belfast had become fire conscious enough to have had all the wooden chimneys replaced by stone or brick fifty years earlier.

The Brigade thus formed in 1800 was the second oldest County Borough Brigade in the United Kingdom-the oldest was I believe the Edinburgh Fire Engine Establishment-and the original Belfast Fire Brigade H.Q.'s was in Victoria Square. The City purchased its first fire engine in 1808 at the grand cost of £26,15 shillings, and 8 and one halfpenny!

The first Fire Superintendent/Chief of Police or Chief Fire Officer appointed-in 1840-was Mr John Cockburn, who was succeeded in 1860 by the much vaunted Captain Eyre Massey Shaw-an Officer of Cork Militia-who fifteen months later was appointed to command the London Fire Engine Establishment. The joint command of Fire/Police ceased after his departure. Belfast was the first Brigade to be wholly equipped with motorised fire appliances, all horse drawn appliances having been replaced by motor fire appliances by 1910.

... Fire Brigade HQ at Chichester St., or Chi', as it was known.

Shaw, a gentleman from County Cork, ultimately became a friend and confidant of Queen Victoria and Prince Albert who were committed enthusiasts of the Fire Service. Prince Albert had a personalised uniform and used to ride to fires in the great 'Metrollops'.

Captain Shaw was the author of many instruction manuals on the art and practice of fire-fighting. His recruitment of Firefighters was almost exclusively based on the premise that ex-members of the Merchant and Royal Navy made the most suitable recruits. He said that these people had an inculcated sense of navy traditions and discipline and were the people most capable of working at heights and tying tricky knots in ropes having spent a lot of their time, as the old crude barroom ditty says, 'swinging in the rigging and wanking on the planking'.

... the 'swinging' old boys, including the farriers, of the B.F.B.

Maybe it had more to do with the fact that a barrel of pork, some hard tack, and a shot of rum would keep the lower decks happy. These were a tough breed of men and as there was no keel hauling at the disposal of authority to act as deterrent or punishment-as in days of yore in the Navy-mean dispositions combined with a love for this daily ration of grog invariably led to indiscipline. It was as often as not those with the meanest predilection and highest in the physical pecking order-the silver backed gorilla-who were self appointed to lead and so the meek certainly did not inherent the earth. It was far more usual for them to inherit a thick ear. All this has changed today- though I have yet to see a barred door yield to a Diploma waving Firefighter-maybe they burst them open Yuri Geller-like with their minds?

Be that as it may, life on a Fire Station is still in many ways akin to life aboard ship with the exception that the shore based establishment is stationary and does not roll, when sober that is. Today's rank structure based as it was on the Merchant and Royal Navy still broadly remains in situ with its references to 'Leading Hands' , 'Divisions' 'Watches' and the Fire Service salute which still remains firmly naval. There is no point in rushing change is there now?

Captain -later Sir Eyre Massey Shaw KCB-was to leave Belfast to become the founder and first Chief of London Fire Brigade-the new boy on the block. Members of this particular Brigade-which according to them is the original centre of the British Fire Service universe-are not noted for their modesty-nor indeed for their knowledge of Fire Service history nor matters technical, and tend-when reminded of their heroic leader's antecedents and his old Brigade-to look somewhat green around the gills.

Fire Station, Belfast.

The collection of Victorian building housing Brigade Headquarters in Belfast was in its hey day a truly impressive edifice. It was constructed in red sandstone and brick at the south end of Chichester Street at its junction with Oxford Street on a rectangular site. It consisted of the Central Fire Station which was a six bay three floor building topped by a truly awe inspiring look-out/hose tower. Situated around a central court/drill yard paved with Mourne granite square sets-served by verandas-were two floor flats for the 'slaves', these were built cheek by jowl-in conjunction with workshops and stables for the horses-which comprised the other three sides of the site.

Many a small boy of the fifties era-myself included-will fondly recall the Brigade's open days when fire fighting displays were given by Chi's Firefighters on those splendid summer evenings. They were held within the confines of the drill yard. We would stand there open mouthed on the first floor veranda that surrounded it-outside the flats in which the Firefighters and their families had lived for decades-waiting expectantly for the show to begin. We would first hear the distant sound of the Station engine room gates crashing open at the front of the Station-then the thunderous roar of the Dennis's Rolls Royce straight eight cylinder-ex. Second World War Centurion tank engines being revved up by their drivers. The fire engines would roar out into Chichester Street and making a sharp left turn speed into the Station yard leaning over at a crazy angle as if about to overturn, but they never did. Screeching to a halt their crews would pile out with much slamming of doors and at the command of their Officers-in-Charge scamper about 'getting to work.' Watching their feats such as scaling the tower solo with hook ladders, being 'shot up' on the turntable ladder or getting foam jets to work was all enthralling stuff. Oh! happy days for everyone then.

Chichester Street or Chi' as it was always affectionately referred to by its Firefighters was built in 1893 and was one of the City's four brick built Victorian fire Stations built at the turn of the 19th century. The others being Albertbridge-1903, Ardoyne-1904, and Whitla-1905. Cadogan Station on the Lisburn Road-euphemistically known as the 'hotel'-and described with artistic abandon as neo-Georgian-was opened in 1954-more than 50 years after the last new Station was opened-to give additional fire cover to the expanding stock broker belt on the south side of the City. The commissioning ceremony documentation relates in patrician prose that... 'An interesting feature of the new station is the fact that no residential accommodation for Fire Service personnel and their families is provided, as members of the Brigade posted to this station enjoy a shift system and are privileged to reside wherever they may please...' my weren't they lucky!

Each Station served a pre-designated fire area within the City's boundaries. The Brigade was organised on a three Watch 56 hour week system-Red, White and Blue- wouldn't you know it-no Green, White, and Orange here, thank you.

In 1968 a full replacement programme for Belfast's Fire Stations began when Albertbridge was superseded by another Station built at Upper Newtownards Road/Knock Road junction known surprisingly as Knock Station. Whitla followed in 1973. Ardoyne was replaced with Westland in 1976 and an additional Station was erected on the Springfield Road in 1981.

The move from Chi' was long overdue not only because of the continuing danger from bombings but because traffic congestion in the area also played its part in interfering with response times to call-outs. No matter how one tries to modernise and improve an old building, it can never economically be made to meet the modern day requirements of comfort, safety, and efficiency standards. The Station's-by now-four Watches-the colour Green albeit reluctantly having been added- eventually moved into an ultra modern Station at Bankmore Street off Ormeau Avenue. Does it have the character of our old fond Chi'-I doubt it-but who knows, perhaps for the next generation it may well have.

Chi's imposing one hundred and twenty foot high lookout hose drying/drill tower had stood silent sentinel over the city centre for over one hundred years. It had witnessed the events such as the coming and going of the old horse drawn steamer pumps-the building of the Titanic-the German air raids of the Belfast Blitz-and the construction of the world's first offshore oil platforms-and more recently over the last twenty five years it has been shaken to its very foundations by terrorist bombings detonated in the immediate vicinity of the Law Courts across the street. Sadly it was condemned some years ago due to structural instability and along with Brigade Headquarters was pulled down.

While Chichester Street was the last of the old Victorian Stations to disappear the people of Belfast can still feel secure today in the knowledge that their community protection will be well looked after unstintingly for another hundred years or more by Firefighters of the next generation who march resolutely on. They will probably be better than we were but they have yet to prove that?

Probationer Reg. No: 399 Wright. A... When I joined the existing 350 Firefighters on the Brigade's establishment on Monday the 29th July 1963 I was initially based at Chi's Training School for my 12 weeks basic training course along with 9 other Recruits. Over the succeeding weeks, after being issued with our kit-which did not include the Helmet for we were not entitled in any shape or form to wear it-we were taught to spit and polish-march and counter-march-salute it if it moved and paint it red if it didn't-tie knots-bandage limbs in first aid and manipulate a host of weird and wonderful things during drill after incessant drill. All done at the double.

It wasn't all serious though. One lunch time as I was climbing through a classroom window during a bit of horseplay I was caught by the Chief and his phalanx of 'inspectors' in flagrento del window so to speak. As his Greatness floated past he observed dryly 'The door has distinct possibilities Wright...'

While all the 'organised' horseplay of the training school was going on we would enviously hear the centrally controlled Brigade mobilising tannoy system announcing 'Fire Call!' after fire call and on occasion whilst we would be involved in ladder or pump drill, due to a large incident in the city, our equipment would be snatched away from under our very noses. It really was quite frustrating to see the duty Watch return in their smoke blackened state and lay out yards of hose and piles of equipment in order to get the appliances 'back on the run' as rapidly as possible. Chi' simply buzzed with excitement and activity. Our education continued unremittingly, visiting this fire risk or that, sitting tests and examinations, practising, practising, practising, until finally the great day dawned after our final examinations when we were presented with out Helmets and given our first postings.

I was initially posted to Red Watch Chi'. So it was with great expectations and not a little trepidation that I reported for my very first Parade with Th-ee Watch. I arrived on Station well before commencement of my tour of duty which happened to fall on a night shift. I had drawn the short straw. A day shift would definitely have made me feel a lot more at ease because it would have avoided that frightening prospect of over-sleeping a turnout. So I decided to avoid that possibility by not going to sleep at lights out, as I climbed the stone staircase of the Station tower to the second floor dormitory of the single men's quarters that evening. How was I going to react-how was I going to handle my first fatality? Curiosity, thankfully, leaves little room for fear.

When I entered the dormitory landing after climbing the stairs that first evening to come on duty, feeling a little uneasy and lost for breath I heard the foghorn like voice of Tommy 'Shorty' Mc Kinistry serenading anyone who was within earshot with one of his bar room ditties. He was one of the day duty White Watch personnel preparing to go off duty. He directed me to my per-sonal kit locker. I was to learn later that this misnomer 'Shorty' belied a five foot nothing character who had a big heart and whose lack of stature was more than adequately compensated for by his other physical attributes. A veteran of the Second World War, he said one of his claims to fame was that he had tried to further the Fuhrer's cause in Europe by being a Sergeant Master Cook in His Majesty's Forces!

It really was a funny sight to see him on occasions-due to his miniature stature-standing upright driving whilst at the wheel of one of the fire appli-ances-no luxury of power steering in those days. Driver's training and abilities were categorised by colour-white, cars and vans-red, appliances-blue, turntable ladders and all other specials. He was one of those elite band of blue drivers in Chi'-although only a Firefighter-who were recognised and respected by all ranks and to whom we, as rookies, naturally learned to look for some of the skills of our new profession.

While jiggling with a key that refused to open the tin coffin locker 'Shorty' demonstrated for my benefit the dexterity required in removing and the refitting quickly the wrongly named detachable shirt collar to the fore and aft studs on his already red, raw neck without actually strangling himself.

Then it was with issue fire-fighting gear consisting of tunic, boots, helmet, belt and axe-to be carried in the prescribed manner- that I made my way towards the pole drop for the two stage decent into the engine room for the 1800hrs Parade. My first Parade. After standing aside and watching the timing and skill of the old hands who just launched themselves fully loaded down the pole hole without seeming to hold on, I decided-on second thoughts that I might be better practising a few dry runs first-just in case I made a heavy landing in the engine room in front of an expectant audience. It is called making an entry but I felt that it was a bit soon for that. I had in mind the Chief of Warrington over in Lancashire who, whilst demonstrating his pole prowess to Civic Leaders at the opening of his splendid new Station, ended up being carted off to hospital with two broken ankles. So I slipped a little self-consciously into the engine room by the stairs.

All the five bays were filled with the red gleaming and waxed appliances. The Brigade was equipped with quite a modern fleet of 15-20 appliances- sounds like something out of a sex shop-because we were not allowed to call them fire engines anymore. Later, I was to learn from experience that they did not remain in that pristine condition without an awful lot of hard work, even at 0300hrs in the morning they would be chamoised down for the third or fourth time on a night shift. Can you imagine the three man crew effort of trying to wipe down a dripping turntable ladder, it really was a depressing task, particularly when you were wet and exhausted.

My name was chalked up on the huge crew rider board at the rear of the engine room listing out all the crewing positions for the five appliances and including the Chief's Driver-a much sought after position-particularly on night duty prior to annual leave. Having learned my driving skills prior to enlistment in the Brigade in the Territorial Army-or as they are handsomely described by their Regular Army colleagues as the Temporary Assh***s-I often fell for the job of Chief's driver. It was an easy wee number. Chiefy was an English man and did not know his way around Belfast, or so he said-but then he had been a Captain in the Army-a Military Cross holder and an Officer and a gentleman to boot-was he not entitled to Batman and Boy Robin?

On occasions some labour saving Duty Officers, who did not like your 'pretty boy image', would have you double up on the 'Mail Run' and hope the Chief in the meantime did not call for his driver-which invariably was the case on night duty-whilst you were hurtling at breakneck speed around all the City's Fire Stations using all the shortcuts and rat runs in a frantic gear crashing attempt to try and break the unofficial record for the shortest circuit time and to try and make it back for a warm supper. Any thing marked 'fragile' in the bulky mail-in this helter skelter-was an open season invitation to have it booted out of the Land Rover mail wagon onto the appropriate station yard.

Although not detailed to ride an appliance or given any really dirty jobs about the station, for anyone keen to see action, it was a complete bore. A full night's undisturbed sleep was seldom possible though the odds in the sleep lottery were a little better. One of the other little perks of the job was that the Chief's driver-when an appliance turned out through the night-had to make the descent into the engine room and close the appliance bay gates. An irksome task on a freezing winter's night but then not as irksome as the poor sods who had just turned out to God knows what.

On one riveting occasion the Chief decided to drive himself to a job in the City centre. When eventually he returned to the vicinity where he had left his car he immediately began upbraiding the pump operator nearby for moving it out of the way of his operations. When the poor Firefighter, who did not really understand the big words the Chief used, but felt in his deeper inner self that he ought to resent them, started to stutter and look even more vacant than usual the Chief, being a sensitive person, started to feel all was not well. Indeed, it was not, someone had just hijacked his car and driven off with it for a joyride. The entire Brigade were deeply affected by this traumatic event, so much so in fact, that every time the Chief passed in the days that

... 'if you were not watching my car, what were you doing?!'

followed everyone seemed just to fill up with emotion and find solace in their handkerchiefs in a paroxysm of coughing and spluttering. Guess who had to wash the fingerprint powder of the interior of the 'returned' car 3 days later?

In the meantime, on this first night, I noticed that I was number 6 in the crew on the Pump Escape or the 'turnout' as it was known. This Dennis/Rolls Royce engined appliance carried a crew of six-two in the front and four in the back of the limousine style cab-a 50 foot timber wheeled escape on the roof with a 1000 gallon per minute pump-a 100 gallon water tank and of course two 1 hour oxygen breathing apparatus or as it was commonly referred to-BA. This carriage wheeled ladder was a direct descendent of the parish pump/ladders of old. In addition the rider board listed out the Dennis/Rolls Royce Pump crew. This appliance of similar appearance carried a 35 foot extension ladder a 1000 GPM pump a crew of six a 200 gallon water tank and of course BA. Both of these appliance supplied the primary life saving role and carried out the bulk of the bread and butter daily work load and could by force of manning circumstances be crewed by five and four Firefighters respectively.

Amongst the Specials, as they were known, stood the mighty Dennis/Rolls Royce powered German built Metz 125 foot turntable ladder pump with its crew of three. This particular appliance was unique in its ladder length, the average turntable ladder length being 100 foot, although at that time the leviathan of them all was a 150 foot ladder in service with the Leeds Fire Brigade in England.

Unusually the ladder crewman rode in an open cubby hole facing rearwards at the back of the enclosed cab. This was an especially exciting place to ride while roaring through the city centre on a  Saturday afternoon, the blur of the startled faces of the shoppers and the overtaken drivers alike as this huge appliance with its creaking and groaning ladders wove its way through the melee with its electric bells hammering away-air horns were to be fitted a short time later. Unfortunately as a piece of operational equipment it turned out to be pretty useless and was later downgraded to 100 feet in length but by that time new concept aerial platforms had been added to the fleet.

The even more specialised end of the rescue spectrum was dealt with by the huge bus-like Dennis/Rolls Emergency Salvage Tender its crew of six covering the whole of the city with its quite simply exceptional range of specialist rescue tools, generators etc etc. a DIY's delight. Everyone agreed it was over loaded but the diverse range of equipment was growing and this gear was required to meet the technical challenges of the daily more complex rescues.

The specialist risks of the docklands and oil refinery were provided for by a Bedford TK engined Foam Tender. This new and highly complex piece of machinery with its 800 gallons of foam concentrate could produce foam out of every orifice but the engine 'wouldn't pull the skin of a rice pudding' and was generally regarded by its three crew members with embarrassed derision when it came to road performance. Up hill and up wind, or both, it was usual to turn the blue lights off as the appliance was regularly overtaken by sneering refuse trucks. It was the stuff of legends that on one spectacular occasion in the right conditions the speed had gone off the clock at 49 mph!

And so it was, on this exciting evening that I nervously placed my so obviously new, regulation folded fire kit and boots, in front of my feet at the lowly position at the end of the muster line at the rear of the appliances. Our personal issue fire kit-compared to that issued today-was quite simply laughable and we knew it. The 'Metro' helmet was state of the art patent leather matching our lancer buttoned serge fire tunics from Glasgow. The wellingtons-well the Duke would have been proud of them-leaked and were punctured by rusty nails at an attrition rate. The undress uniform Service trousers were protected while in action by flimsy ex-wartime National Fire Service individual black rubberised leggings rather in the manner of the chaps worn by John Wayne. These were held up by the Firefighter's individual choice of braces, buttons, or belts or by the cunning use of all three. Above all else though the bottoms had to be held at the regulation 9 inches from the ground. The leather belt, axe pouch, and axe completed the ensemble for the cat walk. The gloves….what gloves?..are you a big jessie ?

Thus equipped we were ready for war. Nevertheless having said all that we were fiercely proud of our Brigade. We knew who we were-and let no one-particularly these part-time Firefighters on the outskirts of our city domain-dare challenge us.

In this period before the 0900 hrs or 1800hrs Parade the engine room would always be awash with hubbub and purposeful bustle although Officers would clearly congregate to hand over information from Watch to Watch. Appliance drivers, those off-going and those oncoming, generally conferred on the state of their chargers for which they were most decidedly responsible. Any 'new' scratches were deliberated over and subsequently disowned by the on-coming Watch Officers. As the magic minute would draw nigh tension would start to build and quiet settle over the engine room for right up the order 'White Watch Dis-miss' the duty watch was required to respond to incoming fire calls.

The Parade call over the tannoy of '1759hrs' would alert all the personnel present to take up their 'at ease' respective positions. The off going Watch-a Watch at Chi' consisted of a Station Officer[Watch Commander]-four Sub Officers-four Leading Firefighters-and 17 Firefighters-would stand alongside their appliance at their rider positions behind their stacked fire kit with the two Watch Commanders out front and the oncoming watch at the rear of the appliance room behind their kit. At the precise moment of the striking of the Parade bell the entire company present numbering roughly 40 to 50 would be called to attention by the oncoming Watch Commander and the Roll called in this well practised twice daily human tide manoeuvre. Upon completion of this essential task the off going Watch would be dismissed and file boisterously away usually to the disdain of the new Duty Officer now that a proper Watch was on duty.

So began my operational life in the Belfast Fire Brigade.

The detailing of riders-BA wearers, to whom distinct safety working rules applied-other duties-and other notes of special interest-would be read out. On this occasion I was of 'special interest' and was welcomed to my Watch for the first time just before the Watch 'fell out' to carry out the essential inventory and safety checks of all the equipment on the appliances. Appliances drivers were always held accountable for any deficiencies that were not discovered and reported at Watch change over time. As a consequence from time to time on large incidents equipment went 'walk about' from other Station's appliances. Accordingly deficiencies were immediately corrected if possible or recorded by him with the Duty Officer for future action.

It was then a case of following the throng up the stairs and into the galley for a cuppa' tea.

The messroom table is famous in Fire Service circles. Until your acceptance is generally approved you try to be unobtrusive as possible and listen to the verbal bandinage of your new colleagues. This is not as it might seem at first glance a superficial look, at you, by them. The new boy will always be drawn into their quizzical probing and chatter. As often as not this is a serious attempt to find out your strengths or weaknesses and equally for you to find out theirs. World wide the mess table is where friends for life are made, or sometimes enemies. It is where after-the-incident scenarios are re-run, decisions analysed, performances reviewed and where personalities and especially senior Officers-for whom there is no place at the 'Table'-are scrutinised.

This inner sanctum of close camaraderie is conducive to the public sharing of many thoughts and hidden fears. Whether they be personal or Service. A place where the very soul is sometimes bared. This is where the critical trust develops between the newly appointed recruit and the Watch. Can they take a gentle joke, can he or she be trusted to hold the line and pull their weight, keep calm, be resolute when the going gets rough? What are their views on righting the ills of the world? The recruit has everything to prove and the Watch nothing. This was made clear to me from the outset during my initial interview by the Watch Commander. So the Watch's assessment will continue until the body corporate has made up its mind both individually and collectively whether you can or cannot be trusted with another Firefighter's life, so the microscopic scrutiny has no idle intent.

Fire-fighters-when you pause to think about it-get everywhere. It does not matter how top secret an establishment anywhere in the world, they will already have been there-done that-and be writing home to Mum. The intelligence system operated through the gossip clearing house of the 'Table' would make the espionage services green with envy. However, even with such an efficacious grapevine there are always better more skilful sleuths to be found. The mighty 'Table' always gallantly bows to the Cooks and Cleaners. They are indeed the Princes of Intelligence. Their predictions are always guaranteed to an accuracy of 100% before even the Great One has thought about it! So consequently as one can see there are no secrets in the Service.

By 1830hrs we would normally be detailed for our fatigue duties-or called either to the station yard for drill in full fire kit or to the recreation room for a lecture. Fatigue duties for the new recruit always seemed to be either the nightly inter-station internal mail run or in the galley setting tables, cleaning dishes and heating up the cooks culinary delights, left prepared for her unsuspecting favourite bunch of boys on night duty.

Stand-down on night duty began at 2000hrs when supper was served by the galleymen. After this the rest of the night was yours to do with as you wished. Providing, that is, fire calls did not interrupt. Some personnel would play snooker, table tennis, or pursue their individual hobbies. Yet others studying for promotion would absent themselves to their dorm and bury their face in a training manual, sometimes individually, some times in small question and answer study groups. The T.V. room was usually the gathering place for the intellectually unscrubbed.

Boots off and lights out at 2300hrs. was diligently adhered to by most Duty Officers.

The general public may jib at the thought of Firefighters sleeping but believe me it is not proper sleep and in any case the intention is to have fully charged rested rescuers. A Citizen's very life frequently depends on it. The body might rest but the mind is like a large pre-programmed coiled spring the slightest unusual sounds awakens even the heaviest of sleepers and the actions that follow are distinctly by sinew rote. Statistically Firefighters live an average of 5 years after their retirement before popping their clogs, now I wonder why? Today's experts tell us of their sleep pattern studies. Any Firefighter could have saved them the trouble. Between 2300hrs and 0130hrs is the difficult time for turnouts. It is the deepest sleep. It still takes a gargantuan individual effort to hit the streets within 20 seconds, really a rather long time, and drive a 10 tonnes fire appliance or dress in fire kit and BA whilst trying to dispel the dream in the head and take in critical information. Enough of the heroism, I digress.

Come bedtime, the new recruit's first night duty is an opportunity for a newly found father figure to take him under his wing to show him how to set his leggings and trousers over the fire boots at the end of the bed in preparation for a quick turnout. Then it is strip down to the underwear, climb into bed, and lights out. Test turnouts even at 0300 or 0400hrs were not unknown as visiting groups wandered around the city visiting bakeries and other 'night workers', but there were other 'unofficial' test turnouts.

It later became apparent that on my first night my mentor had given the nod to the other inhabitants of the dormitory, who were seemingly unconcernedly preparing themselves for bed. When at last peace reigned supreme and just as uneasy sleep beckoned the dorm door burst open-the lights came on-and someone hollered 'fire call'. So of course I was out of bed like a greyhound leaving the trap-into boots via trousers and leggings-trousers pulled up accompanied by attached leggings-by this time I was already on the move thinking-as I made it to the door-that I was doing pretty well having avoided stumbling and falling-and then there was the tricky leap onto the slippery pole. There the whole panicky flight unravelled.

Why am I not moving-not descending-why has gravity not taken over as Newton said it would? There I remain stuck on the pole. By now, of course the other dorms have disgorged their bodies who are doubled over laughing at my predictable predicament. Then I realise the obvious facts, rubberised leggings and rubber boots do not slide easily down a metal pole. Leg pressure and friction need to be very delicately controlled to achieve that. Practice makes perfect and of course I had not practised. Words of encouragement are heard from my mentor amongst the roars of laughter and with embarrassment and difficulty I begin the slow jerky, screeching, and faltering descent to the recreation room below. By the time I make my way back up the stairs, all the spectators have disappeared back to bed satisfied with the outcome of their little ploy. My first christening into the church of Watch humour has just taken place. One day it would be my turn to spectate.

0640hrs came early with the inter station Tannoy crackling into life along with the Station lights being switched on by Controls. Some Control staff wakened the sleepers softly, others took great delight in giving the nervous system an electrifying kick-start. When your life is governed by the 'click' of a tannoy you soon learned to find out before retiring who was on the eleven to nine shift in Controls.

'Were there any calls, did I miss anything?' were my first queries. 'No Allan we had a quiet night.' Was the reply. 'Oh hell!', I thought I wonder when I'll get my first turnout. Up and into the ablutions for a quick wash and shave and then on parade for 0700hrs, galley men excepted. The tasks detailed to be carried out prior to breakfast at 0800hrs included-cars and vans to be washed-engine room gate brass work and front door bell to be brassoed-and a general tidy up of the sleeping quarters, which included dressing the beds with a taut counterpane for the Duty Officer's 'bounce a penny' test. Each job was inspected by a designated Leading Fireman or the Duty Officer and if not done to his entire satisfaction it was done all over again. A well ordered life-thus was ending my first night duty-later I was to get more than my fill of action.

After breakfast at eight o'clock personnel would climb the Tower stairs for a final tidy and wash up, drop the pole into the 'Rec room' and perhaps sit for a while ruminating over the nights events or lack of them.

At 0845hrs the final pole drop of the night duty into the engine room beckoned. The engine room was deserted not unlike the Marie Celeste. Where had everyone gone was my first thought as I looked around and listened intently. A murmur of voices could be heard coming from somewhere-but where? Prowling the engine room I came upon a tidy little nucleus of the young bloods of the Watch at the front of the appliance bays. A regular group-I was later to notice-which would occasionally include the amused married 'old guard'. Apparently the morning ritual included the patient wait for the appointed time-when just around the corner from 'Chi' at next door's Oxford Street bus depot-the scene of terrible carnage in the future-the Ulster Transport Authority buses would unload its morning cargo of suburban female beauties. They would waft past-this elixir of youth-in their droves to the love lorne glances, wolf whistles, or the occasional impertinent tap on the glass of the gates to distract and attract as they hurried past to their places of work in the city centre.

Each of the lads had their particular favourite or two. There was Miss McAfee from Holywood, so named because she worked in a shoe shop of that name. Miss Law Courts no need to explain that one, and Hazel from Comber. It made a romantic prelude to the day if you could raise a smile or an acknowledgement. There were, as in all things in life, veterans of our various exhortations, the Untouchables-those who were either happily married, whose mother's marriage hit list certainly did not include Firefighters-those who looked straight ahead poker faced-or dropped their glances in studied bored disapproval.

A pleasant footnote: Not long ago I was travelling by air enroute from Belfast via Amsterdam to my final destination Oklahoma to visit with my Editor in order to have a final revision of this work completed. Sitting opposite me on the aircraft was a not unattractive middle aged dark haired lady and a little girl who I assumed was her granddaughter. I casually watched as they sat and happily played a computer game together. It gradually began to dawn on me that this lady's face was familiar to me though I could not immediately place her. I am always inclined not to leave loose ends lying around and as the journey progressed I knew I would probably never have the chance to satisfy my curiosity if the moment passed. So I determined at an appropriate moment I would ask the lady where I thought I knew her from. As we were gathering our overhead luggage prior to departing the aircraft at Schipol I popped the question, 'Would your name happen to be Hazel?' She looked at me somewhat taken aback, 'Yes' she replied 'it would'. I continued, 'Hazel from Comber' who used to get off the Ulsterbus in the mornings and run the gauntlet of a bunch of amorous young Firefighters in Chichester Street Fire Station', again she replied 'Yes'. I then introduced myself and in the few short moments we had left I told her the purpose of my journey and that she had got a special mention in company with a few of the other 'Juliets' in my book. She thanked me for making myself known to her, the last passing comment between us was, 'Small world isn't it, imagine thirty five years ago'. She also managed during this brief encounter to relate that she still had contacts with at least one of the modern day era of Belfast Firefighters, who it happens is also known to me. Perhaps those young Lotharios of yesteryear did-n't leave too bad an impression on 'Hazel from Comber' after all!

Once in a while a new wag on the Watch would come up with a carefully thought out strategy which he would hone on the cynical opinions of the more experienced before putting it into action. Some of these complex strategies were meant in military prose to secure the bridgehead established by much pleasant facial contortions and mouthed love bouquets and were usually directed at a receptive regular gaggle of giggling girls, but as in most high risk military tactics there were inherent 'minefield' risks. In this minefield the Duty Office lay at the north end of the love run and Our Highnesses Officers Mess at the other.

Briefly the technique involved a complex surreptitious chain of communications from the south side of Brigade H.Q. which faced the Bus Station-'they're coming'-to the engine room wag who at the precise moment that the girls appeared at the first bay would stride along with them waving and smiling at every gate and making mute talk as the girls walked laughing hysterically on the other side of the glass. This was going great guns until one morning our wag buried his nose straight into the Military Cross brevet on the chest of our Greatness who was making an unscheduled visit to the Duty Office…

However many a brief romance did spring forth from these little morning soirees which were often followed up by a visit by the bachelors of the bunch after nine o'clock, to gaze love struck at their particular heart's desire through their employer's shop window just to endorse the seriousness of their quest.

Testosterone levels were high in those days. These nuptial manoeuvrings would usually be brought to an abrupt premature conclusion by either the Parade bell or an irate Duty Officer trying to preserve the good name of the Brigade.

My first tours of night duty came and went, they were uneventful affairs. Calls were attended, appliances came and went but I always seemed to be on the one that did not move. I began to think that Duty Officer possessed the gift of foresight and was deliberately manipulating the manning rota to prevent me from getting my first call. So there was not much to relate by way of excitement on my three days rota leave to my civilian friends existing in their hum-drum everyday run-of-the mill jobs.

My first day duty soon came around. The second phase of the twenty four hour daily routine of a fire station began. The drill session for the day includ-ed Turntable ladder drill, with a slight variation, I had done Turntable ladder drill before but not this one. Training Officers always seem to be unable to resist the masochistic streak that I suppose most of us possess within us. The Metz T.L. was brought out and the Longworth inertia operated self rescue/emergency escape mechanism was snap hooked onto the securing eye at the head of the top extension. The operator was ordered to extend the lad-der to its full working height of 125 feet. The three man crew which included myself were ordered to fall in at the rear of the appliance. The Leading Fireman conducting the drill told me to put on the leather T.L. safety hook belt, so I had a vague idea what was coming next. It was a kamikaze manoeuvre all recruits and even most sane old hands dreaded. But it was usually only reserved for the new recruits, this was how the nerve was tested, under the full glare of your colleagues scrutiny.

'Right young Wright up you go to the top, hook yourself on, and show the operator a 'clean pair of heels' we don't want you loosing your little tootsies now, do we?'

I should explain. It was the safety procedure to place the toes-rather like a high board diver-as close to the edge of the top platform as possible-the ladder operator would glance up knowing, unless you had boots like a circus clown, the toes would be well clear on entrapment in the scything ladder movements-before he commenced to house or extend the ladder. On this occasion I was to climb the fully extended ladder all 125ft of it!

However it wasn't my toes I was worried about it. It was what I had to do with them when I reached the top that seemed the focus of my mind. So began the long climb to the top, which gave me ample time to reflect. What the hell am I doing here anyway, why did my Dad have to send in that bloody appli-cation form? I was perfectly happy being a wastrel. Who wanted to be a hero anyway it was all a bit blasé these days. On the public display evenings I used to enjoy watching this thrilling display, I often wondered if those guys really enjoyed it, now, as the fella in the big picture, I was about to find out. Ever so slowly the top of the ladder got closer, lovely view over the city, pity I'm not enjoying it. The extensions began to sway and twist. Because the ladder had become 'saddlebacked' from resting in its gallows the top section tended to be very near vertical when extended to its full working height. The purists of this type of insanity used to calculate that in any sort of training movement right or left, the base would stop, and the top platform would whip back and forth over an arc of 16 feet. I always thought it was more like 15feet 11inches myself but what is an inch between the psychotic!

Near the top now-just below the platform-what was I taught in Training School? Unclip the platform from its stowed position-and drop it into the hor-izontal-done-now negotiate over the platform and hook on-show a clean pair of heels-right, I'm hooked on. The ladder intercom crackles into life-as if I did-n't know what was coming-I am instructed to put on the sling of the Longworth and lower myself to the ground. I reach out and round to the lad-der face manage to capture the sling and pull it on board. My legs are like jelly by this time-I wonder if it is them that is making the ladder shake-na!-it's prob-ably the vibration from the engine. Cannot actually see the TL appliance roof but I suppose it's still there otherwise I wouldn't be up here wondering if its down there!

This would go down well as a circus act I think to myself-I manage to put the sling over my head and tighten it around my chest-next I unhook the T.L. belt and begin the precarious climb around the top extension which is doing its best to twist itself from its partners-hope this line has been tested-with that I let go and there is an almighty gut wrenching drop of about 10 feet until the inertia device gets up to working speed and then I watch mesmerised as the rel-ative safety of the top of the ladder recedes. Too soon yet to look for the com-fort of the ground. At the minute I am somewhere suspended between heaven and hell. It seems like I am never going to reach the ground but then before you know it terra-firma touches on the soles of my boots and its all over-for this time at any rate. I look round at my colleagues and they are studying me closely for a reaction. 'Gee that was great fellas who's next?' - it's not me that's for sure-don't you think I lie with such casual dash and elan-as I hand over the Lonsdale belt to the next jelly legged sucker.

Before the next drill can proceed the station speakers click into action and the slow monotone voice of Paddy O'Connor comes over the Tannoy, 'Fire Call, full attendance to Assembly Buildings, Fisherwick Place'. I didn't wait to hear the repeated message, I was off across the yard and into the engine room. The gates had been swung open and the Pump Escape's engine was revving waiting impatiently for it's crew. I was aboard in a flash and didn't even have time to get dressed in my fire gear. Geordie Gordon our driver shouted all aboard and off we sped. Out of the station-right turn-and up Chichester Street adopting a centre of the road position and bullying oncoming drivers to pull into their near side. It was a half mile run to Fisherwick Place straight up Chichester Street past the old Plaza ballroom then the City Hall into Wellington Place and sharp left to our destination. We pulled up outside the Presbyterian Assembly Building seat of Presbyterianism in Northern Ireland. Dressed by this time I jumped out eager and ready to do my bit. No sign of fire-my Station Officer Billy Shanks who strode off followed by his entourage of junior Officers in search of his fire.

I shouted to Geordie 'What can I do.' 'Grab a standpipe and find a hydrant.' This I located at the blind side of the building in question-opened the lid in the pavement-shipped my standpipe-a pipe with an 'L' shaped bit at the top, and waited and waited and waited. It is a tedious fact of entomological life that open jam jars attract flies so it is with the Fire Service whenever we park in the street. We simply attract the dross of the streets, the winos, the weirdoes, the flashers, the retired banana republic dictators, all of course completely off their collective trolleys. Thus it was I had my first experience with this clientele, but I had been warned. The proper technique is to completely ignore their presence no matter how sane they look, or if you have to, converse in their 'speak'. The doorbell might be ringing but nobody will ever answer. They always start by asking 'Are you from the Fire Brigade' the reply to this question are of course legion but being rather pressed for time on this occasion I replied that 'actually I was a member of the Royal Division of the Household Cavalry, that I had left my horse tied to this fire hydrant and it seemed to have wandered off and would he mind keeping an eye out for it' as off I strode.

It was about ten minutes later that I decided to desert my post to see what if any thing was happening so I poked my head around the corner. The Pump Escape was moving off with no Allan on board. I ran up to the Pump and asked the driver what was happening. I was told it was a malicious call and all appliances were returning to station. I asked him to wait while I un-shipped my periscope. This I did in double quick time and climbed aboard the Pump for the ride back to 'Chi'. On return I was given a fool's pardon by the 'Boss' but he shouldn't have left without checking that everyone was on board I thought, but I didn't have the temerity to tell him so. The standing joke for weeks afterwards on the watch was, did anyone see a submarine periscope surface in Fisherwick Place recently? I had been had again!

Back at station those daily jobs that had been due to commence while we were out looking for fires had to be caught up. After the tradesmen had been detailed and sent to their respective hidey-holes, the few remaining worker bees in the hive including myself were given a large pile of unwashed hose from the night before to wash, pressure test, and pull up the drying tower. It was also the work custom-come hail, rain, or shine-to hand scrub and bleach two lengths of hose a day over a table in the yard. The hose was of course pristine white after this treatment but it didn't half leave a resistance to laying out hose on a job through dirty puddles and the like.

The washing and testing duly expedited, the twenty lines or so of reinforced rubber-lined canvas hose were carried round and left at the base of the tower. Each must have weighed about ten pounds heavier wet than when dry. I had been in the base of the tower previously and when you looked up there did not appear to be any light at the end of the top of the proverbial tunnel some one hundred or more feet above. I had watched Watch personnel-while I was in training-equipped with fire helmets and waterproofs loading hose onto the hauling line when it snaked down from above. This was a wet, uninspiring and dangerous job too if one of these snakes decided to defy the law of gravity and come hurtling down through the darkness of the inside of the tower. For this and other sanitary reasons it was plain common-sense to remain inside the tower for the minimum time. One could never be sure that the residue of water that cascaded down, as the hose was pulled aloft, was of the street hydrant variety or from the bladder of a fireman too lazy to walk down the tower the few flights to the ablutions.

The Duty Officer must have admired my prowess at working at heights so much that he had another little delight in store. I was told to take my gear off the Pump Escape exchange it with the Chief's driver and accompany one of my colleagues up the tower to haul the hose aloft. Up the staircase we climbed past the dormitory landing level until we had to exit to the open air where we joined the outside metal spiral staircase for the final climb to the top of the tower. This time I did have time to admire the view while having a breather before going into the top of the tower. The tower at that time was the tallest structure in the city centre. It commanded a wonderful view especially of the cross channel shipping tied up at their berths at the adjacent Donegall Quay. You could almost see down their funnels into the engine rooms.

I opened the access door and stepped inside the tower onto a narrow platform which was built into the opposite wall. At right angles above us were a number of hard wood joists their square ends built into the brick wall of the tower. Their centre sections had been rounded by the countless lines of heavy wet hose that had been hauled over them probably starting with the original copper riveted leather hose in the days of old. A pulley with a well used hemp rope was threaded to one of the cross beams and so we began by lowering the rope to the bottom, which you could not see. A shout would tell us when to start hauling up.

The simple technique at the top was etched in sweat. By the time you caught sight of the hose snake, the shoulders would be coming out at their roots and the two bodies required for the task would be pulling their guts out. When the hose reached the top-one person would grab it while the other held on-the old safety rule of the sea one hand for the rope and other for himself-the female lug was then disengaged from the catspaw knot and leaning out over the black abyss the attempt was made to get one free end over a suitable joist which was accomplished with your third arm as you fed and pulled in unison the up and down of the hose until each half had equalised and was in equilibrium on its beam. Of course just once in a while it would not go as 'smoothly' as this and it was to cries of 'stand from under!' and a dash for the external staircase that the hose would be left to flail itself all the way to the bottom from whence it had just come. The acoustics of the tower added little nuances to the foul language that would float up on the ether. As I have said the personnel detailed for this task would be 'off the run' for calls but I recall on one occasion one of the barmy army I was with when the tannoy went for a fire call simply launched himself onto the hauling line and disappeared before my disbelieving eyes as he zoomed down to catch the call. All this and a malicious call in the space of two hours.

When the initial frisson of life in the Brigade wore off those daily occurrences which might initially have raised an eyebrow rapidly became accepted as part of normal life but they never lost their excitement.

The thrill of a full turn out-all 5 appliances to respond-the sudden purposeful pandemonium. The crew of the first away shouting 'turnout' to make the others stand aside-the thudding feet hitting the pole mats on the floor-the thrust away to avoid a set of boots descending on your hands-the scramble to pull up the other brace and do up the fly buttons or alternatively to pull off the fatigues-whilst listening to the thrice repeated address-the whirr of the starter motors as the engines coughed into life-the crash opening of the spring loaded gates and the slam of appliance doors- the staccato 'all aboard?' followed in a breath by the 'Go!'-the appliances edging forward eagerly to take up their preordained order in the rescue cavalcade-and suddenly in the stopwatch 9 seconds by day or the 20 seconds by night they are all gone…the lonely Chief's driver wandering disconsolately in the clouds of blue exhaust smoke and still swinging corded door trippers and battery charging leads hanging from the ceiling whilst picking his crestfallen way amidst the detritus of oil drip trays, gathering discarded collar and ties, shoes, and fatigues on his way to close the bay doors.

Small wonder then that Station visitors would be thrilled by all of this glamour. The principal actors were too, but there were always extra treats in store out in the drill yard for the ratepayers. Culminating, after a display, in the grand finale by the ladderman of the turntable-ladder in his undress uniform climbing all the 125 feet to the top platform to commune with the Gods-a quick glance around to see if Scotland is visible and then the casual reach around to pull in the loop of the Longworth and with the loop securely in place under the armpits-and with consummate ease the Geronimo step off into space-arms akimbo all the way to the ground- a quick blow on the fingernails, a brief polish on the chest, and then back to boring work. We were all completely feckless youths but we wouldn't have exchanged it for a gold bar and the boredom of an office job. John Wayne only acted the dreams-we lived them.

Most of the Stations at that time still retained their herringbone tiled floors-though Chi' did not-which had been designed to give the horses a better grip when pulling the steamers out of the station and still had the hooks in the ceiling for the automatic harness which would drop down on Dobbin when the fire alarm bells sounded. All the engine rooms had to be kept spick-and-span on the weekly scrub out.

So it was all appliances out into the yard-all engine room doors open-and the white blancoed decorative ropes-this was the era of decorative rope work-hung across to keep out the curious public. This was of course way before the advent of liquid soap concentrate so 'sugee' had to be prepared for this chore This mystical ritual was the privilege of seniority and involved the shredding by penknife of one foot long solid bars of brown soap into a bucket, the adding of mysterious ingredients to choice, and the boiling of all this concoction on the gas galley stove to produce a disgusting looking squirmy brown mess which was splattered by handful over the offending floor-then all in line with the bass brooms and off we would go shoulder to shoulder singing or whistling at the passing beauties and that was only the girls-rub-a-dub-dub 10 men in a tub-and if it was summer well then of course the swill-out jet would simply run amok! Oh!.. what a gay day- we've had a good word hijacked there. It was the apotheosis of camaraderie.

It was not all sweetness and life though. The personnel were controlled by a very rigorous discipline code in which civil liberties and personal rights were regularly and gratuitously abused. Spitting in the yard or other such foul deeds were instantly punishable by the offender generally being given the task of whitewashing out the surface water drains or by other MENSA like tasks. More formal punishments were regularly handed out under the Statutory Fire Service Discipline Regulations. The going rate for example for over-length hair was a £40 fine all on a wage of £9.2 Shillings and 6 pence a week so you learned to keep your hair short and your spit discreet. The principal of discipline as in many other things in life could be taken to the point of stupidity. On one occasion a Firefighter was a couple of minutes late for work and just as the 'Parade dismiss' was given, a turnout occurred. This unfortunate individual was successfully prosecuted with two charges-the first being Awol, absent with out leave-and secondly failure to respond to an appliance. Just think about that-that's an Englishman's logic applied to an Ulsterman.

One of the most humiliating tasks was to be sent out of the Station on routine hydrant inspection duties into the city centre to inspect and flush hydrants on a specially designed bicycle which could easily have carried Two Ton Tessy. As you grunted and clanked along in full fire kit sans helmet, studiously avoiding any kind of eye contact the greatest mortification was to be identified by one of your girl friends or worse still to have one of your colleagues gleefully bellow across the street to deliberately draw the passing shoppers attention to your presence. Up to that you had been doing a fairly decent job of personating the Invisible Man. Let no one tell you that the Provisional IRA had ski-masks first, hydrant duty Firefighters had been using them for years!

It was all very egalitarian in other respects though and we were all issued with white shirts unlike the rest of the British Fire Service which was split along the white/blue shirt-Officer and other ranks lines. Mind you, a working Firefighter wearing a white shirt and a starched collar and tie regardless of the ambient temperatures could be rather hard on your Mum!

Belfast Fire Brigade Politics...I first became aware of the politics within the Brigade during the engine room discussions on this promotion or that as we polished away at the brasses of the equipment on the appliances. Everyone was astonishingly candid about the whole business. Perhaps it goes to show how institutionalised discrimination and corruption had become in promotional terms in the Brigade. It has been said with a measure of certainty that any Brigade simply reflects the community it serves. Discussions would range over which of the short listed candidates for Station Officer up at the City Hall that day for promotional interview would fare better than the others. It all boiled down to who it was felt had the most 'pull' with this Councillor or that, and which Councillor was in the candidate's Orange or Masonic Lodge. When sweepstakes were run on the possible outcome of a promotion race this was the cornerstone upon which the odds were laid-not, you will notice, any minor consideration of merit.

Following my promotion to the rank of Sub Officer in August '69 I remember being informally approached by two members of the Masonic Order-one was a cousin and the other my immediate Watch Commander-asking if I had ever considered joining the Brotherhood. I knew that Lodge members were not supposed to make approaches to potential recruits but nonetheless approaches were made. They were probably thinking that what they were doing they considered to be in my best interest.

My reply was that I had respect for the Order and was aware of its Constitution-that it was, at least in theory, non-denominational, altruistic, and well intentioned-that it carried out charity work-mostly for its members and their families-but that its central theme was, in my opinion, one of self interest and self advancement for its membership. I had taken the opportunity to observe with cynical interest the personality cult of those who were self professed members. Self evidently a number of the senior ranks in the Brigade were members along with a substantial portion of the junior Officer ranks those whom I knew that aspired to climb further up the snakes and ladders of promotion. I was not aware of any Roman Catholic Brigade personnel who were members of the Brotherhood. It was my opinion that in general Masonic members seemed to be the self centred type who would take more out of any organisation than they would ever put in. I felt that I did not have anything to offer the Brotherhood and was therefore disinclined to give the thought of joining any serious consideration.

It was Captain Robert Mitchell MC.,QFSM.,MIFireE, an Englishman appointed Chief Fire Officer in 1962 who had overseen-during the first six years of his administration of the Brigade-how this City Hall approach to promotion procedure was being operated. Probably being a long term pragmatist or cynic depending on the standpoint he was the first Chief in Belfast to introduce promotion by qualification which had been since 1947 a Statutory requirement in the rest of the U.K. I must also say that he was supported and encouraged to this end by the local officials of the Fire Brigades Union even though there were a few closet Masons in their Socialist ranks as well. I have reflected since that this surely was a contradiction in philosophical terms for them but ambition is rarely ethically driven.

I often wondered, after promotion by qualification was introduced into the Brigade in 1969, if the number of applications for membership to the Brotherhood from Brigade personnel had decreased. However the old boy network still operated to some degree after this development and still does today. To become a Chief Fire Officer-the Fire Service Appointment and Promotion Regulations were changed suddenly overnight without explanation-the aspiring candidate has to have completed the Brigade Command course at the Fire Service College. To get on this Course requires extended interview before invited panels. Guess who sends out the invitations and controls the panels? All very subtle but still pure corruption and discrimination for all that. How is a black woman or an Irish Catholic going to go on?

What I had not said to my two friends was that I had quietly carried out in my own private capacity a survey within the Brigade on the number of Officers from Station Officer up to Assistant Chief Officer who were members, and discovered that in excess of 50% belonged to the Masonic Order. All of these were Protestant there being only one Roman Catholic Station Officer in Belfast at that time. He must have had some influence at City Hall level. I often wondered how he made it that far-perhaps he was the Token non-Protestants within the job-which thinned out the higher up the ladder Catholics climbed. This state of affairs within the Brigade was indicative and reflective of what was happening generally in society and employment in the Province at this time.

I was politically naive but due to events that were occurring on a daily basis in the Province from 1968 onwards one could not help but have some of what was happening in society rub off on you and in the process rapidly lose this degree of naivety. By this time as I was now officially part of the 'establishment' I thought it would be prudent on my part to make a deliberate effort to assess what the pecking order and the order of things in general were within the Brigade and make a mental note of it for future reference. It helps to know how people are going to react before they react. History has shown that those who cannot remember the past are doomed to relive it.

Today in Ireland the people responsible for violence have been indoctrinated in tribal history since their youth and therefore do remember history but the question remains why do the people of Northern Ireland have to constantly relive it?

I am sure it is interesting to digress for a just moment to show by example the tribal mindset point I am trying to make. I shall do this by way of quoting an unimportant issue in a way which exemplifies local 'ruling' councillors' mindsets of the period-and as likely as not-still works today-for we are still trying to sort out the legacy in Ireland that we inherited from our well intentioned forefathers-the legacy of bigotry.

On the day my promotion to substantive Station Officer was being put before the Belfast City Council Police Committee for approval I was in the company of a neighbour of mine from Sydenham in east Belfast where I lived. We were in another Committee room in the City Hall pleading the case for the residents of our road objecting to a bus route which had been imposed on our thoroughfare without prior consultation with, or by the agreement of the residents. In the eventuality we lost our case but when we came out I was spoken to by our Councillor for the Ward Hubert Cranston who told me 'You know Mr. Wright you might have won your case if you hadn't canvassed the Nationalist members of the Transport Committee'. I had taken it upon myself to lobby as many members of the committee as I could at their homes. These included Gerry Fitt and Paddy Kennedy prominent in the civil rights movement at that time. Other Transport Committee members that I had approached included Eileen Paisley (wife of Ian) and Hubert Cranston himself. I did not particularly care what their political or religious persuasions were. They were all members of the same committee as far as I was concerned and they were supposed to represent their electorate equally, or so I thought. It was the Belfast Corporation Transport Department that we were opposing not any particular political party.

I had also written to the M.P. for the area Roy Bradford, who was also a Stormont Minister. His huge contribution to the issue was a letter wishing us good luck but with no active support forthcoming. In my political naivety canvassing was what I thought politics were all about. I had not allowed for the party political wormery, the religious barriers, and bigotry that existed. Council Members as often as not served on several Committees within the City Council it is therefore not unreasonable to assume that Councillor Cranston's attitude to my soliciting support from Members, other than Unionist, would reflect the 'unofficial' policy which existed within the Police

Committee who were the political masters of the City's Fire Brigade and thence logically this attitude would translate into an unofficial recruitment policy for the Belfast Fire Brigade. Councillor Cranston had played his Unionist card and by his remarks I could only conclude that my card had been marked for my future in the Brigade as well. As the old saying goes there are more ways to kill a pig than shoving apples up its rear.

At this point I recalled and began to understand what my friend Paul Burns a Roman Catholic friend had said to me before departing the Brigade in 1968. He and I had joined together and he was obviously eager to climb the promotional ladder early in his Service career. During our many discussions he had commented on the lack of future for his 'sort' in the Brigade. He was the only Roman Catholic recruit out of our class of ten in July '63 and the only one of five Catholics in the Brigade of 350 which comprised one Station Officer, one Sub Officer, one Leading Firefighter and two Firefighters. These simple statistics gives the merest insight to discrimination within the Brigade if you were 'not one of us'.

Paul's father-a property developer-had numerous business contacts and dealings within the City Hall. Because of his outgoing, jolly and charming nature he was one of the very few Roman Catholics who was trusted and had the confidence of-if not the local elected councillors-then their administrative officials. He was able to bridge the social and business gap within the Unionist establishment in the City Hall in the early sixties. He knew how the local political and social hierarchy worked and was able to advise Paul accordingly. He had repeatedly told him go East young lad, anywhere except Northern Ireland. As a Roman Catholic he felt his son had no future in the Brigade or the Province and he was right.

Paul who is still my oldest(?) and closest friend eventually became a Divisional Officer in Lancashire County Fire Brigade. On one occasion I recall he was sent to hoist the Union Flag by an Officer who thought he might take the opportunity to raise a cheap laugh out of the situation, so off Paul went as ordered. A short while later the front door bell sounded and the Duty Officer was summoned, 'Did he know?' queried the vigilant frosty Loyalist, 'that the Union Flag was being flown upside down at distress'?...

I often wonder that if Paul could have foreseen the forthcoming overall changes that were to take place within the Brigade within the ensuing twenty years since his departure whether in retrospect he would have decided to stay. Paul, in addition to his father's attributes, was always a determined, dogmatic, and dedicated character to any cause which he chose to pursue. I wouldn't doubt that if he had stayed he could have made Chief here. He had a lot of potential talent which he still retains to this day but I felt it would only have been wasted in Belfast at that time.

Paul-opting for the lesser 'paddy' discrimination in England- later transferred to seek his fame and fortune and to take up a Sub Officer's Instructor's post at the Home Office Fire Service Technical College in Gloucestershire in England.

Around the early and mid seventies there was an exodus from the Brigade of personnel from both sides of the religious divide. It was noticeable that most of the Protestants who resigned did so to join either the Police or Prison Service and most Roman Catholics emigrated abroad or went to England where they felt they would get marginally better deal. There were a number of reasons for this migration-poor pay was one-fear of the uncertain future that staying in Northern Ireland meant for them and their families-and another, and perhaps the principal concern, was that some had already suffered from intimidation within their own communities.

It is safe to say with conviction that in no way did the camaraderie that was shared by individual Firefighters serving together suffer because of religious and political differences or any internal frictions contribute to this glut of resignations. Firefighters are a very close knit bunch of men and women living at close quarters when on duty and are united in a common purpose to serve their fellow man-serving as comrades under arms-each inter-dependant on the other for their personal safety and survival. There is no room for any political or religious bigotry. We all undoubtedly hold our own views on these matters but they are left behind when we enter a Fire Station. I have seldom seen or heard any political feelings expressed but on a few occasions when political and street tensions have been particularly high I have sensed something simmering below the surface I always brought it immediately to the attention of the personnel involved and quickly snuffed these issues out before any animosity or hostilities could be allowed to surface.

Peacetime-The Mundane-The Magnificent-The Melee...Even as I was receiving my initiation into Brigade politics and the terrors of the turnout the Brigade was as they say continuing to go about its lawful occasion. Although every incident is different, the mundane-which is always a trap for the unwary-still continues to go hand in hand with the exceptional, such is the very attraction of Fire Service life.

One of the more mundane tasks at the time-in a city kept warm domestically with coal fires- was the ubiquitous chimney fire. We dealt with these by the thousands particularly at night time and on the dark winters nights. The Fire Service technical manual offers sagacious advice on the four useful ways of extinguishing these tedious events, however in practice-and we had plenty of that-the junior Officers of the Brigade invariably chose to use the top down technique.

This slick operation-carefully thought out to ensure the least possible post incident cleaning for the personnel-involved the use of an extension ladder pitched to the roof-a roof ladder up to the adjacent chimney stack and thence to the offending pot-a hosereel from the appliance was carried aloft-a quick squirt down the chimney-and hey presto on to the next one. Suffice it to say that while the 'troop' was up on the roof-inside the nearest metal dustbin lid was requisitioned, inserted into the fire place with a small shovel-chimney, fires, for the use of-and as soon as the first trickle of water was spotted it was off with the water-a quick tidy around, frequently leaving it cleaner than we found it, and off we would jolly well go. As simple as your uncle Allan.

Of course there were more numerous variations on these contortions than the Kamasutra but I will not bore the reader with this trivia. Just once in a while however one of the crew, the man with a mission on top, could get it just a tad wrong.

So there I was this afternoon in Sandy Row-the pump operator on a chimney fire-catching the admiring glances of the local ornithology and keeping the other eye on the water tank contents gauge as I pumped. Par for the chimney course was about 60 gallons. Well my gauge continued to plummet past this mark until it hit the 100 gallon level. At that moment the Sub Officer who shall be nameless-but was nicknamed 'Desperate Dan' by his underlings-burst forth from the front door and in a classical imitation of a dying helicopter gesticulated to 'knock off' the water. Clearly something was amiss, but what care I. It would appear-according to the householder later-that as she was tidying her upstairs bedroom she was startled by an almighty whooshing noise which heralded the deluge of ankle deep black slurry all over her best carpets from the wrong fireplace. Ah! the joys of command.

In the winter time auntie's favourite backyard cat would migrate to the chimney pots for a wee bit of warmth. This would, of course, bring on a rash of 'trapped cats'. Here the rescue technique was exquisitely simple-'Now, love why don't you go in and put the kettle on while we deal with this tricky situation'-in would go granny-off with the hosereel-quick blast on cat-and oh! look!, how wonderful, tabby's come down!

Have you ever noticed that the entire world could be coming off its axis-your favourite budgie could be lying claws up stiff as board in the bottom of the bird cage-the second flood could be up to your lower lip-and as Noah was pithily recorded as commenting- 'all every one wants to do round here is put the kettle on'?

But t'Army during the Firemen's Strike did not understand the technical subtleties of this type of rescue. On their afternoon, t'Army heroically retrieved the aviating cat and gave it to the grateful owner and then went in for a cup of tea on this chilly day. The cold cat-left to its own devices, cats are like that, completely ungrateful-just wandered off into the street and found another warm spot. After much exchange of pleasantries and self congratulation all round t'Army with great elan and dash jumped up on their Green Goddess and roared off into the sunset straight over the cat which had been warming itself under the appliance exhaust...

Along with farce, and in parallel with the Beast which was starting to flex its muscles, there was pure unadulterated heroism in the Brigade's daily life as well. So towards heroism.

It was the practice of the Corporation Cleansing Department-for routine maintenance purposes-in the summer evenings when the traffic flow was reduced to open the manholes that strode down the centre line of the busy thoroughfares in the City. The objective of this maintenance was to clean out the silt settling pits which lay about 15 feet below the access manholes These pits-about 3 feet deep were set below the sewer line level and were built at intervals along the 5 foot diameter sewer run to intercept and settle/trap the heavier silt in the run-off. Normally check-chains were permanently installed at intervals in the sewer for the safety of sewermen should they loose their footing in a sudden above ground downpour and get swept downstream.

The working technique in this malodorous task for the two men normally involved was to bring in a trailer for the spoil and to erect a free standing wire winch and bucket gantry over the manhole whence the unfortunate sewerman would descend, after a suitable period of ventilation, to his obnoxious, but warm task of shovelling this silt into the lowered bucket. This risky business was long before employers valued or were accountable in law for their questionable working practices.

Anyway, over on the Albertbridge Road in East Belfast the long overdue de-silting was about to take place and the Department set up its operation on a particular bright summers evening. An intrinsic risk in this work is sewer gas-caused by the decomposition of matter-its stealthy and deadly properties are well known to sewermen and Firefighters alike. Sewerland-like a tropical forest with a constant humid temperature-is the adventure playground of leptospirosis, or Weil's disease-a consequence of rats urine-and other, too numerous to mention, unsavoury unmentionable potential killers.

This evening the operation commenced with one man as usual at the bottom filling the bucket and his mate the 'topman' available for bucket emptying and traffic safety above. There was a fair flow of water in the sewer but nothing the bottom man in his thigh boots couldn't accommodate and so he commenced work. All progressed well for a short time but as the bottom man dug deeper into the silt it is clear that he released a cloud of sewer gas and in a few seconds was overcome and collapsed into the water. His 'topman' observing this and after a few moments of calling and getting no response ran to a nearby Public house to raise the alarm and call the Brigade.

In as many minutes as it takes to relate this tale the Pub's occupants spilled out onto the street and made at the run for the manhole-and, without in anyway impugning the heroes involved, Dutch unfortunately did add his Courage to the situation. In spite of the pleadings of the 'top man' to wait for the Brigade one brave soul, deciding to try and rescue the sewer man, climbed down the embedded rungs in the brickwork. The inevitable happen and the would be rescuer was also immediately overcome and fell on top of the sewerman. What happened next was appalling in its predictability-the would rescuer's friend set off down to rescue his pal-and was in turn overcome himself. The sewer water flow rapidly built up around all three victims and in a few seconds this 'plug' of humanity was propelled piston like down into the sewer proper to be brought up some yards further on against the first set of safety check chains…

In our work when an incident starts to slide down hill out of control-and it happens-there is that little that can be done but to ride the death slide and pray…thus it was this evening.

While this tragedy was rapidly unfolding the Pump and Emergency Salvage Tender from Chi' -the Pump from Albertbridge was elsewhere- were hurtling towards the scene completely aware by radio of what was happening as horrified call after horrified call came in for help-the appliance drivers cursing the traffic-urging their steeds on-willing them to get there….

When the God reaches down to beckon forward a hero His choice seems, at times, arbitrary if not a little whimsical…

In the back of the speeding EST was one Firefighter by the name of Billy 'Jaunty' Johnston. 'Jaunty' by name and Jaunty by nature. He was the very bane of the erstwhile 'Desperate Dan's' life. 'Dan' never could get Jaunty to wear his soft cap properly nor 'toe the line'-Jaunty strode about the engine room with his great outsplayed feet-like a fighting bantam cockerel striding through a snow drift-full of self confidence and ready at the drop of an order to give 'Dan' a load of old lip. Of such unlikely essence are heroes made...

As the EST thundered on Sub Officer Miller ordered Jaunty to don a BA and the remainder of the crew get ready with a life line for Jaunty and a rescue line for the anticipated task so that the crew could hit the street running upon arrival. And that is precisely what happened. As the appliance roared into attendance at the, by now, crowded pessimistic scene. The crew leapt into action.

Burdened by now with two lines and clutching an oxygen cylinder-in a well rehearsed drill- pausing for a few seconds to adjust his nose clips on his BA set-and with just a glance down below- Jaunty grabbed the steel cable of the winch with his bare hands-and he was off-sliding fire pole like down into the dark abyss-cutting his hands and arms-and unnoticed, partly tearing the oxygen inlet tube to his mouthpiece.

As he landed waist deep in filth he immediately cracked open the oxygen cylinder to get some life giving oxygen into the foetid atmosphere. Hesitating for a second to appraise the situation with his miners headlamp-he was off down the sewer half kneeling, slipping, and sliding into the pitch blackness-head bumping on the sewer roof-until making contact and starting to disentangle the bodies-giving each one as he struggled alone-a vital shot of oxygen in the face as he strapped the rescue harness on.

And so the rescue went on apace until all those requiring succour were quickly hauled out-that is until his turn came-by then for some indeterminate reason which Jaunty couldn't quite work out in his mind he seemed unable to make his legs work properly as he tried to climb the wall rungs-the ingested sewer gas entering the ripped BA tube beginning by now to take its insidious toll. In an instant the crew above sensing he was in trouble took up the slack on his personal safety line and started to haul their protesting colleague out of his personal whirlpool.

So like so much primordial slime our hero was eventually dragged semi-conscious up into the street to be 'beached' in the gutter and then despatched, a stinking heap, to the hospital. What an undignified end to a glorious achieve-ment-this stupendous solo effort at the sharp end-in the greatest traditions of a great Brigade. Later the hospital bulletin in its sterile prose stated in as many words of the rescued-one did not make it-one was not expected to-and one did.

Jaunty? Well the nurses just got fed up with him ogling them and after about 24 hours slung him out into the street. Desperate Dan loved him for a whole day and the Royal Society made him an 'official' hero. A short while later he drifted on to another job....maybe the personal price he paid was too high? We all missed him. He was most certainly was one of the Glorious Boys of the BFB.

The Albert Bridge, of which I have written previously, has not been includ-ed in the history books millennium's works of architectural art but it does have a place in history at least in respect of the Brigade. This long high bridge span-ning the Lagan joins east Belfast with the Markets area in central down town. It stands there in silent cast iron Victorian sufferance observing the daily flood both beneath-and back and forth across its high broad back-that other tide, those of the industrious ants. But even the Bridge has its place on the history rostrum of best views, as it did on a particular day in the summer of '66.

The Rev Ian as he is chummily known to his congregation decided he would march in prayerful attack formation across the Bridge from the east through Cromac Square to the Presbyterian Assembly Rooms in Fisherwick Place to exchange a few biblical tracts with the errant Presbyterians who had an annoying habit of not toeing the party dogma line. In the event he was a lit-tle late for his appointment due to a tiresome minor skirmish along the way.

He had an interesting Fire Officer in his midst who was one of his disci-ples by the name of Hercules Victor Mallon. Clearly with parents who had great ambitions for him. 'Herky' as he was known to the multitudes was more regularly known to his Fire Brigade 'commoners' as Sub Officer Mallon who at one time in an otherwise illustrious career failed to restrain an enthusiastic recruit driver as he attempted to drive a two storey appliance under a one storey bridge. The Chief's view was that Hercules failed to lift up the bridge in time and was as a consequence demoted one rank for a time.

Meanwhile back at the Markets....Now the 'Markets' area creatively named for the fruit, veg', and cattle markets in the vicinity was a mere hundred yards from Chi's front door. As well being a Republican area and another deprived enclave it had a curious ethos of solidarity. Possibly the gypsy-like nature of the fruit and veg stall holders contributed to this collective characteristic. This amalgam ultimately produced a pugnacious community mindset almost uniquely its own. Even within a Belfast filled with such truculent diversity these fearsome people were treated with a great deal of circumspection by anyone who had occasion to visit their territory. Because quite simply in that great Irish condition they were 'agin it'. So it needs little imagination to conclude that they were 'agin' the Rev's rumbustious march through their territory and-pre-parade-there was much loose talk of 'Custer's Last stand' on a date-the 6th of June-D-Day, which brought its own connotations with it.

The Bridge was not the only silent spectator that Sunday, the on duty Firefighters on stand-down were watching from the top floor of Chi' as well. First came the sound of the drums from the east, then the marcher's banners appeared below the horizon of the Bridge then eventually the placards became discernible as the 'rumpty tumpty' assembly strode over the crest and down into the curve of the 'Little Big Horn' at which point the marching column was lost to the viewers behind the obstruction of the white Portland stone Law Courts opposite. The sound of the band continued for a brief period to be instantly curtailed by a banshee like roar as the good denizens of the Markets went into action. At one point there was what one listening WWII veteran described as a hand grenade going off and then errie silence.

A few seconds later the dreaded tannoy clicked on and announced a fire call to the Post Office in Cromac Square. I was driving the Pump and it was only the Pump to go for some unusual reason. By this time of course matters had long since gone beyond the joke stage in Chi'. It is sensible custom and practice to get dressed in fire kit before attending calls in the immediate vicinity of the station and that is what we did. With the instruction to 'take it easy' I nosed the appliance out of the Station and around the two corners into Cromac Square where we stopped to take a 'look see' before proceeding.

It appears that the night before the march someone had conveniently left two loaded articulated open topped trailers parked in side streets adjoining the Square. They were laden with tons of broken cast iron railway fish plates which by now were scattered thickly across Cromac square around the recumbent figures of many marchers. I vividly recall seeing a Police constable sitting on the edge of the pavement with blood streaming down his face as we looked diagonally across the small square to the dying flames of a Molotov cocktail which had been thrown against the wall of the Post Office. Gingerly picking and clearing our way over to the small fire which we quickly extinguished we were ordered to mount up and just sit there while the Sub Officer engaged in conversation with the local hard cases.

Do not let anyone try to tell you what a riot atmosphere is like. It has to be experienced to be believed. The air quite simply buzzes and crackles with volatile tension and the hair on the back of the neck stands straight out. One wrong move is all that it takes to trigger this maelstrom of primordial emotion off again. So there we sat until the Sub climbed back on board and ordered me to drive, ever so slowly, the wrong way up a one way street and off back to the Station. Apparently it had been 'suggested' that our presence was not desired.

We had experienced similar volatility in the streets during the annual tribal celebrations of the 12th of July and the 15th of August but this was something else.

Still, I suppose it broke up a boring Sunday afternoon for the 'boys'. What was few cracked heads and a good punch up all round, for it all made for great post prandial bar-room talk. Little did we all realise that we had just entered the chilling classroom of urban guerrilla warfare wherein sat our teacher the Grim Reaper gently stroking his scythe, and though we were reluctant students, we had much to learn.

CHAPTER

2

Reaping The Whirlwind ....

Irish Stew-a Recipe for Disaster...It is not intended that the uninitiated reader of Northern Irish affairs should have to quaff deeply of the cup of blood which is Irish history in order to try and grasp the complexities of a religious, sectarian, and political conflicts which has evolved into a continuing 'peak and trough' armed struggle over the past three hundred years between the peoples on the island of Ireland. Nevertheless a broad understanding would no doubt help the reader achieve some perception of history's lessons which have been completely ignored by the protagonists in this present revival of the 'Troubles'. The current 'peak' phase of this conflict has been carried to the very seat of democratic power in the heartland of the British government in London in an effort to coerce British politicians in the same manner that Ulster's political majority electorate have been militarily coerced over the past thirty years. A multitude of obscenities have been perpetrated in an attempt to make the majority surrender their freely elected choice to be ruled from Westminster and not Dublin.

However it is necessary that the uninformed be given some understanding of the historical events that has led to what has become the most determined and concerted military/political effort to date by Republican/Nationalism, to wrest power from the silent democratic majority and give it to some hitherto unknown and unexplained institution within a United Ireland. The Good Friday Agreement of 1998 is simply the democratic alternative to Republicanism's intended military solution to the continuing problem.

Northern Ireland has been allowed to suffer the death of a thousand cuts by consecutive British governments. Each with varying degrees of committment to stamping out terrorism and resolving its self generated political problems. It has had a succession of Secretaries of State appointed from Westminster since its own Stormont Parliament was prorogued in March 1972. They have included government Ministers from Westminster such as William Whitelaw, Francis Pym, Merlyn Rees, Roy Mason, Humphrey Atkins, Tom King, Jim Pryor, Douglas Hurd, Peter Brook Sir Patrick Mayhew and latterly

Majorie Mowlam. Eleven 'Supremos' in some twenty five years, each having had a learning curve to go through and each with their magic solutions.

The appointment of Secretary of State for Northern Ireland is undoubtedly the poisoned chalice of British politics. No sooner would this or that be achieved than these Ministers would be whisked back to London to follow their masters' bidding. Their new political role in government then being dependent on, whether or not, their political star had waxed or waned in the eyes of the respective Prime Minister under whom they served during their sojourn in the Province. Hardly conducive to the continuity of a healing policy in attempting to suture a long running sore which is set in such a volatile environment.

No matter what disinformation the propagandists put out to the listening world the social and political injustices previously complained about in Northern Ireland have largely been addressed, if not yet solved. The beginning of these reforms was begun as far back as 1969. The embryo of the success achieved is borne out by this statement given in the *New Left Review* by one of the founding Civil Rights organisers Eamonn McCann in which he admits,

> *'Instead of uniting the two communities as originally hoped the Civil Rights Campaign was dividing them more than ever. We keep saying parrot-like that we are fighting on working class issues for working class unity... It is a lot of pompous nonsense... The consciousness of the people fighting on the streets at the moment is sectarian and bigoted.... Everyone applauds loudly when we say in a speech that we are not sectarian, we are fighting for the rights of all Irish workers but really that's because they see this as the new way of getting at the Protestants'.*

An honest and forthright statement from one of the minority which is as true in its subtlety today as it was in its candour in 1969.

The Province has slowly bled, suffering the death of a thousand cuts. Its slow tortured execution taking place at the hands of its sons and daughters-'in this land of saints and scholars'-by those who would purport to love its hallowed soil. All in the bloody attempt to unite its people. Proscribed organisations have killed, maimed, and destroyed in the historic cause of Irish Unity an ideal that is by now long outdated in a land where these paramilitary groups have no mandate given to them by the people of Ireland, North or South of a border which geographically divides them. It is only too obvious that those real injustices which are based in the past have been found difficult to remedy in the present.

The Irishman it would seem always reserves his right in the last analysis, to attempt to resolve his political problems by force of arms. But then is this not the recourse by which the rest of the world seeks to resolve the problems between nations when failure to reach agreement is not achieved, when slaughter, violence and destruction is then given the legal and sanctified status of war? So it is quite piously hypocritical of foreign politicians to complain about the Irish doing the self same thing.

Religion is the label that is too often expeditiously and indeed all too readily attached to these 'modern' versions of the 'Troubles'. Apparently it is the reason and justification for the desecration that has taken place in this corner of the British Isles. Violent acts and injustices perpetrated in the dim and distant past may indeed have been substantial contributors to those historical conflicts but not today. How many of today's extremists attend their churches for worship? Damn few I would guess. Religion is often accused as being the vessel for conflict between peoples throughout history. I simply do not believe it is. Those who follow their own particular God within each of the myriad of world religions do so usually in harmony sharing the same broad beliefs one with another. Perception and interpretation of religion is as diverse as each of those followers who belong to it. When dissension does occur within a cult, violence is not normally resorted to. Given these circumstances these religions may fragment and splinter. Splinter groups may form and be led by those who have dissented-in the wish to seek an ecclesiastical power base for their beliefs-but at least in modern times this is usually done without bloodshed.

Christianity is a prime example of this in the western world where within its house there are many mansions-Roman Catholicism-Protestantism subdividing into-Presbyterians-Methodists- Latter Day Saints-Jehovah Witnesses etc.,etc. some of these sects in turn subdividing yet again. It is when differences of belief and misunderstanding occurs between religious factions and when deference to the views of others ceases to be the guiding light amongst religious cultures that physical conflict ensues. While this conflict may be pursued under the guise and name of religion it has little to do with actual religion at all and all to do with the basic animal instinct inherent within the human being which takes over when all reason fails and the will to solve problems by domination, born of killing, surfaces. A lethal mentality which subsumes every other rational peaceful approach and to which any form of reason is an anathema.

"… but I'm an Atheist, honest to God! "

The Province of Ulster sits at the northern end of the island of Ireland. It consists of nine counties although the political map of Northern Ireland only consists of six counties under the jurisdiction of the United Kingdom. If that is not confusing enough parts of the 'south' or Republic, Donegal, lie physically further north than Northern Ireland! The 'Province' as its euphemistically referred to by some of those living within its borders measures roughly 110 miles east/west and 80 miles north/south roughly 9000 square miles populated by about 1.5 million residents. The Province occupies just less than one quarter of the land mass of the island. The whole of Ireland would quite comfortably fit twice into a mid-west state in the U.S. Though whether the 'Doodle Dandies' would want to fit it in or not is a moot point.

Those of a masochistic nature or those who simply 'love a good read' and would seek to be confused further will find an excessive number of books available on Irish history. Written not only by those who record violent events in Ireland but also by those who would seek to solve them. Historians write from the beginning of an event or period and there should the assiduous reader commence. However anyone who chooses to take up the pen and write about any aspect of the Irish problem are to be well advised that in so doing it is with the certain knowledge that there is no 'quick fix' end in sight and all superficial attempts to condense Ireland's history tend to end up with as yet another unintended 'seminal' *work.*

Northern Ireland has suffered in excess of three thousand fatalities over this past thirty years or more of this three hundred year war. History sowed the winds of their destruction, these unfortunates simply reaped the whirlwind.

The Witches Brew…First a 'wee' dash of…History has spun the spider's web for this recipe for disaster. Suspicion, loathing and hatred of English dominance existed within Irish Roman Catholic Celtic hearts from the times of the Reformation when Henry VIII for his own lustful reasons decided that England should break with the Church of Rome. The Irish did not give support nor share in his subterfuge and wished to hold onto the Roman Catholic faith. While this is indeed an extremely superficial statement covering a multitude of events it simply serves to give the reader a toehold on the ladder of history.

The next rung of this ladder is the forfeiture of the northern Irish lands of the Chieftains O'Neil and O'Donnell to the Crown in 1608. The British government of the day decided to 'tie' this land into the Union by means of placing or planting English and Scots settlers on to the by now appropriated lands. This was the so called Plantation of Ulster. During this period of 'civilising' indigent Irish crofters were forcibly displaced from their lands. Naturally this simply fomented and encouraged dissent in those so deprived and it was not long before the understandable backlash came.

It is critical to the understanding of the present day troubles in the Province to seek to grasp the impact that this backlash had, and continues to have, on the very psyche of the Protestants in the Province.

The backlash when it came in 1641 took the form of a series of brutal attacks, hangings, shootings, and massacres perpetrated against both the English and Scots settlers by Gaelic Irish Roman Catholics in- as they saw it- the legitimate pursuit of the preservation of their faith and the recapture of their stolen lands. There is some historical dispute about the magnitude of this genocide but nevertheless the intended effect was to terrorise the settlers into leaving. In that respect it was only partially successful. The Crown's position was to effectively abandon the Planters to their own fate. Naturally this left them embittered, entrenched, and surrounded on all sides by their foes, quite literally on the ramparts fighting to the last man. This deep fear, with some justification, of a second abandonment by todays Crown continues to dominate the psyche of collective Unionism until this very day. It remains to be seen if history does repeat itself?

This pivotal event was some time before William-Prince of the Dutch state of Orange-landed in Brixham in Devon on the south coast of England in 1688 with his Army and decided to grace Ireland with his brand of Protestantism-in order as he saw it also-to defend the faith. The question was which faith? Have you ever noticed how 'Gott' is always 'mitt us'? Well he cannot be with everybody. Now, can he?

William crossed the Irish Sea, to be welcomed by the beleaguered Planters, where he successfully challenged the rule of England's King James I and proclaimed the Protestant faith in Ireland. You could be forgiven for wondering what a Dutch Prince fighting an English King on Irish soil had to do with the natives? What indeed.

Following his rout of King James's Army at the Battle of the river Boyne in 1690 William was magnanimous enough in victory to let those of the vanquished Army who would not join his service be permitted to take passage to other corners of Europe where many sold their services and distinguished themselves as mercenaries in the armies of France and Spain.

Then add a pinch of..... Oliver Cromwell who physically oppressed Roman Catholicism and its followers with his Army of Roundheads-so called because of their tonsorial style and round helmets-were victors of the English civil war over the Royalist Army of the Cavalier King Charles. Cromwell's Army plundered, raped, and killed throughout the length and breadth of Ireland and razed the town of Drogheda to the ground. He was probably more responsible than any other English ruler for the native Irish patriots hatred directed against the English ruling classes for centuries afterwards.

Then a spoonful of . . . . tolerance. It had been observed towards the end of the eighteenth century that this was a time in Ireland when both Roman Catholic and Protestant were settling into a tolerant relationship. However previous social stability began to be replaced by civil unrest due to the perception by Roman Catholics of the privileged position given to the Protestant Church of Ireland within the British constitution as the State church. Roman Catholic political aspirants were urged by their bishops towards loyalty to the British Crown and King George III. They were urged not to upset the stability of the Monarchy as it was already being upset by the American colonist rebels in 1778. This was evidenced by the support of the Protestant Volunteer movement given to the Rebels at the time of the American War of Independence.

A splash of...Patriotic Irishmen both Protestant and Roman Catholic who had sworn allegiance to organisations such as the United Irishmen and the Roman Catholic Defenders were heartened by events in the New World. The United Irishmen drew their support mainly from Protestant professional and mercantile quarters in Belfast and Dublin and were intolerant of the corruption and the lack of democratic politics found in Ireland. Both of these elements, power and corruption, were vested in the Irish political class who ruled from Dublin but who felt equally at home in the corridors of power at Westminster. The United Irishmen had only a vague idea of what new political society they wished to create-save that it would be clean-parsimonious of public money-and based upon the 'people'. This political aspiration was quite unique in Irish politics the inclusion of Roman Catholics in the government of the country. The movement gave a joint openness to both Roman Catholic and Protestant dissenter for a share of political power. These two previously religiously polarised societies eventually united thus swelling their collective ranks and giving their cause a new impetus.

Whiff of vinegar....A religious and demographic population imbalance existed throughout Ireland. Anglican and Presbyterians who were becoming politically more aware were the most prolific in the North with the presence of a Roman Catholic minority. Conversely Roman Catholicism was the primary religion in the rest of the island with a Protestant minority. This position still exists today. The State Church of Ireland hoped, given time, that its view of the perceived flaws in Roman Catholic dogma would eventually erode Catholicism but it became evident by the end of the century that the Roman Catholic religion would not suffer this fate.

A sprig of......Intolerance brought about by social and religious injustice manifested itself amongst the different religions and cultures on the island. Agrarian secret societies existed on both sides of the religious divide. The Roman Catholic 'Defenders' and the Protestant 'Peep o' Boys' formed to give protection to their respective communities against any insurrection directed towards them. Irish society itself was becoming ever more complex. Politically minded Protestant Dissenters and Roman Catholics explored various political options that had been previously denied them. Those political privileges previously exclusively held by Protestants had to be defended against radical Presbyterians and an emerging vociferous Roman Catholic majority that had hitherto not held political municipal or legal office under English rule but who were allowed only to practice medicine and commerce.

Then bring to the boil......Ireland supported a population of some eight and a half million people out of a British Isles total of twenty five million people. By 1798 four fifths of the Roman Catholic population were in rebellion demanding the removal of the Penal Laws seeking, even then, equality of opportunity. These Penal laws were 'laws' passed against Roman Catholics in Britain and Ireland after the Reformation that penalised the practice of the Roman Catholic religion and imposed civil disabilities on Catholics. For example to own a horse over a certain value was to invite its seizure by a landowner. Various acts passed in the 16th and 17th centuries prescribed fines and imprisonment for participation in Catholic worship and severe penalties, including death, for Catholic priests who practised their ministry in Britain or Ireland. Other laws barred Catholics from voting, holding public office, owning land, bringing religious items from Rome into Britain, publishing or selling Catholic primers, or teaching. Sporadically enforced in the 17th century and largely ignored in the 18th, the Penal Laws were almost completely nullified by the Roman Catholic Relief Act (1791), the Catholic Emancipation Act (1829), the Roman Catholic Charities Act (1832), and the Roman Catholic Relief Act (1926).

England under the rule of George III was about to lose its colonies in the New World. France was undergoing a revolution which was fanning the wind of change in Europe giving encouragement to the people of other European nations wishing to be rid of autocratic and tyrannical rule. Britain was aware of the Irish political rumblings. The policy of ameliorating Irish politics by means of an Irish Parliament in Ireland had failed.

This not only plunged Ireland into political crisis but caused political unease and a strategic military problems for the British Isles. Centuries later the position of neutrality adopted by the newly sovereign state of Ireland during the Second World War was also to cause this problem to the British on its Western flank in its struggle against Nazism. Rather than risk having an enemy on its Western flank where the Roman Catholic French would have an ally the British chose to retain a firm strategic presence in Ireland. The were however consequential fears, highlighted by the French, who landed at Killala Bay in the West in September 1798 giving credence to the fear that open rebellion was underway and throwing the Protestant people into turmoil. This bold Franco Irish enterprise was suppressed with great ferocity, revenge, and reprisal.

In 1801 George III brought Ireland into full membership of the United Kingdom. It was within its parliament that the Irish Parliamentary Party debated Ireland's cause on behalf of its people, this uneasy union was to last until 1923. Full emancipation of the Irish Roman Catholics was not countenanced by Pitt the British Prime Minister as it would have violated George III's coronation oath to maintain the Protestant constitution. Several Lords resigned on the grounds that the new administration was formed to resist 'Roman Catholic Emancipation'. As Roman Catholics were not considered by the British political establishment as being loyal British subjects within what was a Protestant constitution their political history was considered as one of sedition and disaffection. This was not true, as at that time, the Roman Catholic Church was eager to reach an accommodation with the State.

Ireland although having an agrarian economy was known as the 'land of the small towns' these hamlets being numerous throughout the country. Farmers traded their produce in the towns and in turn purchased wares and services from the trades people. Each complemented the other and were interdependent, all had to flourish to survive. The 'Great Famine' of the 1840s was to test this relationship with horrific consequences. The 'Famine' was not in fact confined to Ireland but did have the most disastrous results on its population because of their dependence on the potato as a staple diet. It however contributed once again to the re-kindling of its people's hatred for government from England.

In Ireland the British crown which had confiscated lands and property had bestowed them on many of its loyal Lords for services rendered. Those Roman Catholics who were disinherited were taught to hope for the day which would bring the restoration of their religious freedom, ownership of the soil, and restoration of forfeited estates. Some of these landlords resided on their estates. Others regarded as absentees chose to live elsewhere, principally in England. Many engaged managers to administer their estates, livestock and farmlands. Tenant farmers, cottiers and peasants worked the land and herded the animals and paid their dues to the landlord in cash or in kind. None owned the land they worked.

The potato famine was not a plague of mans' making but the 'Great Hunger' (there had been other famines) and how it was mismanaged was. Food did exist on the island but did not reach the needy, instead most of it was shipped to England to line the pockets of absentee landlords. The Irish parliamentary party and British government failed to act in time to relieve the suffering of a starving people. It has been well chronicled that many of the tens of thousands of those tenants, cottiers and peasants who were unable to feed themselves and those who could not pay their masters were evicted from their homes and land by the landlords or their managers with the assistance of the local constabulary, to trudge the countryside in search of food and shelter. Those who could not find it died. Usually the very young, old and infirm. Others who witnessed these tragedies chose to wall themselves inside their homes with their families and await the coming of their ultimate Lord and Master. Many managed to make a passage to England to seek work and shelter. Of those who remained over one million were 'officially' to die of starvation although it was probably more like two million including the 'unofficial'. When it was all over the population stood, if they could, at around three to four millions.

Shortly after this time the English lexicon was expanded by the use of a new word. It was boycott. Captain Charles Cunningham Boycott a retired British army captain who was an estate manager in Ireland. After retiring from the army, Boycott in 1873 became agent for the 3rd Earl of Erne's estates in County Mayo. The Land League, formed in Ireland in 1879 when bad harvests made a famine likely again, told Boycott in 1880 that he must reduce rents by 25 percent. In September 1880, after Boycott had attempted to serve writs of eviction, the president of the Land League, Irish nationalist statesman Charles Stewart Parnell, urged that, without resort to violence, the tenants should avoid any communication with those who refused their demand for lower rents. Parnell's policy was first used against Boycott, who, consequently, was forced to employ workers from Ulster, guarded by soldiers, to harvest his crops. He left Ireland the same year and eventually became an agent for estates in Suffolk. The most recent addition to the English lexicon has been the word 'Brit' this time supplied by the Provos.

Those humane landlords who would have wished to be able to feed their tenants but had not the actual food to do so offered them a passage to Canada or the United States. Intending emigrants had to be physically sound and free of disease. One and a half million people left the shores of their homeland. Eighteen per cent of Ireland's population availed themselves of this option but many died during their voyage to their promised land in the 'coffin' ships so called because the trade was so lucrative any old ship would do to transport these unfortunates. Many of these vessels ending their voyage on the floor of the Atlantic Ocean soon to be joined by the company of the Titanic. The main port of embarkation was Cobh-Queenstown was the English name for the town in those days-near Cork city. Today in Cobh's Heritage centre housed in part of the town's old railway Station where trains left to take so many of the survivors to other destinations of refuge there is a permanent pictorial exhibition depicting the exodus of the emigrants to the New World. Many tens of thousands of third or fourth generation Irish/American relish-when realising that a visitor is from the 'old sod'-in telling you of their justifiable pride in their ancestry. Sadly it is these self same Americans who have been targeted-because of their patriotism towards their ancestry-by the supporters of violence and who have unwittingly added to the financial coffers of the men of death-thus aiding in the injury and deaths of their distant and innocent kinfolk.

Apart from food and succour given to the needy by the Roman Catholic Church many Church of Ireland clergy throughout the island offered sustenance also. Some of the hungry accepted, others refused it, from the Protestant clerical representatives of an English establishment. Those who accepted it were given the pejorative name *'Soupers'* within their communities for their trouble. Hunger and death was not apportioned to the peasant Roman Catholic population alone. The Protestant northern *'Planters'* in Ulster suffered equally appallingly. Throughout Ireland many of the unfortunates took refuge with their families in workhouses. They huddled together on wooden plinths on stone floors. Many died where they lay. The literary genius John Mitchel-the son of a Presbyterian Minister-who was from Newry, records in anguished prose in his 'Jail Journal' the sights and sounds of those pitiful survivors as they entombed themselves in their cottages to meet their doom. Famine graveyards containing their mortal remains can be seen from Belfast-to Dublin-to Cork-to Galway-to Sligo-to Donegal-to Londonderry, all found unity and equality in death.

Not only did an underlying unrest and detestation of the ruling English exist in those who would be free of the yoke of Imperialism it also existed in the Anglicised Irish who directed their ire towards those Irish Parliamentarians who failed to secure food and succour for their countrymen during the period of the Great Hunger. This general unrest began to surface and manifest itself openly around the turn of the twentieth century. But the outbreak of the Great War in 1914 seemed to herald an unspoken truce for a time in this consensus enmity directed at the Crown. The aspirations of Nationalists went into a state of suspended animation for the duration but the Republicans saw the Great War as a God sent opportunity to make their bid for freedom. No conscription existed in Ireland, nor was it permitted under the Ireland Act but nevertheless many of her sons and daughters volunteered to serve in the forces of the King. They fought and died alongside English, Scottish, and Welsh soldiers and sailors. It was the Irish regiments alongside their Ulster counterparts that were formed to become the Irish Rangers who were chosen by the British to become cannon fodder and who fought so valiantly at the battle of the Somme where thousands were slaughtered on that first day on the 1st July 1914 and later at Messines Ridge in 1917.

On one occasion I made a pilgrimage to the 'Old Graveyard' a few miles North of Cobh, to visit the three mass graves of those poor unfortunates whose bodies were not claimed following the torpedoing of the passenger liner Lusitania by a German U Boat in 1915. Twelve hundred innocents perished off the Old Head of Kinsale.

As I wandered through history in the graveyard my interest was awakened when, from the corner of my eye, my gaze alighted on what at fist glance seemed to be a British war graves plot. The stones were not of the classical white Portland limestone which I had seen in the fields of Flanders but instead were of dark grey slate or granite. I stopped counting the headstones when the figure I reached was in excess of thirty. Their inscriptions included epitaphs to many local men who had served in the Royal Navy, Royal Navy Reserve, Merchant Navy, and the Irish Regiments of the British Army. By way of stark contrast close by was a distinctive life size statue dressed in the unmistakable trench coat and trilby of an I.R.A. Volunteer, clutching a rifle across his chest. The inscription on his epitaph read 'Captain Rushelm shot dead by the British Army 1918'. How ironic it would seem are the circumstances in which those three groups mentioned above came to share plots in the same remote little graveyard in the south of Ireland. One group dying at the hands of the Germans who claimed that the Lusitania-an American vessel sailing under a neutral flag at that time-was carrying munitions to aid the British cause for freedom being fought out in Europe. The second group containing Irishmen defending that cause on behalf of the British Crown. The third an Irish Patriot shot dead by the British while fighting for his freedom in Ireland from the British. Once again all found equality and freedom in death.

Following the cessation of hostilities in 1918 the Irish Brotherhood emerged as the voice of Irish Nationalism with James Connelly and Michael Collins as two of its leading lights. Up until this point in time it would appear that although loyalties differed the Loyalist/Protestant northern *'Planter'* culture and the Roman Catholic/Nationalist had in the main peacefully co-exist-ed. Not only were the English interlopers considered to be the enemy but those who would support them and this included the Royal Irish Constabulary and the 'Black and Tans'. 'If you are not for us then you are ag'in us' was the maxim of the oppressed.

Brutality occurred on both sides but the 1916 uprising against British rule in Ireland was successfully and brutally repressed jointly by the British Army, the Royal Irish Constabulary, and the Black and Tans. This latter force was a British auxiliary Police force employed in Ireland against the Republicans from July 1920 to July 1921. This slang description derived from their attire of khaki coats and dark green trousers and caps. When Irish Nationalist agitation intensified after World War I, a large proportion of the Irish Police resigned, to be replaced by these temporary English recruits, mostly jobless former soldiers-though they were publicly described as the scum of British jails-who were paid 10 shillings a day and who dressed in a mixed "black and tan" outfit because of the shortage of Police uniforms. The British government of the day, as usual, went too far and executed many of the Irish Leaders thus creating the first recruitment drive for the Irish Republican Army. It was ever thus.

However in spite of all the hostilities in Ireland the writing was on the wall, 'Home Rule' was on its way.

Irish Home Rule was finally achieved in 1923. Twenty six of Ireland's thirty two counties having seceded from the United Kingdom. It was agreed with the incoming Irish government that six of Ulster's Province of nine counties at the behest of its majority Protestant population would remain united with the rest of the United Kingdom made up of England, Scotland, and Wales. This pleased some but not all. The United Irishmen had sought a united Ireland within the United Kingdom. The Roman Catholic majority aspired to a United Ireland free of British rule. Neither aspiration was fully achieved a halfway house accommodation was reached the classical camel, the horse designed by a committee. The newly created statelet North of the border was christened Northern Ireland. The one to the South of the newly created border was named the Irish Free State. Not until 1937 did the south change its name to the Republic of Ireland.

A Roman Catholic majority that had existed in the whole of Ireland now became a minority within a Protestant majority in the North. An overwhelming Protestant majority with its own devolved government sitting at Stormont on the suburbs of Belfast was seen by Nationalists and many Protestants as a Protestant government for a Protestant people. The die was cast once again in Ireland for a further round of confrontation and violence. It was the usual question who would inherit the future?

Ireland does not have what other countries such as the U.S.A and Australia might call an indigenous population whether they be Red Indian or Aborigine. It was migrant peoples who moved from East to West across Europe who eventually settled Ireland. America was the next stop for some on this long trail of tears. There is nothing purist about our blood line. It contains the genetics of the Celts, the Vikings, the Spanish from the failed Armada, the Anglo-Norman, the Anglo-Saxon in its polyglot. It just so happens that it was the Protestant Planters, an industrious lot, who took the short sea route from Scotland and were the last to arrive on these shores. Or were they? The ancient Kingdom of Dalriada stretches from south western Scotland the short dolphins leap across the North Channel into the eastern Antrim hills. This was the trading and hunting territory of the ancient tribe of the Dalrhys. Maybe the Plantation of Ulster was a second coming?

The U.S.A, Canada and Australia have existed as States for only two hundred years and are eager develop a history of their own. One does not have to be in the United States for long however to see just below the surface the sensitive problems that exist between the races. A continuing embarrassing issue seldom referred to but still alive for all that. Canada and Australia with their increasing influx of Asians could also experience this one day. Let each of them learn the lessons of Ireland in time.

Following the partition of Ireland civil war broke out in the Irish Free State in 1922 over the issue of Partition. The Southern Irish government elected following Partition was soon to change. The newly elected government did not accept the Partition of the island that had taken place and therefore claimed jurisdiction over all of the island of Ireland. This was evidenced by Articles two and three of the Republic's Constitution which has lately been amended by the 1998 Good Friday Agreement. These Articles were to be another ingredient added to the recipe for disaster and were to be regularly used as justification by those activists from that day until this as giving legitimacy for waging a war of attrition against a section of Ireland's population.

The 1920's saw sectarian violence erupt in the North. The same horrors as before were perpetrated on each community by the activists from the other. People were murdered, families were driven from their homes, and many intimidated from their places of work. The situation simmered until the I.R.A. campaign of the 1950's.

The 11th December 1956 saw the opening of a military campaign mounted by the Official I.R.A. This campaign was mainly carried out along the border counties of Armagh, Tyrone, Down, Fermanagh, and Derry and was direct-ed at British Custom Posts and the Royal Ulster Constabulary-The Royal Irish Constabulary was disbanded in the Irish Free State following partition, its con-tinuance was regarded as unacceptable because of its previous role in support-ing British rule-The Royal Ulster Constabulary was the newly re-formed Police force in the North.

The I.R.A.'s desultory campaign was held in check by the R.U.C in the fifties and it finally fizzled out in 1962 the lack of success having being recog-nised by the I.R.A. Army Council as *'not achieving the desired goal'*. In their cease-fire statement issued on 26th February, the Army Council admitted that the campaign had failed to attract any popular support from the Northern Roman Catholic population. The only consequence being that the Nationalist's collective minds had been simply distracted from the *'supreme issue'*- facing the Irish people- **the unity and freedom of Ireland.**

Six members of the R.U.C were killed plus eight I.R.A. Volunteers and four Republican supporters. But the open sectarian conflict that had previous-ly accompanied such conflict did not occur. A lull in any organised resistance was to exist in the Province from then until the late 1960's.

Those of us reared as products of the fifties and sixties within Northern Ireland and who had not been religiously or politically indoctrinated by our parents were blissfully unaware of the educational and social differentials between the two communities. Most of us were also oblivious of our collec-tive history and historical conflicts that had taken place in Ireland. It is strange when I reflect in a Province of one and a half million souls how little we knew of each others culture and heritage. I had only been taught British history at school and it is fair to assume my religious counterparts had Irish history shoved down their throats. Once again the seeds of mistrust and ignorance were being sown by our *'teachers'* during the tranquil period of this tempo-rary respite.

So here we were the flower power children of the sixties. There was not a lot happening on the surface or so it would seem. Who was King Billy and his battle of the Boyne? Who was the Pope? Who cared! We had Elvis, the Beatles, and Mick Jagger with his Rolling Stones. Flower Power had arrived Scott McKenzie and San Francisco was here and the beautiful people were there. Life was great. 'Up King Billy!', 'Kick the Pope!' were the slogans brought out and dusted off once a year around the Twelfth of July. This was all we knew about our past. Ignorance is bloody bliss or so we thought. Confused yet, please read on.

Hubble Bubble Toil and 'Troubles'...Behind the scenes the script was being written and the stage set for what might well be the Final Act in this long running saga.

The military history clock that had run down and ceased to tick on the 26th February 1962 following the I.R.A. Army Councils cease-fire was being wound up again. At that time it was not clear whether or not it was going to recommence ticking again or not.

September 1962-Ruairi O'Bradigh resigns as Chief of Staff I.R.A. Cathal Goulding takes over.

1963-200th anniversary of birth of Wolf Tone a founder of Irish Republicanism. Wolf Tone Society meets to re-evaluate beliefs and strategy following the failure of the 1950's border campaign.

January 1964-Dr. Conn McCluskey and his wife Pat founded the campaign for Social Justice in order to publicise grievances in employment, housing, and electoral malpractice which were being used in blatant discrimination against the Roman Catholic minority.

January 1965-Sean Lemass Irish Prime Minister lunched at Stormont as guest of Northern Ireland's Prime Minister Captain Terence O'Neill. The Unionist Party told him not to take any such similar action in the future without first consulting them.

21st May 1966-Belfast newspapers receive a statement purported to be from the Ulster Volunteer Force stating 'From this day we declare war against the I.R.A. and its splinter groups. Known I.R.A. men will be executed mercilessly and without hesitation'.

27th May 1966-John Scullion a Roman Catholic was attacked on the Falls Road-he died on 11th June-Anonymous caller to Belfast Telegraph claims that U.V.F. were responsible. The first victim of the present Troubles.

26th June 1966-Peter Ward a Roman Catholic barman was shot dead in the Malvern Arms a pub in the Protestant Shankill Road-two others were injured. Five U.V.F. members were charged. 'Gusty' Spence did life for the crime. It was generally thought by the Unionists- whether guilty or not-that this was a political sentence. He was made to serve his full time.

29th January 1967-The Northern Ireland Civil Rights association came into existence. Its members included both Roman Catholic and Protestant but its steering committee contained members of the Belfast Wolfe Tone Society.

7th March 1967-William Craig Minister of Home Affairs at Stormont banned the Republican Clubs under whose name Republicans in the North circumvented a ban on Sinn Fein and its Newspaper 'United Irishman'.

June 1967- I.R.A. Chief of Staff Cathal Goulding says the movement should not be elitist but should engage with other like minded working class peoples in support of the common ideal. In future physical force should only be engaged in when it was 'demanded and supported by the people'.

11th December 1967-Jack Lynch now Taoiseach-Gaelic for Chief or Chieftain-of the Irish Republic pays a courtsey call on Captain Terence O'Neill at Stormont. He was heckled by the Reverend Ian Paisley and his supporters, who shouted 'Keep Ulster British' The alarm bells were ringing loud and clear now in the Unionist camp.

20th May 1968-Five hundred hostile Protestants demonstrated, carrying placards saying 'O'Neill must go'. His car was pelted with stones and eggs.

1968- The Northern Ireland Civil Rights Association held marches and demonstrations throughout the Province. It was these actions and counter demonstrations staged by the opposing Loyalist factions which began to destabilise the tranquillity of the Provinces society, streets, and roads. Law and order began to break down with increasing frequency. The R.U.C. and their companion force the 'B' Specials-recruited almost exclusively from the civilian Protestant population and much hated by Republicans because of their past provocative sectarian performances-found great trouble keeping the peace between the factions.

2nd December 1968-In a speech at the Ulster Hall in Belfast William Craig accused the Civil Rights Movement of being bogus.

9th of December 1968-Captain. O'Neill broadcast to the people of Ulster on T.V. His first words were 'Ulster stands at the crossroads' he asked 'What kind of Ulster do you want?' This question has been posed many times since to the people of Northern Ireland. They have given their unequivocal answer each time, at the ballot box. When will they be listened to?

11th December 1968-Terence O'Neill asks William Craig to resign as Minister of Home Affairs. Craig resigns.

12th December 1968-Terence O'Neill was given a massive vote of confidence from the 'Unionist Parliamentary Party'.

And so it went on. As each historical period of perceived or actual injustice faded with time, it only faded to be replaced by another and yet another injustice, ad infinitum, each following the other with ever increasing frequency. Until the time was reached when each event seemed to have merged with others into a kaleidoscope of political and violent disasters. It would seem at this point in time that the stage has been set for the final showdown.

What had started out as a war of religion in 1690 progressed to a hatred and a desire for the removal of the English from the island of Ireland. Finally mutating into a battle to dominate the freely elected right of the majority to remain part of the United Kingdom. It has been largely an unsuccessful attempt to subjugate the mind and free spirit of a people through a campaign of politically orchestrated intimidation and violence, although the outcome is uncertain and remains to be seen. However the military campaigns have undoubtedly shaken the will of various governments-each with their own political agendas- to adhere to the democratic will of the majority and has sought to accommodate the forces of violence for the sake of political expediency. Never a good idea.

The Restless Natives...In 1968 Northern Ireland was not alone on the stage of world events nor did it hold centre stage. It shared its platform with the swelling ranks of people from other countries who in parallel like-mindedness sought social change and justice. It was a year that recorded demonstrations and marches in a number of European countries and the United States. Parisians, as ever, tolerated its student demonstrations and their barricades. Londoners ignored the Grosvenor Square demonstration held outside the American Embassy in support of the anti Vietnam lobby, a demonstration which finally broke up and degenerated into a riot. Washingtonians were astonished to see the Civil Rights and anti Vietnam marches. Disciplined Berliners suffered the excesses of the Bader-Meinhof terrorist group-who of all these groups-demonstrated publicly for change by the use of premeditated violence. Violent methods which were justified by their leaders because of their perceived lack of progress towards social change in Germany. Their particular methods of terrorism, for political ends, became the role model for other, as yet unknown, subversives to come onto the world stage.

The Northern Ireland Civil Rights Movement was the only group of those mentioned that became a vehicle for those who sought to manipulate it for exclusively Nationalist purposes. Shades of Nationalism could be seen emerging from the ranks of the youthful marchers evidenced by the flying of the Green, White, and Gold of the Irish Tri-colour. To Unionism this flagrant flag waving was worse than a red rag to a bull. This was the final ingredient in the recipe of disaster which brought this cauldron of sorcerers brew to the boil, causing it ultimately to boil-over. We have been trying to clean up the resultant mess ever since.

CHAPTER 3

Towards the Abyss ....

The Brigade is 'Blooded'...The isolated incidents of petrol bombings and attacks against property that we had dealt with during 1968 escalated to the point when 1969 really became the year things began to hot up for the people of the Province. Not least its Firefighters. Tactics of street violence used in the civil disturbances of the 1920s were resurrected and re-learned-with a few devious additions thrown in for good measure-by a new generation of activists within both communities eager to have a go at one another. Petrol bombing was the dominant tactic used amongst these methods of attack.

In the early hours of Sunday 3rd August fire bombing of public houses and the burning of vehicles heralded a 14 day spell of intense activity for the Brigade. The majority of serious fires occurred in an area approximately one and a half square miles, this area was mainly within the Lower Falls which contained high density terrace housing. These nestled around former linen and flax mills which in turn were interspersed with newer industrial properties and city developments. The area housed approximately 20,000-30,000 people. A sustained and prolonged period of sectarian street rioting was taking place in the Lower Falls Road, Balaclava Street, and Percy Street areas. It would usually begin in the mornings and continue into the evenings. Hijackings and the burning of buses and lorries was taking place regularly as these were being used as defensive street barricades. It was estimated that 400 homes were damaged to varying degrees, plus eight industrial premises. Gunfire had broken out. Fear and violence stalked the streets both civilians and security forces sustaining injuries. The Army was having running battles with rioting crowds and petrol bombers.

During this period of intense activity the Brigade attended 416 incidents 37 of which were doubtful intent and had first to be checked out first for safety's sake by senior officers, prior to Controls dispatching men and appliances. So the brunt of the first strike, extreme risk work was carried out by them. During one period from 1400hrs Thursday August 14th until 0600hrs on

Friday 15th Brigade Controls was averaging one call every two minutes. As the backroom boys they too were later to be praised for their splendid efforts and co-ordinating response to all this mayhem.

In the face of this increasing whirlwind of activity Brigade personnel, and the hitherto good order and discipline on the Fire Stations throughout the City, had no option but to 'adjust' to the changing times. This was no longer the Brigade of 'spit and polish'. It simply did not have the luxury of time to be. Fire appliances that were in and out continually were, for example, just left dirty-they still worked the same. When clean recycled hose supplies became depleted hose was put back in the lockers and used wet. In this condition they were heavy and exhausting to work, they burst regularly, and contained dangerous shards of glass and metal etc., from previous jobs. But, no matter, they still carried water. Beds that were turned out from-numerous times throughout the night-were fallen back onto by exhausted and still fully kitted Firefighters-they could still be slept on. The days of the gleaming waxed appliance and taut bed covers were long gone and probably gone for ever.

On the nights between 13th and 14th fire crews had been stretched to the limits of their physical endurance-dodging in and out-knocking down fires after fire-with all the available Brigades resources and equipment being brought into use. During lulls in the battles Officers-in-Charge of appliances would take the opportunity to retire to a safe distance for a period of respite in order to regularly reappraise the fluid situation with the vain hope of avoiding getting men and appliances caught up in further hazardous situations.

On the evening of 13th August Assistant Chief Officer Billy Whyte was in the Control Room at Brigade Headquarters Chichester Street monitoring by radio the progress of events and the safety of several of the crews operating in the Lower Falls. Accompanying him at this time was his friend and colleague, Assistant Divisional Officer Richard Sefton the Brigade's Engineer.

Billy Whyte was a Firefighter's Firefighter who lead from the front. He had joined the Brigade following his demob from the Royal Air Force at the end of World War II and had seen active service in Burmah. He was a fiery dapper little man with a neatly trimmed pencil moustache and a mischievous twinkle in his eye. He engaged subordinates only on his terms. He was respected and generally liked and did not suffer fools gladly.

After having listened to the fireground crews' radio messages for some time he said to Dickie Sefton, 'Lets go and see for ourselves what's happening up there.' The Lower Falls was just within Chi's Station boundary and it would only take them a matter of a few minutes to get to where the action was. They left Controls informing the staff of their destination. Went out into the Station yard and got into the A.C.O.'s Whyte's white Hillman Minx car, which carried a blue beacon and was marked as a Fire Brigade vehicle.

The city centre had that awful deserted errie feel about it as they drove through it that evening enroute to the Falls. From Donegall Place they turned into Castle Street towards Divis Street. At this point they began to see the tell tale signs of street rioting, the bricks and stones that had been used as missiles to attack whomever were strewn over the footpaths and roadways as was the odd burnt out vehicle. At the lower end of the Falls they encountered a fire appliance, the crew were having a breather. Some groups of civilians were up ahead. Then it happened...

As they drew close to a group they just had time to catch out of the corner of their eyes a movement from one of the pedestrian groups. Crash, the windscreen of the car was shattered with a lead pipe and two petrol bombs were thrown in. They were both enveloped in a ball of fire, the car careered out of control mounting the footpath. One of the rioters was struck and thrown over the bonnet sustaining a broken leg, another one of the crowd was crushed against the wall. The car finally came to rest against the gable wall of Peel Street its doors bursting open on impact. Whyte was catapulted out through the flames which were belching from the car's interior. Sefton rolled himself out

"... it doesn't matter let the bastards burn".

onto the ground trying to extinguish the flames that engulfed his head. He was unable to breathe and was beginning to suffocate due to lack of oxygen. As they lay there writhing and screaming in agony an old lady who lived in Peel Street ran over and attempted to extinguish the flames. She then ran off. As Sefton lay on the ground he remembers hearing a voice say. 'They're not Policemen, they're Firefighters!' Another voice said in response...

The fire crew that the two unfortunates had just passed led by Leading Firefighter Jimmy Mc Comish witnessed the whole horrifying spectacle unfold. They ran across, incensed and shocked at what they had just seen. Jimmy Mc Comish screamed at the crowd to get back and with the aid of his crew helped to finally smother the flames. The smell of petrol from the victims clothing and the staff car was intense. An Ambulance was summoned and both Officers were taken away to the Ulster Hospital at Dundonald on the eastern suburbs of Belfast. Both had suffered severe burns to their faces and hands which were to leave them badly scarred and maimed for the remainder of their lives. Even during their time spent lying in hospital suffering terrible agony from their injuries both men were still deeply concerned enough to ask regularly about their colleagues struggling on the fireground.

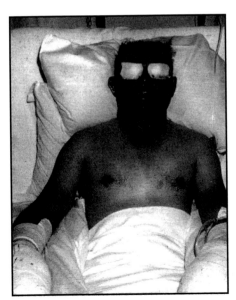

Dickie Sefton recovering in hospital following the petrol bombers dastardly deed.

Although both men received dreadful burns Dickie's were the more serious. He was to spend from 13th August until 24th December in hospital but was allowed home for Christmas. He returned to his sick bed on the 29th December 1969 and stayed there until March 1970. He resumed duty in April and during the next two years was in and out of hospital for treatment which comprised of seventeen operations to his face and fused fingers with extensive skin grafting. This was not to be Dickie Sefton's only brush with the Angel of Death. He was to live to be able to stare it in the face once again some three years later.

Dickie was an avid antique motor collector and restorer. He was the proud owner of 1927 Bean having successfully restored it to pristine condition with the help of another Brigade colleague Billy (Bumper) Young. In 1971 he entered for the commemorative England to Australia rally having been sponsored by Heinz the international food manufacturers. They went overland via France, Austria, Yugoslavia, Turkey, Iran, the via the ill-famed Khyber Pass into Pakistan but there they were thwarted by the outbreak of the Bangladesh war. He had to have the car shipped back to the U.K. but was to try again in October '72, unfortunately this time having to abandon their efforts to reach Australia due to irreparable mechanical failure. His gallant but unsuccessful efforts stand as testimony to his sheer guts, determination, and also to his powers of recovery from his dreadful injuries.

Within the Brigade everyone asked themselves the questions why? Is this the shape of things to come, who is going to be next, how could anyone do that to a Firefighter, sure everyone loves us, don't they? The answer to these questions were not immediately forthcoming. One could only speculate but it was not to be too long before we had some of these questions answered, though not necessarily to our satisfaction and mental well being. There was no chance that anyone could have confused the staff car for a Police car because it had a 'FIRE' sign on it. The general consensus was that at particular time when the adrenaline was flowing, those who where out for blood were determined to get it-if that is how it is described whenever someone has the urge to kill or maim. They did not care who they got just as long as they got it and were able to vent their blood lust and anger on someone. This one incident in all its horror was to be a turning point for the Brigade. It was to determine our future actions when dealing with civil disturbance calls. Although we served all of the community we now knew that we were safe from none. This fear was before too long to become only too painfully obvious. It also created a personal awareness of safety which was only forgotten at your colleagues and your own peril.

This is an extract from a newsheet on this period put out by Chief Fire Officer :

> *'I would like to pay tribute to all my officers and men who rose so magnificently to the challenge and overcame it. Many young men became veterans overnight and many young officers handled situations of great magnitude with courage and efficiency. This is the spirit on which the Fire Service is built and will continue to flourish'*

Robert Mitchell M.C.,Q.F.S.M.,M.I.Fire.E.   August 1969.
I was proud to be one of those young Officers.

Good Heavens ...is there a Problem? Astonishingly it was not until late in 1970 that official, positive moves were made by the Brigade to adopt any anti-riot policy for the protection of personnel and appliances. This was only after strenuous representations from the Fire Brigades Union. This was reflected in the Brigade Circular issued by the Chief Officer 6th July 1970 one year after the above tragedy.

Brigade Circular No:63/70

FIRE APPLIANCES - ANTI-RIOT PROTECTION

Your representatives approached me recently to request the provision of protection to crews in fire appliances during riot conditions. It was suggested that The windscreens and side windows be fitted with metal mesh screens. This request I refused for the following reasons:-

(a) It suggests that you expect to be stoned, and in my view this will undoubtedly provoke stoning.

(b) Metal screens; due to demand for windows in properties are in short supply and take an inordinate time to make-up. I was quoted on a previous enquiry, three months.

(c) The Police are removing their screens for the same reason given by myself in (a).

(d) Restriction of vision.

However, I have always accepted that protection is desirable providing it doesn't inspire attack. It was from this point that the idea of perspex screens was born.

...and in the same Circular...

FIRE APPLIANCES - ANTI-RIOT PROTECTION

You will by now know that steps are being taken with all urgency to fit perspex sliding screens on the insides of the windscreens. The purpose of sliding screens is to enable a broken or shattered windscreen to be knocked out and the perspex will then provide the guard. Windscreens will be dealt with as first priority and side windows replaced with perspex as second priority. Although this will take some time it is being pressed forward. Additionally, bolts will be fitted inside all cab doors.

You will appreciate, I am sure, that precautions - by the checking of routes, enquiries of police and army and a preceding check out by senior officers of incidents goes a long way to ensure that you can do your work without molestation. This, together with your record of initiative and courage should see us through.

...Chiefy with the 'Fire' Cars.

Something of an indecisive attitude had still existed within Brigade H.Q. All staff cars were to be identified with red stick on reflective tape which would hopefully and positively denote them as Fire Brigade cars. Fire appliances had internal plastic screens fitted inside the front windscreens to ward off any possible incoming missile attacks. Door bolts were fitted to the inside of all doors. Personnel were issued with industrial type protective goggles and PVC gloves. Fire crews attending probable civil disturbance calls were not to engage in fire-fighting until the immediate area was secured by the Army or Police. This particular decision was agonised over before being agreed on. Which was to be the lesser of two evils, risk possible attack whilst on your own, or risk it with the security forces in attendance? It was after all they who were primarily the targets of the gunmen. Such were the daily pragmatically difficult decisions of command.

"...so next time you are attacked by an angry mob, just hand out this leaflet which explains that you are Firefighters!!"

This wasn't the only leaflet produced about then. The Official poster produced by the Government of Northern Ireland illustrated a few Firefighters climbing over a pile of bombed rubble under the banner headline 'The IRA Has Planned A Future For YOU...YOU'VE Got 10 Seconds. Terrorism Hurts Everybody'. Was it any bit of wonder that illiterate children threw stones at the Firefighters!

The Fire Service has always jealously guarded its reputation and still does, never identifying itself with the Security Forces for very obvious reasons. It is a completely apolitical organisation. It was rumoured that some of the City Fathers-and it was even said a few Senior Fire Officers would have permitted Firefighters to engage-at the request of the Army and Police-in playing water from high pressure hoses on rioting civilians-or in providing equipment such as ladders to assist in searching premises. These former distasteful and stupid practices can be seen to taking place in some other countries to the shame of the Firefighters involved. The Army eventually brought in their own Salamander water cannons and the Police bought their own ladders. Thank goodness common sense prevailed through strenuous efforts from the Fire Brigades' Union not to let the Brigade become involved with or to be identified as part of the Security Forces. It most certainly saved the lives of our personnel. Nevertheless in one year of operations of the 311 frontline personnel engaged in operations 70 injuries were recorded. As anyone will agree a very large proportion indeed.

There were other official/unofficial operational procedural changes as well. In delicate situations Officers were sent in first to 'weigh up' the situation and where practically possible appliances were not tied in to hydrants and positioned for a quick getaway. If abandonment was necessary, if possible, the appliance radio was to be disabled to prevent the malicious blocking of the Brigade's system. Other more sinister additions were made to the appliances inventories such as larger shovels and black plastic bags for body parts. Of course the 'other side' were gearing up also. Bombs were getting bigger and better and the camouflage of devices as innocent household articles became an art in

... Victim of a 'Sucker Punch'...

itself. Petrol bombs or 'Molotov' cocktails became more efficient. The bombers found that simple petrol burned out too quickly and did not adhere to surfaces long enough so they began to include diesel oil, detergent, or sugars, anything to make the mixture stick more readily. It was time of the assiduous student and many were to be found.

Into the Abyss-July '69 and beyond... The civil unrest of July carried over into August with varying degrees of intensity. For many Firefighters there was no coming off night duty after a quiet night having had good night's sleep and heading out to get a few extra bob on their wee part time job. Oh no, it was straight home and into a nice cosy bed and if your were lucky a warm body to snuggle up to and no hanky panky thank you-no energy. A fifteen hour night duty is a long and exhausting spell if you do not get your beauty sleep so it was essential get the old batteries charged up to be ready for the next onslaught. But of course there were always the silly greedy buggers who burned the candle at both ends with their little day off jobs.

Violence flared between rival factions with increasing ferocity from both Loyalist and Republican areas with gunplay coming more to the fore. Sorties into each other's territories of the Shankill, Falls, Springfield, and Grosvenor Roads took place via the arterial roads linking both communities. Favourite routes used for these incursions were Townsend, Boundary, Dover, Northumberland, Percy and Cupar Streets to name but a few. Over stretched and exhausted Police fought and re-fought running battles with the rioters in streets with place names of countries and battles of yesteryear such as Balaclava, Balkan, Sevastopol and not so yesteryear, Serbia. They eventually lost control of the situation. It was decided by Stormont to ask the Westminster government to send the Army into the Province in force to restore law and order. They arrived on the 15th August. We see now some twenty eight years later how successful they have been since? I remember them marching up the Falls in full battle kit welcomed by the people as their defenders but the honeymoon as we now know was to be short lived.

The 11th of August saw me promoted from Leading Firefighter to the rank of Sub Officer and transferred from Ardoyne to Red Watch Cadogan. My new Watch Commander was Tommy Everett. He had just been elevated to Station Officer rank but when I was transferred to the Watch he was on leave at this time. So I arrived full of beans at my new Station to find myself in temporary sole command of my first Watch. Apart from being a shock to the system it also looked like it was going to be a baptism of fire as well. By this time I was getting used to unexpected shocks having done the rounds of Stations in Belfast since my first promotion in May of the same year. These shocks were by no means finished yet as it was not long before I was to be blooded. Phase two of a young Belfast Fire Officer's learning curve was already underway.

Bombay Street off the Falls became the concentrated target for incendiary attack by Loyalists from the Shankill area. At 0112 hrs 16th August 1969 Sub Officer Bob Oliver, in charge of one Pump From Chi', Station A., attended a call there.

His incident sheet which is typical of this time read...

Bombay Street. 16th August 1969. Call No. 1202.

Call received per TWR(Two way Radio)…

from Assistant Divisional Officer Matthews. Time of call 01.12 hrs.

In attendance	01.12 hrs.
Stop.	01.12 hrs.
Returned	01.52hrs.

Stn. A. White Watch Officer-in-Charge ...Sub Officer Oliver.
14 Houses on fire.....3 jets in use.

To the layman in Fire Brigade language an interpretation of this incident sheet is necessary.

Time of call, means the time the call is received at Brigade Controls.

In attendance, when appliance arrived.

Stop, when fire is under control and no further assistance is required.

Returned, time back at Station.

This call given by the Assistant Divisional Officer indicated that he was in the area in his staff car and talking to the fire appliance also in the vicinity. Having seen the fire he informed the Officer-in-Charge, who had responded immediately. Normally a fire of this magnitude warrants an attendance of at least four fire appliances. Such was the pressure that the Brigade was under at this time only one could be spared. As the houses were already vacated it was a case of a quick knock down job then back to Station. This type of call was typical of one of many when the Officer-in-Charge had to swing by his own tail without backup and simply carry out a holding operation due to fire fighting resources being stretched to the limit.

Over the next several days Bombay Street was to be the focal point of a number of fires and exchanges of gunfire between protagonists. While on day duty a few days later, operations in that area were still chaotic and dangerous, some of the Watch and myself had crowded into the Station Watch room to listen to the radio traffic at continuing incidents. We stood transfixed as we heard one Officer-in-Charge hurriedly transmit a radio message that he and his crew were caught in gunfire and were abandoning their appliance and taking refuge in a Catholic Convent. They then transmitted a message requesting that an Ambulance be dispatched as they had come across a casualty who had been shot in the back and they were rendering assistance. The Ambulance got through into the Convent grounds when it reappeared not only was it carrying the wounded casualty but also the fire crew. How is that for initiative and self preservation!

Later a brief garbled message was received by Controls on the radio from the abandoned Pump, then the radio then went dead. We waited in anticipation to hear what was coming next. We didn't have to wait long. We then heard a repeated clicking sound coming over the radio indicating that the radio handset tranmit switch was being pressed, then silence. A few moments later a voice using incorrect radio procedure came over the air waves. He asked 'can anyone tell us how to operate this fucking pump'. We were all flabbergasted.

It transpired that some of the residents of Bombay Street had commandeered the fire appliance and in the absence of the crew and had quite understandably attempted to put out the fires in their own homes. One of these must have enjoyed the experience so much that at a later date he and his brother were to join the Fire Brigade and at a time and place yet to be ordained by the great Almighty, one was to play no mean part in the salvation of yours truly.

Although Bombay Street was fired by marauding Protestants the Army had been in attendance only a short distance away. On their arrival and deployment in the Lower Falls area the Army had made enquiries with the Police-not being familiar with the demography or topography of the area, in circumstances like this soldiers are trained to use map grid references-where the dividing line was drawn between the two communities of the Shankill and Falls. They were disingenuously told, 'down the centre of the Falls Road'. This is largely true but a few isolated streets such as the Roman Catholic Bombay Street lie on the Shankill side of the line. The Army took up their positions facing the Roman Catholic side of the line with their backs to northern portion of Bombay Street. It was not until Bombay Street was an inferno that they learned they were in the wrong place-and only then because Roman Catholic residents in the southern half of Bombay Street implored them to act in defence of their neighbours across the Falls Road. Which was of course too late to save the Roman Catholic homes on the Protestant side of the Falls. During these next few days this area was considered simply too dangerous for personnel to enter the area. People had been regularly shot and killed. Discretion was considered to be better of valour on this occasion.

Over in the Ardoyne area a pogrom similar to that of Bombay Street was to be experienced by the residents in the Loyalist enclave of Farringdon Gardens. They were living within the largely Roman Catholic Ardoyne. There dozens and dozens of homes were not torched by a rioting mob from the opposing faction but by the residents themselves encouraged by Loyalist paramilitaries. This was done for fear that Roman Catholics were about to evict the residents and claim the homes for themselves. Such was the depth of fear at this time within the respective communities, that they were prepared to invoke a scorched earth policy on their own homes to prevent the 'other side' from

Farrington Gardens - Protestant enclave in Catholic Ardoyne.
The result of a scorched earth policy by occupants.

Burned out homes.
Bombay Street - Bewildered residents the morning after the day before.

taking them over. Ardoyne Station attended this incident but due to a lack of available Brigade resources were powerless to do anything to save the properties which the fleeing residents did not, in any case, want saved.

At Cadogan day duty was followed by night duty, the burnings continued unabated in the Falls. Greeves huge flour mill at the Falls/Conway Street junction had been fired and allowed to burn like a huge beacon on the rising ground of the Falls Road. Around midnight on our first night Controls rang me and said that I was to take the Pump Escape and Pump to Bombay Street and extinguish some remaining small fires in the houses there. We were to proceed without the use of flashers and horns, do the job and get out quickly and quietly. The area was reported to be secure and quiet. Before leaving I quickly briefed personnel what they should expect to see on arrival and my intended actions.

When we left the Station we turned right, down the Lisburn Road for about half a mile and then left into Tates Avenue heading towards Broadway and onto the Upper Falls. We drove past the Royal Victoria Hospital on our right. It had taken in most of the casualties from the shootings and street rioting. As we crossed the Grosvenor/Springfield Road junction the streets were in total darkness. We began to pick out in our headlights the unmistakable signs of battle, debris was scattered everywhere. We drove slowly and with extreme caution, my driver Bobby Moffet picking his way through, avoiding any major obstructions likely to cause a puncture or snag up under the machine. There was a deathly silence as we went along, I was expecting at any moment to hear the crack of a sniper's rifle come out of the darkness. We saw the dark shapes of soldiers on street corners or crouching in doorways looking up at the remaining tall buildings. I thought to myself my God it looks as if World War III has broken out. We were eventually waved down by a young fresh faced looking chap whose rank was First Lieutenant from an Infantry Regiment. At this time the Army had not learned the lesson of concealing their rank markings, Officers were to become a prime target for the sniping gunman. There was gossip at the time that Republican snipers were being offered £1000 a bounty.

I suppose I must have also looked young and raw to him both our officering careers having just begun and now some twenty seven years on both probably over, unless that is, he went on to become a General. He directed me into Waterville Street which led into Bombay Street. I was quite unprepared for what I was about to see. Bombay Street had virtually ceased to exist. Every single house of the dozens and dozens was totally burnt out, only the shells remained. A few small fires still burned in domestic gas pipes but they weren't spreading anywhere there was nothing to spread too. Some of these lead pipes we sealed off others we had to let burn. If we could not seal them they then would have presented a gas or explosion hazard. There was certainly no chance of getting the Corporation's emergency gas squad out.

By the dim light from the flickering fires we saw exhausted young soldiers lying on the pavements, some in sleeping bags trying to get some shut-eye their colleagues standing guard over them. We saw the Convent at the end of the street where our own colleagues had sheltered a few days before. What a bloody mess it all was but over the next number of years we were to become accustomed to sights such as this. On occasions seeing much worse. When I had satisfied myself that there was nothing else to be done we drove out onto the Falls to have a look at things there.

The sight that met us at Conway Street was every bit as depressing as that which we had just left. Greeves Mill which once had been a proud and imposing old six floor Victorian mill now lay as a collapsed mountain of bricks, some on the main Falls Road and some in Conway Street. In its dying moments it had managed to take a number of the terraced houses with it. High buildings such as mills and factories had been used by snipers from opposing factions as firing points to carry out their deadly art form. The buildings had simply been fired in attempts to dislodge the snipers. Everywhere was now deserted. All that we could see and hear was the arcing and staccato cracking from some of their electricity mains junction boxes and the odd flicker from a lone bare light bulb.

... building the 'peace' line.

It was in and around these little back streets that run off the Lower Falls that people had tried to defend themselves against the 'Prods'. Hastily improvised makeshift barricades of paving stones, ripped up from footpaths and commandeered vehicles was the general pattern of street defences for these communities. Citizen Defence Committees had sprung up for each of the main areas. The longer the Army were able to hold the intruders at bay the greater degree of sophistication these street defences achieved.

At that point we bade farewell to the young First Lieutenant to return, much older but none the wiser, to the warmth and safety of Cadogan. Each of us alone and silent with our thoughts all the time wondering what in God's name could possibly justify all this destruction. I still wonder.

By the 15th August the Army were in control of the general area where hostilities had taken place and on 10th September they began to construct a 'Berlin Wall' between the peoples of the 'Shankill' and 'Falls' for their mutual protection. Solemn pledges were given by the Army reassuring the Defence Committees of the protection that would be given by this so called 'Peace Line'. This allowed negotiations to begin towards reaching an agreement for the dismantling of the street fortifications. We in the Brigade held our breaths during this period of respite which we knew would be short lived.

It was agreed between the Army and residents of both persuasions that a peace line would be constructed to give security to and separation between the two communities one from the other and this was duly done. Despite the guarantees given by the Army on the 28th September a Loyalist mob breached the 'Peace Line' and fired five houses in Coates Street. On the 11th October another Loyalist mob attempted to attack the Roman Catholic enclave at the foot of the 'Shankill' known as Unity Flats. They were repulsed by the R.U.C. Shots rang out and Constable Victor Arbuckle a Protestant, fell dead. He was the first Policeman to die during this latest phase of the struggle for supremacy. Murdered by a 'Loyalist'. Within a few short years a young Belfast Firefighter was to die under similar circumstances. Murdered by a so called 'Loyalist'.

This time it was the Loyalist areas turn to be invaded not by a rabble but by soldiers of the Queen defending the Realm against its Loyal subjects. Resistance was noisy and short lived the. The Army contented themselves with a few well aimed shots and the Loyalists melted away. By morning the Army were in control of the area of the fighting. This show of strength at this time was enough to discourage any further organised insurrection. Loyalism could not be seen to be engaging with the Forces of the Crown. The breathing space brought about a temporary restoration of law and order. It allowed for the warring factions to take stock, regroup, and live to fight another day. The Army were by this time fast becoming no ones friend.

The winter of 1969/70 was one of seething discontent for all.

10th October-The Hunt Report commissioned by the government recommended the disbandment of the R.U.C. 'B' Specials and the formation of a more politically acceptable force. The 'B' Specials were an armed volunteer section of the R.U.C. Unlike their counterparts they wore no numbers on their uniforms and this led to abuses at routine road blocks and other activities because no one could subsequently be identified. This was later to become the Ulster Defence Regiment, an arm of the British Army and its biggest regiment. This in turn became politically unacceptable to Republicanism and was eventually absorbed into the Royal Irish Regiment.

12th October-The Army carry out searches on the Shankill and the Ulster Prime Minister Major Chichester-Clark appeals on T.V. for calm. At a Peoples' Democracy meeting Michael Farrell one of the original members of the Civil Rights Movement said 'Now that all the Civil Rights demands have been met, we must work further into the future'..... This statement along with that made by Eamonn McCann today stands as testimony to what the true intentions of Republican manipulators within the movement were. The Civil Rights Movement aims were indeed honourable but it was used as a springboard to resurrect the old Nationalist aspirations for a United Ireland

29th December-The Dublin based Irish Press announced a split within the I.R.A. The Provisional I.R.A. was born. These dissidents later said this schism was caused by their discontentment with the leadership of Cathal Goulding which was due to the old I.R.A. leaderships' recognition of Westminster, Stormont, and Leinster House (the seat of power in the Republic of Ireland).

The death toll for the year in Northern Ireland was 12 civilians and one Policeman.

24th January 1970-heralded four nights of rioting on the 'Shankill' when Protestant crowds repeatedly attempted to break through into Roman Catholic areas. It is not hard to see why the Provos took over the security of their areas.

31st March-2nd April-This period was to become known as the 'Ballymurphy Riots' which erupted on Belfast's Springfield Road. Roman Catholic crowds were to have their turn at attacking the Protestant New Barnsley estate just across the road from the Roman Catholic Ballymurphy.

This former Protestant estate of New Barnsley was now a Roman Catholic one. A busy time for the boys at Ardoyne Fire Station.

May through June and into July saw rioting in-Flax Street off the Crumlin Road-Ardoyne- Lower North Street near the city centre-and also on the 'Shankill' again.

1st of July-The British Home Secretary visited the Province and on the air-craft on the way back to London was rumoured to have said 'For God's sake bring me a large scotch. What a bloody awful country.' It seems that it is the British who are the last to learn that they have been one of the main unprinci-pled contributors to making it what it is.

Falls Curfew...On 3rd July serious rioting broke out following a search by the Army of a house in Balkan Street. Hundreds of troops were rushed to the scene. The security situation deteriorated so badly in the Lower Falls area that the General Officer Commanding Sir Ian Freeland declared a curfew in the area. Shortly after ten o'clock a helicopter flew over the area. From its loudspeaker the words 'This area is now under curfew' could be heard boom-ing out , 'You are to go to your homes and remain there, anyone found on the streets will be arrested.' This announcement was heard by thousands. Residents and their community leaders were in no doubt that the word 'cur-few' was used.

The significance of the word 'curfew' is that a curfew cannot be proclaimed by an Army commander unless a Magistrate has read the 'Riot Act' or a State of Emergency has been declared by the civil powers. No one in the area was aware that these procedures having been announced nor implemented.

This illegal action was to become known as the 'Falls Curfew'. Not since the Second World War had such an event occurred within the United Kingdom. This curfew was to last for thirty four hours. This time it was the Official I.R.A. who decided to take on the British Army. During the gun battles that ensued three civilians were killed and 1,600 C.S. gas canisters were dis-charged. House to house searches for weapons were carried out. Residents were only allowed out of their homes for short periods. Religious worship was restricted. The residents complained that too much authority had been vested in junior N.C.O. ranks such as Corporals and Sergeants who it was claimed acted insensitively. After all, not all residents could be considered to be Republican activists in the area giving succour to the I.R.A. but who else was there other than the Army to do such a dirty job?

The Army were accused of axing down doors, ripping up floorboards, destroying furniture and smashing religious statuettes in their quest for weapons. The curfew along with these actions more than any other events at this time in Northern Ireland's brief history, swelled the ranks of the newly formed Provos.

"...the IRA recruiters at work!".

These heavy handed actions achieved more in recruitment terms for the Republican movement than Cathal Goulding could accomplish with the 1950's Official I.R.A. border military campaign. This lesson in 'how not to do it' was completely and repeatedly lost on the British military and government in the succeeding decades. Before the curfew ended women from the surrounding areas flooded into the Lower Falls with supplies of food for their beleaguered relatives and friends. It is hard to stop a Belfast housewife even with a bayonet!

Irish people have a greater affinity and propensity for celebrating anniversaries. Each community commemorates them separately as a show of solidarity and fiefdom. Seldom are they observed jointly. One only has to look towards the Protestant marches, bonfires, and orange lilies of the annual Twelfth of July commemoration of 1690 Battle of the Boyne-the Catholic Feast of the Assumption of the Blessed Virgin Mary on the 15th August with its marching Ancient Order of the Hibernians-The 1st July Battle of the Somme-and the white lilies of the Republican Easter Rising of 1921.

The 'Falls Curfew' was a situation heaven sent to the Republican propagandists. However in this instance it was not fully capitalised on. But it was not going to be very long before the Army and government gave the 'Derry community something to grieve over' and Nationalists throughout Northern Ireland three more anniversaries to be crossed on the calendar. Crosses which the people of Northern Ireland as a whole would have to bear into the foreseeable future. The three events would be known as Internment Day, Bloody Sunday, and The Hunger Strikers.

Internment Day 9th August 1971 was when 342 men thought to be Republican extremists were arrested by the Police and Army in early morning swoops. Of course it transpired that a lot of these internees were completely innocent and as time wore on-after up to 7 years internment without trial-eventually quite a few of the internees with, by now, very little to lose 'graduated' from this school of terrorism to join the ranks of the Provos Active Service Units when finally released after having been neither charged nor convicted of anything. Internment is still recalled in Nationalist areas-and celebrated as a great recruitment coup in Republican circles and as great own goal by the Brits-by the banging of dustbin lids on the ground. Just as they were on the morning of 'Internment' when this method was used to warn residents of the coming of the Army and Police. I witnessed it on the first anniversary while dealing with a fire on the Falls Road. A spine chilling experience akin to that tactic used universally by riot Police to instil fear into a mob when they are about to charge by beating their batons on their shields.

By the 12th August 1971 twenty two people had died in the worst violence since 1969. Over two hundred and forty houses were burnt out in the Ardoyne. Many Roman Catholic and Protestant families had to flee.

Derry's 'Bloody Sunday' occurred on 30th January 1972 when 14 innocent men were shot dead by the Parachute Regiment on the streets of the 'Maiden City'. This happened during a Civil Rights march against Internment. The troops opened fire upon the demonstrators, reportedly after hearing shots being fired, after being called in when youths began rioting and stone throwing in the William Street area.

During the seven month 'Hunger Strike' of Republican prisoners in the Maze prison nine hunger strikers fasted to death. Margaret Thatcher's government were accused by the Republican movement of letting them die. While in prison Bobby Sands, the acknowledged leader of the hunger strike, was elected to the Westminster parliament. Once again a nice propaganda coup for the Republican movement.

The times of the initial realignment of sectarian areas had almost been completed and the role of the fire raiser was to be shortly to be diminished and over shadowed by the malignant era of the car bomber with all theirs skills and deadly cunning tricks. But first, the bombers had to develop their skill and technology, and that did not come without its 'own gaol' price .

Explosives & Explosions-A Vade Mecum...It seems appropriate to me that at this point in my narrative that I should digress a little to educate the reader on the subject of explosives, fertiliser bombs and other assorted devices which mans' ingenuity has created to seal the fate of dissenters that need convincing of the strength of your arguments.

Hopefully none of my readers will ever experience an explosion in their lifetime nor should my 'education' encourage the feeble minded down a path of dubious knowledge. This technical digression is meant to illustrate how indiscriminate, yet brutally effective a weapon that car bombs are. It is written in the hope of providing some understanding of the violent conditions that so many innocents, did or did not survive, and in which Belfast's Firefighters worked and endured for their 'daily bread'.

Regularly, to the point of boredom, viewers of the violent media see explosives in use in 'Hollywood' epics and other such similar nonsense- but how much does the average person actually know about explosives or their effects- thankfully little. However, if the interest is more than casual then perhaps a deeper but not necessarily an in depth technical understanding is useful in appreciating the effects such devices have on their victims and their surroundings. Any sense of mystique, or even glamour, can easily be stripped away by simply stating that, in the main, commercially available explosives are relatively insensitive, completely stable chemical compounds designed for an engineering function. These chemicals can, if required, be stored for many years without detriment. Home made devices are another matter.

Young recruits to the Fire Service are expected to learn many tablets of stone. Perhaps the first is, not unnaturally, 'what is fire?'. It is defined thus- 'a rapid exothermic[giving off of heat] reaction in matter leading to the emission of energy in the form of heat and light'-this is precisely what an explosion is. It is just the emission rate which is the variable factor. Crudely put, therefore, a bomb is just a very fast fire giving off energy.

"... that's a handy wee light ...".

Paradoxically-the 'slower' the explosion-the greater the 'dwell' time-the longer the energy pressure wave or 'impulse' time-the greater the destruction.

Explosives are however not particularly cost effective nor efficacious means of mechanically demolishing anything. That is unless they are in direct contact with the item to be destroyed. Have you ever seen a birthday boy try to blow out a candle at long range? Broadly the same mathematical rules applies to explosives. If you need to blow something out or down, get as close to the target as possible. It is as simple as that.

No one has really yet produced a definitive work or yardstick for emergency service workers to use when considering, at an incident, how far to evacuate the Public and personnel, when, potentially, they might find themselves exposed to the consequences of an explosion, whether that be from a explosion of conventional commercially available explosives, military, or so called terrorist devices.

Like their military counterpart the Fire Service never 'retreats' it only 'regroups'.

Surprisingly, world-wide, there is no such protocol. Clearly different countries and organisations have distinctly differing views as to how durable, or expendable, their employees or service personnel are.

A pragmatic solution to such a problem should always be based on experience and experience is to be found-it is simply a matter of searching. It is common knowledge that there are explosives and then again there are explosives. The point is purely academic if one is unfortunate enough to be subjected to the effects of one. However, for international transportation purposes, explosives are grouped into Classes by the United Nations, which just goes to prove that it can on occasions actually get something right. A mass detonation hazard is known in the 'trade' as Class I. So if we take a rail car with say 1 ton of Class I military explosives and blow it up and measure the greatest distance a fragment of shrapnel is thrown by the bang we find it is 400metres[x3.3 for yards]. In point of fact, or should that read impact, it is 390 metres . Have you noticed how difficult it is to count whilst you are running ? So, how far to evacuate ? That is best highlighted by a sad tale.

On 29th March 1989 in England in the town of Peterborough in the County of Cambridgeshire a truck belonging to a commercial explosives manufacturer was delivering 1760llbs of mixed explosives-high explosives-detonators-and fuzeheads [a crazy combination if ever there was one]. It got lost and ended up, in error, in the yard of a plant hire company on a small industrial estate.

As a consequence of the truck driving over a speed reducing ramp [a sleeping Policeman in England!] a minor explosion occurred inside the load compartment-this minor explosion caused an incipient fire. The technical reason for this was subsequently determined and is of little account here. The Fire Service, meantime, was called and, knowing it to be explosives involved, arrived in a few minutes and took up position. Standard U.K. Fire Service Standard Operating Procedures [SOPS-since changed] required that an attempt be made to extinguish the fire before it detonated en masse. Approximately 12 minutes from the start of the incipient fire, just time for the personnel to move in to attempt the extinguishment the entire contents exploded.....

'This incident presented a unique opportunity to study the effects of a relatively small quantity of commercial blasting explosive upon a modern industrial estate. By comparing actual damage with what would have been predicted for this situation it was possible to confirm or refine as appropriate, damage/injury prediction techniques.....', so stated the Government investigators for this occurrence. [No doubt the ill-considered Firefighters thought, or have since hoped, that it is 'unique' as well.]

A synopsis of the official report clinically reports the following :

- 14 metres death of a Leading[Rank] Firefighter.
- 18 metres Firefighter engulfed in fireball/vehicles set on fire.
- 25 metres slight burns.
- 1-40 metres perforated eardrums/flying shrapnel, glazing.
- 0-70 metres survivors blown over.
- 0-100 metres structural damage no collapses, nearest concrete building, 20 metres ,intact.
- 0-200 metres cuts, abrasions.
- Fragments 1kg thrown 380-400m away.
- Crater 0.46cm deep by 7 metres diameter.

The report goes on to state....

'Existing models for predicting the consequences of explosions have been developed by analysis of information from a number of sources, including World War II data in which the greatest number of serious injuries and fatalities to people indoors were caused by partial or complete demolition of the houses; people were crushed and asphyxiated by falling debris and dust. In this incident there were no instances of complete building collapse and consequently no related serious crushing injuries......the two closest 'industrial' buildings survived well in comparison'.

As stated earlier the actual destructive force is the energy pressure, shock or blast wave. Many years ago Civil Defence lectures on 'collateral damage' statistics, produced principally by the recorded effects of nuclear test explosions on buildings, repeatedly used a particular example which was taught to Fire Service students. ....If it was possible to seal a building and apply 5llbs per square inch pressure internally then it had been regularly demonstrated, by the recording of nuclear pressure waves, that any conventional brick built building would, quite literally, fall apart at the seams......

Analyses of various incident based pressure wave statistics produce an interesting snapshot for the uninformed as to how objects or building are likely to perform or react in any explosion, nuclear, or otherwise.
Pressure[psi]Expected Damage Produced by Blast.

0.2.	Annoying Noise [137dB].
0.4.	Loud Noise [143dB] Sonic Boom.
	Typical pressure for annealed glass failure. Toughened, or fully heat tempered glass is 3 to 5 times stronger than plain annealed. Laminated glass is even stronger.
1.0.	Partial demolition of house - made uninhabitable.
1.3.	Steel frame of clad building slightly distorted.
2-3.	Concrete or cinder block walls, not reinforced, shattered.
3.0.	Steel framed building distorted and pulled away from foundations.
3-4.	Rupture of oil storage tanks.
5.0.	Wooden utilities - poles, snapped.
5-7.	Nearly complete destruction of houses.
7.0.	Loaded train wagons overturned.
7-8.	Brick panels, 8-12 inch thick, not reinforced, fail by shearing or flexure.
9.0.	Loaded train box cars completely demolished.
10.0.	Probable total destruction of buildings.
300.0.	Limit of crater lip.[Calculated in the instance of the Peterboro' explosion-a model prediction].

Given this background knowledge therefore how does a 'home made' bomb compare technically with its commercially available plastic explosives cousin?

It not really necessary to know much about the chemistry of explosives it is just helpful to compare like with like for a simple logical understanding to develop into an informed conclusion. This methodology could well be summed up as Comparative Testing or more crudely as The Camels B**ls Theory. To buy a good camel it is only necessary to stand in the desert whilst a 1000 camels march past; at the end of the day by comparative testing a purchaser is bound to know a good set when he sees one.

Similarly in respect of explosions if a lay person is supplied with key comparative statistics in respect of the velocity of detonation, the energy, and the gas volume produced, it will be possible to arrive at reasonable conclusion. Here are some such 'interesting' averages:

VELOCITY OF DETONATION.

| Commercial | Ex: | 8,000 metres per second. |
| Fertiliser | Ex: | 3,700 metres per second. |

ENERGY LIBERATED.

| Commercial | Ex: | 5,000 kilo Joules per kilo. |
| Fertiliser | Ex: | 2,600 kilo Joules per kilo. |

GAS VOLUME.

| Commercial | Ex: | 750 decimetres cubed per kilo. |
| Fertiliser | Ex: | 1,000 decimetres cubed per kilo. |

It can reasonably be concluded then that fertiliser based explosives produce less energy than their commercial cousins, but at a slower speed of detonation whilst producing significantly more, high temperature gases, over a longer time period. In point of fact it is almost possible to see the explosion develop. Hence the longer dwell or impulse time, the powerhouse of explosives.

Without strict control on production, unlike its commercial cousin, fertiliser bombs' power output can be very variable but as a general rule of thumb the output is, comparatively, about 60% as powerful as the 'real stuff'. It follows then that a two ton bomb's output should rate the value of about 1.25 tons in commercial equivalent terms.

A crude analysis of all these figures leads one to conclusions which parallel many eye witness statements from those who were unfortunate enough to find themselves in the vicinity of an explosion. The descriptions, to the uninitiated ear, of, in the case of commercial explosives a 'crack' with little or no flame propagation, as opposed to, in the case of fertiliser bombs, a thud, usually with substantial flame propagation in the form of an unmistakable, all consuming and igniting 'mushroom' fireball which literally gives the bomb its characteristic acidic 'flavour' in the mouth.

Apart from the Angels how then do victims in close proximity to the explosion-rather than its consequences-survive at all? This can quite simply be attributed to their distance from the point of detonation. There is however the codicil of a long history of pressure waves performing in a quirky and fluky way in differing circumstances. As some surviving Firefighters in Belfast are glad to be able to testify to.

For sake of understanding a simple inverse mathematical rule applies, the pressure wave decays-markedly-with the cube of the distance from the explosion. Aren't maths wonderful! Put simply this means that the effects of the pressure wave dissipates rapidly as the gas/fireball vents and expands away from the point of ignition but still with this unpredictable or fluky element, which is probably related to the air or gas flow around objects or buildings in its path. Conversely, it then follows that if the wave 'dwell time' is long or delayed-or confined-or as its known technically, 'tampered' in anyway, the resultant damage inflicted will be all the greater as the pressure wave fluxes back and forth all the while magnifying until like the proverbial evil Genie it escapes.

The progenitors of the use of 'fertiliser' bomb against civil targets are the Provisional wing of the Irish Republican Army. Necessity, as they see it , has indeed been the mother of invention. Although this type of explosive material has been in regular daily use in the U.S. in quarries and elsewhere for decades before hand the technology seems to have escaped the misdirected use of idle hands until it was exported back across the 'pond'. It is worth bearing in mind that these bomb manufacturers, have, in striving to achieve the high level of technical expertise taken over a quarter of a century to hone their skill to the edge of perfection in this black art. British Army Officers up in Bronte Country on the North Yorkshire Moors at one of their many secret whizz bang training sessions will unabashedly inform you that PIRA[Provos] are very good at what their good at. However, it has not been without cost to the IRA in terms of 'own goal' mistakes along the way as they built up their technical know how.

The Great Public may suppose that any yobbo' can get on the Internet acquire the knowledge, then collect the bits and pieces necessary, as indeed they can, sling them together, have a little test in a secluded spot, and hey presto you have the recipe for a functioning device. The fundamental questions are however-is the device going to be reliable- and is it going to function correctly every time ?

How technically difficult is it to make such a fertiliser bomb ? Therein, of course, lies the actual skill and accumulated expertise. Clearly it is not as simple a matter as it superficially appears. It obviously takes chemical engineering knowledge-explosive-electronic-and mechanical engineering skills-allied with management acumen, to put it all together and bring it to a successful conclusion. To achieve this objective it may well be necessary to 'buy in' this type of technical and managerial skill from the international market.

What type of fertilisers make up into a good weapon ?

For fertiliser bombs, pure, or nearly pure, ammonium nitrate is the favoured base material and is usually readily available in all its forms in the farming communities. It is a good strong oxidising agent-that is a compound that as well as being a little unstable itself-contains in addition its own rich supply of oxygen-a dangerous combination. Earlier reference was made to the fact that explosives are effectively just fast fires. You may recall the old fire triangle from your school chemistry days. To make fire oxygen, fuel, and a source of ignition are needed. The two properties of the triangle oxygen, fuel, simply need the third , the initiator or source of ignition, allied with a little devious tweaking, to perform.

Ammonium nitrate's explosive properties were recognised by scientists as early as 1867, more than 130 years ago, when a patent was first issued for its use with various sensi-tisers and nitroglycerin. Its first widespread use was to replace some of the nitroglycerin used in dynamite. Its first use as an ingredient in non-dynamite explosive materials was in a blasting agent called Nitramon, introduced by Du Pont in 1935. In 1955 a patent was issued for a blasting agent using fertilizer-grade ammonium nitrate with a solid fuel sensi-tiser.

Unfortunately the properties of ammonium nitrate were later to be recognised by the Fire Service throughout the world following a disastrous explosion at Galveston in Texas in 1947. In this disaster ammonium nitrate exhibited one of its unseemly characteristics, that of being highly unstable when heated and confined. The incident involved a fire in a cargo vessel carrying bulk ammonium nitrate. Suffice it to say that after an initial determined effort, the local Fire Department, in conjunction with the ship's crew, decided as a means of last resort to smother the fire in the ship's holds, by battening down the hatches. In the subsequent colossal explosion that followed the ship and crew, the Fire Department, the port area of Galveston, the town, and over 500 people were obliterated.

It was concluded that the confining of the ammonium nitrate in the holds had led to a runaway chemical chain reaction. Following from that it is clear that when ammonium nitrate is sensitised, by what ever means, and then confined in any substantial vessel or container, it is potentially lethal. Ammonium nitrate the chemistry books tell us is, as we now know, an oxidiser, which, by definition, must be kept out of contact with organic combustibles. It reacts with a huge range of materials, but most particularly with, charcoal and organic fuels, both carbon based. When mixed properly and uniformly with these finely divided materials it can, given the right 'encouragement', react explosively. Common mixtures used in the past have been-coal dust-hydrocarbon fuel oils-diesel-kerosene etc., -and sugar. Thoroughly and carefully mixing 2% to 5% of these carbon based elements with 95%-100% pure ammonium nitrate will further sensitise the ammonium nitrate and make the resultant mixture relatively unstable.

Even though sensitised it will nevertheless in this state require a substantial shock from a combined device consisting of the usual-electronic timing device-a battery supply-a percussion detonator or booster-and an augmentor-that is, plastic explosives of one form or another to set the chain reaction going. Essentially also, the mixture will have to be confined, to allow, in milliseconds, the development of the exothermic chain reaction. This is normally achieved by containment in common metal containers e.g. milk churns, beer kegs etc. which have of course the inherent 'advantage' of producing mutilating shrapnel from this witches brew-and if not enough shrapnel-worry not-literally pile in some bolts and nuts, ball bearings, nails etc.,-whatever. A hideously effective weapon, what more is there to be said .

It takes an especially warped kind of mind for this type of work-the question should always be posed-not that it matters-who or what warped it in the first place?

CHAPTER 4

Ardoyne .... servant of two Masters ....

Fortress Ardoyne…From my first promotion to Leading Firefighter in May '69-and subsequent advancements up to and including the rank of Station Officer- I had chalked up some ten transfers within Belfast. Time spent serving on Stations was interspersed with periods in the Brigade's Fire Prevention Department. All prior to my move as Watch Commander to Blue Watch Ardoyne in January 1972.

The Chief had seen to it that I was well grounded in the administrative and operational skills of my new rank and able to cope effectively with whatever might come my way. He and other senior Officers must have had misgivings about my ability to shoulder the responsibilities of the rank during such a hectic period, having risen so fast to the dizzy height of Station Officer. I had simply been in the right place at the wrong time or visa versa whenever the dice of promotion by qualification was cast. It was either sink or swim and I thought I was a good swimmer.

So it was on 21st January 1972 that I arrived on transfer from Knock Station to Blue Watch Ardoyne with a much travelled kit-bag containing my fire-fighting gear and a few personal effects. I was by this time used to travelling light and at short notice. When I arrived there were a few old familiar faces were there to greet me.

Big Tommy Woods an experienced and long standing Leading Firefighter a veteran

Ardoyne 'Smoke Eaters' of yesteryear

from the Irish Guards during the Second World War and Sub Officer Sammy Hill an old friend and colleague from Cadogan. Then there were the 'boys' as we affectionately call the workers of the Watch, Firefighters Billy Skelly, Gavin McWhirter, Alan Lyle, Davey Doyle, Charlie Hughes, Trevor Smith, Geordie Richardson, John McDonald and finally Davey Williamson, whose family owned a Funeral Undertaking business a short distance down the Crumlin Road. I remember thinking to myself that Davey's family were well positioned for business and that he would come in handy in the event of us having to handle serious casualties where other might be minded to flinch I would expect him to be able to carry on. These were the initial members of the Watch. Personnel of a Watch change on a fairly regular basis in the Fire Brigade due to the ongoing process of transfers that can occur for a multitude of reasons. These were the nucleus of an outstanding bunch of men. Ah!.. yes, I remember them well.

Ardoyne's fireground covers a large area of both North and West Belfast. The main arterial routes in the North being Crumlin, Shankill, Cliftonville, Oldpark, Ballysillan, Antrim, and Falls Roads. These roads enclosed side streets of high density Victorian brick built terraced dwellings. Housing the families who for generations had supplied the textile mills and factories of the area with their labour. Only a small number of these mills still continued in production the others having become casualties of the synthetic fibre boom of the late fifties and sixties. Some of these redundant buildings having been sub-divided and let as single units in what were now multi-occupancy industrial estates.

West Belfast had developed during this period as a large urban, seemingly uncontrolled housing sprawl with little industry. It comprised a number of estates like, Ballymurphy, Andersonstown, Whitehall, Moyard, New Barnsley, Highfield, Springmartin. These estates were bounded and intersected by the Upper Springfield, Upper Falls, Whiterock and West Circular roads.

Self imposed segregation had always existed within these enclaves whether it be of Republican or Loyalist persuasion. They had polarised even more since the late sixties each religious/political group feeling more secure within their own tribal boundaries. Some estates such as New Barnsley which was previously regarded as Protestant had undergone a complete population reversal due to the pogroms and the fact that it was an isolated Protestant out-post on the Upper Springfield Road Nationalist area. Ardoyne, Shankill, and Crumlin Road areas had substantially remained unchanged as these had long been 'tribalised' as either Loyalist or Republican. This was the simmering cauldron that Ardoyne Station and which its three Watches served.

I could readily identify with both sides of this religious and political divide as I had been spawned and brought up in a back street working class environment within a mixed community which had been at peace with itself during my formative years. Belfast people are the 'warmest greatest wee' people in the world, as many a visitor will testify to but put the two different factions together and it won't be long before they find something to argue, if not fight about. Their different inherited histories and cultures making them suspicious, fearful, and hostile towards one another. We're all accidents at birth whichever side of the religious divide we're born into. Just created to be exploited by those 'on the hill'.

The Station itself was sited halfway up the Crumlin Road, on the hub of the wheel that joins Upper/Lower Crumlin Roads, Woodvale Road, and Twaddell Avenue. It stood elevated on a plain just above the Holy Cross Catholic chapel. The 'doyne's Firefighters' looked after the fire safety needs of the community whilst the Chapel was entrusted with the spiritual needs of its flock. If one had had a mind to, you could have literally freewheeled on a bicycle from the very top of the Crumlin right into the heart of the city centre, a distance of approximately three miles. Large grammar and secondary schools in close proximity catered for the educational needs of both religions and in a way probably perpetuated the system of segregation from which the whole community suffers today. These schools were frequently the focal points for minor verbal and physical skirmishes between pupils and parents when either going or coming from school. There was always a Police or Army presence at the school 'release' times. I first witnessed this spectacle on a previous tour of duty as a Leading Firefighter in '69. This daily jostling always added a little bit of variety to life in Ardoyne if you ever got the chance to get bored, which was not often.

About this time whenever the name of Ardoyne Station came up in conversation with Brigade personnel-whether it was for outduty purposes from their base Stations, or for transfer- it would either solicit an internal silent groan accompanied by a sickening feeling in the pit of the stomach or a sudden rush of adrenaline and excitement. Either feeling was entirely dependant on the demeanour or fatalistic outlook of the particular individual involved. Remember at this point in time this was where most of the 'action' was taking place in Belfast and it definitely was not for the faint hearted.

Ardoyne like the other old Victorian Stations in the city was a Spartan barracks of a place. More reminiscent internally of a workhouse than a Fire Station. Attempts had been made over the years to bring it into the twentieth century and make it a little bit more habitable for its residents, but without much over-all success. These efforts only served to give parts of it a superficial facelift which made the 'unimproved' portions look even more Dickensian. Original bare floorboards were covered in linoleum, cream or brown painted walls were wallpapered, and plastic upholstered easy chairs were provided. The engine room floor was still laid with the original herring bone tiles designed to give the horses that pulled the old steamer fire pumps a better grip on the floor when responding to a call.

Some of the ground floor flats which used to house the Firefighters's families were utilised as offices, bedrooms, stores, T.V. room and galley. The Station Watchroom situated at the front of the Station-had long since been vacated due to periodic gunfire in the immediate vicinity of the Station-in favour of a reinforced concrete shelter that had been built into the structure of the engine room during the Second World War as a defence against Luftwaffe air raids. The external windows of the dormitories and other rooms in the out-side wall abutting onto Mountainview Park-where our Assistant Chief Officer Sydney Pollock M.B.E.,G.I.Fire.E., lived-were protected by steel sheeting for protection of personnel and the Station in case of attack from petrol bombs or stray bullets. Stray bullets had on several occasions winged their way into the Station yard and the old Tangy Shed where the wartime fire appliances of the same name had been garaged and which now housed spare machines and Ambulances. On one occasion a bullet whizzed past Jimmy Greeves's nose and buried itself in the yard wall, and on another, bounced off the concrete floor of the shed at Bobby Malcolm's feet. A concrete blast wall was built in the Tangy Shed to obviate the possibility of injury happening in the future. Pretty picture isn't it? More reminiscent of a nuclear fall-out shelter than a Fire Station.

After settling in that first morning, I took a walk around my little 'palace' to refresh myself with what changes if any, had taken place. I went into the Tangy Shed, where I spotted A.C.O. Whyte's staff car which had been taken to the Station for storage after it had been petrol bombed. I peered into the partially burnt out interior. As I had been told previously-there adhering to the inside of the partially shattered, smoke blackened windscreen-which his face had struck that night in July '69 -was part of his little pencil moustache complete with blackened skin.

In the afternoon I took the Pump Escape out with its crew on a topography run into the Station area to familiarise myself with the quickest and most direct routes to different locations in the Station ground. We drove down the Woodvale Road and turned right into Alliance Avenue towards the Springfield Road, then right again heading in the direction of Ballymurphy, Highfield, Moyard, and New Barnsley. I could not help recalling as we drove along, those times not so very long ago, in the early sixties-whenever I was courting or having 'partied' in these neighbourhoods and missed the last bus into town-the number of occasions that some of my friends and myself had trudged down those dark and lonely streets. Walking along late at night alternately passing through Republican and Loyalist areas enroute to home via the Grosvenor Road, Boyne Bridge and Sandy Row. I had never been so much as molested by even a passing female on any of these occasions-shame really. One stood more chance of getting 'duffed up' going through your own townland of Sandy Row than up here. God I thought, no chance of walking these streets now alone now, day or night, even in company.

Our second day duty saw us dealing with a bus that had been hijacked from Ardoyne bus depot just across the way from the Station. It had been abandoned on the roadway at the Alliance Ave/Berwick Road junction with its engine still running. Petrol had had been poured inside and used as the igniting agent. The fire by the time we arrived had taken hold and was going well so I ordered the crew to get a jet to work.

We nearly had it extinguished when we heard the distinctive and unmistakable crackling sound of low velocity gunfire nearby. It seemed to be emanating from further down Berwick Road. We may have known roughly which direction it was coming from but we sure as hell didn't know where it was going. I didn't have to tell anyone to abandon operations, this was immediately done instinctively. Everything was dropped and we all scattered, seeking the nearest shelter. I dived to the ground and lay on the roadway in the lee side of a fairly high kerbstone, praying it would be high enough to give me protection if anything was to come my way.

The gunfire abated as abruptly as it had begun. I do not recall there being any Army present in the immediate vicinity. It was probable that the gunman was letting of some steam at the bus depot. The Army had a billet in there and as the bus hijacking had clearly failed to have the desired effect of bringing the Army out onto the street he thought a few token rounds might do the trick. Fire-fighting operations were quickly wound up, the bus by now nearly having burnt itself out. It never failed to amuse me at bus fires-and there literally have been hundreds such fires in Belfast-how reliable the good old diesel engine is. Although not designed for this type of treatment whenever the vehicle had been 90% burned out including the aluminium skin-yes-aluminium does burn like everything else when hot enough-as often as not the engine, which seems to have a mind of its own, could still be heard ticking over merrily as if to say, you can't stop me, you can't stop me.

When we returned to Station some of the lads exchanged pleasantries in my hearing in the engine room after dismounting whilst getting out of their fire-fighting gear. It was to the effect that they hoped-'Wright wasn't going to be a jinx,' or as they say in Belfast a 'skud'-and that this was not going to be the shape of things to come and me only newly arrived. While the gunman that day may have been off target with whomever he was firing at the lads of the watch most certainly were not. For many a true word is spoken in jest.

Clonard Street-Little and Large...On Thursday 9th March 1972 shortly after arriving on Station one morning and several minutes before commencing day duty at 0900hrs we heard the distant thud of what was undoubtedly an explosion. Wonder where that one was, was the thought that immediately flashed through my mind? It wasn't long before we found out. At 0910hrs while I was present in the engine room and the appliance crews were still carrying out their Watch changeover appliance equipment checks we received a call from Controls over the callout speakers, 'P.E and P to an actuated '77' at Clonard Street Falls Road'. As I swung on the pull cord to open the P.E. bay gates a passing male pedestrian shouted in, 'That's a bomb in Clonard Street'. How the hell does he know? I thought. The Bush Telegraph must be working well this morning. Clonard Street is about three miles away from the Station by road and he certainly did not hear it on any news broadcast.

We turned right out of the Station and headed down the Woodvale Road and down onto the Shankill about three quarters of a mile. Through the traffic lights at Agnes Street and along to the end of Northumberland Street right onto the Falls. Thank goodness no heavy traffic, up the Falls about 400 yards and right into Clonard Street. As soon as we turned in the picture told the story. Where there had been a complete row of neat terraced houses, there was now a huge gap, I estimated some 60 feet wide, it contained a mound of smouldering debris. The partially demolished remains of two houses on either side were at the extremities of the gap. Their roofs and floors hanging at a precariously dangerous angle, as if sliced through by a giant, blunt guillotine, the bedrooms still containing some of their furniture. It only took a split second for the picture to register and to comprehend what had happened.

As we dismounted from the appliances an Ambulance crew carried a stretcher past us towards their waiting Ambulance. It contained the apparently lifeless-or was he unconscious? -body of a young man dressed in a dust covered heavy black overcoat, his face blooded and bright red. Civilians and Army were scrambling over and clawing wildly at the rubble with their bare hands. The appearance of a respected uniform as often as not has a settling and reassuring affect on the public in times of an emergency. We were that respected uniform. Someone has to try and bring discipline and order into affairs whenever tact has to be employed in what can be a tense atmosphere, especially with the Army present. It was always better to slip into the situation quietly and not to try and throw your authority about. Remember the honeymoon by this time was over with the Army and they were the interlopers, we were not. As we approached I knew thinking time was needed but not available. A quick assessment of what we had to do was required. Do something immediately, just as long we're seen to be helping. So I called to my Sub Officer Bobby Bloomer to instruct his crew to assist in the removal of the debris. Without issuing any further orders we formed a human chain and began to transfer the smaller bits of debris out onto the street. The crowd seeing this followed our example. What had been confusion and panic started to settle down into order. I shouted that there was too many people standing on top of the rubble hindering the possible recovery of casualties and some moved off.

There came a shout from the direction of one of the partially demolished houses. 'Hey Firefighters over here, there's someone here'. A few of us stumbled over the debris and entered the remains of the house. The first thing that caught my eye was a perfectly formed kidney lying alongside a bare leg that was protruding from the rubble and was wedged against the wall. It was distorted and obviously badly broken. I remember thinking this is a woman. I shouted for someone to get an Ambulance man and a plastic bag and this was done. I gently lifted the kidney and placed it in the green bag. Almost immediately two civilians arrived with a stretcher. We began scraping away at the surrounding rubble where I felt the rest of the torso lay. Life was obviously extinct. As we scraped away it became increasingly clear what we were exposing was an oozing bloody mass of pulp, no gender was readily identifiable so I called a halt saying. 'This is going to be messy one lads'.

The only way I could visualise extricating the body with the least amount of distress to all involved was to try and wrap it in a canvas salvage cover out of sight of the civilian helpers with little or no actual handling. God knows to what extent actual handling would only cause further dismemberment of the body. A cover was duly brought and we began to carefully wrap the cover completely around and under the remains, rubble and all. When it was felt the body was enveloped I said to the two civilians. 'Place the stretcher alongside lads'. This they did. Then to my boys I said. 'Right now we straddle the corpse end to end caterpillar fashion, wrap our arms around it and lock our hands underneath. Give me the nod when your ready and then we lift'. Four of us straddled the bulging mass. All went well until we began to lift then pieces of 'things' started to come out from inside the cover. Fortunately the two boyos with the stretcher saw this happening before the lifters did and hurriedly pushed the stretcher in underneath, saving an already messy situation that threatened to thwart our efforts. My own lads moved aside quickly but unfortunately for me, the stretcher bearers in their excitement and haste to remove the stretcher before I was able to step aside lifted me stretcher and all. Needless to say you can imagine my horror and disgust at finding myself straddling this disgusting mess. When this grim task was complete and we had all taken a few deep breaths and regained our composure we went outside to assist in the search for further casualties.

As we dug from the top of the mound of rubble down we began to unearth feet after feet of intestine, along with other larger pieces of human remains which had to be bagged and given to the Ambulance crews. These remnants would ultimately used by pathologists to assist to in identifying the deceased. I overheard a few nasty remarks beginning to be directed towards the Army from the crowd. It was then that the Major in charge of the patrol who were from the 1st. Battalion the Gloucestershire Regiment approached and said. 'The crowd's beginning to get a bit restless'. 'So I've noticed'. I replied. At this point I decided to call together the Officers-in-Charge of the attending appliances and drivers. In fact whoever I could readily summon for a quiet little update and briefing on the situation. The crowd were not getting restless with us but with the Army. This was a local tragedy and the Army clearly did not belong there. If anything untoward was about to break out we were going to be caught up right in the middle of it. After the initial flurry of rescue activity had settled down and without any survivors having been located it was just possible that some of the hotheads-having learned from previous experiences-might be looking for someone to vent their spleen on. Some of the crowd were already beginning to melt away a sure sign that gunplay was about to be brought to the fore. I do not know whether or not the Major sensed this but in any event he began to re-deploy his men to less exposed positions. It seemed to me that it was time for us to do the same.

Several of us gathered in a small circle at the kerbside alongside the driver of Chi's Emergency Salvage Tender, Willie Shellard. I pointed out how the situation might now develop and said. 'Spread the word quietly and quickly to the rest of the lads to make their way back to their respective appliances in preparation for return to Station'. 'There's very little we can do here now. If anything does break out don't wait for me to give the order to move. Even if you don't have your full crew on board move away to a safe distance and wait. It's not us they'll be after. Anyone left stranded will be 'O.K.'. Just as I was finishing my pep talk I happened to glance down at the ground in the middle of where we were standing. 'Oh my God what's that', was all I could utter, as if I didn't already know already . 'Somebody get an Ambulance man back here quickly before anyone else sees it'. Lying at our feet was a section of skull with a matted dust covered mop of hair still on it.

As I looked up at one of the seriously damaged houses I noticed a Sacred Heart religious icon still hanging on the bedroom wall. On the sagging floor a baby's cot balanced precariously. I called to Bobby Bloomer. 'Bobby see if you can get up there without the floor collapsing and check out that cot'. Bobby disappeared to carry out his task. Thinking we had witnessed all the horrors we were going to that morning, a dog was soon spotted carrying an arm in its mouth. Then a leg was retrieved from a nearby roof. Other large portions of human remains were also recovered. Before I gave the order to make up and return to Stations the Major came over once again and said, 'Dirty job, well done.' 'Your not bloody kidding.' was my reply. With that we departed and returned to Station. There was no eruption of violence at the scene as we had feared. Perhaps respect for their dead was the reason, who knows.

We got back to Station just about lunchtime. I was pretty weary and with the mornings horrible events still searing through my conscious mind I walked into the duty office, Big Tommy Woods who was Officer-in-Charge that day of the Turntable Ladder whose services had not been required at the call was standing there with the juices from a pig's trotter that he was chewing on, running down his chin. 'Want one Boss' he shouted. 'Fuck off Tommy', as I made a mad dash for the toilet.

What had happened that day at Clonard Street was what the Security Forces had by this time christened as an 'own goal'. This was confirmed at lunchtime by the news media. Initially it was impossible to say for certain how many dead there were but it was thought that three persons had died in the explosion. However it was subsequently established-following investigations by the Forensic and Pathology Departments-that in fact four males had perished in the explosion while handling gelignite.

That night at home I was viewing the local new's coverage of the explosion. I saw Bobby Bloomer-who I had completely forgotten to ask what his investigation of the baby's cot had revealed-on the television screen, he was passing something down from the bedroom floor to an Ambulance man. The next morning on duty I asked him 'What was it Bobby?' ' It was just another part of a skull we found'.

This is perhaps an opportune moment to explain the origin of code '77' used in the original call to this incident. Because terrorist organisations were monitoring radio messages of the security forces and the emergency services, it was thought prudent to give different levels of call a code number. What could be simpler for simple firemen to remember than numbers? '66' unactuated device, '77' an actuated device, and if I recall correctly a '99', which was to evacuate a Station because of a bomb nearby, to a previously designated adjacent rendezvous point which each Station had. The code, which was also an attempt to keep the ghouls away, sounded very impressive but did not really serve a useful function after a time. I recall when on out duty to Chi' one day as O-I-C I was supervising the reversing of some appliances back into the engine room when I spotted a flat bed lorry on the weighbridge outside the High Courts opposite. It was loaded with scrap metal. Never gave it a second thought. When the appliances were safely tucked in their bays I got a '99' call. It was the lorry on the weighbridge and of course we had to drive close to it in order to evacuate to the Sand Quay. It did indeed go off, although it was not one of their better efforts. The alcohol in my blood still runs chill when I think about it even now.

Little Clonard Street...Several weeks after the Clonard Street explosion Blue Watch Ardoyne responded to another '77' call to Little Clonard Street but on this occasion it was to a suspect car. Whenever I heard Clonard Street come over the call out speakers my flesh crawled and I prayed that this was not going to be a repeat performance of the last attendance to the area. Controls announced the address as 'off Leeson Street' but we were not exactly sure where off Leeson Street. The Army had initiated the call and gave our Control Room staff the minimum information. I was only to learn this after the incident. Controls would normally pre-warn the Officer-in-Charge if there was any suspicion of gunfire in the area. The information gave me the impression we were simply attending a standby while an Ammunitions Technical Officer checked out the vehicle.

Our route to the incident was the same as that taken to Clonard Street except that we turned into Lesson Street to the left some 50 yards before Clonard Street. As we turned in at speed from off the Falls I did not realise that we were virtually on top of the incident. The Lieutenant in charge of the Army foot patrol had heard the approach of our two tone horns and as we rounded the corner we nearly ran him down. He waved frantically at me to turn into Little Clonard Street, which we did. Whenever I had dismounted he pointed out the suspect car further down the street. It was then that I noticed one of the

"... nice try son, ... pity! ... the sniper lives at number 13!!"

Army Saracens parked nearby in a rather dishevelled looking state. It's armoured superstructure was covered in what appeared to be building rubble. I said to the Lieutenant 'What happened here?' 'See that space' I looked across to where he pointed in Lesson Street where there had been a house there was now a large hole, the roof still bridged the gap between the adjacent houses. 'Sniper in the roofspace, fired at us through the roof slates'. 'My driver drove the Saracen through the house to try and dislodge him'. 'Did you get him?' "Fraid not, he got away'. That did not surprise me, it was a favoured ploy by the Provos when using a common roof void in a row of terrace houses to have their escape route preplanned along the length of it emerging at a point some distance from where they would have been operating.

I noted that in attempting to dislodge the gunman the Saracen had structurally damaged the two occupied adjoining houses. The resident of one of these was on the street remonstrating with the Lieutenant about the damage to her property. Being concerned, I suppose, with more pressing matters he appeared to be oblivious to her protestations. In an attempt to solicit solace from some quarter she turned to me. 'Look at my house mister'. She shouted. 'Look what the bastards have done, what am I going to do?' This was one of those times when a little sympathy and diplomacy was required and which might be to our advantage. I went over and tried to console her by saying. 'Look love, contact the Housing Executive and tell them your house is badly damage, they'll either start emergency repairs or re-house you'. This seemed to assuage her immediate temper. Local knowledge being a wonderful thing, my next question to her was my immediate priority-'Are we safe here love?' 'Yes love, don't you worry son you'll be all right'. Spoken like a mother I thought; 'It's those bastards there'. Said she, pointing to the Lieutenant.

The Ammunitions Technical Officer eventually arrived and did his party piece with a small explosive charge, the car bomb turned out to be a hoax. On that particular call the Army did not bother to evacuate the nearby residents as is usual when a suspect car is about to be blown. We had to radio for an Ambulance for an old dear who took a heart attack when the controlled explosion went off. I could not help but think after this incident, what a tit for tat situation exists between the Security Forces and the Provos. It is the residents that usually suffer in this deadly game of cat and mouse. This may also have been the Provos way of telling the Army after Clonard Street 'own goal', 'We're still in business'.

S ilver City...From the commencement of the additional build-up of its ground forces in the Province in 1969, the Army had commandeered and occupied various buildings for the purposes of observation posts, communications/control, and billeting of troops, throughout Belfast and other towns in the Province. These included a diversity of premises that ranged from the long term vacant, prestigious Grand Central Hotel in Royal Avenue, in Belfast's city centre, gravitating to the lower end of the housing market which included Police Stations, spinning and weaving mills, bus depots and church halls. At one time in the early days they even wanted to install an observation post in Ardoyne Fire Station. This was resisted vigorously and thankfully common-sense-from the Brigade's point of view-won the day. There was very little in the way of luxury in these requisitioned establishments. Most of them were barely habitable for the troops. Basic utilities such as sleeping quarters, toilet and cooking facilities had all to be installed.

A number of custom built 'forts' were also erected, in what was considered by the Army to be sensitive Republican areas, where they needed a presence from whence they could observe the onset and execution of Republican clan-destine operations and also to give their patrols the advantage of a quick response to incidents. Silver City on the Monagh Road was such an establish-ment. The nick-name Silver City in this instance was derived from the fact that generally the 'forts'-for speed of construction-were mainly erected from galvanised corrugated sheet metal, surrounded by high fences made from the same materials. It was to this particular 'Silver City' that my two crews, with myself in charge, were to pay my one and only visit to such an establishments, with near disastrous consequences for some of the inmates.

Night duty once again at Ardoyne and the Pump received a call to a hut on fire on the Monagh Road-run of the mill-nothing to get excited about. A reduced attendance of one Pump was required, therefore I was not required to go. On this occasion Leading Firefighter Sammy Mason was Officer-in-Charge of the Pump. He was a good very experienced Firefighter with a droll sense of humour, which comes from being raised on the Shankill Road. He was a seasoned veteran of the 'Troubles' and knew the Station area well. Fifteen minutes after the Pump departed, another call was announced from Controls, this time it was for the Pump Escape, with me in charge. The address was designated as the Army post on the Monagh Road. When turning out from the Station I thought-Sam's fire has either spread to the post or it was the post all along and he now needs assistance-the latter was to be the case. We pro-ceeded quietly to the address-the 'fort' was approximately three miles distance from the Station-so we went , via the Upper Springfield and left down the Monagh Road. The 'fort' stood on its own, between the housing estates of Ballymurphy and lower Andersonstown. When we arrived the place seemed to be very quiet, but as the appliance approached the main gate, hidden eyes had been watching, for the main gate immediately swung open to admit us. We wound our way in through the chicane type entrance the short distance to where we rendezvoused with the Pump.

Sam was not immediately visible but what I saw and heard was a partially collapsed, single storey hut, belching smoke accompanied with spasmodic loud cracks. I also saw a hose line disappearing into the tangle of metal. Sam came out from the still erect end of the hut. 'What's going on Sam,' I asked. 'We had to withdraw, those are rounds of S.L.R.(self loading rifle) ammunition going off, when we arrived we were only told that it was a dormitory that was on fire not that it contained rifles'. The rounds were not loaded in weapons but contained in the rifle magazines and although they do not have the same velocity when discharged from a magazine nevertheless one would not like to be on the receiving end of a 7.65mm calibre round whether or not discharged from a rifle barrel. This was my main concern, discretion being the better part of valour at that moment. He pointed out also that the dormitory adjoined the fort's Ops room and he had decided to leave the dorm to its own fate, in the meantime concentrating on creating a fire-break between the two, as the Army were most anxious that their Ops room should be protected and preserved.

Personnel continued to shelter behind the appliances until the sound of the exploding ammunition ceased and I gave the order to make an entry into the hut. Upon entering the burnt out shell we immediately smelt the distinctive sweet smell of burnt timber, cordite, and the choking taste given off by the pungent fumes from the bedding. What had been a dorm was now a smouldering, blackened mess. During damping down we recovered the metallic skeletal remains of nine S.L.Rs- their wooden stocks and butts having been incinerated-along with one very sad looking 9mm. Browning pistol hanging in its webbed holster and belt. The information that Sam had gathered relative to the possible cause of the outbreak was inconclusive. Apparently a foot patrol had just come in shortly before the outbreak was discovered and had unloaded and left their kit and weapons in the dorm before going for their supper. There did not appear to any obvious source of ignition and security would have been too tight for a terrorist incursion. The only possible explanation as far as we were concerned was the old favourite of a carelessly discarded cigarette or malicious ignition by one of the soldiers. So we all went home none the wiser.

During his stay with me at Ardoyne-because of his local connections on the 'Shankill'- Sam had obtained a photograph of a murdered Loyalist. He showed it to me one day on Station. It was of the body of a Loyalist U.D.A. leader from the Shankill area who, up until the day of his death, had still crossed the 'Peace Line' each day into the 'Falls' to attend his place of work. It was taken in the morgue after his body had been recovered from a van in the Falls area. It showed him on the Ambulance trolley. His face had been badly beaten and he was naked from the waist down. His scrotum had been cut open and what had been some of its contents hung out. The remainder was lodged in another place. Some time later a local B.B.C. news team, did an investigation into some of the sectarian murders that had taken place in the Province around this time. One of the cases he reported on was that of a man from the 'Shankill' who had been abducted and held in a van. His squeals of pain and cries for help could be heard beyond the confines of the van. His body had been mutilated, it was suggested, by women. He must have died an agonising death from this barbarism.

This type of abduction and barbarous murder was not confined to one faction or the other of these 'Christians'. Extremists from both shared in the ritualistic torture and murder of their victims. Most notorious of all was Lenny Murphy and his gang *'The Shankill Butchers'* who scoured the streets in the late seventies for innocent Roman Catholic victims to vent their blood lust on. Murphy was never convicted of these crimes but met his Maker at the hands of a Republican assassin. It was reported that he had been fingered by one of his own. His gang were convicted and jailed in February 1979 for a total of nineteen murders.

Spinning Mill...It has been mentioned in a previous chapter that each Station and area had its own particular character-from the mainly residential of Cadogan through the mixed industrial and residential-that the Stations of Whitla, Ardoyne and Knock Stations stood sentinel over. Each patch also had its proportions of population that were further subdivided, owing their allegiance to this or that respective religious and political leanings. The North and West of Belfast were heavily populated by both communities, who were fearful and suspicious of one another as had been demonstrated by their recent actions. There were those in each community who declared themselves to be their citizens self appointed guardians. Guardians who not only opposed one another at times but when it suited joined forces to confronted the Security Forces. The Republican factions were prone to use this 'my enemy's enemy is my friend' philosophy more so than the Loyalist. So it can be seen that the

Brigade's activity level directly reflected the peaks and troughs of the activities of the paramilitaries as they pursued their military objectives.

I mention this because it will be seen that although I write about my many experiences and incidents in Ardoyne it has to be noted that there was a distinct difference in the nature of incidents in say Knock as opposed to Ardoyne. Although these operational activities are reported some years apart, the differences remained constant. Of all the station areas Ardoyne was the area more directly involved with the paramilitary street violence, much more so than any other districts. Chi' figures greatly in the story, for it was the personnel there who took the brunt of the incendiary and bombing attacks that were launched in the commercial heart of the city in the early seventies. Similar attacks seldom occurred in the residential locations. It was very fortunate indeed that the I.R.A. did not know how close the Brigade was to being down on its knees and if had continued with its scorched earth policy the City centre could quite easily have been razed to the ground. Each Fire Station in any Brigade is interdependent for support, one on the other, from time to time. Because Chi' was so heavily under pressure outlying Stations were frequently mobilised into its area to give this support. This is a story of such an attendance from Ardoyne. It does not rate as being one of the classic fires of the period, or indeed in the annals of the Brigade's history, but has its own complexion and memories for me.

It was a quiet April evening in 1973, quiet that, is in terms of Mother nature but not in terms of the continuing Provos incendiary campaign that was being mounted within Belfast's city centre. Appliances were scurrying about the city attending a number of calls. Our call to duty and turn to become involved came to Ardoyne at 1830hrs that evening. The call was to a large haberdashery store, the Spinning Mill, in Royal Avenue nearly opposite to the Army's billet in the Grand Central Hotel. When our three appliances arrived on the scene, there was no mistaking that we had the makings of a good working job. No fire was visible, just thick black smoke which you could have cut with a knife billowing from the first floor veranda windows. Two adult male figures were seen on the roof, entreating us to rescue them. The turntable ladder was put in position and a textbook walk-down rescue was carried out. Personnel were put onto the veranda with a view to penetrating into the building-plate glass windows were smashed to make entry- hoping against hope that a flashover would not occur when the fresh air reached the interior-which in the event did not occur. I was reasonably familiar with the building from my time in Fire Prevention. It was of concrete monolithic construction with mushroom supporting columns, it would be a safe tight structure in a fire, not prone to collapse but difficult to ventilate. I was reluctant to commit B.A. men because of this, not knowing where the seat of the fire was. At this point I ordered my Sub Officer Sammy Hill to make an entry via the ground floor in an attempt to locate the fire.

Just about now Assistant Divisional Officer Dickie Sefton and Divisional Officer Billy Beggs arrived from Chi'. They must have been in the Officer's Mess when they got the call because when they got out of the staff car Mr. Beggs put his helmet on back to front. He was a visiting officer from the Northern Ireland Fire Authority who was to become the third C.F.O. of the new Northern Ireland Fire Brigade in due course.

Amalgamation was only a matter of months away and I suppose their Officers were having a wee look into the 'big smoke', to see how the 'creme de la creme' operated. Feeling rather proud of myself, my turntable ladder crew having just effected a copybook rescue, I reported the fire status to both Officers who seemed oblivious to what I was saying and didn't state if they were taking over control or not but simply waltzed off to places unknown. I wish to God that they had taken charge-I had just sent a 'make up' message for further additional Pumps-for this fire was for me and the attending crews one of the most frustrating and exhausting that I had ever experienced, before or since. It took something like two hours to eventually locate the seat of the fire. One of the B.A. teams stumbled across a service staircase tucked away out of sight on the ground floor which led up to the first floor where the fire was raging in a clothing storeroom-happy days-we began to win the game. By this time water was pouring down through the building and into the ground floor showroom, the fitted carpet between the display gondolas was floating about two inches off the floor. When I walked on it I felt as if I was walking on a swampy quagmire. As I descended into the ground floor from the service staircase-the smoke was beginning to clear and steam was rising from the hot water that flooded into the floor from above-through the steam and smoke towards the front of the shop I could just discern the figure of someone moving about. As I drew closer I perceived the figure of one of the visiting Officers dancing around the floor with one of the window mannequins in his arms whilst wearing its 'borrowed' blonde wig. He was completely oblivious to me which was just as well for by now I was doubled up in a silent convulsion of laughter and as I had not made my presence known I decided to make a hasty exit.

"... mind if I cut in, Sir??"

The wig was recovered and brought back to Station as a memento for big Tommy Woods-who was completely bald-to wear on special occasions. At around ten o'clock as darkness closed in I was relieved by Davy Vance and his crew from Whitla. I was sitting on the pavement in Rosemary Street at the side of the premises, coughing my guts up and gasping for breath, I was never so glad to be relieved as I was then. Who says fire-fighting is glamorous, if it wasn't for the beer and laughs who would do it?

Mr. Goldstone, the proprietor of the Spinning Mill-which was the 'in place' to buy material, if you could not get it there you could not get it anywhere-was one of the very few business men in the City, that I know of, who by way of appreciation for our efforts, gave us carte blanche to call with him anytime and make a cheap purchase from his store. This building later became the first Argos store in Belfast, prior to them moving to occupy new shop premises in Cornmarket. of which more later.

No-Go Palmer Street…'No-go' areas in Belfast and Londonderry became quite fashionable in the early seventies. Fashionable is probably an incorrect description for they were anything but fashionable. These 'local arrangements' were introduced in the Province's two largest cities by the self styled guardians of both their respective communities on either side of the religious and political divides. The Loyalists no-gos' growing tit-for-tat in response to that of the Republicans. Their perceived intention was to give protection against violent incursions by one or other faction of the opposition's' activists. This was the 'official' line but in practice these no-go areas proved to be a front to give cover to the community's own covert, illegal activities and to prevent access to the Security Forces. An example, of one of the less sinister activities was the setting up of pirate radio Stations by the Ulster Defence Association-one being named 'Radio Free Nick' broadcasting on 242 metres-the other 'Radio Free Ulster' on 318 metres transmitting out of Linwood Street. They broadcast daily from 3pm playing music and giving out local news and propaganda. As long as 'Free Derry' had their no-go area the Loyalist ones were politically tolerated. Some of the barricades that blocked access by road into each area were permanent structures. These were constructed with steel H beams cemented at an angle into the roadway or large concrete blocks or even a combination of both. It took the Army's operation 'Motorman' on 31st July 1972 to dismantle the long standing no-go area in 'Derry. Following which the Loyalist barricades were taken down voluntarily.

In the Loyalist areas of Belfast each no-go enclave was controlled and patrolled by companies of the Ulster Defence Association. When on patrol they could be seen driving about their designated area in open backed Land Rovers dressed in battle fatigues. Some were wearing Boer type bush hats and sun glasses or face masks and carrying various forms of displayed weaponry, such as pick axe handles and cudgels, only they knew what wasn't displayed. They were a frightening and intimidating sight for strangers seeing them for the first time and these 'guardians' were a law onto themselves. By the end of June 1972 fifty permanent barriers had been erected in West Belfast which included the Woodvale, Shankill, and Oldpark areas. The rest of the City sported some one hundred temporary barricades which posed a problem for emergency appliances who needed rapid access. It was 'C' Company of the U.D.A. that controlled the section of the Upper Shankill within which Palmer Street lay. This area was bounded by Cambrai Street, Woodvale Road, and on the side where any threat from Republican activists was expected, the Crumlin Road. The Ardoyne lay just beyond the other side of the Crumlin. Only three road routes were passable into this area and it was incumbent on each Station Officer to continually familiarise themselves and their crews with these entrances. They could be changed at any time and without notice thus causing a delay in response time to an incident that occurred beyond the barriers. To this end some liaison for mutual benefit took place with these communities within the no-go zones.

Whenever no-go areas come up in discussion, which is rarely, Palmer Street is always first to spring to my mind. Just as I was about to crawl out of bed for breakfast one morning while on night duty-'fire call to a house on fire in Palmer Street enter by Cambrai Street entrance'-was the call that boomed out over the Tannoy from Controls. It was daylight by this time. It wasn't far and the traffic was light so we had no need of flashers or two tone horns. We found our way into the street speedily and easily. There ahead was an end terrace house with smoke belching from the open hallway door. It was a large size end terrace unlike most of the other high density kitchen houses in the immediate vicinity, it even had a front parlour. A quick look in through the front door and I heard the crackling of flames upstairs. Two B.A. men with a jet were ordered in and told to ascend the staircase. The other boys of the crew fed the hose up to them. We heard them thrashing about with the jet up above us, so the fire was indeed somewhere up there. Following up as the smoke quickly thinned with other crew members who were able to take over the branch, I told the B.A. men to by-pass the fire and begin a search of the bedrooms for possible casualties and to ventilate the premises of smoke. The fire was on a half landing and had begun to spread up towards the front main bedroom, it was starting to get extremely hot.

As we waited crouching on the landing, several minutes passed before the B.A. men reported back to me. One came to the head of the stairs outside the main bedroom and shouting indistinctly through the speech diaphragm in the face-mask of his breathing apparatus. He was calling for me to come up. It is one thing that every Firefighter dreads finding a body. So up I went and he pointed over towards the double bed that was still covered with bedclothes that were partially burned and blackened. One of the lads pulled back the clothes. No, it wasn't a body, but what was snuggled under the clothes was a World War I vintage rifle. The thing was nearly red hot but I lifted it and pulled back the bolt to see if it was loaded, it was. For safety sake I decided it was best to eject the rounds that I could see in the breech, five came out. I went back down the stairs and out into the street leaving the rifle in the bedroom. All this time there was no sign of the occupants of the house which was sparsely furnished.

What the hell was I to do about this bloody rifle and its ammo, remember this was a no-go area. That meant no Police, no Army, no law and order except the U.D.A. Who do you pass the buck to here Allan I thought as I walked towards the appliance with five .303 shells in my pocket. What a dilemma, who needs this kind of aggro, why didn't I finish serving my apprenticeship as a fitter, or go to sea as an engineer as I had always wanted to, why me? I could not report it to the authorities over the two way radio at that time, for both I.R.A. and Loyalist para militaries were able to monitor emergency appliance channels. I could not take it away with me as a keep sake. What would Sandra say if I came off night duty with a bloody rifle or even the shells? Maybe the owner had a licence for it and uses it for duck shooting-or perhaps its an off duty soldier who lives here and he likes to take his work home with him?

Then walking towards me, unwittingly, was the answer to my prayers, it was one of the local U.D.A. leaders whom I knew from seeing him being interviewed on the television. As he approached he must have noted the consternation on my face, 'Everything alright Chief '? he asked cheerily. I dropped my voice and spoke to him, 'if you call finding a fucking loaded .303 rifle in a bed alright I suppose it is. What do I do with these things?' as I took the five rounds from my pocket-he snatched them from me. Who was I to argue? 'If the rest of the bloody stuff goes off in there your bloody plastic helmets won't save you', he said. I didn't have to ask him what he mean't. I knew, a case of out of the frying pan into the fire. I told him that I had a 'mixed' crew and that I could not expose them to seeing anymore than they had already seen for the sake of their own self preservation. What you don't see you cannot worry or talk about. He said that the 'Nailer' was on his way. I hadn't heard that expression before or since-'we'll get him moved' was the final response I got from this U.D.A. leader. Just before we left that morning to return to Station a van arrived and some locals started emptying the house of its entire contents, the 'Nailer' was one of them. He was a jaunty looking little fellow but looks were probably deceiving. He was casually dressed in jeans and matching jacket with a distinctive, green 'Robin Hood' type hat perched on his head. He was in fact the local home guard, part of 'Dads Army' We didn't hang around long enough to see what else was brought out of the house besides furniture.

Shortly after this episode we were to attend another call to Palmer Street. This time it was to be more dramatic and with tragic consequences. In the interim period the no-go areas in the Loyalist areas of the city were being relegated to the history books, or perhaps they were to be kept in cold storage for another day? The barricades were dismantled and life had returned to what

120

the residents in these areas had come to know as 'normality'. In Belfast terms that is.

It was a Sunday evening when we received another fire call to the street. When the appliances turned in past the house we had previously been at we could see some distance up the street that a kitchen house was going well. Some of the residents who were out in the street were going frantic. The women yelling and screaming and motioning to us to hurry. It was clear even then that life was at risk. The appliances were prevented from getting closer to the house than fifty yards, being obstructed by vehicles parked opposite to one another on each side of the narrow road. As we dismounted I yelled at the Officer-in-Charge of the Pump behind me for two B.A.. wearers and a jet to be run out as we all sprinted towards the house. The jet and B.A. men arrived almost as soon as I did, the neighbours were shouting that there were children upstairs. The front living room was an inferno.

There was little or no smoke, it was so hot, with the flames leaping out the front door and window, licking up as high as the first floor and beginning to take a hold on the staircase. As the jet was brought to play on the fire in the front room, from a relatively safe crouched position, in the little vestibule hall-way, I told the B.A. men to make their way up the staircase, for search and rescue. As they were doing this the screams of some of the crowd changed to 'they're downstairs, they're downstairs' my heart sank. If they were upstairs they might have had a chance but downstairs, no. I shouted for the B.A. team to come back down. They didn't need to be told twice for they were being cooked trying to get up the staircase. The heat was intense, there is nothing as hot as a little kitchen house that is 'going well'. I needed them to try and pen-etrate the fire in the front room aided by their B.A's. with its supply of cool fresh air. It only took a few minutes for them to quell the fireball that was the front room. The flames disappeared rapidly and were replaced by rising scald-ing steam. The walls were so hot the plaster exploded off the walls whenever the water from the jet touched it.

Visibility improved slowly through the fog of steam, one of the B.A. men shouted, 'here S.O.' I knew they had got something. I looked and against the far wall of the tiny room was the skeletal remains of what had been a settee and on it the small charred figure of a child. The figure was lying reclined on its back we could not identify the corpse as being a boy or girl. The sad news quickly reached the gathering crowd outside, the yelling and squealing changed to subdued crying from the women. The names of two children started to be muttered by some of the crowd, we had only found one. Poor little Samuel was what I remember hearing. He was the child on the settee, I don't recall the name of the second. The settee was close to a fixed gas fire in the hearth and between the two I could see a large lump on the floor which was covered by the plaster from the walls and ceiling, I wondered what it was. We scraped away the plaster and found the body of the other child an infant. I enquired from a bystander where the parents where. I was told that the father was probably at the local drinking club and the mother visiting a neighbour nearby.

The other B.A. team by this time were searching upstairs, when one of them came down he drew me to one side and said 'S.O. there's a hand gun and a rifle butt upstairs'. Oh no, not again I thought. By this time the Police and Army had arrived and also the local friendly neighbourhood U.D.A. leader who I had encountered at the last call to Palmer Street. He sauntered up to me, here it comes again I thought, I was right. He knew there were weapons in the house as did the Police but he got to me first. He made the approach and asked if they could be got out. I told him that there was no one allowed in at the moment as it was still too warm and that there were two fatalities inside. As far as was concerned I was still in charge of this as a fire incident no matter what other implications there might be for the Police or the Army.

No sooner had he U.D.A. man walked away than a plain clothes detective introduced himself to me and asked, in a nudge nudge, wink wink manner if I had seen anything. I knew what he was after but I told him the same as I had told the last chummy. He would be able to go inside when the place cooled somewhat. I did mention as a tease to him, that there were cases of tinned foodstuffs in the kitchen and it was obvious from the cardboard boxes in the hallway which had been on fire and giving off a lazy blue flame that they contained high proof alcohol. The residents had not been buying early Christmas fare that was for sure.

Things were just too tragic at that moment and I simply did not wish to know about any weapons or who might or might not be interested in them. My intention was to vacate the scene as quickly as humanly possible. What the Police or what anyone else found on our departure was their affair not mine.

At times like this that Firefighters suffer mixed emotions-could they, should they have done more-anger at the carelessness of the parents-frustration at the appalling waste of it all. It was indeed a time for mixed emotions. In the distance I saw the sobbing mother of the children being comforted by neighbours. It is always the worst kind of fatality to attend when a child is the victim, it affects everyone involved. The children are the ones who suffer for a parents' moment of in-attention or the unintended neglect of their guardians. Guardians could be prosecuted under the Childrens and Young Persons Act but who is going to prosecute a parent who has just lost a child? They will suffer themselves for the rest of their lives, I am sure that is prosecution enough.

The damage was so severe to the living room that I could only surmise at the supposed cause of fire. The gas fire, though out at the time of my investigation, had its on/off switch in on position. It was therefore reasonable to assume that it was lit prior to fire-fighting operations. The position of the infant, on the floor between the settee and close to the fire, indicated to me that it had been crawling about the floor and had probably brushed against it and had caught fire, thus igniting the settee with the sleeping six year old Samuel on it.

The foregoing two episodes are only examples of a few of the type of events that were undoubtedly encountered by many other Officers-in-charge of appliances at incidents throughout the city. These were seldom talked of openly to others, except among those personnel directly involved. Because these incidents relate to events that took place in a Loyalist area it does not necessarily follow that instances such as I have related were exclusively peculiar to Protestant enclaves only. The fact that arms were so easily and accidentally stumbled upon by ourselves, probably testifies more to the lack of guile and cunning displayed by Loyalist para militaries at that time rather than a failure in a well oiled organisation. These weapons were clearly intended to be used in the defence their own homes so immediate access was therefore required to them although part of the blasé attitude was probably attributable to the fact that the Security Forces did not intrude into these streets during the no-go era. It was the Republican elements who were the sworn enemies of the Forces of the Crown. It was they who had the time to plan attacks, to choose the killing ground and who therefore had less urgency in retrieving their weapons for immediate use, or perhaps because they were better organised?

I could recount at least two other incidents that I experienced around this time but not in any great detail or with any great degree of conviction, as my conclusions were arrived at more by suspicion than fact. One was a call to a block of flats in the Moyard region of the Upper Springfield Road when we extinguished a fire in a flat that I assumed, not unnaturally to be Republican field hospital because of the two metal framed hospital beds and drip stands that were present. The other was when I was investigating a smell of smoke in a property in Islandbawn Street off the Falls where I had occasion to ask the tenant of the adjoining premises if I could check her property for signs of fire and if their was anyone upstairs. The house was a barrack of a place and I did not want to disturb anyone either in bed or carrying out their ablutions. The answer to both my questions was yes and no respectively. However when I opened the door into one of the bedrooms I encountered a man with a heavy growth of beard, lying on a mattress on the floor, peering out at me from under the covers. I could see he was heavily bandaged around the right shoulder. Neither of use spoke, eye to eye contact was all that took place, and then I quickly and quietly withdrew. This was the time when exchange of gunfire was a regular occurrence between the Provisionals and the Security Forces.

Simple little questions that begged an answer like these have bugged me all these years but, just as in the case of those incidents of Palmer Street, when in Rome do as the Romans do, do not intrude. You are in an alien world. Just take care to look after the interests of your crew, yourself, the Brigade, and your colleagues, those who might have to follow in your footsteps one day.

On 28th January 1973 Dave Fogel the local U.D.A. leader who had departed Belfast suddenly with his family, in an interview with the *Sunday Times* revealed there was a power struggle going on within the U.D.A., 'We are mixing with dangerous and evil men out for their own gains and not for the interests of the ordinary working-class Protestant people of Ulster'. He said he hoped the two working class communities could eventually unite. Incidentally Dave Fogel was an Englishman.

Corry's Timber Yard...Corry's timber importing business is a family run affair and has been one of the longest established importers of the product in the Province. Their original premises were at a dockland site and in more recent times they had developed a larger capacity storage area on the Springfield Road. They were one of the few timber firms to stock exotic hard woods back in the seventies. I know, for I used to enjoy roaming around the timber sheds looking for a particular piece of Teak or Mahogany when I used to do a bit of boat building.

Timber yards have been a favourite target for terrorist firebomb attack for a number of reasons-but then what has not been a target in Ulster? On the 10th and 14th February 1972, McCue Dick's and Corry's timberyards within the dockland area were both firebombed. Corry's Springfield Road site was targeted on the 18th July 1972. Timber yards were easy targets, first and foremost because of the combustibility of the raw material, secondly, because of the difficulty of giving adequate surveillance and security to the long boundary fences required to enclose such extensive sites and, lastly, as any Firefighter worth his salt who has experienced fire-fighting a timber stack fire knows, the difficulty of control and extinction once it really gets going.

The tale of this particular conflagration has a particular twist in its own tail, one that is not to be experienced during the course of normal fire-fighting and cannot therefore be allowed for, or indeed anticipated.

Night duty once again at Ardoyne, 'Fire Call Full Attendance' to Corry's timber yard Upper Springfield Road. Up and at it lads, here we go, was the cry as we turned out that evening, anticipating and planning the route in my mind as we ran to the engine room. Sharp right out of the Station acute right again into Twadell Avenue down to the junction with Ballygomartin Road, turn right four hundred yards and left into the West Circular, picking up speed now on the straight half mile run to the 'T' junction with the Springfield and we are there.

Looks like a good one, I thought, as we turned into the West Circular Road. I could see the glow in the dark night sky, lighting up the site at the far end of the road. No need to give any initial orders to the crews it was obvious jets were needed and it did not matter how many initially, the more the merrier. Divisional Officer Johnston arrived on our tail along with Chi's Emergency Salvage Tender and immediately made an assistance call to Controls for a 'make up' of more appliances. A number of timber stacks were starting to get going well, fanned by a strong breeze. The first two jets were got to work from a downwind position directly into the face of the flames in an attempt to prevent spread to adjacent stacks that were close to the boundary wall. Just beyond the wall was the Whitehall housing estate. As the number of water jets that were being brought into play increased, drivers were beginning to report that water pressure was dropping, but the fire was still growing in intensity. More Pumps and more hose were requested.

I found myself taking shelter from the intense heat behind a flat-back trailer, in the company of two branchmen and another Fire Service uniformed figure whom I could not immediately identify, when without warning there was an unmerciful bang. All three of us started in panic and wondered what it was. Then we realised that it was just one of the tyres of the trailer that had exploded with the heat, thank goodness that was all it was. It was at this moment I realised who the previously unidentified Firefighter was-it was the Chief-what a surprise to see him in the thick of things on the fireground-you did not see Chiefy in the middle of it very often on the fireground- that was usually Mr. Pollock's the Deputy's role.

No need for Johnty or I to worry now, He was the Man, who was going to take charge! Fire was beginning to spread to the stacks at the boundary wall because of the intense radiated heat, we could see steam coming off the roofs of several of the pensioners bungalows that were adjacent to the wall on the other side. This estate was a no-go area which had been barricaded to prevent access by the Security Forces. A request from the people of this neighbourhood for fire appliances to be sent in for protection was met with caution by Brigade Controls, however Assistant Divisional Officer Dickie Sefton and two pumps one of which was from the Northern Ireland Fire Authority, that had joined us from Castlereagh Station, were dispatched to survey the scene and if neces-sary aid the residents of the houses that were under threat of becoming engulfed by lateral fire spread. The Assistant Divisional Officer was sent in on the clear understanding that he would be accompanied by a local priest.

One of our principal worries was that the fire would spread to the wooden slatted storage sheds where it would be even more difficult to put out and would in addition expose men to the risk of structural collapse. Through sheer doggedness and gutsy determination of the branchmen holding their ground and preventing the seemingly relentless spread, the fire spread was finally held, surrounded, and contained.

Just when we seemed to be getting on top of the situation, Johnty came up to me, saying, 'Allan we have to withdraw all appliances from the area'. 'Why?' was my short obvious query. Apparently a radio message had been received from the P.I.R.A. using the two-way radio in Assistant Divisional Officer Sefton's staff car, from within the housing estate. Dickie Sefton and the Castlereagh crew were being held hostage until we vacated the scene, if we did not, Assistant Divisional Officer Sefton would be shot. Poor Dickie, captured for the third time. There was to be no question about this order either on my part with Johnty, or on the Chief's part in dialogue with the para militaries on the other side of the wall. The word was quickly spread to all the crews.

No one, at that moment in time, other than the Chief- because we all had been totally committed and engrossed in subduing the mini fire storm that wind conditions had assisted in bringing about-knew how many personnel or appliances of one sort or another which were in attendance at the incident or

126

in what capacity they were deployed. Hose lines were hurriedly shut down by drivers, and any equipment that was easily portable was carried out of the timber yard. The fire was simply left to go its own merry way. Such a shame after all that effort.

Drivers were directed to take their appliances and park them along the West Circular Road. Eventually there was a wagon-train of thirteen fire appliances lined along the road, a sight to behold. Perhaps not unusual in some of the bigger U.K. Brigades but for Belfast it was the biggest gathering we were ever likely to see. After this enforced retreat the fire crews and appliances were released at 0400hrs though Dickie Sefton was held for another half an hour.

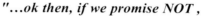

"...ok then, if we promise NOT ,

to let him go will you quit fire-fighting?? "

When he was released he reported that on his arrival at the barricades the accompanying 'priest' had disappeared. He was seized and spread-eagled over the bonnet of his staff car with a gun held to his head. His captors noted his name and address from his driving licence and told him if he identified any of them he would be 'dealt with'. The fire crews were allowed to deal with the fire that by now had broken out in several of the pensioner's bungalows. When released he was informed that a bomb had been placed on one of the fire appliances, when he inquired which appliance it was on he was told 'that's for us to know and you to find out'. A subsequent search of the appliances did not reveal any bomb. His captors also ripped out his radio hand set so that he could not contact Controls. Poor Dickie was not to have much luck with car radios. At a later incident while investigating a fire in a garage in Tates Avenue, which is in a Loyalist area of the city, he was seized by members of the opposing faction of the I.R.A., the U.D.A., who whilst brandishing cudgels demanded his car keys. These were reluctantly handed over under on the threat of a beating, or as it was put 'you can do it the easy or hard way', Dickie quite understandably, chose the easy way. The car was driven off and later found intact but minus its radio, which had been professionally removed.

Without digressing anymore we must needs return now to Corry's. Some crews including my own proceeded to Chi' to the hose store to replenish stocks and take a breather. Yet others returned to their respective Stations. While at Chi' I spoke to Johnty and asked 'what next?'. He told me that the Army was moving in with their armoured Salamander fire appliances in an attempt to control the fire and hold it in check and if all was quiet by the morning we would return to finish the job. Far from putting me at my ease, this last tit-bit of information made me feel decidedly uneasy, especially in view of the fact of what had happened to Dickie Sefton and company. Sometimes lightning does strike twice or thrice, even in his case.

Nonetheless the next morning a reduced attendance of appliances returned to the scene and as the fire was on my Station's ground we drew the short straw. Things were very quiet, the Salamanders were still putting water on the smouldering timber stacks and had prevented any fire spread to the timber storage sheds, in fact they had done quite a good job under the circumstances. It only remained for us to leave a minimal number of personnel there to damp down. There was no more threat from the para militaries. Little did we know that Johnty had slipped back up to Corrys that night and directed the army's firefighting efforts from inside a Salmander. He was not about to let the Provos completely thwart our galant efforts.

It was my responsibility to make out the K433 fire report-as it was then-on the incident. On these report forms there was a section at the end for any comments on any relevant points in relation to fire prevention matters. This information was gathered and collated by the Home Office Fire Research Department for statistical analysis into causes of fire and so the information gathered could be used to research and develop improved methods of fire fighting, fire prevention, and fire detection. This gathering of information still continues today but in a much more sophisticated manner since the introduction of information technology, which has touched on all aspects of all our daily lives.

Even in the seventies Home Office Fire Prevention Notes and Technical Bulletins, laid down basic requirements with regard to the safe distances between timber stacks on an open storage site and adjoining property. The stacks that were on fire beside the boundary wall and adjacent to the housing estate were, in my opinion-and according to the current Home Office advice-not only too closely stacked together-but were also too close to the boundary and the domestic housing on the other side of that wall. Self evidently a number of houses were in fact damaged by the fire. I thought it prudent that I should make mention of this in my report for future reference in case of another possible similar conflagration. Some weeks later a 'messenger' in the guise of Assistant Divisional Officer Graham was sent up to the Station by the A.C.O. to speak to me regarding the content of this section of my report. I was asked to remove it. I had known that I might be walking on thin ice as far as the Brigade was concerned, when I had recorded my observations. This had been a terrorist initiated fire which had spread to Roman Catholic housing, however two wrongs do not make a right. As everyone knows rules are made to be broken and if a little extra storage space can be gained, no harm is done. In my experience that is usually the business man's way of thinking, until he is caught that is, or something goes wrong. This time they were caught and something had gone wrong, luckily for everyone concerned without disastrous consequences.

Now why was an Assistant Chief Officer who never had any fire prevention experience telling me to change my fire report? I told the messenger that if the A.C.O. wants the report changed he can do it himself and sign to the fact accordingly. He left with a faint little smile on his face as he walked away and the issue was never raised again.

5

Murder and Mayhem ....

The Belfast/Bangor Railway Line...Prior to the 'Shankill Butchers' going on their rampage of sectarian murder and mutilation in the mid seventies, torture and murder was taking place throughout the City in Loyalist areas on Roman Catholics by 'Loyalists'. Yet others murders were being perpetrated by Republicans as a form of punishment or control on their own kind.

It was always prudent on the part of anyone who commuted to Belfast to work to listen to the local early morning news bulletin prior to commencing their journey into or across the City. Prudent that is in order to avoid possible delays due to bomb scares, fire bombings, or civil unrest. All of which resulted in serious traffic delays. When living in East Belfast and Stationed at Ardoyne I carried out this ritual before leaving to go on duty every time. One morning I heard on the news that the unidentified body of a young male had been found near the Belfast/Bangor railway line at Sydenham. He had been shot through the head. I lived at Sydenham and the line ran past the bottom of our road. Before I got out of the house the phone rang, it was the Station Sergeant from Strandtown Police Station. He informed me, that upon hearing the news of this murder on national radio, the sister of our neighbour Eddie Curran had telephoned the Station to enquire about her missing brother. She had said that she was concerned about his safety because his was a mixed marriage and he lived in a Protestant area. She had tried to contact him by phone but was unable to get any reply from him or his wife. In order to reassure her the Sergeant rang me to request if I would go to the city morgue to identify the body. Not being particularly keen to carry out this gruesome task I remarked that the news report had stated the victim had a black panther tattooed on his left forearm. I was adamant that Eddie had no such tattoo. He thanked me and I thought that was that.

Shortly after getting into Ardoyne that morning I received another phone call from the Sergeant. This time the question and request was couched slightly differently with clever use of the English language. Instead of me making a positive I.D. he asked that I make a negative one, that is to say, identify the corpse as not being that of Mr. Curran. I could not get out of that one. So I handed over charge of the Station to Sub Officer Sammy Hill-borrowed Brigade transport-booked off duty via Controls-and left enroute for the old single storey brick built Victorian city morgue. It was situated on the old sand quay where the barges used to discharge their cargoes, just across from Chi'. When I arrived I was received by two very nattily dressed C.I.D men. They escorted me inside. I had my uniform cap pulled well down over my eyes, not quite knowing what I was going to see. I think my two escorts realised my apprehension. Whenever I observed the body I saw that the corpse was dark complexioned whereas Eddie was fairish skinned. A post mortem had already been carried out on him. He was stitched up the middle roughly, like a sack of potatoes, no finesse here I thought.

One of the officers unceremoniously took hold of the chin of the victims and thrust it to one side in order that I might have a side view. He then lifted the tattooed arm for my inspection. I said to them that the body was not that of Eddie Curran. I later learned that this poor soul was a young chap from Carrickfergus named Henry Russell who had obviously strayed from his usual haunts and paid the ultimate terrible price. That is the way the tribal boundaries worked then in Belfast and still do....

Bodies in the Boot... At 2300hrs on 1st July 1972 while on night duty at Ardoyne, the tannoy system from Controls crackled into life and announced, 'Fire Call! Pump only, to a car on fire Landscape Terrace, Crumlin Road'. Landscape Terrace was only about three quarters of a mile straight down the road from the Station just above Crumlin Road Prison. A car on fire only warranted a reduced attendance turnout of one Pump. I was therefore not required to go. One of my Leading Firefighters Tommy Woods was Officer-in-Charge. As I lay in bed I listened to the muffled sounds of the crew responding from various parts of the Station to board the appliance and heard it departing the engine room enroute to the incident. I must have dosed off shortly after this. It was the sound of someone coming into the duty office outside my bedroom that awakened me. I looked at my watch, it was 0115hrs 'Is that you Tommy, only back?' I shouted, 'Yes' was the reply, 'That must have been some bloody car on fire'. I bantered, 'Bloody well was' he retorted as he came into the room. 'What'ya mean' I said. 'Two bodies in the boot'. Oh shit, I thought and at that I sat up.

He went on to relate to me that when they had arrived at the incident and approached the vehicle it was well alight inside. The Army who were present had told him that they were suspicious of the vehicle, a Ford Cortina, as it had been stolen. He had told the crew to knock the fire down quickly and retire to a safe distance, which they did. The Army Ammunitions Technical Officer was summoned and on arrival set charges to blow the boot open. This was duly done without any subsequent additional explosion. On inspecting inside the boot compartment to everyone's horror, it became immediately apparent that two bodies had been secreted there.

A cursory examination determined that that both had been male. They were later identified as a forty three year old who was a member of the Roman Catholic Ex-Service Mens' Association and a nineteen year old English youth who had been on holiday with his companion in death. It was also established they had both been badly beaten prior to death. They had been subjected to a 'Romper Room' type execution-Romper Room was a kiddies playroom T.V. programme of this era-a methodology which was 'popular' around this time amongst some para military factions The crude analogy being that the perpetrators of these heinous murders tortured and played in a cruel childish way with their victims before killing them. Theirs was a particularly agonising and brutal murder.

T elstar...The cover of darkness seems to be the time when those who would perpetrate evil seem to relish carrying out their hideous crimes. It was certainly no different in my experience during the period of my posting at Ardoyne Station when our activities seemed to be at their peak at night time also. This time it was to be a Republican faction that had carried out the execution, the details of which were recounted to me. I say recounted because it was one of those crimes that was never officially recorded anywhere as such and which so many families have had to bear silently. Not only never seeing their loved ones again but never to have been made aware of the facts surrounding their disappearance or where their mortal remains might still lie.

Once again I was to be disturbed while in bed. The Dutyman Alan Lyle came into my room one night about 2200hrs. He said there was a guy in the Watchroom who wanted to report a murder. I told him tell this guy to report it to the Police. Alan said he had already told him this but the fellow wanted the Army and refused to leave. I reluctantly got out of bed put on my trousers and shoes and proceeded across the Station yard towards the engine room, thinking wearily to myself oh! Lord what have we got here. The Station was blacked out and I did not immediately see the shadowy figure in the corner of the engine room, just as I did, he began to approach me. I said to him he had better come into the office. I retraced my steps across the yard and entered my bedroom/office. I motioned him to sit down. As he sat down on the bed I took note of his appearance. He was short and stocky with shoulder length mousy hair and had a disfigurement that I was always going to remember. He wore a combat jacket and was somewhat dishevelled looking and not a little agitated.

I said, 'You want to report a murder'. 'Yes' he replied. 'You know it's bloody dangerous for us to get involved with anything like this. We're in a very dodgy position here. Would you not go and use a phone somewhere else?' 'There's no public phones working about here' he said. Of course I knew this was a fact but it was a good try anyway. 'Do you want to tell me what happened?' I enquired. At this point I really did not know what to think and was apprehensive about this character and for my own safety. Little did I know that some of the boys who had been with Alan Lyle in the Watchroom also shared my feelings. At this point the phone rang. It was Joe O'Kane from Controls, he asked 'Allan are you alright there' I said 'Yes Joe, why?' 'The Watchroom rang and said you had someone on Station.' I interrupted him, not wanting my visitor to pick up the drift of the conversation and maybe panic. 'It's O.K. Joe if I need anything I'll give you a ring.' and I put the phone down. I had not taken my eyes of my visitor for a second. Returning to our conversation I said to him 'Well tell me about it, do you really want to report this to the Police?' 'Not the Police, the Army', he said. 'Tell me your name first' 'It's Charlie Farley and I live in the 'Doyne' he said and went on to tell me what he had witnessed. 'I was keeping Watch outside the Shamrock Club-a local Republican shebeen-I was in the Forces and if you've been in the Forces you're not allowed into the P.I.R.A. So I got the job of keeping dick. They brought an old friend of mine out of the club at gun point. He crawled along the pavement begging for his life and they shot him in the head. It was awful'. I sat there listening absolutely transfixed. He continued, 'His body was put in a manhole into the sewers. I ran off in case I got it next for witnessing it.'

After listening to him I said 'Are you sure you really want to report this'. 'Yes'. ' I hope you know what your doing'. He then gave me the number of Ardoyne bus depot where the Army had a post and told me to ask for Captain Johnston. The depot was only about one hundred yards from the Station. Before I could carry out his request, the phone rang again. 'Hello' I said, somewhat irritated thinking it was Controls again. The voice replied. 'This the

Station Sergeant Tennent Street-Police Station-are you having some trouble up there' 'No' I said, 'Hold on a moment,' I covered the mouthpiece and said to Charlie 'It's Tennent Street Police, will you talk to them?' 'No, the Army'. At that I spoke to the Sergeant again telling him 'No, everything is O.K. here Sergeant if I need you I'll give you a call,' and put the phone down.

I dialled the number Charlie had given me and the phone was answered after a few rings by an English accent. 'Hello Ardoyne', I said, 'Can I speak to Captain Johnston.' There was silence for a moment, the recipient of my call must have been thinking about it. Then he said, 'Who's calling?' ' I have some-one here who wants to speak to the Captain.' 'Hold on' he replied. After a short time another voice came on asking who I was. I said , ' Is that Captain. Johnston ?' 'No this is Captain Williamson, who is that?' he said, 'Officer-in-Charge of Ardoyne Fire Station here. I have someone with me who wants to speak to you'. At that I handed the phone over. His first words were 'This is 'Telstar' I'm coming in,' was all he said. He listened to what the other party had to say and then put the phone down. I was horrified. This fellow was obvious-ly an Army informer. What an appropriate name for an informer I thought. 'Telstar' was the first ever communication satellite launched in 1968. After this the only words that I could summon up were 'I hope you know what your doing'. I led him up the Station yard bypassing the engine room, to the side entrance where the turntable ladder was sitting. Opening the wicket gate set into the main gate, I watched him make the lonely walk off into the pitch blackness of the night. When he had gone I went into the Watchroom where some of the boys were still sitting. I said 'Well you know what that was all about, I don't need to tell you to say nothing to anyone. Let's listen to the news in the morning and see what transpires'.

Once again I crossed the Station yard to my bedroom, got undressed and slipped into bed. All the time my mind was still a whirl at the developments of the past hour or so. Still thinking about it I managed to fall asleep. Less than an hour later it was the voice of Alan Lyle that awoke me once again. ' Station Officer, Station Officer, this guy's back again, this time he's got the Army with him'. Oh no! Not again, was all I could think, what the hell now? 'Where is he Alan?' I said, 'In the engine room.' Up I got again, trousers and shoes on, across the yard and into the engine room which was still in darkness. No sign of any-one, I walked warily up towards the front gates and as I drew level with the door of the old Watchroom-which had to vacated due to the threat from stray bullets some years before-I saw two figures inside-one my recent newly made acquaintance Charley-the other a tweed sport's coat and twills type chappie.

'Mr. Wright I'm Captain Williamson'. As he spoke, he produced an I.D. card from inside his jacket and thrust it into my hand.

Right enough it said Captain Williamson on. It also stated that he belonged to Army Intelligence. 'I believe this chap has reported seeing a murder to you.' 'Scared the shit out of us too he has!'. At this he turned around to his tout and gave him a stern rebuke. 'You should never have come near the Fire Station, never do anything like this again!'. Silence from Charlie. 'I want you to forget that this happened tonight'. 'Forget what?' I replied, trying to bring a little sarcastic humour into the affair. 'I've already told my men not to mention anything to anyone'. With that I let the both of them out through the front gate. I went back into the Watchroom where the boys were still congregated in the expectation of knowing what was happening. I simply told them what had transpired and repeated not to say anything to anyone. Off I went across the yard once again. It was more difficult than ever to get back to sleep my head was buzzing even worse than before, following this latest revelation.

The implications of all this were becoming clearer-all the pieces were beginning to slowly fall into place, as events unfolded. Charlie was an Army informer. That is why he had been so insistent that the Police were not to become involved. He was not on their payroll. It was widely known that the Army and Police did not fully share their intelligence information, perhaps understandably. To do so could have compromised the safety of both the tout and his controller. Captain Williamson and myself immediately realised-and I suppose so eventually did Charlie-the foolhardiness of coming to the Station. God only knows who could have been watching. If it was Republican para militaries it could have been misconstrued by them that the Station was being used as a rendezvous point for Army and their informers with all the consequences that would bring on us all. Perhaps if we had been in such a desperate position as Charlie we might have dived into the first port of refuge also.

The next morning I listened to the local early morning news. There was no mention of any murder having been reported. This did in no way contradict what we had learned the previous evening, in a way it supported it. If the Police had known about the murder it would almost certainly have been reported to the media. However on Tuesday 15th February 1972 the Army investigated shootings in the Butler Street area of the Ardoyne. It was reported that men had been blindfolded and shot as punishment for committing robberies and violence. This investigation occurred around the time Charlie had called at the Station. For my own benefit in order to help corroborate Charlie's story I looked up the Belfast street directory of that period to see if the family and street names he gave existed in the Ardoyne and indeed they did. During ensuing calls in the Ardoyne I always kept a lookout for this 'Will o' the Wisp' without success.

It was not until some years later that I spied him in the Crumlin Road courthouse while I was attending a Fatal Accident Inquiry Inquest. I recognised him by the deformity of his left hand. I often wondered how long 'Telstar' , like his celestial counterpart, continued to transmit his messages to his controller or perhaps by now he is with his Heavenly controller somewhere out there in the Ether....

Near Miss... It was some time after this event through the Republican grapevine that the Brigade received word that Firefighters were to be targets if they co-operated with security forces. This report was published in the Belfast Newsletter. I remember the morning on day duty in Ardoyne I heard the news, my flesh crawled with goose pimples.

That same day Sub Officer Sammy Hill and I were in the Station area attending several malicious bomb scares. He was in charge of the Pump and I was with the Pump Escape. We were separated and standing by at different incidents. Controls called us on the radio and asked if we were available to attend a fire call to the Post Office in Alliance Avenue in the Ardoyne, the reply was to the affirmative in both cases. I was attending a bomb scare at a petrol filling Station on the Crumlin Road nearly facing Ewarts Mill just below Flax Street. Sammy and his crew were in the Cliftonville/Oldpark Road area not far away from the incident. Both appliances booked mobile to the call almost simultaneously.

We set off, turning off the Crumlin Road, right into Flax Street, passing on the right the Army billet in the old Flax Street mill, then a left, into Brompton Park, quick right, into Jamaica Street. By this time we could see the smoke coming from the direction of Alliance Avenue. I knew this was no hoax. I remember seeing, out of the corner of my eye people watching us drive past as they stood at their front doors. We were approaching the Jamaica/Alliance junction at speed where I knew we would be making a left into Alliance. That left turn that never took place. When our appliance was about fifty yards from the junction the Pump turned directly into our path from Alliance Avenue, we had been unwittingly on converging courses, a Cardinal sin for fire appliances. I knew Sammy should have gone straight on. What had he seen that made him turn left into Jamaica Street? Both drivers managed to stop their respective machines before they collided head on. Sammy Hill was gesticulating at me wildly with his arms. My interpretation of his sign language was that he was motioning for us to retreat. I thought 'if that's what wee Sammy wants that's what wee Sammy gets'. Trouble was we really did not have any room to manoeuvre. So I jumped out of my appliance and ran to the rear to make sure no one was behind. Before I could tell my driver he started to reverse at speed. I thought I was about to be run over but I managed to grab the levers of the wheeled escape ladder mounted on the rear of the machine and hung on for dear life. This exercise was more by instinct than a deliberate thought process I did not want to be left floundering in the middle of Jamaica Street, not knowing what had contributed to Sammy abort his approach to the fire. As we reversed away Assistant Divisional Officer Dessie Graham in his staff car turned in on the same route that we had travelled, nearly crashing into our rear with me suspended from it like a side of beef. He also managed to stop and quickly got into reverse. I am sure all three fire appliances must have looked a pretty sight proceeding as we were along Jamaica Street two in reverse one pushing the other two as it were. I learned later that we had reversed over a dog as we made our hasty exit.

Whenever we all got clear of the scene Sammy and I dismounted obviously anxious to know what the hell was going on. Sammy informed me that as he drew near to the bend at the bottom of Alliance before making his final approach to the fire-which turned out to be Fusco's ice cream and newsagents-the roadway in front of the appliance had been raked with machinegun fire. Someone did not want the Fusco's fire extinguished and it was not open to argument. It seemed too much of a coincidence in my mind after what had gone on recently. Coupled with the public warning from the Provisionals regarding the Fire Brigade that this was probably a friendly but very intimidating and sobering warning. If it was, they certainly had the knack of getting their point across. Sanity however prevailed through the good offices of senior Fire Brigade Union Officials and contacts with Republican sources. The threat was lifted, when they were told that it would be counter-productive to their own community safety if Firefighters' lives were put under threat as they would be unable to attend calls in the Republican areas in the future so putting the residents safety in jeopardy....

MR Kelly... It was a Sunday morning, about 0730hrs, guess what, lying in bed again thinking about going off duty at nine for a lovely three days rotary leave. Some of the best experiences in my life have happened when in bed but I would not like anyone to think that I had a fetish about it. Boom! the room and my bed shook. 'Fuck!' that was close. Train of thought shattered-out of bed-across the yard and into the Watchroom-on the phone immediately to Controls enquiring if they had received any calls regarding the explosion. 'No not as yet Allan', was the answer, I put the phone down. A few minutes later over the speakers, 'Fire Call to an actuated '77' at Kelly's newsagent's shop on the Upper Crumlin Road'. This part of the road had some very nice properties on it and was considered to be the posh end of the road. Kelly's shop was a converted detached house with living accommodation over. Both appliances turned out and we arrived within seconds. It was a quiet Sunday morning and even after such a loud bang, there were relatively few spectators about. It was immediately obvious what had happened. A small blast device had been placed on the ground outside the shop window which was shattered as was the first floor one. Mr. Kelly who was a quiet little middle aged man came out to meet us. I asked if anyone was injured, he said that he was not sure. He still seemed a bit dazed and shaken. I went inside and up the stairs to check and went into one of the bedrooms. I was surprised when I saw that his son was in his bed and still sleeping soundly. The bed was littered with the fragments of broken glass from his bedroom window. We helped tidy up and then left. Within six months Mr. Kelly was shot dead by para militaries. They put six bullets into him. Obviously whatever message they had tried to send him with the blast bomb had fallen on stoney ground….

Ballysillan Incident…The Ballysillan Road branches off the Upper Crumlin Road approximately half a mile above Ardoyne Station and extends some three miles in a Northerly direction where it joins the north bound Antrim road from Belfast. A pleasant enough thoroughfare serving an area which is largely residential with small shops dotted occasionally along its route for the convenience of its residents. It was late one wet cold winter's evening that the Station received a call to a petrol bombing at a house on the road nearly opposite the junction of the Ballysillan/Oldpark Road. On arrival I could see that the house was fully illuminated and whilst walking up the long garden path to the front door, which was open, I could smell the sweet unmistakable sickly aroma of petrol. Going into the hallway I received by an Asia gentleman who was obviously the occupier. By this time I had also noted that a quantity of sand was scattered about the hall and several empty buckets were lying around. The occupants had obviously been prepared for an attack and were successful in extinguishing the fire themselves, fortunately without much damage having been done and without injury to the themselves. Full marks, I thought to myself. I told the crew to check if there was any further signs of fire and I began to question the occupier what had happened.

He told me that this was the latest of nineteen attacks of one kind or another that had been made on his home. On this occasion not only had they received two petrol bombs in the hallway that night but the rear of the house had been strafed by machine gun fire. My immediate response to him when I was told this was to ask did he not think that it was about time he considered moving house. I also enquired why his home was being targeted as it was. His was a mixed marriage he replied. Where was his wife I enquired further? He told me that she was on night duty at the Royal Victoria Hospital. By this time his young daughter had joined us still in her night clothes. He continued to tell me she had been in her bed at the rear of the house when it had been machine gunned and had jumped up out of bed after the first burst of gun fire. At this point I went upstairs to have a look. There, above the child's bed were two holes in the wall plaster presumably made by the gun fire. If the child had jumped up as the firing was taking place she would surely have been mown down.

I went downstairs and went outside to the back garden to inspect for any other damage. The back of the house overlooked what was the Protestant estate of Benview. As I surveyed the bullet holes that had raked the back of the house I thought how lucky the child had been and suddenly realised how exposed I was at that moment, standing there in the darkness, probably close to the gunman's firing point. Before leaving the scene I offered my sympathies to the man and reiterated if it was me I would be out of it. By this time he must have felt more inclined to respond to me than he had hitherto whenever I had initially broached the subject. He told me that he was an owner occupier and he had made approaches to the Northern Ireland Housing Executive for them to purchase the house but to date without success. As we drove back to Station I could not help thinking of the irony of the situation. In a sectarian conflict such as the Province found itself in who wouldn't the bigots target. Was this man and his family Roman Catholic or Protestant Pakistani? Probably Roman Catholic Pakistani as the fire had come from a Loyalist area. What a crazy world.

The **Rattle of the Thompson Gun...**18th April 1972, another day to remember at Ardoyne. How many more was there going to be? At 2000hrs on that still April evening we got a fire call to premises on the Grosvenor Road-near the notoriously infamous Lesson Street-some four hundred yards below the Royal Victoria Hospital. The address was in Chi's area and so the call took us out of our Station fireground. Chi were obviously busy elsewhere in their area that night.

The location of the call was close to Arundel Street where my Father's recent ancestors had settled when they had moved to Belfast in the late eighteen hundreds from the 'sticks'. He used to tell me about his very first job as a twelve year old messenger boy in the 'Royal' and one day how he had stood and watched the horse drawn Ambulance clattering up the Grosvenor Road with a casualty from Harland and Wolff's shipyard enroute to the hospital. Little knowing that it was actually his own Father who lay mortally injured inside it. Yes, I knew the area well. I had visited my aunts and uncles and played there manys the time as a child. The 'Royal' side of the road was mainly Protestant, the Lesson Street side mainly Roman Catholic. Both communities had co-existed peacefully and contentedly enough, that is, until the start of the present 'Troubles'. We arrived to find a derelict shop on fire.

As I pulled up we found a detachment from the 2nd Light Infantry in attendance. I knew the soldiers to be from this Regiment as my brother-in-law was serving with them at that time. It was common practice in those days-in areas of possible sectarian conflict-for the Army to give us cover in case of attack from a riotous crowd. This procedure had been introduced in the early days after personnel had been stoned, petrol bombed, and some seriously injured. Street violence and rioting had largely died out by the seventies and this practice by the Army of providing cover was now considered by most Officers to be of dubious value, due to the rival gunmen and bombers having taken over from the riots. Some of us had made our uneasy feelings on this subject known to Senior Officers and Union officials. My own view was that it was the Security Forces that the gunmen and bombers were after, not us, and the Army's presence was more likely to attract trouble rather than prevent it.

A small crowd had gathered on the other side of the road to watch proceedings. I noticed our boiler-man from Chi' wee Jimmy Rodgers was one of them. The crowd was orderly and I told the young Lieutenant that I did not need his services. For some time now Officers had known that with the Army's presence the Provo's would orchestrate an incident, perhaps by getting youngsters to fire a building, such as this incident we were attending. The Provo's would in the first instance have selected their most advantageous shooting positions and escape routes from that location. Officers-in-Charge of appliances had wised up to this tactic by now but the Army recycled their troops on three monthly rota basis and if a particular regiment or platoon commanders had not done their homework or had not been in the Province before they had to learn all the tricks of the trade from scratch just as we in the Brigade had done at the beginning.

The ominous sign of a pending attack on the Army at an incident would usually be the crowd starting to melt away, but this did not happen in this instance. The young Lieutenant did not respond to my request to leave and remained in the vicinity. Bobby Bloomer was the Leading Firefighter in charge of the Pump crew. The crews initially got to work with a jet and it was not long before the fire was beaten down. Within half an hour I ordered the boys to start making up the gear prior to returning to the Station. I was helping one of them, Charlie Hughes-remember Charlie and his brother Jimmy from Bombay Street in 1969 the unofficial 'Convent' pump operators-who was up the fifteen foot ladder at the time, to feed the hose down to the ground when I heard the rat-tat-tat. My immediate thought was that it was the sound of someone twirling a 'corncrake', a handy noisemaker used at football matches. It only took a millisecond for my thinking to change on this. I immediately felt a thud on my gloved right hand which was at that time holding the string of the ladder six inches away from my head. I certainly heard and felt the whoosh of bullets passing over and around me. As I threw myself headlong down onto the pavement, I remember shouting 'I'm hit'. If I could have crawled into the joints in the paving stones at that moment I would have. As I lay there hugging the pavement I felt the rest of the volley whoosh over my head. The only thing that I could think of was, is the next one going to go up my backside. I felt completely naked and vulnerable. I was frozen to the ground and afraid to move. At that moment big Charlie jumped down from the ladder onto the ground and grabbed me by the scruff of the neck and with me half crawling and he half dragging me we made into the shelter of the derelict shop that we had just extinguished the fire in. We tumbled in through the gap in the wall that had once been a doorway and as no flooring existed we fell the couple of feet down through the floor joists into the sub floor. We were quickly joined by two members of the Army patrol diving headlong in through the window and doorway and they landed unceremoniously beside Charlie and I.

Then all hell broke loose again, rat-tat-tat, rat-tat-tat, rat-tat-tat, All I could think of now was how vulnerable we were. Was this gunman going to come in for the kill? I envisaged him suddenly appearing, standing in the doorway and spraying us all with bullets. We did not know how close his firing point was, only that it was from somewhere close on the other side of the road. Fortunately my fears were not realised.

When we thought that the firing had ceased-one of the soldiers who knew I was hit-ripped his field dressing from the butt of his Self Loading Rifle and I gingerly took the glove off my right hand. As I did so I wondered what sight was going to meet my eyes. When my hand was exposed it looked as if the right fleshy side of it had burst open like a rotten tomato. The soldier quickly wrapped his dressing around the wound. I did not feel any real pain and there really was not that much blood. Just a feeling of numbness. I recall thinking that it felt as if I had been struck a sharp blow on the hand by a school ruler or pointer.

That was phase one over. As usual there is always the comic side to serious events and this episode was not going to be any different.

When the firing had commenced some of the boys had taken cover behind the Pump, one of them was Bobby Bloomer. Due either to exhaustion or shock and in an apparent state of semi-collapse, he ended up slumped at the rear of the machine. Those nearest to him thought he was the one who had been shot. In the meantime my driver, Billy Skelly, drove the Pump Escape up onto the footpath close to the wall opposite the doorway through which I had been dragged-in order to give protection-so that I could get back aboard. Seeing the appliance move into position those who thought Bobby was the casualty grabbed him as he came around from the rear of the Pump and insisted on bundling him towards the Officer's door on the P.E. for boarding. He resisted whilst protesting all the way to the appliance. While I was still lying inside the building trying to collect my senses I saw poor Booby being pushed and shoved by his colleagues, trying to get him into the machine. It was his pride that was the only injured part of him at this moment. Finally his protestations prevailed and he was able to convince his concerned helpers that it was not him, but 'the boss' who had been shot. So they immediately ceased their well-intentioned onslaught on him.

I was then helped aboard and along with the rest of the crew Skelly commenced the short drive up the Grosvenor Road to the 'Royal' past my ancestral home in Arundel Street following the same route that my grandfather had taken in 1914. We stopped outside the entrance to Casualty and Emergency Admissions which at that time was entered via the Falls Road. Some of the boys accompanied me down the stairs to the lower level where I was met by the staff and taken into the examination room for an initial examination. I was

"... but! BUT!! .. Sorry Boss ... serious casualty!!"

stripped of my fire-fighting gear and was asked by the female casualty doctor if I was hit anywhere else other than on my hand. Although I said I was not I got a full examination anyway. She informed me that sometimes when a person is hit by gunfire they can not tell immediately if they are hit anywhere else on their body due to shock.

I felt totally euphoric at that time without even having received a single drug. I suppose it was the reaction setting in because I felt so lucky to be alive. Shortly after this time Sandra my wife arrived. She had been told of the shooting and had been collected by Divisional Officer Leslie Johnston from our home. She looked more shook up than I felt. When I reassured her about the non life threatening nature of my condition-she told me her appearance was not due to concern about me!- but more to the fact that Johnty-affectionately known as 'Fangio' by some of his older longer serving colleagues-had driven the staff car at speeds of up to ninety miles per hour on the way up the Grosvenor Road becoming airborne every time he hit a security ramp. Johnty always relished any excuse for a high speed burn-up and never ever drove at what one would call normal speeds. I have it on good authority that 'Johnty' managed to either seriously damage or write off three staff cars before his retirement from the Brigade. I can quite believe it.

I was informed by the Doctor that I would have to have the wound excised of dead skin and then stitched up. At about 2300hrs I was prepped to be taken to theatre though still blackened and stinking of smoke. I was lying in the anaesthetic room on a trolley with both arms outstretched on armrests like a crucifix. My injured hand for support and my left ready to receive the knock-out injection, thinking to myself, what a way to spend Easter. The anaesthetist was about to administer his magic potion when proceedings were brought to a halt. Another casualty of a shooting had been brought in, her needs, it appeared, were more urgent than mine. I was to lie there for the next three hours until two in the morning. At one stage I desperately wanted to do a pee and wouldn't you know it. Not a nurse in sight-a bit like buses they only travel in pairs- what a predicament. I could not move unaided from my crucifix position. When a nurse finally did show up I told her of my bodily needs and that I was afraid of taking short while on the operating table. Her reply was, 'you'd better not, but I'm new here and I don't know if there's a toilet on this floor'. Anyway she brought me a bottle but by the time it arrived the notion had left me. A bit like going to the dentist with toothache. I lay there listening to the sounds of the other gunshot victim being operated on next door. Finally my turn came.

Trying to regain full consciousness in the recovery room after my operation I struggled to get my leaden lids open and my bleary eyes in focus. I was not sure whether I was having heavenly hallucinations or was still asleep and dreaming? Reality came in the form of smacks to the cheeks and the recovery ward nurse calling 'Allan, time to wake up its all over', which eventually brought me back to full consciousness. No, I hadn't still been asleep, I hadn't been. Not more than six feet away in the adjoining bed when I finally got my eyes in focus I found I was looking at a beautifully proportioned curvaceous female back and posterior lying in a recovery position similar to my own. The only cloud to partially obscure this heavenly vision was a surgical dressing placed over part of her posterior. What a funny place to get shot? When I had time to examine my clothing I saw that I was not dressed in much more of a presentable way myself. What a state of undress to make a new acquaintances or to meet a lady. At a time like this who cares anyway? She had been the other casualty that I had heard being operated on while I lay in the anaesthetic room. She had been hit by a stray bullet that previous evening, while driving through East Belfast.

Later that morning-having been removed to a ward and whilst Sandra was being entertained by me recalling the previous night's exploits- the Chief Officer and Assistant Chief Officer Pollock, arrived at my bedside to pay their respects. I hoped it was not their last! The visit began amicably enough on both sides of the bed, that is until I raised the subject of the Army's presence at incidents. I told the Chief that he had already been informed by a number of Officers that this type of incident, in which I had been injured, was likely to occur due to the Army's presence. That the young Lieutenant's dedication was commendable, but that his pig-headed determination to carry out his task to give us cover when he had been told by me that I did not require his services, had directly contributed to this fiasco.

At this juncture the Chief lost his composure and began a tirade of how, when he as an Army Captain in the Second World War, at the battle of Monte Cassino he had stood on rocky ground with German machine-gun bullets bouncing off the rocks all around him. It was pretty obvious that the man was under considerable strain, my incident coming on top of his attempts to administer a civilian Brigade in urban guerrilla warfare conditions. I knew that he had won the Military Cross at this particular action. My thoughts however were that he considered us only bloody stupid Firefighters who were expected to be subject to this type of risk as part and parcel of our normal duties. Soldiers expect to be fired on and are trained and equipped to return fire, so where did this leave us? Are we going to be issued with weapons next-I thought not ? The only personal protection we had-our personal issue of fire axes-had been withdraw from each man without explanation. Presumably for fear they might fall into the wrong hands or a Firefighter might take the law into his own hands. A Firefighter feels very naked without one. Departing abruptly from the bedside the Chief stated he was on his way to see the Army's General Officer Commanding Ground Forces regarding the matter. I heard no more from him after this on the subject of Army 'protection'.

During my six weeks on sick leave following the shooting I kept in touch with events happening within the Brigade, one of which particularly upset me. My own Blue Watch Ardoyne had attended a terrorist fire at Mitchell's in Northumberland Street a large wholesale firm. Some of their products included optical equipment such as telescopes, binoculars, etc. It was reported to me later that wholesale theft of a large amount of this equipment had taken place. Recorded below is a transcript of the messages received by Control Room staff. It gives some indication to the size of the fire. This incident is narrated as it gives an indication why at a different time and place the matter of looting had to be resolved. It gave me no pleasure to know that it had happened on my fire ground while being attended by my Watch of which I was so proud in the short time that I was to spend with them.

CALL No 549
25th April 1972 Northumberland Street.
Attendance- 2P.E., 2P., 2T.L.P., 1H.P.P. Stations-'D'/'B'/'A'/ 'C'.

Call received per Army Exchange Telephone.

Officer-in-Charge… Assistant Divisional Officer Matthews.
Time of call   -1226hrs.
Informative   -1229hrs.
Stop message -   -1508hrs.
Ret. to Station-   -1817hrs.(26/4/72)
Stop message reads-Building 100yds.by 50yds. well alight.
10 jets, 2 T.L.P.jets, 1H.P.P. jet in use.

Other tit-bits of information were relayed to me during my time off. I was anxious to know what had finally happened to the Pump crew immediately after my rapid departure from the fireground on the night of the shooting. I learned that Bobby Bloomer had departed for Chichester Street to report on the incident to a Senior Officer. On arrival he and the crew, who were obviously still shaken up, were ushered into the Officer's Mess and given a strong bumper of the 'hard stuff' and asked to recount their experience.

Having left the fireground in somewhat of a hurry any gear not already stowed had been left behind. The crew was ordered to return that evening and collect it. It was discovered that the bullet which had struck my hand while I held the string of the ladder, had passed through the wooden string. Other bullets had lodged in the bodywork of the Pump. A.C.O. Pollock was heard to remark in company that the bullet which struck me 'was only a ricochet'. I wondered how he came to that conclusion not being there himself? Was this his way of playing down the incident on behalf of the Brigade? Ricochet it was not. Nonetheless if it had been it would have had no less a capability of killing someone. I attended several Brigade meetings and functions of one sort or another during this convalescent period. Senior Officers never failed to show me off in company. I felt I was being used as something of an oddity, a curiosity, representing as I did the first Firefighter to be shot during the present 'Troubles'. They seemed to enjoy the reflected glory of it all. A feather in the Brigade's cap, another kind of blooding, a coming of age, into the real world that was Ulster 1972.

In June 1972 Bernard Falk of B.B.C Television was visiting the Province. He and his crew were putting together some local footage for the Beeb's national evening new's programme Nationwide. I had returned to duty at Ardoyne and was about to come off night duty at 0900hrs when I received a phone call from my old friend and mentor Jock Hall in Controls telling me that he had told Bernard about my shooting and that he would like to interview me about it in the engine room at Chi'. The Chief had given him permission to speak to whomsoever he wished in the Brigade. I called into Chi' on the way home through town and met Bernard. He and his crew set up their equipment in the engine room and the interview got underway. I recounted the incident, displaying my scar for a close up to the camera all the while aware that nearby we were being observed by a uniformed figure who I could not identify at that time. When the interview concluded I was approached by the figure who it transpired was Assistant Divisional Officer Matthews. His first words were 'Why were you being interviewed? Who gave you permission to give an interview'? I was not long in satisfying his curiosity but could not help thinking from the aggressive tone of his enquiry-that apart from some people who revelled in the reflected glory-equally there were those I surmised who felt it should have been them who were shot. Little green men kept popping up everywhere and I do not mean leprechauns. If they had the gift of second sight and known what was to happen within a few short months to the second member of the Brigade to be shot they would not have felt so jealous. The second Firefighter to be shot was not to be as lucky as I had been.

The Fire Brigades Union through their locally based solicitor pursued a claim on my behalf for criminal damages from the Northern Ireland Office. This claim was settled out of court within a year or so. The initial offer was two hundred and fifty pounds, which I refused. My solicitor suggested asking for a sweetener which amounted to an additional fifty pounds. I reluctantly accepted. It was pointed out to me-in the cynical language that only the legal fraternity can speak-that it was not the potential of the seriousness of injury that might have been caused, or how the injury was received that decreed the amount of a financial settlement- but the actual injury itself, which after all was only a minor cut to the right hand that required seventeen stitches....

Footnote...In the intervening years since this personal incident and simi-lar incidents affecting other members of the Brigade I have read exten-sively, consuming many of the authoritative works relating to the intelli-gence war-a war within a war. This has not only provided food for thought but has served to confirm my suspicions of just how exposed we in the Brigade were to the threat of injury and death during this period. This intel-ligence war was fought between the Security Forces and, principally, at that time, the Provisional I.R.A.

In 1972 a certain Brigadier Frank Kitson arrived in the Province. He was a counter insurgency expert and veteran of anti-terrorist campaigns against the Mau Mau in Kenya, communism in Malaya, and EOKA in Cyprus where he commanded a Battalion. He had written two books on the subject entitled 'Low-Intensity Operations' and 'Gangs and Counter Gangs'. His posting was therefore not just a coincidence. He took command of 39th Infantry Brigade which in fact gave him military control of the City. The Provos quickly learned of his pedigree and his writings.

The army had sustained a number of casualties and deaths of their per-sonnel in the Leeson Street/Lower Falls/Grosvenor Road area, an area controlled by 'D' company part of the I.R.A.'s Belfast's 2nd Battalion. It was Kitson's job to try and stem the haemorrhaging flow of his soldiers' blood. The gunman who had fired on our crews fired from the corner of Leeson Street.

Kitson has been credited with setting up the Military Reconnaissance Force a secret grouping even within the Army. Covert surveillance was one of the tactics used. A man would be surreptitiously secreted in the roof space of derelict premises, such as the one we had fought our little fire in. They were tasked to observe the movements of suspects in the area. It was a game of 'cat and mouse'. I have often wondered whether the Provos were aware of a possible Army spy in the roof space of our building and had the building set alight, not only to dislodge their target, but to draw further mil-itary forces into their line of fire. It is called killing two birds with one stone, only this time I was very nearly that bird. Because of the unsched-uled interruption to our fire-fighting operation we never got the chance to check the building out for possible casualties so we will never know the answer to my hypothesis. Perhaps the young Lieutenant knew something I did not, hence his reluctance to leave when entreated by me to do so. Another question which also begs an answer is why was the Chief Fire

Officer after his visit to me in hospital in such a hurry to consult with the Army's General Officer Commanding (N.I.). Did he perhaps also know something that we did not?

My reading of 'THE DIRTY WAR' by Martin Dillon revealed more of the intelligence war. It revealed how little the Brigade personnel on the ground really knew about what was going on. As usual intelligence was being operated on a 'need to know' basis and clearly where even our personal safety was concerned we simply did not need to know. Note the defusing of a bomb by Major Calladene in the Co-op building-whilst we were still in it-completely without our knowledge. Some knowledge of the advance in bomb making skills of the P.I.R.A.-bomb makers skills by the mid seventies was well tuned-would have been useful to know if only to prevent Firefighters thumping and banging around suspect cars that had been set alight. In their thirst for knowledge the P.I.R.A. traded knowledge for weaponry etc., as required. The Provos were the first to use the mercury tilt switch. It was generally thought that it was first used to kill Airey Neave, but before this use it had been successfully tested in Ulster on an unsuspecting victim in a car bomb, before being approved for use in Neave's murder in the underground car park of the Houses of Parliament in Westminster.

It was indicative of the poor working relations between various groupings within the   security forces-secret forces within forces- RUC Special Branch-Army 14th Intelligence-SAS-MI5 & 6- that the left hand did not know what the right was doing. A fine example of this was the car bombing of the Belfast Taxation Office. Army Intelligence had penetrated the bomb team through an informer and knew of the plan to plant the bomb. They substituted the fuse with a dummy one and knew when the bomb was being planted. But they failed to tell the A.T.O. He treated it as a live bomb with a controlled explosion. As I have said elsewhere when is a controlled explosion not a controlled explosion when it blows the building down. His controlled explosion set off the main charge. So it was around this time that the RUC decided to set up what was called 'Task Force' to attempt to co-ordinate intelligence information between groupings. Naturally high on this Task Force's list of 'Need Not Know' was the good old Fire Brigade as usual.

Summary Execution?...
Summary Execution?... During the years that the Army have been present in the Province, allegations of summary execution have often been laid at their doorstep. Controversy has arisen, even after the judicial process has run its course when the outcome of those few cases that have been tried, have not

satisfied one party or another, usually the bereaved relatives of the deceased. Having related murder and attempted murder, in this chapter, which had been instigated by the para militaries, it would be inconsistent on my part not to give a paragraph on one more incident which I made it my business to unofficially enquire about.

The Ambulance Service had for years-for sound operational reasons-based several of their Ambulances in Ardoyne Station. The Ambulance crews that manned the appliances carried out some sterling work in the area during all the phases of the present conflict and we often found ourselves working alongside them at incidents, whether it was assisting in the removal of casualties or picking up the pieces. Surprisingly on the Station we had little contact, they having their allotted quarters, we ours. Late one evening, during the hours of darkness whilst in the Station we heard the sound of gunfire. Because of the frequency of gunfire that was within earshot from time to time we had become quite good at identifying whether or not it was high or low velocity round, or even the type of weapon that was being fired. Someone might say 'that's an Armalite' or perhaps an S.L.R. or a Thompson. This evening it sounded like the high velocity crack of an S.L.R. Shortly afterwards one of the Ambulances left the Station yard always an ominous sign. Within an hour it had returned and I saw its two man crew open up the rear doors and begin to clean out the interior casualty carrying area. I went over to enquire where they had been called to and the sight that met my eyes surprised even me. The interior was awash with blood and they were carrying away and disposing of stainless steel basinsful of it. I asked where the incident was and was told in the Ardoyne. Apparently the Army had shot a guy through the head.

It was the Parachute Regiment, the 'Paras', more than any other Army Regiment who were responsible for subduing the Ardoyne area's terrorist elements. They did this very successfully with very little casualties of their own to show for it. Several days after the shooting when a Para foot patrol was passing the Station their Corporal in charge came in asking if could he use the loo'. Before leaving the Station-being the inquisitive person that I am-some extremists would say I was nosey-I could not resist the temptation to ask him what had happened regarding the shooting a few nights before. He was quite willing to divulge the information and told me that sentries in the Observation Post within bus depot were changing guard-the off going squaddie had reported to his opposite number that he had been watching someone in Alliance Avenue through his night-sight who kept popping his head above a backyard wall. The both of them then began to jointly observe the scene, it happened several times again but on the last appearance, it was assumed that the person had taken up an 'aiming position' and was promptly shot through the head....

Ardoyne's Cease fire?... The P.I.R.A. Cease-fire that took effect from 22nd June 1972 was reported as having been broken on 9th July. Well, we on Blue Watch knew that it was broken a little earlier and at a different location, than was officially reported. On a quiet Sunday evening, some of us were sitting in the T.V. room waiting for the evening's T.V. entertainment to commence. I was following the early evening news, when I heard what I thought was the sound of shooting. Not possible I mused to myself, there is a cease-fire on. Then this first sound was followed by another distinct rat-tat-tat. This time we all looked at each other in surprise and apprehension. Immediately following this I was called over the Station loudspeakers to the Watchroom. As I rounded the corner from the yard into the engine room I saw Tommy Woods standing at one of the open engine room gates peering to his right. He shouted to me, 'they're firing at the Army from across the road'. 'For God's sake Tommy come inside', I yelled, which he did, closing the gate and coming to meet me. For there was absolutely no chance of me venturing anywhere near the front of the engine room. He said that the Army had a 'pig'-armoured car-placed at the tangy shed end of the Station and that someone had opened up on it from the roofs of the single storey shops opposite. We waited for about ten minutes-no more firing occurred-we both advanced to the engine room gate and opened it cautiously and looked down to our right. As we did so, an apparition wearing a steel helmet appeared from around the corner of the gable end and pointed to the shops, mouthing something we could not hear, so I gave him the thumbs up and disappeared inside. We heard the 'Pig' start up shortly afterwards and move off, only then did we nervously venture out to inspect the scene at the Tangy shed end of the Station. What we saw were three bullet holes embedded in the brickwork of the wall. A near miss for someone.

There had been no news of a break of the Provos cease-fire at that time. This came later on that evening when we watched the scene unfolding at Twinbrook, a Roman Catholic housing estate in West Belfast, where Martin Bell-one of the B.B.C's news team in the Province at that time-was reporting the scene of an Army Saracen, confronting head on, a lorry loaded with domestic furniture.

It was following this confrontation that the official cease-fire ceased to be a cease-fire. At 2100hrs the I.R.A. issued a statement from their Kevin Street office in Dublin which said that the truce had been broken by the British

Troops at 1700hrs at Lenadoon. Apparently this particular incident had occurred without a shot having been fired. Active Service Units of the P.I.R.A were instructed to resume military operations.

So there you have Ardoyne Fire Station, more interesting than the average fire Station, don't you think?

"...don't just stand there. Get in here with the rest of the watch!! "

CHAPTER 6

A Shotgun Marriage ...

Pre-Nuptial Agreement? As part of the United Kingdom's local government reorganisation, big being considered to be better, the Belfast Fire
Brigade was scheduled to amalgamate with the Northern Ireland Fire
Authority in August of 1973 which was the other Fire Brigade which served
the Province.

The decision to amalgamate was due to the recommendations contained in
the 1971 report of the Review Body on Local Government in Northern
Ireland. A contributory factor to the decision may also have been the continuing terrorist campaign in the Province which by the early seventies had
brought a fire damage bill in excess of 40 million pounds sterling. However it
is difficult to quantify if in fact this was one of the reasons for amalgamation,
but nevertheless the unification of the two Brigades would in fact decrease
their annual operating budgets. I would be inclined to think that government
was simply following suit with the local government reorganisation of the rest
of the United Kingdom's Fire Service. Prior to 1973 fire cover had been provided by the Northern Ireland Fire Authority, a statutory body established by
the Fire Services Act (Northern Ireland) 1969 and by the Council of the
County Borough of Belfast. The 1973 Fire Services (Northern Ireland Order)
enacted a single Fire Service for Northern Ireland under the control and management of a new Fire Authority. On the 1st October 1973 the Fire Authority
took over all Officers and employees of the previous authorities and created a
command structure with its Headquarters based in Lisburn with five
Divisional H.Q.'s in North Belfast Whitla, South Belfast Knock, Londonderry,
Ballymena and Antrim. The composition of the Elected Members of Fire
Authority itself would consist of seventeen members four of whom would be
nominated by Belfast City Council, four would represent the interests of the
other District Councils, and nine would be nominated by the appropriate
Minister.

The N.I.F.A. had essentially been a part time Brigade with the vast majority of its Firefighters part time Retained personnel who manned some 52

Stations dotted throughout the Province. One wholetime Station staffed by professional Firefighters existed in Londonderry, Belfast had six wholetime Stations. On amalgamation personnel figures were approximately 500 professional whole-time personnel and 650 Retained, making the newly formed Brigade one of the largest in the United Kingdom.

Derry had dealt with more than their fair share of civil disturbance calls, carrying out some sterling work in the course of their duties. It was the Firefighters of 'Derry who had taken a terrible pasting in the early years of the 'Troubles' with the heart of their beautiful and ancient city, being torn apart by bombings and incendiary attacks. It is not for me to tell their story that is for someone else.

Amalgamation was, essentially, an operational reorganisation of the two Brigades, with administrative reorganisation taking second place. Hedley B. Reid the Secretary to the Northern Ireland Fire Authority, who wielded more internal political power than the Chief Fire Officer, saw to it that administrative power for the newly amalgamated Brigade remained firmly vested in Lisburn Headquarters and not in Belfast. They were to be brought together, jointly under a newly constituted Authority, entitled the Fire Authority for Northern Ireland-abbreviated as F.A.N.I. -it seems that it took a lot of imagination to produce that new title from the previous two Brigades' names, I prefer the abbreviated version myself. The Fire Brigades Union had also lobbied vigorously and campaigned for amalgamation of the two Brigades in the Province in the interest of increased efficiency and the elimination of duplication. Without the Union's activity it is doubtful whether this concoction would have ever taken place. The amalgamation was eventually to be seen by local Union officials as a take-over and not an amalgamation and was considered to have been the greatest mistake as a representative organisation that they ever made.

Prior to amalgamation, to oversee the marriage-clearly a marriage with no recourse to divorce-the two Brigades convened a Set-up Committee. It comprised Senior Officers and administrators from both Brigades but the Fire Brigades Union was excluded. Prior to Stormont being prorogued in 1972 the Union's senior officials Jock Hall and Ken Kernaghan requested a meeting with the then Minister for Home Affairs, John Taylor. The necessity for the presence of the Union on the Set-up Committee was put to him citing that they and they alone upon the creation of this new Authority would be the sole industrial relations representatives representing the rights of Northern Ireland's

Firefighters for whose Conditions of Service they were responsible at National Joint Council level. The arguments were successfully put across and they were duly given their rightful place at the table.

It was in fact the Union who made contact with the National Joint Council for Conditions of Service and advised them that the newly formed Brigade should be encouraged to join this employer/employee forum. Belfast had held membership within it for sometime but the Northern Ireland Fire Authority had not and its personnel had not therefore enjoyed the enhanced conditions of service that the City's Firefighters were in receipt of automatically when agreement was reached on issues at National level with their employers.

In the event an invitation to F.A.N.I. to join the club was duly extended by the N.J.C. It is doubtful that if this little subterfuge had not been used and the Union at local level had tried to coerce the new regime into joining, that a long hard struggle would have ensued before all personnel enjoyed the benefits to be derived from the membership of the N.J.C. On completion of its task, members of the Set-up Committee gave themselves ex-gratia payments for their trouble, all, that is, except those from the Fire Brigades Union.

Financing in the case of the N.I.F.A. was to be transferred from Stormont and that of the B.F.B. away from the local rates. Direct financing was to come from the national exchequer via the Transport Division of the Northern Ireland, Department of the Environment, this being the body with responsibility for the Brigade.

During the months preceding amalgamation, rumours abounded within the Brigade with respect to who the new Chief Fire Officer was likely to be. Those who would be King set to work each in their own way, setting out their stalls, and displaying their wares to the King makers. It was hoped, not unnaturally, that our own Chief would apply and get the post. He had been an excellent administrator and had been instrumental in the introduction prior to Amalgamation-at the behest of the Fire Brigades' Union-of the National Joint Council, Conditions of Service. This was one of the F.B.U.'s better decisions. It gave Belfast personnel parity with the rest of the U.K. Fire Service in terms of working conditions. Something which the N.I.F.A. had not yet achieved, but which they were about to achieve under amalgamation. Retained Firefighters at this time, did not even have an undress uniform to wear for walking out.

Sadly Robert Mitchell had taken all the flak from numerous quarters over the past five years who seemed to be somewhat of a tired and spent force. He did not submit himself for candidature, probably already aware, having been given the nod, of who was being groomed for the post. He was glad to bow out, take his golden handshake for services rendered, and retire back to his roots in England. The spirit of 'Monte Cassino' had disappeared. They say 'you never miss the water until the well runs dry,' we certainly were to find that out.

Some punters were putting their money on Belfast's Assistant Chief Officer, Sydney Pollock he was, and indeed had been, a fearless inspirational leader, and a tower of strength to personnel on the fireground during the height of the civil riots and fire bombings in the City. He also did not apply, probably having again been given the wink with respect to what his new role would be in the new Brigade, that of Assistant Chief Officer.

In the interim period between Mitchell retiring on 30th April, 1973 and amalgamation in August, Sydney Pollock was appointed by the Belfast Corporation Police Committee as Acting Chief Officer. He was so keen to see himself as the last Chief of the Brigade, that he had his name inscribed, for posterity, on the plaque that hung on the wall of the Officer's mess. This plaque bore the names of all the previous Chiefs of Belfast Fire Brigade from Mr Cockburn Esquire on to Sir Eyre Massey Shaw an through to Robert Mitchell MC,QFSM,MIFireE. Someone must not have agreed with his sentiments as the plaque was defaced, the gold lettering denoting him as Chief being rather crudely scraped off. However, his appointment as Chief is recorded on the Roll of Honour of Chiefs in the 'Conferring of the Freedom Of the City' on the Northern Ireland Fire Brigade on the 21 August 1992. So although this respected Officer did, rather belatedly, get his just recognition, the Firefighters of the City never did.

Unless of course, you count this granting of the 'Freedom' to the Northern Ireland Fire Brigade as another belated accolade. An accolade which is recorded on a parchment Certificate of Election contained in a silver casket inscribed with the words...

Presented to

The Northern Ireland Fire Brigade
On the occasion of the presentation of the
Certificate of the Election and admission as a
Freeman of the City of Belfast.

The Parchment contained therein reads thus...

This is to certify that on the 21st day of August 1992
THE NORTHERN IRELAND FIRE BRIGADE
was elected and admitted as a Freeman of the City of Belfast
in recognition of the contribution it has made to the life of
the City and as a mark of the gratitude felt by its citizens
to the personnel of The Northern Ireland Fire Brigade, many
of whom daily risk their lives in the service of others.

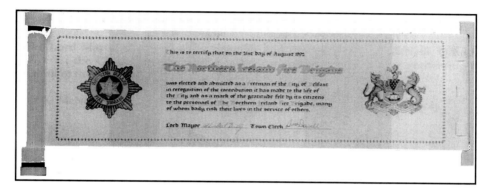

We are apparently, as the illustration above depicts, all 'officially' certified now... so bring on the white coated attendants.

In the ritual photographs which followed the 'certifying event' swinging in the breeze behind the Union Flag under the cupola of the dome above the heads of the posing Firefighters was a large political banner which read... 'BELFAST SAYS NO!'...did they mean us?

In any event it was Mr. George Morrison CBE; QFSM; MIFireE, who was to be the first Chief of the newly formed Northern Ireland Fire Brigade He was rather an aesthete but clearly his art form made him uneasy when mixing with 'common' Firefighters. His father had been a Belfast Firefighter and he and his family had lived in Ardoyne Station. George Morrison was a Divisional Officer with N.I.F.A.

Unfortunately, or fortunately, Chief Fire Officers do not merit a place in the written annals of history save that they have been exceptional in some way or other. This piece will have to suffice for the first Chief of F.A.N.I. He can rest content that he achieved his goal of a place in history that of simply being F.A.N.I's first Chief Fire Officer. In accepting the post of Chief Fire Officer he also accepted an inferior salary to that which the post merited. It was once again the F.B.U. who successfully campaigned to have this increased and be brought in line with comparable Chiefs' salaries in the rest of the U.K.

It has been attributed to Mr. Morrison when he was interviewed, post retirement, that he suggested that by the 1970's the F.B.U. was trying to assume many of the roles of management. Whatever the truth of this observation, it was hotly disputed by some former F.B.U. members **('Forged in Fire'** history of the Fire Brigades' Union 1992). However if it was true perhaps the F.B.U. leadership would have felt justified-based on experience, and according to them would have been better positioned at that time, to have an objective opinion-as opposed to his subjective one-to be able to judge what was good management as opposed to bad. It is always worth bearing in mind that Unions tend to exploit weak management.

In the ensuing ten years or so that I served under his administration, I came to view the Chief as a person who was well intentioned, humanitarian, and responsive to the needs of the individual but who also tried to be all things to all men. This seldom works in reality, better to be perceived as a hard man from the outset, then everyone knows where they stand, I speak from experience.

It was to become painfully evident in the early months of the marriage how little the new administration appreciated how instrumental the F.B.U. had been in bringing about National Conditions of Service to the Firefighters of Ulster and how seriously they took their role of safeguarding Firefighters against personal injury and in keeping the Brigade as a neutral and impartial body during the early years of civil disturbances. The old Fire Authority was something of an autocracy. They had never had to deal with national issues as most of their personnel did not then belong to the F.B.U. and therefore did not enjoy National Joint Conditions of Service. Their employees had always had to play catch-up with Belfast Firefighters. This administration due to its inexperience of industrial relations were suspicious and reluctant to deal openly and freely with the Union. But for the perseverance of senior local union officials such as Jock Hall (Regional Chairman), Archie Culbert (Regional Secretary) and Ken Kernaghan (Executive Council Member), trust would never have been built up and the chasms bridged. Jock must have made an impression on someone in authority somewhere along the way, for after his retirement from the Service he was invited to become a Fire Authority Board Member himself, almost a unique appointment. Presumably because of his superior inside working knowledge of what made the Brigade tick.

Jock could have hypnotised an adversary with his eloquence, his melodic Scottish twang and his Celtic charm. Thirty years or more spent in Ulster since settling here after leaving the Royal Air Force at the end of the war and marrying an Ulster girl, had not diminished either. Archie who incidentally was a co-member of my recruits course, was of a more stoical nature with quiet determination, and Ken was so soft spoken one had to lean close to him to pick up his low dulcet tones for fear of missing out on what he was saying. They were a formidable negotiating team who really 'knew their onions' and knew in which direction they wished to steer their membership. Despite the early hiccups and difficulties associated with getting amalgamation of the ground, not only did the Belfast membership owe them a huge debt of gratitude but also those Firefighters in N.I.F.A.-who were not members of the Union-all benefited equally from improved conditions of service.

It was the F.B.U. nationally that dragged the British Fire Service yelling and screaming, despite itself, into the twentieth century and helped make it what it is today. It was their considered submissions in the sixties, on the future role of the British Fire Service, presented to the government appointed Holroyd and Cunningham Departmental Inquiries that were accepted as the way forward, and not the employers. The employers failed over the years to satisfactorily implement these recommendations with the result that the Fire Service today, as a constituent part of the nation's public service bodies, has been stigmatised by government auditors, for not giving value for money. It has been pressured into becoming, along with the Health Service and Education Boards, during the Conservative Government's tenure of office, a money driven service and not solely the caring one we would wish it to be.

The part played by the F.B.U. in shaping the British Fire Service, prior to Prime Minister Thatcher's Union bashing legislation of the eighties, could not be compared with those militant trade unions that she was out to bring to heel.

The F.B.U. not only looked after the welfare of its membership, having its finger on the pulse of the Fire Service nationally, when some employing Fire Authorities and Chief Officers did not, but the organisation was also successful in influencing governments with respect to the requirements needed to improve fire safety legalisation for all the Public in the U.K. It imposed a standing and continuing national ban on overtime in the job, to the earning detriment it must be said of its membership. This apparently paradoxical manoeuvre was designed to create employment prospects for potential new recruits. It has always championed higher standards of fire cover and fire prevention and safety when government have and are still trying to hive off fire safety to other bodies who have less of an understanding of it than today's modern Firefighter. Today because of government economic policies it is fighting a rearguard action to maintain all these 'casus belli' in the interests of public safety.

Consummation?... It had been decided   that the previous N.I.F.A. Headquarters in Castle Street, Lisburn, would serve as the new headquarters for F.A.N.I. It seemed to the Firefighters of Belfast that it was to be, the tail that was to wag the dog, morale at this time was very low. George Morrison appointed his new command structure, several of Belfast's previous Senior Officers were promoted, including Sydney Pollock, and transferred to H.Q. Then the new Chief's attentions were   focused on the City and its Stations.

Those Officers who sold out and transferred their loyalties, took their thirty pieces of silver, doffed their caps to their new masters and departed from their Belfast colleagues. They disappeared into the celestial Black Hole that was Headquarters and were seldom seen or heard of in any meaningful way in Belfast from that time on. It had been hoped, during the transitional period, that their voices would be made heard giving advice and opinions in the light of their experiences gleaned as wholetime professionals within the City how it should continue to be run. Their voices were either not raised or were ignored. This lack of adequate communications and liaison; something that should have been seen as being crucial at this time was to prove instrumental in helping to ferment the industrial unrest that was to surface before long in Belfast. Belfast Firefighters felt very let down and neglected.

A City Brigade once administered as a whole, was divided into two divisions, divide and conquer. This move did not bring about any advantages but caused the two newly appointed Divisional Commanders of what was now 'A' and 'B' divisions; considerable headaches and administrative problems. Mr. Morrison then instructed that any existing insignia or Belfast coats of arms displayed on Stations be either obliterated or removed. The wheel eventually turned full circle in 1992 under the leadership of Mr. Ken McNeill a prodigy of the old N.I.F.A. whenever the old system of administering the City Stations was readopted.

Any service if it is to function efficiently and uniformly must have its bible as a datum line to work to. This in the Belfast Brigade, as in most other U.K. Brigade's is a set of Brigade Orders which is applicable to that particular Brigade alone. They are continually updated and amended as circumstances change and dictate. They evolve and expand over a period of time in order to allow for certain operational contingencies. They were not created overnight and as such were just as applicable after the Amalgamation, as before. Brigade Orders can be likened to the Queens Regulations which Her Majesty's Armed Forces conform to. They are a set of instructions which everyone is obliged to know and are able to refer to when the need arises. They apply equally to all.

Following the Amalgamation Officers-in-Charge in Belfast asked for guidance if the old Brigade Orders still applied, none was given. If they, myself included, had not decided to continue to apply them as a yardstick the City's Stations would have been operating in a vacuum. Up until my retirement in 1989 only a handful of new Brigade Orders had been promulgated. It appeared to me and others that anything that stank of the old Belfast Brigade was taboo even if it were necessary, an attitude which is hardly conducive to the efficient, smooth operation of a wholetime professional Fire Brigade.

...the last generation of the 'Boys of the B.F.B'.

Prior to Amalgamation, whispers had percolated down from City Hall that Belfast's Firefighters were to be given the freedom of the city. It would have been a fitting tribute at this time, not least for the deeds done since 1969 but for the service given to the people of Belfast since 1845. This idea along with the identity of the Belfast Fire Brigade were buried at one and the same time. Not until 1992 was this honour bestowed on the Northern Ireland Fire Brigade, some twenty three years too late for those who served then, in the City's own Brigade. Following Amalgamation, it took all of fifteen years for old loyalties to die, veterans retired and have been superseded by young fresh minds and bodies, who now have new loyalties, be it to the profession or themselves. Mr. Morrision as Chief has come and gone. In fact the Brigade is on its sixth Chief since he was first appointed and has only now gelled and finally become, as one.

Increased funding that was once refused, with the old stiff upper lip attitude that we can cope, had been accepted, be it ten years late or not. It was being used to finance a ten year expansion programme begun in 1987 under the auspices of Mr. W.Beggs MBE,GIFireE, who held the reins of office, from 1985 until 1987, with the objective of building additional Stations throughout the Province, including the provision of new and more technically advanced appliances and equipment, to continue the never ending fight against the common enemies, of fire and disaster.

F .A.N.I's Legacy-F.A.N.I.-ing Around...When writing a book which portrays the humanitarian role of Firefighters, a work that could not have been written if it was not for mans' inhumanity to man I felt that it was relevant and hopefully not too oblique a point to briefly address one of the fundamental problems which has led Ulster and -by the overspill factor-the Brigade to the very brink of disaster.

Discrimination in employment is but one of those fundamental problems. Even though the Brigade was to be at the focal point of many terrorist actions it was not to be excluded, for self evident reasons, from the social action/reaction to employment discrimination either. This complex topic is the subject of much debate by the wispy haired academics of this world but I will hope to do it limited justice if only in respect of the Brigade. I should be at pains to point out to the reader that what has gone on in Ulster in employment discrimination is not peculiar to our society alone just in case we are held accountable for all the ills that bedevil human nature and its society. Some understanding of the human psyche-and that most complex version the Ulster psyche-is required in order to best appreciate the reason-if not the peculiar justifications-why.

In the beginning-in any superficially stable society throughout the world-a small ethnic, religious or cultural minority's presence is welcomed and smiled upon benignly and they are accepted by the dominant majority who mentally place them at the bottom of the social ladder. Small-being the operative word-since ethic minorities are looked on as adding colour and culture to that particular society. It makes the society feel good about itself. It is when the minority population grows to larger numerical proportions-in a natural social evolutionary cycle-and when it begins to flex its legitimate social muscles and demand or demonstrate for parity of esteem which are peculiar to its own culture and political aspirations that it may be perceived by the majority, rightly or wrongly, as becoming a threat to the status quo in areas such as employment, housing, etc. These staples of a comfortable life having previously been regarded as the exclusive entitlement of that dominant majority. When the issues in question are ignored or handled insensitively by the political majority's representatives it is then that both parties to the debate may adopt intransigent positions and produce the fertile soil for violence to eventually manifest itself. In the realm of world affairs Ireland has never had a monopoly on the ills produced by an unjust society.

In 1977 the Fire Authority-reformed by the Local Government Act of 1974-which by now encompassed the whole of Northern Ireland Fire Service signed the Declaration of Principle and Intent which is described in Section 6 of the Fair Employment (N.I.) Act 1976 (F.E.N.I.). The new Brigade had committed itself to policies to 'protect equality of opportunity in employment in accordance with the letter and spirit of the Act by every means at its disposal'.

In 1979 the Fair Employment Agency received a complaint from a Roman Catholic that he had been unlawfully discriminated against in the matter of promotion within the Brigade, the complaint was not upheld. The newly amalgamated Brigade establishment was 1032 strong by this time. During their investigations into this particular allegation the Agency found there was a suggested imbalance in favour of Protestant employment in the accumulated statistics supporting this perception. The reported figures were 82% Protestant representing 846-16% Roman Catholic representing 165-and 2% who could not be assigned to God or mammon. Comparative figures for the BFB in the mid sixties reflect little pro rata percentage change since that period set against a comparative workforce of 350-82.5% Protestants-17.5% Roman Catholics. As compositional information, it appeared to the F.E.A. that Roman Catholics might not have the same equality of opportunity for entry into the Fire Service and the possibility for promotional advancement that Protestants appeared to have.

This initial examination of the Brigade was part of a broader political issue which was a major consideration with the central U.K. Government and was a portion of that current Government's concerted attack across a broad spectrum on the ongoing malaise and bone of political contention -discrimination in employment-which had troubled the Province for decades. The next deep investigation of the Brigade was embarked on as a constituent part of the continuing terms of reference of the Agency and was an investigation carried out in parallel with other contra-policy investigations of a number of other employers in the Province to determine their employment policy relating to Roman Catholic/Protestant employee ratios in their respective organisations.

Notwithstanding the outcome of the 1979 Brigade investigation it was due to a perceived imbalance and discrimination in employment against the 'minority' within the Brigade that it was decided by the Agency to cast the net wider and investigate the Brigade's employment policies both written and unwritten. So in 1982 on the basis of these provisional figures the Agency under its statutory powers decided to conduct an in depth investigation under Section 12. of the Act into the entire employment practices of the Fire Authority.

Initially it was intended that the investigation should only cover full time employees but following representations from the Fire Authority the Agency decided to extend the scope of the investigation to include the Retained, part-time, members of the Service. The terms of reference for the investigation also included-the recruit selection and promotion procedures of the Fire Authority, in order to establish if these existing procedures had any disparate effect on Roman Catholics and Protestants-the subsequent career paths of those recruited into the Brigade in the year 1974 following Amalgamation-and the qualifications of those who joined the Service in 1974.

It was clear that relatively fewer Roman Catholics than Protestants had successfully taken the initial entrance examination to the Brigade. The report states... 'Sect.12 Para12.5. The examination of wholetime recruitment conducted in 1983 by the Agency indicates that the Protestant success rate in being appointed was more than three and a half times that of Roman Catholics'. Did

164

they take anything other than figures into consideration? These facts may have had their roots in the segregated education system that continues to exist today in the Province. In other words Roman Catholic's may simply have been disinclined to apply to join what they have been educated to perceive-with justification-as an 'establishment' organisation with institutionalised discriminatory employment policies.

The report goes on to state...'Sect.12 Para 12.6 The major differences in the success rates of Protestants and Roman Catholic applicants appeared at the selection stages in which the marks awarded to candidates were dependent upon the objective judgement of individuals'. How, unless interviews are to be conducted by computer operated robots and even these have to be programmed by humans is an interviewer supposed to select a successful candidate? In my opinion Para 12.6 simply and succinctly bears out what I have previously contended in that it contradicts the Agency's laudable aim in trying to achieve impartiality in selecting candidates.

In practice confidentiality regarding a candidate's religion is simply a nonstarter in Northern Ireland. Recruiting proceedings are supposed to be observed by the employer's Monitoring Officer exclusively and interviewers are not entitled to know the religious aspect of a candidate's profile. Yet here we have a quango agency-in what is clearly a contradictory statement-accusing the Authority on the one hand of exercising discrimination by not employing enough Roman Catholics and on the other encouraging it to pursue a positive discriminatory policy, presumably, by knowing how many interviewees there are of one persuasion or the other at the initial interview stage? This is Alice in Wonderland thinking!

It also appeared that the Agency enjoyed the luxury of not being held to public account for this soirée into the realms of fair employment. This was confirmed by the use of ambiguous words in the Report. Words such as *'indicates'* and *'may'* quoted in the two paragraphs of the report which are not the concise and positive *'shalls'* and *'wills'* language of legislation. They convey to those who wish to perceive them as being-on the one hand-'definitive' -and yet to others as- 'flexible' especially those who wish to interpret them for their own ends. Presently the F.E.A. is there to be used not only by those who have grounds for feeling genuinely aggrieved which was the intended spirit of the Act-but just as in other enacted legislation such as the Health and Safety Act, once the flood gates of compensation have been opened-it is there to be exploited by those who would wish to use it for their own financial gains.

Following the introduction of the Fair Employment Act it was only a question of time before the religious card would at last be officially brought into use in the Brigade, if only as a test case, as happened in 1979. It is probable that this, I hope, genuine 'testing' will never completely disappear from the Brigade nor perhaps should it.

The Authority through the Brigade Training Officer voiced its objection to the imposed religious monitoring as a result of the F.E.A. activities. Their stated position being that selection must always be made on merit and that to identify candidates on the basis of their creed would be to introduce religion as a criterion where it did not previously exist. The Brigade's Training Officer Divisional Officer Dessie Graham who was also responsible for recruitment had told them so during their investigations and deliberations. Pointing out, as the report reflected, that the Brigade, had been left with a legacy from pre-amalgamation days and that it was virtually impossible to redress the imbalance in a relatively short space of time. The Agency failed to mention these important aspects in what should have been a fair and balanced report. The report's credibility was fatally flawed in this respect. It deliberately gave a false impression to the public that job discrimination was still being practised and risked causing personal religious animosity within the Brigade where hitherto none had existed. This did not mean, however, that change should not be brought about. It was simply the manner and the methodology that was to be employed that was the contentious issue at shop floor level in the Brigade.

The terms of reference given to the Fair Employment Agency regarding fair employment did not cover nepotism nor glad handing which are also forms of discrimination which apply to all employees not just minorities perhaps if it had it would have been interesting to see what would have been contained in their report then with regard to the father/son ratio of employment and Freemason promotion within the Brigade, but this again was largely a legacy of past recruitment policies.

Dessie Graham the Officer at the centre of this F.E.A. investigation was a man of integrity and conviction, so much so that having previously served as a Station Officer within the old Northern Ireland Fire Authority and having fallen foul of its titular, diminutive, pint sized head Chief Fire Officer George Murphy-what he lacked in stature he made up for with bombast-Dessie resigned his post and was accepted into Belfast Fire Brigade as a Firefighter. Now that takes guts, strength of character, and trust in one's fellow man to take a rank reduction of three places on the promotional ladder. Even if-and only if-a vague promise of a rapid return to his former Station Officer rank at some future date had been given-he nevertheless putting his family's existing standard of living at risk to the point of principle. It was a leap of faith into the dark.

It was analogous, that just as Dessie was prepared to start from scratch with a leap into the dark so it was with all the Province's employers in respect of establishing the fair employment legislation as good custom and practice. Of course this against the expected backdrop of the cries of foul from many of those bigots that haunted the workplace. In a Province torn apart by extreme violence for thirty years trust in the new employment legislation did not exist at its inception. Only with the passage of time and most recently the advent of the Belfast Good Friday Agreement of 1998 has it begun to grow, but there is still along hard road to march.

After two years of supposed in-depth investigation the Agency in 1984 produced a whole thirty page riveting report. The complexities of the report did indeed reveal that there was an imbalance in the Roman Catholic/Protestant employment, recruitment and promotion ratios which needed to be redressed. This imbalance, it concluded, was not entirely the fault of a relatively new administration this discrimination having partially had its roots in previous the administrations' recruitment policies. It also concluded that Roman Catholic recruits and promotion examination candidates were not as successful as their Protestant counterparts. So the wheel turned full circle during the two year investigation and stopped just about where it had started having come up with the same answers which were known at the commencement of its investigation. But then justice had to be seen to be done. The Agency report did not inform the Brigade of anything that its senior ranks were not already aware of.

So is this quango the guardians of the good and the virtuous squeaky clean itself. Well I am afraid not. The Latin expression Quis custodiet ipsos custodes says it all…Who does indeed guards the guardians?

Perhaps the Fair Employment Agency would have done well to investigate itself from time to time or to sup from its own cup of medicine. It has, to its public humiliation, been obliged to in more recent times. The Fair Employment Agency-established from a clean paper sheet-had not been in existence for very long until it was forced to concede publicly that its own organisation had a problem which it had not inherited as a 'legacy'. That of an 'imbalance' in its own work force. The Fair Employment Agency then had to advertise in the local press to fill posts within its own organisation, stating that the Protestant section of the community were under represented   therefore applications would be welcome from that sector of the community. I have heard of shooting yourself in the foot but never of opening the mouth to replace the foot that was already in there!

It is an ironic fact that in 1995 a disgruntled employee of the Agency initiated an action against it. The Commission appointed one of its own officials to represent the plaintiff against its corporate self and the Agency surprisingly won. The more profound question was not who won but who really lost? This risible situation could only happen in Northern Ireland. I could be forgiven for asking Alice for another cup of tea at the Mad hatters tea party just about now.

It is an interesting foot note to the Agency's activities that when the Agency published a report on the Ambulance Service, it stated that they could not find any evidence of employment discrimination, but nonetheless the Service should employ more of the minority anyway. Poor old Ambulance Service when you are seen to be right, you are still wrong.

The principle of fair employment is a commendable one, but the Fair Employment Commission seemed to be only interested in playing the numbers game. The intended target   employment ratio for the Brigade 60/40-60% Protestant-40% RC was meant to reflect the approximate religious divide in the community at large. These figures were to be achieved by ability alone in recruitment although-for whatever reason-presently that does not seem possible. It would appear that the solution will be that this imbalance will be artificially redressed for political expediency sake through what appears to be the hidden agenda policy of reverse discrimination. If that occurs I fear for the future of good employee relations and stability on the shop floor in all spheres of employment not just the Fire Service. The reality based on experience, particularly in the U.S., is that reverse discrimination does not work. It breeds resentment leading to open hostility and recreates the very discrimination it was meant to address. Today it is quite rightly called Tokenism.

There exists today in Northern Ireland a residual and underlying suspicious discontent in the workplace that employment by ability alone is not the name of the game but religion is. Twenty seven years ago the civil rights marches were undertaken by those who were aggrieved and marched to demand equality in voting, housing and the workplace. A situation now exists in the workplace where those imbalances through fair employment legislation, on paper at least, have been partially redressed. If equity is to be achieved and maintained whilst preserving goodwill in a society where none previously existed one must look to impartial policing of the policy. The issue of fair employment needs in what is an ever changing society, will have to be regularly re-addressed and amended to meet and match those changes. The Fair Employment Agency has quite rightly had it's fair share of criticism since it was established. It has had a poor beginning but at least it is a beginning. With the imminent introduction of European legislation in respect of fair employment policy in which the organisation will have to prove its adherence to fairness rather than the complainant prove their case a move which should be viewed by all as being a more rigorous form of in house policing than the victim having to prove the discrimination and thus should be more acceptable to all parties, but we shall see.

F **irefighters's Strike 1977-78...** For decades the Fire Brigades Union-which represented some 70,000 Firefighters full and part-time-had attempted to secure for the Fire Service a national pay formula that would reflect Firefighters's worth in comparison with the upper level of semi-skilled manual wage earners in industry. Firefighters are forbidden to have a second job. In spite of this their wages and income on occasions were supplemented by 'moonlighting', earning wives financial contributions, and in some extreme cases State Benefits for their children. Union officials maintained that Firefighters were at the very least entitled to the national pay average plus 10% for his skills, long hours, shift working and the hazards they had to face. Each annual wage rise was seen to be eroded by inflation and exceeded by those awarded to industry. Although non-producers of wealth Firefighters do contribute to the wealth of a nation-by saving life and property-by reducing the nations post incident health care bills-reducing direct loss fire-bill-and by eliminating the consequential loss of production and subsequent industrial and domestic rebuild costs.

In 1967, the Government appointed the Holroyd Committee to carry out a Departmental examination into the structure of the United Kingdom Fire Service which reported its findings in 1970. While dealing primarily with the organisation of the Fire Service, this report made a significant statement on pay. Another Departmental enquiry under Sir Charles Cunningham in 1971 was then given the task of evaluating the Firefighter's job. Both reports broadly concurred with submissions given to them by the F.B.U. that Station cleaning chores should be dispensed with and Firefighters should be more gainfully employed in fire prevention work with a more structured approach to training, technical education, and promotional advancement. Cunningham added that the job should be re-evaluated every two years due to the changing nature of a Firefighter's job within the community. Pressure through these reports was therefore put on employers to assess the value of a modern Firefighter and to work towards a permanent pay formula.

Unfortunately at this time the governing Labour party, in attempts to control inflation-which had soared as high as 27% with average earnings increasing by 26.6%.-hardly what a Labour government had in mind-introduced a grand scheme called the Social Contract between the Government and the Trade Unions. The simple concept of this was that in return for favourable economic and social policies Trade Unions were to moderate their wage claims. Simple schemes for simple minds.

The Fire Service was caught in the middle of this major policy shift just at a time when they thought they were making progress towards their own pay formula for the future.

There was at this time general discontent throughout the Service, especially amongst the younger generation of Firefighters. There had been a steady drift of personnel away from Brigades into better paid professions and jobs in industry. Unofficial industrial action had already been taken in several Brigades notably Glasgow and Liverpool and the F.B.U. Executive Council was the body that had to police these limited actions. At meetings held during the year by the National Joint Council-a joint employer/employee body which set pay and conditions of service for the whole of the U.K. Fire Service personnel-employers had agreed to pay only the amount central government was prepared to sanction-that being 10%-this of course was entirely unacceptable to the rank and file membership of the Union.

At the recall conference of 300 union Delegates held in Eastbourne on 7th November Terry Parry the F.B.U. General Secretary beseeched delegates not to vote for a general strike. He asked the Delegates, against a background of much heckling whether they were they prepared to let old people and childrens' homes and city centres burn down-shouts of 'Yes!' from the floor was his answer.

Let no one be under any illusions that these answers of 'yes' were in the least bit glib rhetoric. The decision to strike was the greatest moral dilemma ever to afflict individual Firefighters in the U.K. The choice to go on strike was, contrary to media opinion, a moral dilemma which each and every

Firefighter had to address in his own heart before reaching an decision whether or not to strike. The employers to their eternal shame played this violin to the galleries of pure theatre. The only questions to be addressed and answered in this scenario was who were the master cynics and the truly immoral. I believe it was cynically immoral for each and every one of those involved on the government/employers side to put personnel into this stark position of choice by failing to pay a decent working man a decent living wage. Since these momentous events employers have over the intervening decades tried to mumble this cant again on a few occasions but it won't wash anymore. The Public are not stupid they all know political expediency and exploitation when they see it.

Even though a dispensation not to strike was offered to the Belfast Firefighters by the F.B.U. Executive Council due to the continuing terrorist campaign in the Province, defiant words for strike action were also echoed in Belfast by the F.B.U. membership. Before the commencement of the strike on 14th November 1977, Merlyn Rees the Home Secretary made a ministerial broadcast in a desperate attempt to avert the stoppage and echoed the General Secretary's words. An Officer from the Berkshire Brigade which covered Windsor came out with the retort 'We will not turn out even if the Queen is trapped in Windsor Castle'. Poor Mr.Rees, this was the second time he was unable to avert a strike.

The game of brinkmanship was now being played out each participant hoping the other would blink first. Belfast City Council-who feared an I.R.A. onslaught on the city-along with Yorkshire and East Sussex local authorities called on government to make Firefighters a better offer. Even Margaret Thatcher who was in opposition in those days-suggested we should be paid a little more. In the actual event of the strike the P.I.R.A.-apparently because of their socialist ideals-resisted the temptation to embark on a scorched earth policy in Belfast. What a strange collection of allies and bedfellows we had.

At one of the final meetings in Chi' prior to the Strike the Executive purportedly received a coded telephone call from a 'Captain McVeigh' stating that if the Firefighters went of full strike their action would be viewed by the Loyalist paramilitaries as aiding and abetting the P.I.R.A. and as a consequence in future every Firefighter must consider himself a 'legitimate' target. The membership that night still voted to go ahead.

In the early days of the strike even the para militaries seemed unsure which way to jump this was reflected in the local press at the time...

Belfast Newsletter Wednesday November 23,1977.
UVF Leans on Firemen to Turnout in Shankill…

The Ulster Volunteer Force last night denied that it had 'forced' firemen to break their strike in Belfast. But it admits to applying 'pressure' to them. A spokesman at the outlawed organisation's headquarters stated: 'We did not threaten the men at Ardoyne fire station. We simply told them that life was in danger at the Shankill Road fire which resulted from a bombing.' We told them it would be in their best interests to get down there.' They seemed a bit reluctant to react. But we said that if they did not take a fire engine out to protect the old people who lived at the back of the burning Gillespie and Wilson store, it would be taken out anyway'. 'No weapons were produced. And in no way were the UVF trying to undermine the firemen's strike. 'We support them wholeheartedly'. ….He recalled that the Provisional IRA had put out a statement claiming it was modifying its campaign in deference to the firemen's strike action, 'If the idea behind that is that the Provos are going to hit at obviously easy targets in Loyalist areas, they'll have to think again'….

But the government was not the only object of the UVF's criticism…. Explaining the action of its observers who went to 'monitor' the Gillespie and Wilson blaze, the UVF spokesman claimed it took the Army '15-20 minutes' to get its three Green Goddesses to the scene'. 'It quickly became clear that the soldiers were not capable of bringing the fire under control', he said. There was a threat to old people's homes at the back of the burning building. That's why the approach was made to the firemen at Ardoyne'.

The body whom the Union thought might give the strike support the Trades Union Congress representing the whole of the Trade Union movement in the U.K. refused by one disgraceful vote to lend their support to the Firefighters. This just goes to show that the physically impossible is achievable and that it is possible for Trade Union leaders to speak with their collective head buried up a government's nether regions. These lickspittals chose to toe the government line. Other rank and file trade union members were disgusted with them for not throwing their weight behind the Firefighters. One wonders if it had not been a Socialist government what the result might have been. The Firefighters employers had plenty of company when it came to cynical and immoral posturing.

The deadline of 14th November came when those Firefighters on duty the night of the 13th came off duty at 0900hrs and joined their colleagues outside their Stations on the picket lines. The first strike in the Fire Brigades Unions history of fifty-nine years had begun against the policies of a Labour government. On that first day throughout the U.K. the strike claimed 98% support.

The battle was on to win the hearts and minds of the Public. It was another battle the government was to lose unequivocally. Members of the Public came to the picket lines regularly with gifts of food and most important of all encouragement. Those who pulled picket duty on the unofficial rota for Christmas Day 1977 are never likely to forget it.

I and a number of other colleagues went on the picket line as a token of support for the strike on more than one occasion but I did not go all the time. My reasoning was that the strike was solid and did not require any bully boy tactics. I was more interested in getting out and slogging to support a young family and a new mortgage. This did not endear us to all of our colleagues and had slight 'Coventry' implications at a later date but by then I had risen in the ranks so any intended effect on me was lost along the way. I lost more financially than most of my critics, local Union Officials saw to it that I and other like minded did not get our token £9.00 from the strike fund donated by the Public. So it was a difficult time all around and the sadness of it all is seared into our very memory and souls. Times were indeed hard before, during, and after this righteous struggle.

The government did not expect the strike to last more than perhaps a few days. Their opinion was that a well-publicised tragedy with a consequent loss of public support would destroy the moral of the strikers. They entirely misjudged the mood of the Public and the resolution of the Firefighters. Tragedy there certainly was, unfortunately, the first one took place in Belfast with the death of an infant and young girl in a house fire in Ligoniel in the north of the city.

Government as part of its contingency plan nationally, had briefly trained and put on standby 9000 troops along with 850 1950's 'Green Goddess' Civil Defence fire appliances, to take over the duties of the Fire Service throughout the U.K. Their equipment was inferior compared to that of the Fire Service, the tallest ladder they had extended only to a length of 30ft, there was no rescue/cutting gear and their appliances were, quite frankly, designed for a completely different role. Meanwhile the Brigades' own fire appliances stood idle in their engine rooms throughout the U.K. The government had no power to requisition them without an Emergency Proclamation made under the Emergency Powers Act 1920 which Parliament needed to approve. The Firefighters had already anticipated this manoeuvre-and had hit the 'money button'-for all strikes come to an end. The government knew that Firefighters had threatened to 'black'-condemn to the scrapyard forever - any appliance used in strike breaking. Some personnel I know in Belfast had taken the precaution of temporarily disabling machines in the event of this happening and yet others had borrowed emergency rescue equipment to put in the rear of private cars and vans to create a 'shadow' Brigade. It was clear that tragedies were to be averted at all costs. We could all be cynical, the masters were already teaching us a few tricks of their trade.

Fears and suspicions were borne out that our colleagues in the Retained service in the Province-who were paid for every turnout-would not support the whole-time membership in their struggle. The Retained Firefighters Association had been making inroads into their ranks and had gained a number of members. In addition, the National Association of Fire Officers-now consigned to the dustbin of history-a 'professional' body representing Fire Officers only had a small number of members throughout the Brigade. It was these two groups who came into Belfast-the Retained to fight fires-and the N.A.F.O. members to act as pathfinders and toadies for the Army. Yet more financial cynics. There were also a small number of conscientious objectors to the strike within Belfast, I believed there was a place for them, a larger number of the membership did not. It was always the F.B.U. that had blazed the trail for Firefighters' pay and conditions. Unfortunately I have yet to see any non-participants to any dispute who make material gain from the pain of others be conscientious objectors when it comes to refusing the benefits that have been derived by the struggle of the majority.

Industrial relations during this period were extremely volatile both locally and nationally on the basis 'if you are not for us then you are agin us'. Following the dispute there was to be an awful lot of bitterness and open hostility directed at these disloyal individuals and groups whom it was felt, with justification, as well as helping themselves financially had helped to prolong the strike by a matter of weeks. N.A.F.O. members who mostly hid themselves from the real world and only skulked around at night operated from Headquarters were later completely ostracised for their trouble. A favoured banner and slogan-during the stoppage-of the striking F.B.U. members was 'N.A.F.O. needs PAXO'-an allusion to a popular turkey stuffing. Well they certainly had Christmas and Thanksgiving come round regularly for many a year after. Clearly the strike left and, still leaves, a huge legacy of bitterness behind it.

Open resentment and hostility was directed towards the Retained service for a long time afterwards. I felt the saddest thing of all was the case of one young conscientious objector who objected on genuine religious grounds who was hounded out of the job when it was all over. The administration stood by and watched this happen. In spite of their convoluted reasoning these personnel had shown loyalty to the job but there was none shown by the 'establishment' in return when it came to the crunch. I suppose it is called riding the tiger's back.

The government propaganda issued to the news media was lyrical and disingenuous about what a wonderful job the Forces were doing and the full power of propaganda through the British Broad Casting service was blatantly used against the Firefighters. Wonderful and valiant in theory perhaps but to the skilled eye of the Firefighter watching the Army/Air Force/Navy's feeble efforts the actuality painted a different picture. Their 'technique' was simply one of flooding buildings until the water poured out the doors. An objective observer only had to drive through one's own fire area to view the burnt out shells that stood testimony to how successful they really were. We had a great deal of sympathy for the troops personally, quite a few of whom subsequently joined the job when they gave up the Queen's Shilling after their military service, having acquired a taste for the profession after these government inspired 'experiments'. These, mostly young boys, were quite simply terrified of what they were being asked to do. They found out the hard way that Fire Service work is not for the uninitiated or untrained and is definitely an acquired 'taste'.

Aside from the community's financial loss, industry and commerce suffered substantial and increasing fire losses during the period of the strike although the government suppressed the publication of fire loss valuations at the time. Undoubtedly behind the scenes, the insurance underwriters were feeling the pinch and their lobbying to have the strike brought to a speedy end could and did bring enormous pressure to bear on the government. A glance at the statistics later showed that fire loss had almost doubled from £250 millions to £450 millions in just one month. Therefore, it pays to pay your Firefighters.

Following a few carrots which were dangled in front of the Union, which after consideration were rejected, a comprehensive settlement was finally reached in late December underwritten by Jim Callaghan's government.

This gentleman-I am glad to say-personally and directly experienced the ire of the Firefighters when he attended the Trade Union Annual Congress conference at the seaside town of Blackpool in Lancashire. I heard the tale later. I think Callaghan should be advised-whether he realised at the time or not-that this particular morning when he arrived at the conference hotel to address his fellow Socialist political prostitutes that he was the victim of a carefully contrived ambush. It was a particularly mean morning with sleet driving in off the Irish Sea the conditions matched the mood of the over 1000 uniformed Firefighters their wives and in some cases babes-in-arms. The media were of course there in force as were the boys in blue who were policing the event for security purposes. Throughout the strike, the Police with the exception of one or two clowns, were sympathetic. They realised their turn might come one day. So in the Prime Minister's pre-arrival ground rules briefing it was agreed between the F.B.U. reps and the Police that his car would be directed into the open area in front of the Hotel's reception area. It was a part of the 'arrangement' that no harm would come to him. The 'crowd' would be 'held back' by a corridor of Police officers who at an appropriate point would be simply 'overwhelmed' by the Firefighters. That is precisely what happened. Callaghan's car was swamped by Fire Service uniforms and he was trapped in his rocking and bumping car for a few minutes until the Police 'regrouped' and managed to half carry, half bundle, their by now white faced and shaken precious charge into the Hotel.

Apparently mutual congratulations were exchanged all round and then it was off to the local pub to view it all on the television! The publican thought it was his birthday as nearly 1000 customers filed in the front door and then out the back clasping a hot drink.

By the time Callaghan reached the podium to speak to his Socialist pariah chums he was-to the collective delight-obviously seething. Quite obviously, fear had been replaced with anger. It helps the morale of strikers to remind politicians forcefully and personally from time whom exactly the Masters are and where the politicians' place is as our Servant. I am sure the illustrious ex-Prime Minister will remember the day that this particular portion of the electorate reached in and touched him.

The detail of the post-strike agreement amounted to the phasing in over two years of a pay formula which was to be linked to the upper quartile earnings of the skilled industrial sector thus preventing any further wage drift in the future. This was accepted by the membership and return to work took place on 16th January 1978 each sides honour having been preserved.

This pay formula has been the envy of other public sector workers when they saw how equitable it was. It rewards and reflects annually, in financial terms how well the country is doing by how much the industrial worker receives in wage rises. The bigger the cake the more there is to be distributed fairly. However over the years, apart from the present financial stringency of government towards the public sector workforce, employers have tried without success to diminish the benefits that have been derived from this formula.

Like the national miner's strike of 1984-85, the Firefighters' strike left a scar on the Fire Service which has taken years to close, if not to heal.

Availability or Danger Money?...One could not adequately and fully cover this period without interspersing the dialogue with the occasional mention of other matters affecting the internal workings of the Brigade. It would not do to give a false impression that all was sunshine and roses from an administrative point of view. Issues other than Firefighters's safety came into play and one of them is tackled now.

The British Fire Service, functions under the legislation contained in the Fire Services' Act. The Province has the Fire Services (Northern Ireland) Order 1984 it but is basically the same as the legislation applied in the U.K., but with a few subtle differences. The duties of the Fire Authority, contained within this Order, empowered a fire authority, amongst other matters to...

Permit it, subject to arrangements entered into by the Department, to employ the Brigade and its equipment outside Northern Ireland. Perhaps this was the original first cross border executive that is currently the subject of so much political debate?

The foundation of all these duties was based on the premise that the Brigade thus formed was only obliged it to meet efficiently all 'normal' requirements. This is and remains the grey area that the Fire Service in Northern Ireland has operated in for this past thirty years of civil disturbance and terrorist action. The question naturally arises, what is a normal requirement, is it a ship, or an oil refinery fire, or is it a building fired by bombs, some of which may not yet have gone off? These unique additional hazards expose personnel to risks other than they would expect to encounter at what the Fire Service previously classed as a 'normal' fire or incident of other classification. I have not, as yet, heard any spokes-person from any quarter in the Province, proffer an interpretation on that one. This question if raised, would in my opinion be tantamount to opening a legal can of worms. The fact of the matter is of course that if an answer was forthcoming and as a consequence this put present day operational ongoing activities of the Service under threat, it would not receive a welcome from those who would wish us to leave sleeping dogs lie. This is purely a matter of academic debate at the moment but the fact remains that should a massive loss of Fire Service personnel life occur in a terrorist act in the Province the lawyers acting for the Defendants-that is the government- in any future litigation may well put another spin on the currently assumed view.

From the very outset of the present 'Troubles' Belfast Firefighters-as any other Firefighters would do-saw it as their job to attend incidents of this type. This they regarded as being part and parcel of the trust placed in them by the community, to help protect life and save property. After all, who else was there better qualified, equipped, and trained to do the job?

Everyone was happy to see them perform this dangerous and onerous task, not least of all the City Fathers at City Hall. After the first few years, it became apparent, that incendiary and bombing attacks were not about to abate in the foreseeable future. The Firefighters began to feel aggrieved that their efforts should be recognised in some small tangible form even though the Firefighters themselves were not sure what form this should take. Whether it should be in a corporate manner by, for example, by the Brigade receiving the ancient rite of the 'Freedom of the City' or in some other way. This matter had not been addressed on their behalf by the City Councillors nor by their accredited Union representatives, and the feeling grew in strength that the sense of duty that personnel had displayed and were displaying was being exploited to some degree, by the City Fathers. It appeared these Councillors were happy to let them pick up the bits and pieces of human jetsam caused by the atrocities and obscenities brought about by terrorist actions whilst little was being done in recognition.

As I have indicated financial reward was not the primary motivating force, at this time, behind the personnel's thinking. They simply wanted some tangible form of recognition that their efforts were being appreciated. However as these unofficial feelings became generally know at the City Hall and the response was a thundering silence the pragmatic Firefighters decided that if it was not to be laurel wreaths and plaudits then it had better be cash. Following a request from the membership, representations were made by the Union to the Chief. He in turn brought the matter to the attention of the Police Committee, that personnel wished them to make a payment in consideration of the extra hazards which they were continuing to deal with. It was hardly surprising that initially this proposal was rejected.

Rumours filtered back that some Councillors thought that Firefighters status was on a par with the Council's refuse collectors. How to win friends and influence the work force? This attitude was regarded as a gratuitous insult and was treated with the contempt it deserved. Other Councillors considered us to be only water squirters. Water squirters maybe, but it is how, when, and where the water is squirted that is critical to the safe and efficient extinction of fire as most of these morons appeared not to know. They were, after all, only in charge of the Fire Brigade. Squirting water on a Council flower bed is vastly different to squirting it on a terrorist inspired fire. Of course by the time this diplomatic initiative was over by the councillors most Firefighters were minded to go up to the City Hall and squirt on their flower beds with the use of their personal water tanks! A profound lack of willingness, to begin to comprehend our role seemed to pervade their thinking. Perhaps they felt we were trying to hold the City up to ransom. This collective Council attitude only served to antagonise personnel further, but the job continued to get done, for the moment.

Mr. Jack Lewis, Chairman of the Police Committee, a friend and confidant of the Chief Officer, and an ally of the Brigade, who always took a sincere and meaningful interest in its activities had an understanding of the mood that prevailed at the time. In company with other sympathetic members of the Police Committee-one of which was Eileen Paisley, wife of the Reverend Ian- was lobbied in her home by Jock Hall. Eventually common-sense prevailed and in 1971 the princely sum of £2.00 per week was awarded, but not before an agreement was entered into by the Union.

Although the stalemate was broken personnel in order to receive this pittance-which almost amounted to an insult-were to enter into an agreement whereby they would make themselves available for callout purposes, when off duty, in the event of a major conflagration, whenever extra personnel were required. This did not seem unreasonable, and it was agreed. The Union also had to agree that any agreement reached on the allowance would not be used nationally as a lever to have similar payments introduced into other Brigades in the U.K.

All of this was fair enough, but the Police Committee were not to give in easily regarding what the allowance should be called. It was strenuously insisted by the F.B.U. that the award would not be called 'Danger Money' but should be called, 'Availability Money.' It was feared that some stupid Officer might insist on full value for money at an incident and to prevent this no official recognition was to be given that extra dangers were being undertaken. Acceptance of these terms, in my opinion, undermined the Firefighter's genuine claim that the primary intention of the request was not financial, but was to gain recognition for services rendered over and above normal risks.

My personal view at that time was that I would prefer to forego the academic argument -whether the award should be called 'Danger Money' or not- than work under the threat that other public services worked under namely the R.U.C. and Prison Service who carried out their 'normal' duties against the backdrop of intentional threats to their lives. Not for two salaries, would I wish my family and myself to be targeted and subjected to that kind of continuous worry although representatives of the Police and Prison Service had their negotiating eyes on this struggle of the Firefighters as it unfolded. It was not long before they submitted their claims to their respective employers for a similar allowance. They however learned from our mistakes and had the amount consolidated on their incremental scales. This had been the one major flaw in the outcome of our Union's negotiations and was never to be redressed.

In keeping with similar situations before the financial carrot had been dangled and not unlike other workers before and after this event, the temptation to refuse the offer was overcome- the pittance was accepted- and local politics won the day. The matter would raise its ugly head again before long, under the new Fire Authority, but with more resentment than hitherto experienced and also more disastrous physical and industrial relations consequences.

This arrangement stayed in place for several years, without the benefit of an automatic built in review procedure. No voluntary offers of an annual increase were forthcoming from the new Brigade whose personnel were not in receipt of this payment. So I suppose the new Chief just thought the matter might go away. He was sadly mistaken however. Eventually the matter was once again broached, along with the issue of the general dissatisfaction that personnel felt about how the Belfast area was being administered from Brigade Headquarters. This had been left simmering on a back burner for sometime, immediately following Amalgamation, and on the next occasion the problem re-arose it was to be F.A.N.I. in the hot seat this time.

Meetings which had been held throughout the Belfast Stations to discuss these and many other major irritating issues which culminated in an unofficial general meeting, which took place in the Labour Club rooms in Waring Street.

It was well attended that evening and feelings were running high. The Fire Brigades' Union were not officially represented, as the local Regional Committee could not see its way to agreeing to support the intended drastic action that was going to be rumoured.

The evening of the meeting a number of junior ranking Officers in Belfast put their heads on the chopping block, by declaring their position and stating their views on a variety of topics at the meeting. For my part I had sent an open letter to the Chairman of the Fire Authority outlining some of the grievances felt by personnel in the Belfast area. I read out the contents of this open letter to the membership at the meeting, but its contents were barely heard over the din and heckling that erupted whenever Mr. Stewart, a Board Member from the Fire Authority and the Fire Authority's representative to the National Joint Council in London, appeared on the platform to address the meeting and give the Authority's point of view on matters. For him it must have been like walking into the lion's den, but then perhaps he was used to it as he had previously served on Belfast City Council. In any event he was booed down and any sympathetic message he might have had fell on deaf ears.

This Jim Stewart was not 'The Man Who Shot Liberty Valance' although he had been High Sheriff of Belfast and at later date was to hold the office of Lord Mayor for two consecutive terms. A third term usually followed, which it invariably did for Unionist Mayors with the inevitable bestowing of a Knighthood. Neither occurred. Mr. Stewart's tenure of office was not extended. Hypothetically speaking the signboard above his fish and chip shop on Belfast's Donegall Road might have read 'Sir Jimmy Stewart's, Fish and Chip Saloon'. Any American visitors at that time who still visited the City to view the bomb sights, would surely have felt quite at home thinking that their own home spun film hero had received a royal accolade and had decided to set up a saloon-not on a film set- but in good old downtown Belfast.

Their had been a lot of hard political wheeling and dealing done and old political scores settled following the upheavals that had went on during negotiations prior to and immediately after Amalgamation. Was Mr. Stewart's third term and Knighthood a casualty of this?

Enough of fantasising and back to reality.

No dramatic decisions were taken at the Labour Rooms meeting but it was decided to once again approach the Regional Committee for support. This time they could not ignore the strength of feeling of the members and eventually

*"... after what Mr. Stewart said about the Firefighters, the cod's not the
only thing going to be battered around here!!"*

they agreed to speak to the Fire Authority. Their meeting with them bore no
fruit. The local press had since the days of the National stoppage reflected the
deteriorating state of industrial relations...

Belfast Newsletter Wednesday November 16th 1977.

*...The system worked by the old Belfast Fire Brigade was virtual-
ly foolproof and was being continuously improved as suggestions
and ideas came from the firemen involved. At present, under the
Fire Authority, there appears to be a suppression of initiative and
that's just one of the main problems. The men listed other factors
involved in a continuous process which is they say responsible for
the deterioration of the Service. 'If the public knew what was
going on behind the scenes they'd ask for a public inquiry'. Some
of the major points they raised:*

· *Gross understaffing.*
· *Poor recruiting because of poor wages.*
· *Almost a complete breakdown of industrial relations.*

· *Poor maintenance of equipment.*
· *Hose bursting while in use.*
· *Slum conditions of work.*
· *Non renewal of uniforms forcing men to wear tatty and torn clothing on duty.*
· *Erosion of a polished control room system.*
· *Civil service running the uniformed Service.*
· *Severe financial restrictions.*

'It all began with the amalgamation of the old Belfast Fire Brigade with the Fire Authority, 'One of the first things the new Authority did was to split Belfast into two almost totally separate bodies. Now the city is being worked very inefficiently. One hand doesn't know what the other is doing'.

'The lack of a decent living wage and the administrators refusal to recognise the firemen's union as a legitimate negotiating body has caused animosity between the men and the authority. This has resulted in large scale resignations of experienced men and this has caused great shortages of manpower. There have been something like 60 resignations since the beginning of the year. With the big turn over in staff it obviously reduces the efficiency of the Brigade. It means that young inexperienced men are being thrown in at the deep end and are having to fight major fires with only the bare minimum of training. Team work is important in fighting fires and you don't get a chance to build up that type of teamwork because of staff turnover. The younger men don't look upon the job as God's gift and they are becoming more and more militant to have improvements in their wages and conditions'.

The momentous decision was then taken, with great regret, that no further civil disturbance calls would be responded to by the F.B.U. members. This was to include all of the Brigade not just the F.B.U. members within the Belfast area. We were well supported by the boys from Londonderry but were not so sure of the part time Retained personnel's feelings. As Fire Brigade trade unionists they had always been a weak link, and had only begun to take a serious and active interest in representation when they saw after Amalgamation the benefits that were to be derived from being Union Members. Up until this point, membership had been patchy and fragmented. Having the benefit of full time jobs of their own they believed that they did not need representation by the Union even though on occasions Fire Service employers had used them as pawns, to subvert the aspirations of the wholetime service. Was this to be one of those times? Were our fears to be realised? We just had to wait and see.

The British public, generally do not realise that the U.K. Fire Service is a two tier service, in that different standards of recruitment, and promotional qualifications apply between the Wholetime service and Retained. The anomalies that prevail have never been seriously addressed by the Home Office. Probably the Home Office are fully aware of this anomalous situation but are content in the interest of financial frugality to let this situation prevail.

Not long after the commencement of the industrial action, Barnett House on the outskirts of south Belfast, an historical and architectural gem of a building and repository of artistic artefacts, was bombed by the I.R.A. Two of the fundamental questions arising from the possible consequences of the industrial action were answered simultaneously. The terrorists had not come out in sympathy with us, and Retained personnel had responded to the call, but not before serious structural damage and destruction to some of the building's treasures had occurred.

The fact that Retained personnel had turned out to the incident, I suppose, mitigated the sick feeling one had in the pit of the stomach, and diminished the public hostility that was undoubtedly directed towards us from the Belfast people, whose lives and property were entrusted to us and which we purported to protect. I wonder how members of the Fire Authority felt at this moment in time? The affair reflected little credit on all those involved.

Following this unfortunate but inevitable incident, the unofficial action was brought to a rapid and successful conclusion largely by the efforts of senior local and national union representatives such as Ken Kernaghan N.I. Executive Council Member and Terry Parry, General Secretary of the F.B.U. Members of the Northern Ireland Congress and the Irish Congress of Trade Unions also took part in the mediation.

Sandy Scott of Harland and Wolff was a particular friend to the Union and its membership at this time. The Police Committee finally conceded the point having eventually acquiesced with the practicalities of the argument rather than the spirit. The new sum of £4.00 per week was agreed on, but not before another incident had occurred at the Belfast Gas Works, an incident of greater magnitude with a more disastrous outcome in human terms which the Brigade had attended but had no control over. The finality of this incident having been determined before our arrival.

The issue of 'Availability Money' was still not to go away for yet a third time. The problem recurred that there was still no annual review built into the final agreement so the thorny arguments surfaced again. Before any similar action was contemplated by personnel the Fire Authority for Northern Ireland-who by this time were running the show-would not agree to a further increase. Following further approaches again by the F.B.U. to the Fire Authority the Authority clearly influenced by their 'lords and masters' at the Department of the Environment agreed to send the case to an independent arbitrator. Both parties obviously believing this move would get them off the financial hook. It was in fact the Union's case for extra money that won the day. You can imagine the surprise of both parties to the argument particularly when the arbitrator came out not only in favour of an increase, but that the amount paid should be reviewed on a regular basis. The final sum now awarded was to be £12.00 per week. This decision justified the validity of our original claim and to some degree restored our faith in the system that had tried to treat us so shabbily by comparison with other Services, but it was quite a struggle. By the conclusion everyone was sick to death of the whole affair. So sometimes victory can be a bit pyrric. The bill for the balancing of my personal account was not to come in from the 'establishment' until some years later.

Mlilestone on a Blood Soaked Road ....

BLOODY FRIDAY: 21st July 1972.
  '26 Explosions. 11 Dead. (incl. 3 soldiers) 130 injured'

This was the headline in the Belfast Newsletter 21st July 1972. There is little left to say that has not already been said in one form or another about this day, it was simply another day of infamy in Belfast and the Province's troubled history. It was also the day that stretched the resources of Belfast Fire Brigade to the very limit and to the point of being almost overwhelmed.

Listed below in chronological order is a catalogue of the incidents attended by the Brigade, transcribed for me from the originals, by one of the Control room staff on duty that day in the Control room in Headquarters at Chichester Street. It is not quite complete but it does give a slight insight into the scale and enormity of the horrors that were perpetrated that day on the citizens of Belfast but it can never reflect in its Service language the true horror that was witnessed by those who were there, either as victims, or as rescuers.

It will be noted that the messages are brief in nature and do not contain the usual protocol and niceties that are observed either by the Officers-in-Charge sending radio messages from an incident or by Control Room operatives receiving them. This was due to the intense workload that had to be dealt with both on the ground and in Controls over such a short time span.

TIME OF CALL	ADDRESS	ATTEND
14.06.hrs.	East Bridge St. '77'. No fire.	PE., P.,E.S.T., T.L.P. Stn. 'A' Red Watch.
Officer-in-Charge... Stn.O. Fell.		
14.16.hrs.	Garmoyle St. '77'. Explosion. No fire.	PE., P., E.S.T., T.L.P., F.O.T. Stn. 'B'/'D'/'A'.

TIME OF CALL	ADDRESS	ATTEND
Officer-in-Charge...Stn.O. Gotch.		
14.24.hrs.	78-80, Botanic Ave.	PE., P.
	'77'. Serious fire.	Stn. 'C' Red Watch.
G/Floor shop 1 jet.		
Officer-in-Charge... Stn.O. Fell.		
14.32.hrs.	Brookvale Ave.	PE., 2 Ps.
	'77'. Explosion.	
	No fire.	Stns. 'D'/'B', N.I.F.A.
Officer-in-Charge... Stn.O. Magill.		
[Attendance supplemented by N.I.F.A.]		
14.32.hrs.	Limestone Rd.	
	/ Antrim Rd.	P.
	'77'. 30 Casualties.	Stn. 'B'.
Officer-in-Charge... Sub.O. Farling.		
14.46.hrs.	Ormeau Ave.	PE., P.
	'77'. Explosion.	
	No fire.	Stn 'C'.
Officer-in-Charge... Stn.O. Savage.		
15.00.hrs.	Liverpool Bar,	
	Queens Quay.	E.S.T., T.L.P.
	'77'. Explosion.	
	No fire.	Stn. 'A'.
Officer-in-Charge...Sub.O.McCabe.		
[Unusual attendance-Brigade reserves running low.]		
15.06.hrs.	Star Taxis.	
	Crumlin Rd.	P.
	'77'. Building well alight.	
	2 jets.	Stn. 'D'.
Officer-in-Charge... L/Fm. Rowntree.[Minimum attendance.]		
15.07.hrs.	Bus Station	
	Oxford St.	PE., P.,
Officer-in-Charge... Stn.O. Gotch.		Stns. 'B'/'A'.
15.10.hrs.	Eastwoods	
	123-125, Donegall St.	PE., 2Ps., T.L.P.
	'77' Building well alight.	Stns. 'E'/'C'/'D'.
	7 jets, 1 T.L.P. jet.	

TIME OF CALL	ADDRESS	ATTEND
Officer-in-Charge... Stn.O. Fell.		
[Under resourced .]		
15.15.hrs.	Sunningdale Pk.	PE., P.
	'77'. Explosion. No fire.	Stns. 'B'/'D'.
Officer-in-Charge... Stn.O. Magill.		
15.29.hrs.	Salisbury Ave.,	N.I.F.A.,+ P.'E'.
	'77'. Gas main. 2gall. foam ext.	
Officer-in-Charge... L/Fm. Parker.		
[Under Officered.]		
15.29.hrs.	Creighton's Garage	P.E., N.I.F.A. 2Ps.
	Lisburn Rd.	
	'77'. Building well alight 4 jets in use.	
Officer-in-Charge...Stn.O. Mallon.		
15.32.hrs	Bus Station,	
	Glengall St.	E.S.T.
	'77'. 4 Single deck buses,	
	1 wooden hut.	Stn.'A'.
	1 jet in use.	
Officer-in-Charge...Sub.O.McCabe.		
[Inadequate attendance-Brigade creaks again.]		
15.33.hrs	Smithfield Bus Stn,	P.
	Smithfield Sq.	
	'77'. Explosion. No fire.	Stn. 'B'.
Officer-in-Charge... Sub.O. Farling.		
16.47.hrs.	Kennedy & Morrison,	
	Kent St.	PE., P., T.L.P.,
	'77'. Fire first floor.	
	1 jet.	Stn. 'A'
Officer-in-Charge... Stn.O. Fell.		
17.05.hrs.	Europa Hotel	
	Gt.Victoria St.	2Ps., E.S.T., T.L.P.
	'77'. Standby.	Stn. 'A'.
Officer-in-Charge... Stn.O. Everett.		
[High Rise Hotel-most bombed in the world-media base.]		
17.08.hrs.	Smithfield Bus Stn.	
	Smithfield Sq.	PE.
	Fire-roof space 1 jet. Stn. 'E'.	

TIME OF CALL	ADDRESS	ATTEND
Officer-in-Charge...	Stn.O. Fell.	
17.24.hrs.	Sydenham By Pass	PE.,
	'77'. no fire.	Stn. 'C'.
Officer-in-Charge...	Stn.O. Savage.	
18.46.hrs.	110, Donegall St.,	P.
	Fire-roof space 1 jet.	Stn.'C'.
Officer-in-Charge...	Sub.O.Oliver.	

****

So it was a busy day for all involved including those who orchestrated it.

The two incidents which will always dominate my memories of that day-although I was not on duty but still on sick leave recovering from my gunshot wound-were the explosion on the Cavehill Road when three civilians were murdered and the bomb outside the Bus Station in Oxford Street. One of those murdered on the Cavehill Road included Stephen Parker the fourteen year old only son of a Belfast minister the Reverend Joseph Parker, who later said...

'When I got to the mortuary I knew there was a boy, the body of a boy, there. I looked immediately for someone with fair hair, but of course, it was all singed and burnt black with the explosion. I thought immediately though, it's not Stephen. Then I looked again. I recognised the shirt as similar to the one Stephen was wearing, but again it had been affected by the explosion. The belt was a Scout belt-he was a Scout, and a few days before he had put those studs all around the belt and stood there getting me to admire them. I asked one of the men to look in the pockets, I wanted to be sure. Anyway, he looked in the pockets and found this box of matches-trick matches-that Stephen had used that evening before to fool me-then I knew it was Stephen'.

Tragically the Reverend Parker had for some time recorded the totals of the slayings that took place in the Province and had the statistics displayed on a board-for the uncaring world to see-outside his church in Donegall Place East directly opposite the side of Belfast's City Hall-now he was to add his son to this chilling list.

Eventually on the 27th October that year he announced that he and his wife were to emigrate to Canada. Some months before he had founded the 'Witness for Peace' movement, but claimed that his colleagues had not invited him to preach in their churches. He stated, 'I am extremely disappointed how things have gone for me. I am a very sad man, a very lonely man, and am amazed at the attitude of some of our clergy to the present situation. I am leaving my country and my church because I have been completely ostracised'.

I personally recall at around this time that the Protestant clergy-except those who were politically active-were in general very slow to come out publicly in support of the peace cause-I wondered if they ever would. Reverend Parker was like a voice crying in the wilderness, I shared his deep disappointment. He more than any of his colleagues understood the pain and anguish that was being endured by those who had lost their nearest and dearest.

The other act of infamy that day was the bombing of the Bus Station in Oxford Street, which is just around the corner from Chi'. Personnel from the Station when the heard the explosion as the Station shook immediately responded on foot to render assistance joining other would-be rescuers at the scene of the carnage. I can still recall that horrific camera shot of Assistant Divisional Officer Jackie Schofield, along with others, using a long tailed shovel to man-handle the charred corpse of one of the six victims at this incident into a salvage cover.

A small number of the less injured were brought into Chi's engine room by personnel for first aid medical attention prior to the arrival of Ambulances to transport them to hospital. As well as the injured from Oxford Street being brought into the engine room a group of shocked children who had been in the vicinity were also brought in and given succour and comfort by the lads. This care included donating cans of Coke. It was during these efforts to offer comfort and first aid to these walking wounded who were suffering from shock or minor cuts that the Chief made his presence felt in the engine room. His contribution to proceedings was to remonstrate about the untidy mess of bandage wrappings and Coke can ring pulls that littered the engine room floor. When in a crisis and in doubt be seen to be doing something even if it is making an ass of yourself. It is called leadership.

Following the events of that horrendous day in Belfast it was reported by the media that a coded warning of what was about to happen regarding the Cavehill Road bomb-that subsequently killed these three people-was picked up on the Army radio network at 1410hrs-a warning was reported as having been given one hour before the blast, by an independent female witness. That evening a statement was issued by P.I.R.A. stating that warnings had been

... human remains covered by sacks from the local coal yard.

given half an hour prior to the first explosion to the following organisations-
The Samaritans-Public Protection Agency- Rumour Service, and the Press.
Even if all, or part, of the reported warnings are true, due to the sheer scale of

the bombing operations, little time was allowed between the warning and the actual explosions for the security forces to take the vital evacuation precautions to save lives. Patently they were certainly too late for those who were killed and injured on Bloody Friday.

Personnel on duty this day were too busy going from incident to incident to be frightened. It was take a deep breath, tighten your belt, and make sure you had a set of spare underwear in your locker. All the devices had gone off so it was case of arriving assessing the situation and playing it by ear. The mood in whole city was tense and expectant no-one knew what was going to happen next. We all thought this was the P.I.R.A's final push. Time has shown us it was not. Subsequent events demonstrated that this day of infamy was only a beginning.

So endeth this lesson.

The following is a passage taken from the 1996 book *'Blood On The Flag'* the autobiography of an Irish freedom fighter James Malone.

After the Easter Uprising against British rule in Ireland in 1916, many active Irish patriots were summarily interned. Some hundreds of them were interned in Frongoch Army camp in Merionith, Wales. Along with James Malone was another internee Richard Mulcahy his dormitory Captain. Mulcahy addressed his men on how to comport themselves on their release.

> *'Freedom will never come' he said 'without revolution, and I greatly fear the Irish are too soft for the purpose of revolution. To bring revolution to a satisfactory conclusion we need bloodthirsty, ferocious men who care nothing for death or slaughter or bloodletting. Revolution is not child's work. Nor is it the business of saint or scholar. In matters of revolution, any man woman or child who is not for you is against you. Shoot them and be damned to them!*

'My heart went out to him.' said Malone.

Michael Collins-the 1921 Irish rebellion Leader-years later proclaimed Malone as his favourite spy.

Mulcahy and Malone's 'hearts' may have come and gone but these words live on. All the 'Bloody Fridays' in Northern Ireland since then stand as testimony to this murderous ethos, their contemporaries have seen to that.

McGurk's Bar...December 4th 1971 was a cool crisp evening. Blue Watch Knock-to which I had transferred as Watch Commander in March for a short period-had commenced night duty at 1800hrs. Training drills and lectures had been carried out because 'come war or go war' the routine work must go on and supper had been taken at 2000hrs. Personnel were now on their stand down period. Each had drifted off to various parts of the Station to do their own respective thing, playing snooker, table tennis, Watching T.V. or studying. After supper I had gone to the Station's workshop to check on a possible dodgy exhaust on my own car. While there, Bertie Jones, an old friend and colleague from previous times at Knock -who had moved on to greener pastures-called in to have a yarn.

The time was just around 2100hrs whenever we heard the sound of a distant explosion that reverberated off the drill yard walls. We did not know it then but in the fraction of a second that it took the sound to register on our ear drums seventeen innocent lives were being snuffed out and seventeen souls were on their way to meet their Maker. Shortly after hearing this, both of us strolled up the Station yard and went into the Watchroom. I asked the six to two (6pm-2am) dutyman on Watchroom duty, if he had heard over the radio where the explosion was, 'Yes', was his reply, 'Whitla Street's two appliances with Station Officer Vance in-charge and Chi's Emergency Salvage Tender have just booked in attendance at a '77' in Great Georges Street, no further messages yet.'

This sounded ominous, sometimes when you arrive at an incident you will either immediately request assistance or give a preliminary informative message, which indicates to Controls what further requests for assistance they might expect from the scene. A few minutes delay, or the pregnant pause as it is known in the trade, may signal that the situation is serious-has not yet been fully assessed-or that the Officer-in-Charge and his crews are so up to their eyes in it that there hasn't been time to request assistance immediately. It was some little while before this message was received.

When Davy Vance's first informative message it came stated that Mc Gurk's pub Gt. George's had been destroyed and there were a number of casualties. Little other detail was given at this time. Again experience dictated that it was unwise to give too much information regarding casualty status, over the air waves, as persons other than those to whom they were directed would normally be listening-including, probably, the very people who perpetrated it. This can lead to an unnecessary invasion of the incident by ghoulish sightseers which can hinder search and rescue operations and cause traffic congestion. Lack of information unfortunately also frustrates listeners such as ourselves who may well have a future vested interest in affairs.

At 2230hrs Controls rang me and told me that I was to proceed with the P.E. to Gt. Georges Street for 2300hrs and relieve Whitla's crews. A Pump from Chi' with a Sub Officer-in-Charge, was to accompany my Knock's appliance. I was also informed that returning Senior Officers reported at least seven fatalities and that more were expected. Four hourly reliefs are usually the norm at tasks such as this, but if you've had a rough job, its great to see relief crews arriving earlier than you anticipated. I knew by this time that D.V.[Davy Vance] and his lads were dealing with a really nasty job and would be glad to get back to the Station for a welcome breather no doubt. This was not D.V's first experience nor his last of horrific incidents. He once got a call to an actuated '77' at Bawnmore, a Catholic and Republican housing estate on the Shore Road. When he arrived he found a badly damaged car that had been in a lock-up garage. They began to find pieces of dismembered bodies but one of the macabre features was when one of the lads saw a sightless head peering out from behind the car's radiator grill.

I briefed my lads on what the current situation was at McGurk's and what we were likely to encounter. It was probable that more casualties were buried and it was going to be a dirty and loathsome job. We left the Station at 2240hrs the city centre was devoid of traffic so we made good time and arrived at Gt. George's Street at 2250hrs I looked for D.V. to report our arrival and to receive his situation report, and finally for him to do the required legal hand-over of operations to me. He wasn't immediately visible. I didn't need to be told the state of the building for it was painfully obvious. What was left of Mc Gurk's pub was by now a steaming, smoking, mound of bricks and timbers which protruded from the rubble like a pile of matchsticks. An unsupported end gable wall still stood, a rope had been slung around it and secured to a stake in the ground, to prevent a possible collapse of the wall inwards onto rescuers and any survivors there might still be trapped underneath.

It was a surreal ghost like spectacle that met our eyes. There was little sound from the would be rescuers and onlookers, and no sense of urgency seemed to prevail. The flood lights from Chi's emergency tender generator illuminated the phantom like figures of Firefighters, soldiers and civilians as they disappeared and then reappeared again in the thick fog of smoke and steam that still rose from the rubble. The acrid sickly smell of explosive still hung in the air and could be tasted on the lips. Observing these sights in those first few minutes, I felt the realisation had already set in by all those involved that the fight to save life was lost shortly after it had begun.

I saw Sub Officer Walter Wilson appear sliding and slipping down off the pile of debris- 'Wally' was an old friend of mine and had been best man at my wedding-I approached him. ' Well Walter, what's the situation?' 'Bloody awful Allan,' he replied in a distressed tone, 'When we arrived fire had broken out underneath the collapse. We could hear people screaming for help underneath, people's hands were reaching up out of the rubble. I held one person's hand and was speaking to him. As we put the water on, it turned to steam and then they yelled as it was scalding them, what could we do?' What could I say to this? What could anyone say? It was like trying to comfort someone just bereaved, the usual platitudes are of little help. All I could was to let Walter get it of his chest and then reply. ' I know Walter, nothing, a bad situation to be caught in. Go on back to the Station and try and get some rest' and with that we parted.

I then spoke to D.V. who reiterated what Walter had said. He also informed me that it was thought about twenty people were in the premises when the bomb went off. He had recovered seven bodies up to the point of our discussion. At least one body could be seen through the mass of matchwood which had formed pockets in the collapsed building. D.V. also mentioned, that the

... all in a night's work ... The author in the white helmet.

195

owner's fourteen year old daughter Mary McGurk had been reported as being upstairs with a school friend James Cromie.

Without prolonging the agony of having to explain anymore to me-as it was all too self evident-both he and his downcast crews boarded their appliances and departed for Station and no doubt welcome break.

My next thought was obvious. Where do my crews start searching. Davy had given me a lead. As we knew someone was upstairs I told Bobby Bloomer my Leading Firefighter to order the crews to start digging near the surface under the remnants of the overhanging bedroom. It wasn't long before we began to unearth what turned out to be a bed mattress and it was pulled clear. Then Bobby shouted, 'Boss there's something underneath here'. As we scraped away with our gloved hands, what looked like buttocks covered in navy blue knickers started to emerge from the rubble. Digging down further exposed the trunk and we saw that the corpse , was in fact a young girl. She was bent over double, in a head down position. What a pathetic sight it was. It looked as though she had probably been smothered by the very debris that we uncovered her from. A young life taken before it had barely begun. What an appalling waste.

The Army in their haste to recover casualties suggested bringing in a Scooby Doo-a rubber tyred excavator with tined jaws-to use as an assistance in the removal of rubble. I advised against this, as it was possible to cause further injury to persons alive and trapped-or to the human remains due to lack of sensitive handling of the corpses. Bodies should always be treated with respect because they belong to some bereaved family. I have always thought in my professional judgement that employing mechanical earth removing equipment for this type of activity is fraught with insensitivity and practical rescue problems. Make haste slowly is by far the best way. The Army, however, being the Army, my advice fell on deaf ears.

The next thing I saw and heard was this Scooby Doo being driven onto the site. So much for the advice! This had the effect of making the civilian rescuers very restless. Gerry Fitt-a very important local political-now Lord Fitt-and the clergy who were present sensed this and they tried to calm what might well become a nasty situation. For my part I approached the machine's driver in an effort to tell him to be careful and keep the bucket as low as possible on the basis if you cannot beat them at least you can control the worst of their ham fisted efforts-that I would watch the debris for him as he dug-before I could make myself understood to him, what I feared happened. There was a violent uproar and a howl of horror from the crowd. Silhouetted against the floodlights was the ghastly vision of a body of a male person impaled on the spikes of the excavators lifting grab. At this the crowd surged forward-some helped to remove the corpse of the poor unfortunate from the spikes-others immediately started to remonstrate with us and the Army. I repeated my views more forcefully this time and in the event that was the end of the Scooby Doo being used during my stay at the scene. Who knows whether that particular casualty was alive or not before being 'rescued'.

As we recovered bodies, and even before we had them fully clear of the rubble, a Catholic priest was immediately at hand to administer the Sacrament of Extreme Unction-commonly known as the Last Rites-to the deceased. Of all the Fire Service personnel there that night, I could not help but notice one young Firefighter previously unknown to me who dug like a veritable little terrier. In fact I had to order him to take a breather as he was in danger of burning himself out before we got our relief. I found out that his name was Michael (Chalky) White a recent recruit to the job. Recruits were finding that there was no time allowed for the gentle introduction to the dark side of our work as in peacetime. Our paths crossed on many occasions at jobs from that time onwards.

During our spell of search and rescue-only there was no rescue-we recovered five bodies. But that growing total for the Grim Reaper was not yet complete that night. One more person was to lose his life in the vicinity of Mc Gurk's Bar that night. Before we left for Station at approximately 0100hrs we heard a shot ring out, it came from the North Queen Street area, just around the corner from McGurk's. The Provos were active in the area, and their marksman claimed the life of one Major Alice Hankey-he was hit in the head by a sniper's shot and was mortally wounded that early morning.

Other crews worked throughout the night and by morning fifteen bodies had been recovered. D.V. and his crews came back to finish what he and his lads had started. One person was rescued alive but sadly was to succumb their injuries a short while after. The owner of the pub lost his wife and daughter in the explosion. Because no-one admitted this explosion the only reaction was that of the newspapers and news media. These in general reflected the sadness and disbelief of the populous that such an act could be perpetrated on innocents. Members of the UVF were subsequently charged with the massacre. Recently some idiot of a Sunday Times journalist tried to resurrect the event by nonsensically claiming that some of the dead were members of the IRA, anything to fill a column inch or two.

This was, at that time, another record entry of loss of life for the history books, a direct result of the to the 'Troubles' in Ulster. The bombing was later announced to have been the work of the Ulster Volunteer Force and was at that time the worst single incident in the Province. But then as we know, records are made to broken. The law of averages dictated that this one was bound to fall, sooner or later and I hoped I wouldn't be around when it did, but I was. The roll call of death for that year stood at 249 people dead as a result of violence in Northern Ireland-170 civilians-66 Army or U.D.R. personnel-and 13 R.U.C. Since the beginnings of civil unrest a total of 927 people had died. More innocents were to follow.

The Gasworks Own Goal... The old Belfast Corporation Gasworks had stood on its thirty acre site since Victorian times. The site-bounded by the river Lagan on its east side-the north end tucked in behind part of the domestic housing that made up a section of the 'Markets' area-and on the west side, behind the quarter mile long boundary wall that ran from Cromac Street into the Lower Ormeau Road. The Cromac Street area was Roman Catholic/Republican and the Lower Ormeau, Protestant/Loyalist during that period. Not until the population movements and redevelopment of the 'Markets' area in the late seventies did the Ormeau Road change its religious and political complexions. The Gasworks complex straddled this political divide.

Its was a well favoured and executed, typical brick construction by the architects and construction professionals of that period and its retort houses and support buildings were built to last. The entire site was overshadowed quite literally by an enormous 250ft high gasholder-of innovative German design-rising Leviathan like above its comparatively diminutive accompanying gasholders. This city land mark was technically unusual in that unlike its peers which visibly twisted, rose and fell in response to the demands of the consumers the gas pressure in this holder was controlled by a huge piston which rose and fell, unseen within the confines of its outer shell. Recently although the site has all but been cleared for redevelopment, the City Council in its occasional flashes of wisdom have seen fit to preserve the old clock tower for posterity, complete with it clock, all crowned in glory by a copper sheathed bell shaped cupola, resplendent with its natural and distinctive verde-gris colouring.

The Gasworks had served the City and the surrounding dormitory towns of Holywood, Bangor, Newtownards, Carrickfergus and Lisburn well over its

Old Gasworks site

long period of operational working life. I remember as a boy tramping along the length of Donegall Pass-which ran at right angles to the Lower Ormeau Road-on my way to and from school-seeing over the wall, the bucket conveyor belts carrying the coal up to feed the long line of smoking retorts, and on occasions being sent by my mother down to the Gasworks to buy some of the by-products of these retorts, such as coke or tar.

During the late sixties the Corporation had taken the decision to build a new 'state of the art' gas plant alongside Shell's newly constructed oil refinery within the east Belfast Harbour Estate to produce the City's gas supply for the future. The new gas plant was to be supplied with its raw material of petroleum naphtha-an extremely volatile by-product of Shells' manufacturing process. So it was decreed that the old gasworks production plant was to be run down and demolished, with the exceptions of the gas-holders and distribution system which was to continue to be used to store, pressure regulate, and distribute the new methane product to the city and suburbs.

While watching television one evening, whilst on night duty with White Watch Knock-the window of the T.V. room looked out in the general direction of the City centre-without warning, suddenly, through the drawn curtains we could see an expanding glow rapidly increasing in brightness. When we jumped up and pulled back the curtains back, we saw what can only be described as a massive fireball growing in intensity and rising skywards like the huge mushroom cloud of a nuclear explosion. There was no obvious sound of an accompanying explosion. Those of us that witnessed this apparition could only gaze in amazement for the few brief seconds that it took for the fireball to expand to its zenith and then to dissipate. What the hell was that, was all I could remember thinking to myself. The Brigade was at that time in dispute with personnel over the issue of an increase in the amount of emergency call out availability money which we were to be paid. No agreement had been reached on the matter and we were therefore not attending any civil disturbance calls. This is what flashed through my mind as I made my way down to the Watch room to monitor the radio, to ascertain if any appliances had been dispatched to the incident. If we at Knock were able to see it from some four miles distance, then the rest of the City must have seen it as well. God help anyone who was in close proximity to that fireball. More than anything else I was anxious to know what it was that had gone up so suddenly and with such a spectacular display.

Within minutes I heard Cadogan booking in attendance at the 'Gasworks', then Chi's Emergency Salvage Tender and T.L.P. Almost as soon as they arrived Controls gave Knock's P.E with me in-charge the call to attend. There was no time to consider or even ask if it was a civil disturbance call or not. I just responded. Assistant Divisional Officer Magill an old stalwart from Ardoyne days, arrived at the same time as my appliance, and we were both greeted by Sub Officer Tony King from Cadogan. Tony reported that one of the main gasholders had exploded, that there was little fire but after having carried out a cursory inspection he could not account for one of his crew. Norman told Tony to withdraw all personnel, then both he and I started to make our way into the site to locate anyone who might be missing and to ascertain the extent of the damage .

As we walked gingerly along the approach path from the main gate, looking ahead into the blackness trying to pick out discernible objects we could the see somewhere up ahead the flickering glow of small pockets of fires danced eerily in the darkness silhouetting pipework and small buildings nearby. Where I knew one of the gasholder should have been there was only a huge gaping space. Where had it and its contents of one and a half million cubic feet of gas gone? As we approached the chain-link perimeter fence that surrounded the gasholders enclosure the picture began to become clearer. There was an obvious pattern to the flickering flames which formed a circle around the circumference where the gasholder used to be. It then dawned on me that the gasholder had done exactly what it had been designed to do, in other words, when it empties its contents it had mechanically housed itself below ground level in its huge tank of water. Shining our torches as we drew closer to the fence, and fearful in case of any sudden eruptions of unburned gas pockets, I began to distinguish what looked like a body lying beside the fence. Was this the Firefighter Tony had thought was missing? With thumping hearts Norman and I moved closer to have a look. We shone our torches on what indeed was a corpse. The first place that the pool of light from my torch illuminated was its feet. Who ever it was had been wearing brown suede shoes. So it definitely wasn't one of ours.

We shone our torches further along the peripheral path and the next thing to meet our eyes was a full leg lying just beyond a complete torso. Looking at the corpse further back-I had forgotten in the few seconds I had looked away, I looked back to determine if he, for it was indeed a man had two legs, and yes the corpse had. So now we had three legs from self-evidentially two corpses. The question was where was the rest of the body belonging to the third leg? Norman and I went back to the main gate and told Tony of our discoveries, by this time he had located his missing Firefighter and him given a 'rocket' for his trouble. Although there was not a fire of any significance to deal with nevertheless hose lines were ordered to be run out into the complex close to the pockets of fire-they were not to be extinguished, for fear of a build up of gases-just kept under close observation in case of any possible fire spread. All appliances were to return to their respective Stations except one, a presence was to be maintained throughout the night and it was agreed that I should return at first light with a crew to try and establish exactly how many casualties there were and what had happened, although by now we had a fair idea.

At first light I proceeded with the P.E. to the Gasworks to relieve the remaining crew, the fire situation had not deteriorated through the night and the mortal remains of those killed still lay where they had fallen or were blown. Leading Firefighter Bobby Malcolm and myself began a closer inspection of the scene by now having both the benefit of daylight and a night to think about the situation. The body that lay against the chain-link fence was intact but had been blown open along the front centre of the torso, exposing the chest and abdominal cavities. The Army were still searching for the body to which the third leg belonged. As I gazed up at the chainlink fence I noticed what looked to me like clothing rags, hanging from it and fluttering in the breeze. We walked round to the river side of the fence and began to notice what would have passed for mince meat, lying scattered over a wide area of ground, that's exactly what it was, only it wasn't from an animal but from a human being.

Eventually we began to assemble a picture of what had actually happened on the previous night. Provisional IRA Active Service Unit bombers had been transporting a bomb in the direction of the Army observation post which was situated at the South side of the site which they planned to attack. They had stopped in the lee of the giant gasholder, presumably to prime their device, which had detonated prematurely. The bombers had been blown to smithereens the larger pieces of the body having been shredded by the chain-link fencing. What we saw hanging on the fence were the last vestiges of one of the bombers clothing and what we had found on the other side were the last remnants of his mortal remains.

When the bomb had detonated so close to the base of the holder it had torn a hole in the skin of the structure causing an initial escape of gas telescopic, the top half fitting into the bottom half and when the holder is which had ignited. These gasholders are made in two halves and are empty both sections together as one, descend and are housed below ground level. The holder relies on the pressure of the volume of gas contained in it at any one time to elevate the structure. The weight of the top half in turn acting as a piston, imparting downward pressure on the contents giving it the required pressure to flow into the pipelines and distribution system. When the blast ripped a hole in the holder allowing the initial loss of pressure, the piston effect took over forcing gas out at an ever increasing speed, discharging the contents in seconds and causing the huge and spectacular fireball that we had witnessed. It was too slow a release of energy to be called an explosion in the true sense of the word, where a rapid release of energy and gases takes place thus causing blast damage, and luckily there was no damage to other adjacent gasholders in this instance. As Bobby and I discussed the scenario Divisional Officer Peter Neeson arrived from the Communications Department, Brigade H.Qs. He brought a video camera along that was on trial/loan from the Fire Service Department of the Home Office. He asked me to give a running commentary on what we suspected had happened whilst he videoed the scene. This was probably the first occasion a video had been used for such purposes in the U.K. Fire Service, but their popularity has grown in recent years and they are now considered an essential training aid.

One of my crew on this occasion was a relatively new recruit and as all Firefighters have to sooner or later experience their first corpse, I asked Jim if he would wish to avail himself of the opportunity to go over and have a look at the body lying beside the fence. As he walked away my attention was momentarily directed towards a small outbreak of fire on the tank periphery where it had disappeared at ground level, I sent some of the lads over to investigate. By the time I turned back to Jim he had already seen the corpse and was standing leaning over a small wall being, as I thought, sick, but before we could offer comfort, his head flew back, his helmet coming off at the same time and he fell on the ground in a complete faint. It was only a momentary thing and he came round straight away, more embarrassed than hurt. Unfortunately for him this was not to be the end of his embarrassment. Putting a brave face on it he got up and began to assist in running out hose towards this new outbreak of fire. This necessitated going past the fatality, as he ran past the body I saw him avert his gaze to the left in order to avoid eye contact. He promptly tripped headlong over the full length leg that lay just beyond the body. Clearly this was not his day. No more can be said.

As we prepared to leave the scene and return to Station in time to go off duty at 0900hrs I was sitting in the appliance with the crew just outside the main gate. What we witnessed, was for me, one of the most disgusting and degenerative acts of barbarism I am sure I have seen in my service in the Brigade. An action by those who, presumably were ordered into the Province to prevent such atrocities in a so called civilised society. I felt it was more in keeping with a scene from a big game hunt in Africa, when the trophies are being exhibited after the kill. The Army had obviously been collecting bits and pieces of the human remains scattered about the site. We watched inside the main entrance as a young soldier held aloft a large plastic bag containing some of these human remains which were clearly visible-as he was being photographed by his colleague-whilst saying into the camera-'Taig meat'-a pejorative term for Catholic.

Now while it was clearly a case of 'us or them' with these young Army squaddies and poetic justice might have ruled the day, personally if it had been me in their position I would have simply been content to be alive the morning after.

Some years later I got to know someone whom I didn't know at the time of this 'own goal' who was there that morning. We were swapping 'war stories' when he surprised me by disclosing to me that he also had been there at the Gasworks that morning as well, helping to collect remains for the pathologist's office in order to help identify the three corpses which it was later disclosed was the actual the number of P.I.R.A Volunteers who perished during this operation. He and his colleague were working together, when one of them found a human tongue. One asked the other what was to be done with it, the reply was 'well there's a body stick it in his mouth'. The next day both of these men were called in before their superior officer, who said, 'right, which one of you two is the joker'? Silence, they did not know what was coming next, 'I've just received a phone call from the pathologist office', saying he has a corpse with two tongues.

La Mon... La Mon was yet another example of mans inhumanity to man in Northern Ireland. Twelve innocents from the 'Collie Club' were slaughtered one evening in February 1978. Whenever a terrorist bombing is launched against an industrial or commercial target the terrorists know full well what the potential consequences of a successful attack can mean, even if these consequences are not immediately and fully comprehended by the public. An attack can embody one or any multiple combination of acts leading to potentially disastrous consequences. The more obvious being-fatalities and injuries to people-destruction of property with consequent loss of jobs- business and production-rebuild costs and personal injury compensation claims. The imponderables that are difficult to quantify are the mental scars that are left directly on the individuals involved, their relatives and friends and the residual affects of fear and disruption that have been foisted on the community. All of these ingredients contribute to making the attack a success in the eyes of the perpetrators. It is not unusual that all of these set of circumstances should come together in a bombing. When they do they have the most devastating effect. This was to be the case following the horrific fire bomb attack on the La Mon House Hotel on the 17th February, 1978.

Gransha Mills was an old Huguenot settlement built by James La Mon on this site in 1794. The original sandstone door lintel which reads, 'This House was built by James La Mon 1794. Stone Mason J.F.Orr', can still be seen in the old Huguenot farm house. It was purchased by the Huddleson family in 1922 from Danny Lamont a direct descendant of James La Mon. The Huddlesons-being of farming stock farmed and kept a dairy herd until 1965, when Isabel Huddleson decided to open a farm guest house-thus creating a hostelry to provide catering for celebrations, functions, and wedding receptions and as a means of supplementing their farming income.

The success of this initial venture was evidenced by the rapid decline in their farming activities and the obsolescent dairy buildings were soon taken over for use as dining areas and a restaurant. An alcohol licence was obtained in 1971.

La Mon House Hotel is situated on this old site which is some four miles beyond the East Belfast city boundary. It still nestles barely visible, hidden behind trees, just of the Gransha Road and is equi-distant between Belfast and the satellite small towns of Comber and Ballygowan. It enjoyed solitude, peace, and tranquillity and was a relaxing and convenient haven for those wishing to resort to its pleasant, secluded surroundings for food and drink, up until that fateful night.

The La Mon-the creation of the Huddleson family Isabel and Wesley-was as a family run business. The partners employed around 200 full and part time staff. It began as an old country dwelling and since its inception had expanded both structurally and business wise, to become renowned for its quality of food and warmth of reception by its hosts and their carefully chosen, professional staff. I remember fondly, myself and friends on many occasions, tucking into the seemingly inexhaustible-all you could eat-special Sunday and evening buffets. Oh! blissful days and nights. This was all to change for the owners, staff and patrons on that night in 1978.

Red Watch on night duty at Knock Station were the custodians of East Belfast's fire safety that evening . At around 2020hrs a call was received to an actuated *'77' at the 'La Mon House Hotel.'* Chi's Emergency Salvage Tender and Ladas Drive Retained Station were also mobilised, the attendance address coming within the Ladas Station's response area. La Mon was some three miles distant from the city limits but Knock were also obliged to attend as it was within their Shadow Boundary response area. All the appliances that were responding that evening converged on the outer ring road at the Castlereagh Road roundabout and left the City via the Ballygowan Road. None of the fire crews knew what horrors lay ahead that night. As they sped along the Ballygowan Road enroute to the incident they passed Roselawn Cemetery which was to be the final resting place for some of the guests who had been enjoying themselves just a mile or so away down the road in the La Mon .

When the first crews arrived the building, which was mainly single storey was well alight, people who had managed to escape the inferno were running about, panic stricken, yelling and screaming, some searching for friends and relatives, yet others were suffering from varying degrees of burns. The tasks that confronted all would-be rescuers and Firefighters alike was a daunting and simultaneous one-a serious fire had to attacked, contained, and extinguished-searching BA crews whilst they worked had to be protected with jets of water as they searched to locate and rescue missing persons trapped within the building-existing obvious survivors had to be calmed and treated. All in all it was a nightmare scenario of mammoth proportions for the Fire and Ambulance Services.

Because the La Mon was located in a rural setting water supplies were yet another major problem. Augmenting water supplies had to be found and secured. Although there was two hundred gallons carried on board each pumping appliances even when relayed jointly from one Pump through one another it was well understood that this supply would not last long nor hope to quell the blaze and would only 'buy' a calculated breathing space. An immediate 'make-up'-a call for further assistance-of additional appliances was requested from the fireground by radio though given the disastrous rapidity of the spread of fire through the buildings this call was primarily for man-power purposes to attended to the self rescued casualties. Use was rapidly made of a small stream that ran along the periphery of the hotel grounds to augment water supplies but it was to be one of those incidents when the cause had already been lost even before the appliances had been dispatched from their Stations to the inferno. Hotel staff were evacuating the building following the explosion when an anonymous caller gave a telephone warning-'Better late than never' is not a luxury that can ever be applied in bombings.

Even if fire appliances, as a pre-emptive action, had been standing-by before the fire bombs had been detonated, it is unlikely that the fire could have been successfully contained, given the intensity of the firestorm effect of the fire complimented by the stiff breeze that blew that night.

Devices had been armed and placed outside the large patio windows of the dining room. These devices contained a do-it-yourself cocktail of petrol and other ingredients designed to burn and maim, in a similar manner to those of the U.S. napalm bombs of the Vietnam era which also killed, burned, and maimed, so effectively. When these devices detonated they instantaneously discharged a fireball blast into the room in which forty eight guests were dining. The unfortunates received the full effects of the fireball blast. There was no chance of escape. Twelve of the forty eight in this room were to die instantly-all Protestants-twenty three others were injured- and only thirteen got out safely scarred only in their minds. The fire crews stood witness to the corpses of people which had been burned alive where they had sat or stood, while their bodies were instantaneously incinerated.

Whenever the fire had passed its zenith Alec Withers the attending Senior Officer concentrated his attention on the burnt out area of the dining room where the 'Collie Club' had been enjoying their peaceful and harmless function. He ordered further water jets to cool down the smouldering and charred remains. As the steam and smoke slowly dissipated he was able to walk through the room-he saw the distinct shapes of corpse after corpse after corpse-shrouded by ash-silhouetted and frozen in death in the macabre shapes in which they had fallen at the moment of their deaths. Later the Police were to take the unusual step of publishing pictures of some of the corpses of the deceased. The day following in pre dawn swoops the Police arrested and held twenty suspects for questioning in relation to the outrage.

In those first few months of 1978 over one hundred explosions had already taken place in Northern Ireland. My old colleague Bobby Bloomer had a son who had recently joined the Brigade. His son attended the incident that night, this was certainly was his baptism of fire.

La Mon was eventually, to rise Phoenix like from the ashes, the rebuild cost was some £2.5 million pounds. The Huddleston family regrouped after the horrific consequences of that night and rebuilt a bigger and more luxurious establishment which has also thrived and prospered. When the name of La Mon is mentioned, anyone who remembers the horrific events of that night automatically identifies it in their mind's eye, as an act of infamy and a night that is a milestone alongside all of those other milestones scattering the roads of Ulster that have lead to nowhere, save to more pain and suffering.

The following evening the Belfast Telegraph carried on its front page an article entitled 'The Way to La Mon' with an effigy of twelve coffins and ghosts struggling out of them.

The following few pages are Isabel Huddleson's personal recollection of the night of 17th February 1978. Seven family members of hers which included two children were in the La Mon that night.

'On the night of Thursday 17th February 1978, we had a full house booked with customers enjoying dinner in the Grill Bar. The 'Collie Club' had booked for sixty, forty eight eventually arrived for dinner in the Peacock Suite. The 'Junior Motor Cycle Club' had booked approximately five hundred for dinner, four hundred seated in the Main Banqueting Hall with one hundred Juniors in the Gransha Room for their great prize giving evening, my children were included with two friends from school. I had full staff rostered approximately two hundred in all. The security guard arrived at 7.30pm to take control of the building, which he checked, locked off back and front of the hotel and put up signs for everyone to enter by the Banqueting Reception; as was the practice on all evenings when we had large numbers of diners to control; thus controlling access and entry to the hotel, everyone was searched.

At approximately 8.20pm I was in the kitchen, hosting the 'Collie Club' function, soup and main course was served, main course flats lifted and the six waitresses went to the pantry to collect the chosen sweets. I walked round the Peacock Suite and counted guests while I enquired if everyone had enjoyed their meal. The atmosphere was of a happy gathering. I returned to the kitchen and the six waitresses (included three from the same family) were lined up with their trays awaiting my instruction to serve sweets; at the other servery in the kitchen; while my head chef was putting out the meat flats to the other five hundred guests in the Banqueting Hall; with my son Wesley and James the Banqueting Manager in charge. I had just called to the girls to serve the sweets when the unmerciful thud rocked the building and lights either went out or flickered sufficiently for me to return to the Peacock Room, just a few steps away . As I tried to enter the room smoke was blinding me, I turned and came out and a second thud blew the dining room door open and hit me on the back. My staff were leaving assisted by senior members, we all thought something like equipment had blown up but we never suspected a bomb. I called to my son Wesley and James to bring torches to see what had happened to the dining room. People started to come out they were all blackened. I stretched out my hand to help, a man said 'don't touch me', he had no flesh on his hands. There were two other

208

doors from the Dining Room, Reene started pulling people out, putting a table cloth over her mouth to breath . A member of the band came up to me and said he had just answered a call box in which a voice stated to get out there was a bomb at La Mon and he replied 'too late it has gone off'.

We ran to Reception and the other entrance to the Dining Room and formed a human chain by lying on the floor, as it was almost impossible to breathe standing up but there appeared no sign of anyone else left in the room. We retired to the car park, and I found my children who were being looked after by a guest, we were sure we had left no-one in the building. It was not until later that Firefighters broke the news that there were bodies in the room.

Later as I put together a table plan of the room for the Police, they were to confirm that a table of six that were sitting at the patio windows had perished at the same table. Twelve of the forty eight 'Collie Club' members died. My nephew Michael had served the McCracken table wine and had went to the bar for the change when the bomb exploded. My nephew Michael had heart complaint and died approximately six months later. We lost twelve customers on that terrible night but the families of the injured and deceased suffered much more.

If the bomb had been placed at the large banqueting area; which was completely surrounded by a perimeter fence; it is unthinkable what the death toll could have been. Such was the extent of these mindless, murderous animals who planted this terrible torture on their own human race.

But I rest assured they will meet their Maker for the justice they deserve. My thanks to all who helped us, as surely we needed strength to continue'.

Isabel Crawford nee Huddleson August 1996.

Her Majesty Queen Elizabeth II sent her sympathy offering encouragement to Mrs Huddleson to carry on and extended an invitation to attend Buckingham Palace.

'Before' the Holocaust.

'After' the Holocaust.

The **Abercorn Restaurant and Donegall Street...** Although the Abercorn restaurant and Donegall Street bombings were two separate and distinct outrages, I have chosen to link them together, because they had a number of things in common. They were the two most horrific bomb outrages that were carried out in Belfast during the month of March. They were deliberately directed at civilian targets-they were intended to slaughter and maim innocent people-no adequate warnings were given-and the Fire Service along with the other emergency services were left as usual picking up the bits of humanity that the bombs tore asunder.

...removing a victim at the Abercorn.

Saturday 4th March, 1972 was to be the first of two days in this month when an atrocity was to be perpetrated on innocent civilians in Belfast. That day a small explosive device was placed in the crowded Abercorn restaurant in Cornmarket, in the heart of the City. Two people were killed and 130 injured. Two sisters who had been shopping for a wedding trousseau, each lost both their legs. Later the bride-to-be recovered and went on to be married. Life must go on.

I had been crossing through the city centre in the late afternoon-enroute to Ardoyne for night duty-I remember passing the bottom of Ann Street and was able to see up the full length of the busy shopping street to Cornmarket. Flashing blue emergency lights were in abundance and pandemonium seemed to be the order of the day-but I could not stop to offer assistance. I heard the news when I reached my Station that the Abercorn had been bombed. Speaking afterwards to Lloyd Brown-one of the first attending personnel-I learned just how horrific the injuries were that people had sustained. The device had been placed in a very confined area. Lloyd recalled that when he entered the restaurant people were in a complete state of shock and he saw numerous people with limbs missing. Dismembered feet and hands lay all over the place, Lloyd and a colleague recovered two different feet from the debris. There were people with penetration wounds caused by splinters from the restaurant's furniture lodged in limbs and torsos. To ease the excruciating pain of one girl with a leg from one of the chairs through her thigh Lloyd lay down on the floor in an effort to support this girl to keep the shrapnel fouling the floor from increasing the agony of her personal nightmare and to give her moral and physical support until an Ambulance crew could take over. Following the incident B.B.C. Radio interviewed Royal Victoria Hospital surgeon John Robb who had treated the injured on their arrival at hospital. He described even more graphically, the mutilations of the innocents that had occurred that day.

The 20th March was to see another multiple death bombing in the city centre. This time in Donegall Street. Chi' received a call to a suspect '77' in the vicinity of Donegall Street, Davy Vance responded as Officer-in-Charge, fortunately the appliances got stuck in a traffic jam at the bottom of Waring Street, which lead into Donegall Street. Before they could extricate themselves from the congestion the responding crews heard a bomb explode nearby. The delay in being unable to proceed probably saved the crews from death or injury for they would have arrived within seconds of where the car bomb had been placed and would probably have parked their appliances in the vicinity of the bombers vehicle. The old maxim rang loud in Brigade personnel's ears, *'Would be rescuers should not become victims'.*

When the crews eventually arrived at the scene the sight that met their eyes was simply one of carnage. The car bomb had been parked close to the Belfast Newsletter premises. The Police had received a hoax warning, the exact location of the actual bomb was not given. The Police who had been directing people to where they thought was a place of safety, instead, inadvertently, directed them even closer to the car bomb. Six people died, including two off-duty Policemen, who had been assisting with the evacuation and three of the City's refuse collection men, who were working at the rear of their bin lorry. More than one hundred other people were injured. On Friday 23rd March P.I.R.A. issued a statement saying that adequate warning of the explosion had been given.

To give some appreciation-if not understanding-of the ferocity and intensity of the violence and conflict which had taken place prior to and during this period, here are some of the published casualty figures.

Since 'Direct Rule' was introduced on the 24th March 1972 up until the 7th May that year eighteen civilians and nine soldiers had been killed. There was one hundred and nineteen explosions Province-wide. Six weeks prior to

... photographed from the Belfast Newsletter.

'Direct Rule' twenty eight civilians and thirteen soldiers had died, there were one hundred and seventy explosions. By the 10th July 1972 since 1969 there was a total of four hundred and seventeen dead and in 1972 alone two hundred and six people died violently in Ulster. This set against a 'peacetime' murder rate the lowest in the world.

Listed below are a series of some of the more serious incidents that took place in Belfast during the months of February and March 1972 which further illustrates the concentration of terrorist activity that took place within a very short time span.

Tuesday	1st February 1972.	*18 fires overnight in Belfast.*
Wednesday	2nd February 1972.	*8 car bombs and two buses burned.*
Thursday	3rd February 1972.	*9 buses damaged since Monday.*
Friday	11th February 1972.	*5 explosions in Belfast.*
Monday	14th February 1972.	*5 explosions and fire in Corry's timber yard.*
Tuesday	29th February 1972.	*20 cars wrecked in car showroom on Shankill Road.*
Saturday	4th March 1972.	*Explosion in Abercorn restaurant 2 killed 130 injured.*

Monday	6th March 1972.	*Car bomb in car park behind ABC cinema Grosvenor Road.*
Thursday	9th March 1972.	*4 killed in explosion in house in Clonard Street.*
Wednesday	15th March 1972.	*2 Ammunition Technical Officers killed Grosvenor Road.*
Monday	23rd March 1972.	*6 killed and 19 seriously Injured in car bomb explosion Donegall St.*

In addition to the above list of mayhem and murder the Belfast Corporation Transport department had, from 1969 up to June 1972, lost 84 buses with 100 damaged. 'Ulsterbus' which served the remainder of the Provinces transport requirements lost 130 buses, the majority of which had been the target of incendiary attacks. Later buses on specific routes through specific enclaves were deliberately targeted to ensure that the transport Authority would remove the service entirely to that area. This was to allow the proliferation of 'black taxi-cabs' which were controlled and run by the appropriate paramilitary organisation in order to fund sometimes ordinary criminal activities but mostly to finance the day to day running of the military movement. This general pattern of criminality/terrorism was to continue in varying degrees up to the present day. It will eventually become a civilised Mafia like organisation when peace finally breaks out staffed by people who know how to make an easy living and will leave a criminal legacy for generations to come.

'...missed the bus to heaven's gate...'

214

Looting... All the Fire Brigades in the United Kingdom have as their foundation emblem an eight pointed star with the individual name of their Brigade, its motto, and coats-of-arms mounted within an encompassing red circle concentric to the framework of badge in toto. This badge is displayed either as a cap or helmet badge worn proudly by personnel or depicted on the side of fire appliances as a handy focussing point for vandal marksmen. Throughout the ages other emergency services world-wide have adopted the eight pointed star or stylised versions of it, in one design form or another encapsulating their own particular insignia whether it be flames, bugles, or ladder etc,. However disappointingly, it is not widely known by who those who wear the star with pride, what its origins were.

The star in fact is not a star at all but is a variant of the cross paty, adapted and adopted, in the 11th century by the religious/military order of the Knights Hospitallers of Saint John of Jerusalem during the time of the Crusades. The Knights Hospitallers were primarily an organisation providing care and succour to passing pilgrims on their way to the Holy Land. The period equivalent of today's McDonalds.

The eight points or *'Tenets'* of the cross were said to represent the knightly virtues of *Tact, Perseverance, Gallantry, Loyalty, Dexterity, Explicitness, Observation and Sympathy*. All the virtues one would expect to find in those who would seek to give comfort and aid to those in need. It is rare however to find all of these attributes in any one person whether or not they serve in a humanitarian Service. Some of the qualities missing from many individuals could be replaced by less audacious ones such as *'Greed'* and *'Avarice.'* It is perhaps regrettable that the Belfast Fire Brigade did not have as its emblem this eight pointed star to act as a guiding light to some of its members but Belfast in fact displayed a round badge sans star which was unique in the British Fire Service. Belfast Corporation's Latin motto was *'Pro Tanto Quid Retribuamus'.* A less literal and certainly a less flattering translation of this Latin expression might read *'For what we give, what shall we receive?'* I am drawn to think of those moving and fitting words spoken by President John F. Kennedy at his inauguration. *'Think not what your country can do for you'. 'But what you can do for your country?'* Sadly whether consciously or not, some of the Brigade's personnel were to besmirch their own virtue and unforgivably the virtuous and laudable motto of the Brigade by literally taking its motto at its face value. These uniformed malefactors were not content with the City's remuneration for services rendered but preferred to augment their daily bread by looting. Perhaps, and it is no excuse, when the world around you goes crazy the ethically weak can be expected to react that way, who knows.

Yes indeed-looting-a rather stark and odious verb to find used in a book about the Fire Service, did take place by Brigade personnel. Its meaning is described succinctly in the dictionary as 'plunder'. This is one of the more polite descriptions. Either way, it is at its best, an obnoxious anti social practice, and at its worst, simply criminal conduct. Human nature being as diverse as it is, and given people with different behavioural and social values, it is inevitable that these basic features must factor in concert with greed, avarice, jealousy, covetousness to determine those who are inclined to engage in this deplorable practice. In my Mum's plain English it was all about how you were brought up and knowing right from wrong! In a few Firefighter's cases, imagined need, perhaps but never real need. This practice was considered by some as a 'perk' of the job. Who gave them the right to determine that and in so doing bringing shame on the honest majority? Whatever it is that stimulates and motivates someone to partake in the practice it is not a pretty sight to behold when you see it with your own eyes. It is a form of temporary insanity that seems to completely overwhelm the normally decent behavioural patterns of previously rational people.

I can fully understand why military law allows for the shooting of people who do it but I'm not quite sure if this would have applied to the members of H.M.Forces or the Public in Belfast, during our unofficial civil war for it was really never put to the test publicly, at least to my knowledge. Most ordinary people will never witness the act of looting, only those who have can begin to appreciate what it is like to see a person someone you used to respect, out of control with that wild eyed look, oblivious to all else that is going on around them, completely engrossed in the act. I have even been asked on the fireground, by one long serving Firefighter for permission to steal from a home which had been vacated in a hurry during what was then, Belfast's version of ethnic cleansing the looting of civil liberty. What clinical unemotional terms these two words ethnic cleansing are. These terms cosmetically and conveniently hide all the misery and suffering that is the reality of such events-the fear etched in the faces-the former residents scurrying along the street clutching those few prized possessions-as neighbour after neighbour torches their pride and joy to prevent the 'other side' from moving in or looting. The Great and the Godly sitting around their negotiating tables later have not 'tasted' these unsavoury 'treats'. What would they really know about it.

Shortly after I joined the service in '63 I became aware that looting went on. My first posting after leaving the Training School was to Red Watch, Chi'. A call was received to a house in Divis Street, afterwards to be nicknamed 'Our Uncles', which lay at the lower end of the Falls and Castle Street not far from the city centre. I wasn't on the first attendance, and for a house fire it was unusual for relief crews to be needed, but needed they were. Before we relieved, the first crews returning to Station were talking gleefully about a large amount of cash which had been discovered in the house. When I arrived on the relief crew I saw that it was a terrace house and on entering discovered that it was quite literally a slum. Fire had broken out downstairs and had spread up the staircase to the first floor. I was detailed to help clear out the debris from this floor which entailed shovelling it out through the first floor window into the yard below. Shovelled out along with the rubble were half crowns, shillings and florins. While doing this I and my colleague were interrupted by a Divisional Officer and a Sub Officer who ordered us to quit what we were doing and leave the room. As we left I thought it strange that they closed the bedroom door behind us and several minutes elapsed before it was opened again and we were ordered back to work. This Divisional Officer retired within a year or so of this incident having completed his pensionable service. He and his wife bought a little hotel over the border in County Donegal in the Republic and lived there happily ever after but I didn't think a Divisional Officer's retirement pension would have stretched that far?

We were then told to clear out under the double-bed. Beneath it we removed old timber butter boxes, which took up the floor space under the bed, and these in turn were stuffed full of shoe boxes containing unopened pay packets, from the old County Down Railway, that dated back to 1948, with the name Feeney on them, there were also wads of white five pound notes and red ten shilling ones. The amount marked on the packets varied around eight pounds and some odd pence. Other boxes were found buried on the staircase, half covered by fallen plaster. By this time the friendly local constabulary began to take an interest, I remember one constable coming casually into the room, trying to look nonchalant and 'matter of fact'. At one point he saw a basin on top of a tallboy and tipped it up for a wee nosey, I don't know what he expected to find but I'm sure it wasn't what he got. As he tipped it over he was covered from head to foot in urine. He literally got the wee all over his wee nosey. We pretended not to notice, he left the room quicker than he had come in amidst much tittering.

We were ordered to take the boxes down and leave them on the pavement for collection by the Police, for transportation to a bank, there must have been tens of thousands of pounds in them. The car that came to collect the boxes didn't have the appearance of an official Police vehicle to me. The Belfast Telegraph published a photograph of the haul in its evening edition that night. The next day I was surprised at the number of Firefighters I bumped into scurrying about the city centre. I am sure the banks wondered at the stampede of grannies and granddads with so many grandchildren to be cared for, who all of a sudden needed to cash in their old notes before they became invalid.

Then there was the Ulster Transport Authority goods yard fire on the Grosvenor Road in the mid-sixties. A goods train from Cork in the Republic of Ireland had caught fire or had been torched as it sat on the sidings. The ten wooden box car wagons contained bottles of spirits which included, Hennessy Brandy and Cork Dry Gin, Waterford crystal, and foodstuffs such as the new Cadbury's development brand of dried Smash instant potato mix. It was a fierce fire, cases of booze could be heard exploding deep within the closely stacked box cars and gallons of blue flamed burning liquid would drop through onto the railway tracks below. It took about four hours to quell the blaze but the salvage operation and damping down lasted for days and days and days. During this period great care was taken by the attending crews to ensure that the wagons containing the spirits were uncoupled from the others and kept well cooled by water jets just in case anymore of the precious nectar was lost and consumed by the greedy fire, instead of slaking the thirst of the humans for whom it was created. Water damage to the Smash wagons caused their contents to swell and pour out all over the platform and trackside. It was like ploughing through a waist deep snow drift.

I was stationed at the old Albertbridge Station at the time and it was funny to hear old 'Betsy' the Second World War Merryweather Major Pump return to the Station yard after a spell of 'salvage', with the clinking of glass coming from within the deep recesses of her bowels. Many a hot toddy was enjoyed after that fire. It was reminiscent of 'Whiskey Galore' only on this occasion it was 'Brandy Galore', or then again, it could have been called 'Smash and Grab' or 'the Great Train Robbery'. Whatever you care to refer to it as but I dare say many a fine piece of Waterford crystal still adorns a few china cabinet displays of many a retired Firefighter in and around Belfast to this day.

It was not until the fire bombing campaign of Belfast's commercial city centre in the early seventies that I realised the endemic proportions to which looting had, by then, reached. However, hopefully the ordinary householder should harbour no fear for their present day property, on reading this. There was and perhaps still is an unwritten code of 'ethics' relating to personal private property although as we have just seen even that was not sacrosanct. These 'code of the unethical' arguments were used by some in an attempt to justify looting and included the statement that it was coming off a broad back-namely the insurance company-a multi-national-or that the goods would be destroyed anyway, which undoubtedly they were but all this is weak justification for common or garden theft.

I shall never forget my wife Sandra who in the early days of our marriage was a travelling representative for a company selling sewing machines, coming home one night from work and immediately saying to me, 'I never thought I would be ashamed to admit to anyone that my husband is a Firefighter.' When I asked her why? She related to me that she had been demonstrating a machine to a couple who had a shop in the old variety market called Smithfield, near the city centre and which was a landmark flea market in Belfast at that time. This permanent enclosed site had multi-occupancy shops and sold just about everything from a needle to an anchor. Joe Kavanagh had several shops there and his sales motto was 'I buy anything.' I knew, as did the rest of Belfast that it had just undergone a serious terrorist fire attack and damage was extensive, the wife of the house said to Sandra, 'you should have seen the stuff the Firefighters were carrying away'. Sandra just nodded politely. The 'Toolbox' shop apparently was a popular target by some of the Brigade personnel during that particular salvaging expedition. I already knew what a fiasco it had been through the Brigade grapevine. So in keeping with the ancient custom we all got 'tarred with the one brush'.

A practice that was once an exception to the rule was fast becoming the rule. This was mainly due to the upsurge in the number of large conflagrations happening in the city centre. Some considered it an added perk of the job and a ritual to be indulged in. I was given many accounts where water jets were secured in position and allowed to play on the fire, whilst branch-men went off to have a 'wee look around'.

One Officer-in-Charge's exploits earned him the sobriquet of Ali Baba, he didn't quite have forty thieves under his command but the number he did have were well enough organised in that they were able to account for a considerable amount of plunder during the height of the fire bombings in Belfast's city centre. Personnel on one occasion had operations so well honed and were familiar enough with the internal daily movements of the Brigade duty driver that arrangements were made for him to collect an amount of selected timber. This was from the scene of a fire bombing which occurred at one of the main timber importing merchants in the dock area. 'GLE' was the favoured vehicle for such operations, 'GLE' being the registration of the old 1950's Ford box van used for general duties and internal mail runs. It had been bequeathed to the newly amalgamated Brigade in 1973 from the N.I.F.A. as part of its contribution to the new order. GLE was something of a joke and embarrassment to those personnel detailed to drive it. This wagon was more reminiscent of a Black Maria used in one of Stan Stennet's 1920s Keystone Cop movie epics. It always attracted quite a few stares from the public as it rattled through Belfast. Many a nervous ride was taken with 'GLE' by some personnel riding shot gun over its contraband cargo. Who would ever think of stopping a 'Paddy Wagon' even if it was painted red?

By way of a light-hearted interlude in what is a serious matter, most incidents do have their funny side, I'll call time out for a few sentences to relate one of these stories, pertaining to the end use of ill gotten gains. I recall the time whenever a chemist's shop in North Street had been burned. It had a large quantity of condoms in stock, some of these, due to the volume of water that had been used to extinguish the fire were by now floating out with the excess water along the street to find their way into the sewers. No doubt this would ultimately have been their eventual destination anyway, however in this instance, they had not fulfilled their ordained function. A large number of these contraceptives were rescued from going down the tubes, as it were, with the probable intention, in some cases, of being used for their original purpose. But of course you always get the wag on every Watch and every Station and so the creation 'The Phantom Condom Bomber' had arrived on the scene.

All he needed was a good supply of the missiles, loaded with the correct size of charge, the advantage of height, and the eye of a good marksman. With this combination and of course an Watch Commander with a sense of humour, he could keep a Watch at bay and in fear for hours, moving from one secret vantage point to another, striking at will. Some poor unfortunate, would be going about his lawful business on Station, when splosh, a direct hit or a near miss. Either way they would usually be deluged by a condom bomb, filled to near bursting point with water. Personnel were to be seen cowering in corners, reduced to quivering wrecks, unfit to respond to fire calls, due to the attacker having the advantage of the element of terrorist surprise not knowing where the next one was coming from. It was a harmless way of letting off steam, settling a grudge, evening up a score, or just plain devilment. Everyone was a target and everyone a potential terrorist, it was the very odd sourpuss who took exception to the prankster. In many cases a truce had to be called before 'operations' got out of hand but this truce was usually at the behest of the Watch Commander, of course if he could be found that was. Unless you have seen one of these weapons filled it is difficult to believe the volume of liquid they can hold. This is either overkill on the manufacturers part or pandering to the male ego. I once found one on my bed in Cadogan, filled to capacity, about to go off. It was like trying to man-handle a large jelly, without it being on a plate, and of course 'whoosh !' off it went before I could get it into the bathroom.

The Fire Brigade were by no means the only culprits in the 'liberating' of goods game at this time. I recall the fire in the Athletic Stores. This was a well stocked sports shop in Wellington Place which is alas no more. Following the fire a few seemingly injured parties were spotted limping stiff legged in the direction of Queen Street Police Station, just around the corner. I often wondered whether their golf handicaps improved after this 'liberation' of equipment. Then there was one of the many fires that engulfed the main Co-op building in York Street. A few drab green military Bedford four tonners were enlisted and seen, backed up into the loading bay at the rear, to 'salvage' a number of electrical appliances. Those were the days boys, weren't they?

At times during an upsurge of incendiarism-prevention of looting being better than cure-I would periodically, assemble personnel of whatever Watch and Station I happened to be in charge of at the time and address them on the subject. It was my type of terror tactics. My theme would simply be, that I did not wish to be an accessory, before, during or after anyone else's fact. I would go on to say, if caught, these thieves stood a good chance of not only being prosecuted, but would lose their job, all their pension rights, and monies already contributed thereto. I left it at that. It was obvious however, that on many occasions my words had simply fallen on stony ground. How do you save people from themselves?

There was the odd occasion when we returned to the Station from a call when I would find a little 'parcel' sitting on my bed-immediately without opening it to see what it contained I would go straight to the Station Watchroom and announce over the loudspeaker system, that if anyone had misplaced a parcel it could be collected from the Watchroom. I would then wait for a reasonably respectable length of time, so that no embarrassment would be caused, and return to the Watchroom from whence the little 'gift' would have disappeared.

I always felt how kind and thoughtful Firefighters were, which in human terms they are indeed the salt of the earth, but on occasions like this I preferred to forgo their milk of human kindness in case it went sour.

It was increasingly obvious to all concerned that this state of affairs could not be allowed to continue, for it had become endemic in Belfast. Personnel were eventually officially warned of the dire consequences of their actions, if anyone was caught thieving. The question was who was going to pull the plug? It didn't turn out to be anyone from the Service. I don't believe anyone from senior rank down to junior, would have felt confident enough to enact a purge for fear they would have had the finger of suspicion pointed at them or have had lies and accusations directed towards them, perhaps even threats of retribution. Fire appliances were even searched on occasions by Officers-in-Charge before leaving the fireground. Police were aware of what was going on, but no positive proof had been forthcoming, and eventually an example had to be made of someone. The sacrificial lamb of the 'Cinderella service'; was about to be handed to them on a plate. Let he that is without sin cast the first stone. It had not officially been cast as yet, but it was about to be, by he that was without sin, the department store Argos. Remember the Argos discount store fire in Cornmarket? The Fire Brigade will never forget it. Following their fire the Argos management had found that a lot of the stock which had not been involved in fire had been 'moved to a place of safety'. This was reported to the Police who themselves had taken refuge in the building after the conflagration. The evidence was too substantial and the pressure from the management too sustained for the complaint to be ignored, the Police were bound to investigate the whereabouts of the wandering goods, and they did.

Enquiries lead the Police to the Brigade. It had been reported amongst other things that a Firefighter was seen openly flaunting wrist watches, displayed up the full length of his arm, having 'rescued' them from the fire. They set up their investigation team in the recreation room of Chi' and interviewed all who were in attendance at the fire, and also the subsequent relief crews. One of the investigating officers was a namesake of mine, whom I didn't know, but who was years later to become a good friend. Eventually a number of personnel were charged with theft and receiving stolen goods. Nine Firefighters were arrested and eventually they were prosecuted in court and were convicted, their ranks ranging from Firefighter up to and including Sub Officer. They each received varying lengths of suspended sentences. Some years later in discussion with Ferville-the investigating Police officer who had a soft spot for the Brigade and its personnel-told me if they had all sung dumb 'we would never have got any convictions'. Not even the Police's hearts were keen to pursue the issue, but pursue it they did. Perhaps they were fearful of throwing bricks out of their own glasshouse?

While the solicitors in any one of the cases of the accused might reasonably have argued in mitigation that in the case of his client this was the first time that his client had ever been accused of this, or any other type of offence, it really does not butter many parsnips. What he actually meant and what he should be stating is that this is the first time his client has been caught for the offence of looting. That is how it was with the light fingered gentry within the Brigade and unfortunately this one publicised incident was only the tip of the iceberg.

Speculation was rife as to whether or not the convicted personnel would be charged under Fire Service Disciplinary Regulations. Eventually all of them were charged with a number of offences, such as theft and bringing the Service into disrepute. At a Disciplinary Hearing each were found guilty. All nine were 'Dismissed from the Service'. An example had to made and they were to be the example. Having been punished once in the courts, they now received a second and more severe one- the loss of their livelihoods-personnel who belong to any disciplined service and who are subject, in this case, to the Statute Law of the Fire Service Discipline Regulations can, will, and should, suffer a similar fate. If only to preserve the good name of the Service and the integrity of the vast majority of those serving in it. However in law this form of punishment can quite rightly be construed to be a double jeopardy and would not ordinarily be permitted, but that is the price of the Public's trust in us.

Some may say that this should be the case, in a public service where trust is paramount. I do not know if the Disciplinary Hearing, chaired by the Chief Fire Officer, allowed any other pressures or bodies to influence the final decision that these men should be ejected and rejected by the Service. I cannot help feeling along with others that clemency could have been exercised in some of the cases and a less harsh punishment awarded, in view of the exemplary service that had been displayed by some of these individuals during their service in the Brigade and especially throughout the 'Troubles'.

While the convicted looters were punished their families suffered terribly, they were scarred for life. One was the son of a senior Brigade officer, another was an old childhood friend of mine, who was in the process of carving out a brilliant career for himself. He had already achieved several commendations, one being for a magnificent rescue carried out in a bombed multi storey car park. His excellent record of service, and those of the others, did not even have the effect of tempering the Chief's punishment. This particular individual did not recover mentally or financially for years after this silly and unfortunate episode, but they did not heed the warnings.

They all lost not only worthwhile careers, but also their dignity and self esteem as well. Their innocent families paid a terrible price for their stupidity. It was a high and unforgettable price to pay for a few cheap trinkets. They undoubtedly were used as scapegoats and examples, not only to the rest of Brigade personnel but also to warn and remind all those who served in any public role where there was potential for looting that this was the name of the game.

All promotions in the Fire Service come from the ranks. Join as a Firefighter, retire as a Chief, in theory at least. Old habits in spite of all these warnings die hard. Firefighters and junior ranks were not the only ones to have indulged themselves in the past. I am sure there were a lot of sighs of relief and mutterings in certain quarters along with the phrase 'there but for the grace of God go I.' The question was did this incident have a sobering effect on the Brigade? If the experience that I witnessed, not long after with certain person- nel is anything to go by, I doubt it.

I attended as Officer-in-Charge of first relief crews at the terrorist burn out of an old warehouse that housed Dunlop and Hamilton a firm of electrical wholesalers in Franklin Street, Belfast. I positioned two man crews on each floor level for the purposes of damping down whilst 'doing my rounds' I fin- ished up on the top floor which was now open to the heavens.

Through the steam and smoke I could see my two crew men rummaging through shelves which had held domestic electrical goods. They obviously were not looking for pockets of fire. I made them aware of my presence and admonished them for what I suspected they were up to.

I finished by saying some people never learn. If this small incident was anything to go by, how was the rest of the Brigade going to act post Argos?

CHAPTER 8

Close Encounters ....

Head to Head... Shortly after the Army had arrived in the Province a 'Close Encounter' of the Military kind was to be experienced initially by the Brigade administration but which eventually was to include the Fire Brigades Union and was to reach unofficially as far as the highest level before it could be resolved satisfactorily in the interests of the safety of Belfast Firefighters.

The Army in the interest of protecting both the community and themselves in known Republican terrorist operating areas were continually on the lookout to secure the best possible tactical positions for security posts which would also serve as safe accommodation for their own troops. Their gaze was to rest for some time on Ardoyne Fire Station. Due to its geographical position at the hub of the arterial wheel of the Crumlin Road/ Upper Crumlin and Woodvale Roads, on an elevated site, it was to be a prime 'target' from their point of view for the purposes I have mentioned. It was also to be seen for those same reasons, by the ever vigilant F.B.U., as being a prime target by the P.I.R.A. for attack against the Army who wanted to co-habit-and not because they missed their spouses-with Firefighters who were already in residence. The C.F.O. had already been approached by the Officer Commanding the Army Garrison serving at that time in the Ardoyne area, he had informed the Union of the situation, who expressed their serious misgivings about the proposal.

However word had gotten out to some of the Fire Brigade personnel on the Station, who mistakenly thought this was somewhat an unpatriotic view that the Union was taking. These personnel accused the F.B.U. officials of being communist inspired. Nothing however could have been further from the truth, socialists maybe but communist certainly not. These Loyalists asked to have a meeting with the Chief Fire Officer which was granted. Their representative Jimmy McComish met with the Chief on the matter and he put their misgivings and misguided views to him. This rankled the Union Officials and they in turn met the Chief and informed him of their intentions. They had concluded that under no circumstances would they permit their membership to share a

Fire Station with the security forces and during the meeting they also took the opportunity to express their displeasure that he had permitted an unofficial meeting to take place with Mr. Mc Comish over the head of personnel's official representatives. The Chief apparently expressed his regret and shared their concern over the entire matter and the meeting closed on the understanding that the Union had to do what the Union had to do in the interest of its membership and that any stance the Union might take on the issue would be done without any interference from him.

Following these exchanges a meeting was arranged between the Army and Union officials which was to take place in one of the recreation rooms at Ardoyne Station. At the meeting the Army O.C. responsible for the security of the area put forward a very convincing argument for the exigencies of his Service. This O.C. was accompanied by another person, who while all the discussion ensued, remained sitting quietly in a corner, sucking on a pipe. This character clad in civilian attire was completely unknown to the Union officials. He never spoke, he just observed. The Union told the O.C. that they were aware of his dilemma but that he should also be aware of theirs. The usual intense arguments developed in that the Firefighters had to be seen to be completely impartial in the discharge of their duties. For the sake of their own safety and their survival as a group of people Firefighters could not possibly be seen to favour one section of the community, including the Security Forces, more than another. Up until this point in the Troubles it was a matter of fact that Firefighters had been allowed by this faction or that to go to the aid of all those in need no matter what their political points of view might be. Their presence was welcomed by all and the Union was simply not prepared to jeopardise those tacit agreements with any or all of the warring factions which would undoubtedly compromise this collective integrity and allow their membership to be put in more danger, with the soldiers present on their Stations, than they were in already. Jock Hall, the F.BU. Chairman, in concert with his Officials, was adamant that if the issue was forced on the Brigade, that they, not the administration would withdraw all personnel from the Station and house them in nearby accommodation, which would in fact probably have been an old Civil Defence Auxiliary Fire Service building. Each party to the debate, which naturally was speaking from a subjective and not an objective view, might under normal circumstances have seen the validity of one another's arguments but on this occasion was not about to, given the critical safety issue and the fact that the Brigade's impartiality and reputation was at stake. If Martial Law had been in place the Army would simply have requisitioned the property and ejected the Brigade. The meeting closed with nothing having been resolved.

A short time after the confrontation, the Union having meanwhile addressed the Ardoyne membership and admonished them and their unofficial representatives for being 'Oh ye of little faith' for not trusting the motives of the Officials. A short time later word was received from the Brigade that the 'Status Quo' would prevail. This word had come from the highest office in the Province, from that of Merlyn Rees no less, the then Labour and Socialist Secretary of State for Northern Ireland. Apparently it transpired that the gentleman sitting in the corner sucking his pipe had been his observer. Wiser councils than that of Her Majesty's Forces had prevailed, it is a great pity that it was not always like that in the land.

S **pies?...** From a very early stage in the 'Troubles' it was abundantly clear-due to the sectarian nature of violent events that were taking place in Ulster-that Firefighters were liable to be innocently sucked into a role other than that of protecting the community from the ravages of fire. Great emphasis-for all the sensible reasons-was placed on the neutral role of Belfast Firefighters both by the Union on its membership and by the Brigade on its personnel at the insistence of the Union.

While the following few paragraphs are purely speculative on my part it is not inconceivable in the light of what has just been related regarding the possible use of Ardoyne Fire Station for military purposes and the 'Telstar' incident and the fact that the security forces-in the interest of protecting the community had used various subterfuges over the years-that some military or clandestine intelligence body, somewhere sometime, might just try and use the Brigade as a platform to launch covert surveillance operations within terrorist areas to gather intelligence information. Bearing in mind the fact that the Fire Brigade had unrestricted access and movement within all areas without hinder or encumbrance from the local residents and para militaries-enclaves where the security forces would definitely not have been welcome. Given these circumstances it is ironic that in so called 'peace' time recent events have shown that it can no longer be guaranteed that any uniform is either respected or safe from attack, whether it be the bus driver, postman, Ambulance paramedic or Firefighter. The incidents of attacks on Fire Service vehicles and personnel has risen steadily over the years.

It is not my intention in the following paragraphs to threaten the present neutrality or integrity of the Brigade's privileged position but certain seemingly innocent events took place in the early seventies within the Belfast Brigade that were not in keeping with normal custom and practice and raised suspicions with myself and some colleagues regarding whether or not the Brigade had been penetrated by members of the intelligence services and was in fact being used unwittingly as a vehicle for low key intelligence gathering operations. All Brigade personnel were put under what was sometimes near intolerable strain in the 'routine' sense without the need for this perceived additional threat to our safety. It is to be assumed that our Chief would most certainly have been made privy to such operations, but even that remains a moot point whether he did or not.

During one of my frequent extended out-duty tours to Chi' from my base Station, the purpose being to cover for an absent resident Watch Commander-Chi' at that point in time was not permitted by the Home Office to operate with a rank less than that of Station Officer-I would, during a spare moment, especially when my friend and mentor Jock was on duty in the Control Room, dander in to see what was happening in the City operationally. It was during one of these visits that I met a white haired, middle aged chap who was introduced to me as a Walter. He and Jock had at least two things in common, these were that they each had snow white hair and were Scottish. Walter was supposed to be a photo journalist from one of the national fire magazines. Apparently he had been given permission by the Chief to monitor the Brigade's operations. He had been issued with a fire uniform, assigned a personnel locker and was allowed to ride on the fire appliances while responding to incidents. On occasions he had the use of a staff car and like the Chief was assigned on occasions a personal driver to guide him around the city. Following this initial meeting I bumped into him on numerous occasions on the fireground, where he could be seen snapping away with his camera. However he showed less interest in photographing the actual incident and more in snapping away at the gathered civilian onlookers. His driver was often asked to go into areas were the Brigade was not attending an incident.

On those occasions when we did converse in the quiet of the Control Room he was always anxious to accompany myself and some of my friends to our nights out in the City, perhaps to a night club or a musical pub, which were still functioning in full swing, up until the Abercorn and a few others were bombed out of existence. He never volunteered any personal information about himself which seemed unusual to me and being something of a gregarious animal myself I always resisted the offer for him to accompany us for he seemed to have little to contribute to the craic. I just had a gut feeling about him that something did not quite ring true. Perhaps I had been in too many Army camps during my brother-in-laws time in the Forces not to smell security forces when I saw it. He was seen on one occasion by one of our Orange brethren to be wearing an Orange Degree emblem and was asked some searching technical questions about it and his Lodge membership. His embarrassment was obvious in his inability to satisfy the curiosity of his interrogator.

Walter was reported to be lodging in a flat in the largely residential Edwardian area of the Antrim Road near to where three army sergeants had been entrapped by female Provo sympathisers into attending a party. These soldiers were subsequently shot dead in the flat by Provo gunmen. His interrogation by our Orange colleague and the murders occurred at about the same time. He was not seen on station again after this and we had no trace of him. It was the Police who came to Chi' to clear out his personal locker. If he was a spy one can reasonably assume that he knew his cover was under serious threat. Perhaps Walter mistook the pugilistic threatening appearance of our colleague and could be forgiven for mistaking him as a member of a Loyalist illegal organisation. Or could it quite simply have been that things had got too hot for him in the Antrim Road area?

After his departure from the scene I would scan the national fire magazines. I never did read or see anything that was accredited to him, perhaps there was nothing to find?

About this time there was an exodus of personnel from the Brigade usually to the Prison Service or to the Police. Some personnel of both religious persuasions moved to England or abroad with their families simply finding their personal circumstances untenable in the Province whether this was due to living in the wrong area or not being able to cope with the pressures of the job. Some Protestants were under pressure to join Loyalist para-military groups and Catholics similarly under threat in their own area by the Provos or in the case of Catholics were harassed out of the country by the Army.

There was the unusual spectacle of traffic coming the other way, that is, into the Belfast Fire Brigade from England. These men, it was reported, had either transferred from English Brigades or had joined Belfast on being demobbed from the Forces. Some stayed, some moved on unexpectedly after a short sojourn in the Belfast Brigade, where to, I do not know. It was the uncharacteristically high turnover of personnel that raised suspicions in the Brigade at this time.

One chap knew all the basics that a recruit would learn from drill books-or be taught on the drill ground-this is that each member of the drill crew was numbered and carried out a specific task assigned to that crew number. This particular guy who was supposedly an experienced Firefighter from England but unusually he did everything by the textbook on the fireground. The question arose in a number of peoples minds did he just learn it from a book? He was ex-Army and on his demob had stated he had joined an English Brigade. An inquiry was made to this Brigade about him but the inquirer was told that he did not use the surname he was using in Belfast whilst serving with the Brigade in England. Another ex-Royal Navy chappie who married into a local family, heavily involved in the Ulster Defence Association. Before he returned to an English Brigade he asked a Brigade colleague if he would like to earn a few extra quid each week. The inducement was apparently for low level intelligence information. One can but wonder in the light of this knowledge were we in the Brigade being spied on as well a spying ? I am sure we were.

The Billy Boy... During my spell at Ardoyne between 1972 and 1973 a recent transferee joined the Watch in May 1972. He had served a while in the Army before eventually being transferred to my Watch. Billy was a young, quiet, inoffensive looking lad. He was dark and swarthy-lean and slight of stature-with a tattoo on one of his arms depicting the sailing ship Mountjoy breaking the boom, at the siege of Derry in the 1600s-no need to enquire which foot he kicked with. I would see him on Station going about his work routines and training in a diligent manner. He took orders well and without question-unlike some- this was probably attributable to his background of Army training. He was one of the few lads who I was never able to get close to. He only stayed a few months with me and was transferred away to another Station. Some months later there was a bomb explosion at the Hillfoot bar on the fringes of the Loyalist Braniel estate on the outskirts of East Belfast. It was not long before the Police apprehended the suspects for the crime-in fact they caught them before they had travelled less than a mile from the scene-at the Castlereagh roundabout. One of the group who was charged and sentenced was Billy. That was the end of his career in the Brigade and also his freedom for a while.

Blissful Ignorance... Then their was Doyle at Ardoyne. Davy was a Dubliner with an accent that you could have cut with a knife. He had been in the London Fire Brigade and had married a Belfast girl while both of them were working in London. He transferred to Belfast Fire Brigade and both he and Evelyn moved from London and settled in Belfast. Davy and I became close friends. The both of us lived in East Belfast at the time and when it was convenient we would share the travelling up to Ardoyne. Occasionally enroute to the Station our journey would take us up the 'Heel and Ankle'(Shankill) going on night duty and if there was time to spare we would stop of at one of the many hostelries on the road to have a quick embibement. Invariably it would be the Horseshoe Bar, a pub owned by the father-in-law of another colleague of mine Tommy Dawson-'Banker' to his friends-a famous gambling quote of his when relating to a racing certainty. My skin crawled when the news broke during the trial of the 'Shankill Butchers', that the Horseshoe had one of their favoured local haunts. Their modus operandii was to pick up innocent Roman Catholics from off the streets, usually at night, torture and then kill them. God only knows who Davy could have been standing beside in the bar-for he was just like any other Roman Catholic to a murdering extremist-he would have been fair game, particularly if they were in the wrong place at the wrong time.

Loyalist Captive… Alec Withers was a product of the nationally adopted Junior Firefighter Scheme which was a compromise between the employers and the Fire Brigade Union. It was a halfway house between the employers desire to introduce a direct Officer intake into the service and the Union's total opposition to two tier entry as it was known. This scheme gave two years career training before recruits were posted to Stations, thus giving these Junior Firefighters something of a technical advantage over the raw entrant Recruit who only got three months of initial training. Alec was a junior Firefighter in the first induction of this type of recruit in Belfast. In 1973 he had already passed both his Statutory Leading Firefighters and his Sub Officers Examinations. The day prior to him sitting his Station Officers Examination in February 1973, he left his home in Russell Park between 9am. and 10am. to go and do a wee painting job. As he drove through the fashionable residential area of Cherryvalley, he saw a car parked at the roadside with its bonnet up.

High-jackings were rife at this time in the City-his natural intuition told him not to stop-however the Firefighter in him made him decide to stop and offer assistance. For his pains these would be 'breakdown' hoaxers set-about him, and bundled him into the back of the car. They covered him with a blanket and drove off with him in the rear of the vehicle. Alec was taken to a shed-he did not know exactly where-and was told to 'get the fuck out' from the car. They tied his hands behind his back, took his identification credentials from him for inspection and began to interrogate and threaten him. They seemed agitated and nervous. Alec thought about whether or not he should plead with them-in Ulster, if you fell into the wrong hands and gave the incorrect answer as to which side of the religious divide you belonged you could-as had been demonstrated by other terminal incidents-finish up dead. He did not know who his captors were or what organisation they owed their allegiance to so he decided to remain silent.

They obviously had been waiting to kidnap someone but had they got the wrong man? He was finally transferred into another car still under the concealment of a blanket. They drove for some time and eventually when he felt they were in a country lane, the car stopped-he received a dig on the jaw and was bundled out and his abductors drove off. He waited for approximately fifteen minutes before beginning to walk along the lane. Eventually his ordeal came to an end when he was spotted by a passing motorist, by this time was 12.30pm. This event was not exactly a fitting prelude to his final swotting up for his examination the next day, but he passed and never looked back since.

'**O**fficial' Captives... Fire Prevention staff are there to give advice to the general public on matters of concern relating to fire safety, as well as to business and industry. This entails from time to time having to go to visit domestic property to inspect reported faults in chimney flues. It was on one such visit that the next close encounter occurred. Leading Firefighter Jimmy Armstrong-driven by 'Slim' the hydrant maintenance man-paid a visit to a house in Quadrant Street off Cullintree Road in the Lower Falls area one day, to inspect it for a possible defective flue. While there several of the 'boyos' from the Official I.R.A.-P.I.R.A. as yet had not broken away-burst into the house, demanding to know who they were, what he was doing, and why was he was looking up the flue. One of Jimmy's interrogators was waving a handgun which was visibly trembling in his hand. This situation was the ultimate dread of anyone carrying out their daily work in Belfast at this particular time when tensions and suspicions were high within each community.

Immediately realising who he was confronted by, and startled at having been taken unawares by this sudden intrusion, Jimmy began to explain the purpose of his visit. They were not going to readily accept his explanation. By this time they had brought 'Slim' in from the van. Both men were then taken out and bundled into a McCausland's Ford Transit hire van and blindfolded. Then the serious questioning began. Obviously Jimmy and 'Slim' could give no other answers but the truth about their identities, but the interrogators were not going to be easily satisfied. They were driven around, in what Jimmy thought was the local area, while the questioning continued. At one point three shots were discharged from the gun directly behind Jimmy's head. By this time the questioners were pressing him for answers he could not give. Jimmy who was a Roman Catholic from the County Derry town of Dungiven thought that at least this pedigree would suffice, but not so. The only other thing he could offer was, that this father-in-law worked in Ross's mill on the Lower Falls Road and that he could vouch for him if his captors were prepared to investigate his alibi. A runner was sent to the mill and his father-in-law asked for. When he appeared he was told that his son-in-law's life depended on the answers that he gave to the questions that were asked. One of these questions being 'does he talk with a funny accent' He must have passed the test, for Jimmy and 'Slim' were released after being held for three hours.

What Jimmy had not known at the time of his and 'Slim's' abduction was-and God only knows the possible tragic outcome if he had know and how it might have shaped his answers to the questions posed by his captors-was that 'Slim' was a part time Reserve Constable with the Royal Ulster Constabulary, the enemy.

Felix The Cat... Felix the Cat is the unofficial logo of that branch of British Army Royal Engineers responsible for unexploded ordnance disposal-bomb disposal. Unfortunately Felix's personnel were to exceed their quota of nine lives by four during the early learning curve period of their prolonged stay in the Province. It was sometime before they learned, as the Fire Service did, that property is expendable and replaceable, lives are not. A total of thirteen Ammunitions Technical Officers were needlessly lost before it was decided to adopt as standard practice, the use of the remote controlled tracked robot that was specifically developed for investigating and dealing with explosive devices. The use of this essential tool has now become standard practice for Security Forces who are confronted with similar situations-with a resultant drop in Service casualties-and is used by other Security Forces throughout the globe. Northern Ireland has proved to be a useful test-bed throughout this period of strife for testing and developing many new innovations in the field of bomb disposal. Attendance at non actuated '77's' usually involved standing by while the Ammunitions Technical Officer attempted to make safe or neutralise the device, which could range from a simple incendiary to a bomb within a building or a massive car bomb. Like any other profession the outcome of each incident had varying degrees of success, some amusing, some tragic, here are a few that I and some of my colleagues witnessed.

Major Calladene was one of the senior Ammunitions Technical Officers in the Province. He had many successes under his belt but achieved with great risk to himself and his staff. Following an explosion and fire at the massive Co-Operative building in York Street 7th March 1972, the Brigade's personnel were damping down in the carpet showroom section where the main body of the outbreak had occurred. Unknown to them this Major was attempting to defuse an unexploded 30lb. device that had been left on the floor below them. When Assistant Divisional Officer Schofield the Officer-in-Charge of the incident became aware of this there was hell to play with the Major for not informing the Brigade and for exposing the personnel to extreme hazard in this foolhardy way of working. Since that event personnel were inclined in the Brigade, whenever his name came up following this incident, to refer to him as the 'Mad Major'. On the 29th March after successfully defusing a 150lb. bomb on a lorry parked in Chichester Street-not far from Brigade H.Q.'s-he proceeded to the report of another car bomb in Wellington Place in the city centre. Here his luck ran out and he was killed while investigating the vehicle.

It was Wednesday 15th March 1972-as the old soothsayer's said beware the Ides of March- when Chi' received a call to a suspect car on the Grosvenor Road. The appliances parked a safe distance away while two Ammunitions Technical Officers, N.C.O.'s, investigated the vehicle. Having helped to lay out hose lines in readiness for any possible fire that might follow a detonation, a colleague of mine Bobby Malcolm was watching with other personnel as these N.C.O.'s approached the vehicle. There is no other way to describe what happened next other than the car blew up when they had nearly reached it. Bobby told me that he-in company with everyone else present-saw them literally being blown apart. The Spectre of two human beings disintegrating so suddenly and disappearing before their very eyes was a shocking and horrendous sight and left everyone stunned and appalled.

Bomb disposal is literally a game of cat and mouse played out between 'Felix' and the bomber. The bomb makers tries to outwit the A.T.O.'s They in turn employs all the skills and techniques learned-and on occasions had to rewrite the book-to achieve a successful outcome which of course included preserving their own lives. Not all bomb alerts are genuine, the threat and subsequent scare of a hoax bomb attack to the public is real enough. Nonetheless all warnings must be answered and responded to by the security and emergency services. It has been shown over the past thirty years, that it is enough for the would be bomber to issue a warning, even if that warning is a hoax, for it to achieve the desired goal, and accomplish all of the aims of a real attack.

Disruption and fear are effective enough weapons in their own right. A well timed series of hoax calls can tie up a city's traffic system for hours bringing the industrial and commercial life to a halt. All calls must be investigated to treat only one with indifference can spell disaster for someone. The Army in Ulster along with other public services has paid a heavy price in death and injury in attempting to protect the fabric of society. The bombers have also had a price to pay in their learning curve in trying to destroy it.

I cannot help thinking that one of the contributory factors to such a heavy loss of life on the part of the Army is the fact of belonging to a disciplined ser-vice-personnel, no-matter what their role-because they are trained and expect-ed to do their duty-will take the extra risk that might endanger themselves. The human psyche being what it is the 'system' will unconsciously put pressure on individuals in a number of subtle ways. This may take the form of mental con-ditioning-blind obedience to orders-perhaps fear of not wishing to be branded a coward-or the threat of retribution such as disciplinary action for not seeing an action through to its final conclusion, no-matter what that conclusion might be, when tasked to do so. Blind obedience to orders frequently leads individ-uals away from the luxury of exercising discretion and excuses the necessity of having to justify their actions at a later date to their Masters. As we all know the military graveyards throughout the world are full of soldiers who obeyed orders.

The next few incidents are not as macabre as the previous two but are I feel tinged with a touch of humour.

Army 1. Everton 0-or is it the other way round that I remember this one. No, it is not a soccer result as you might think, but one of the counter produc-tive attempts by an A.T.O. to defuse a delicate situation. It was Friday 9th June 1972 in what, to date, had been a very busy year for the Brigade. Day duty at Ardoyne and I received a call to a '77' at the Everton bar at the Everton Street/Crumlin Road junction. When we arrived the A.T.O. was in attendance. He told me that there was a bomb reported in the blue Ford transit van which was parked at the gable end of the Everton bar in Everton Street. These was a hostelry that I had never frequented but I knew it was a pub well known and beloved by its locals. After having parked well up the Crumlin Road and set-up our equipment in readiness for a possible fire, I spoke to the A.T.O. and asked what his course of action was going to be. His reply was a new one on me. I had not seen this particular technique that he intended using, demon-strated. before. He proposed that he was going to fire a Carl Gustav rocket launcher with a blank rocket shell in it at the van. This is going to be interesting I thought, and it was. I positioned myself at an oblique angle to the pub. A little way up the Crumlin Road I could just see the rear of the van. It was parked parallel to the gable end of the bar with its tail end facing out at right angles to the main road.

"...seems a bit harsh for illegal parking!!"

I watched as the A.T.O. got his Carl Gustav ready crouching down preparing to fire some fifty yards away directly astern of the van. He was on the same side of the Crumlin Road as myself. There was a sudden woomph as the projectile left the launcher and almost simultaneously an earth shuddering explosion distorted our eardrums, as the missile pierced the rear doors of the van and found its intended target. Debris rained down all around us for what seemed ages. When the dust settled and we were able to view the scene, there was little or nothing left of the van, nothing that was immediately recognisable that is. There was however a huge hole in the gable end of the Everton that you could have driven a lorry into, but the building still remained standing defiantly. It transpired that the size of the bomb contained in the van was approximately 250lbs. This was one of those situations-if circumstances had been reversed and it was the P.I.R.A. in action-when the Army might have described this shambles as an own goal, only this time the P.I.R.A. supplied the ball. Perhaps this was one of those times when the A.T.O. did use his discretion coupled with a little improvisation. He certainly achieved a spectacular and impressive result from this particular game.

The above action would, I suppose, be described as a controlled explosion by the news media. Only where do you draw the line? When is a controlled explosion not a controlled explosion? I suppose when the object of saving property is defeated by one's own preventative actions, no matter how well intentioned. I'm sure there must have been a few red faces and a few ribald remarks passed in Army messes from time to time when these type of occurrences went awry. What was one pub more or less in this great game.

One other memorable occasion was the famous news footage taken from the vicinity of the Europa Hotel-the most bombed hotel in the world-of the Hamill Hotel, a frequent haunt of the red light girls, which used to stand nearly opposite the Europa on Great Victoria Street. The news broadcaster announced that a bomb had been placed on the first floor and that the A.T.O. was about to carry out a controlled explosion. What happened when he set off his charge was a slow motion action film shot of the gable end of the Hamill Hotel being blown out into Amelia Street. Well you cannot win 'em all. There was many a forlorn red light client that night.

The streets directly behind Belfast's architectural gem of a City Hall, which is the centre piece of Donegall Square and the City contain many old Victorian buildings which are themselves of great architectural interest. The occupancy in these buildings has changed over the decades from the warehouses and factories associated with the clothing and linen trades, to what is now a predominantly high density office environment. A large proportion of these buildings house public service and government departments, thus making them a legitimate target for the terrorist. High emphasis was placed on security of the buildings, making it difficult for devices to be brought inside, however this did not remove their vulnerability to attack by the car bomber.

The P.I.R.A.'s concerted city centre car bombing campaign of the early seventies took a heavy toll of these institutions. Although not many building were razed to the ground by either fire or blast-only a few new city centre car parks were created-millions of pounds worth of damage was inflicted on the properties. This damage was of a largely superficial nature and the buildings stood testimony to the Victorian techniques of sound building construction. In many cases, however, the damage caused had the desired disruptive effect on the work processes carried out within the respective institutions. Office staff would have to retrieve their work and whatever undamaged equipment there was and be re-housed in other temporary accommodation until repairs could be effected. It was the crews from Chi' who attended the majority of these incidents preventing resultant fires storms from developing which would only add to the mounting financial costs to government and insurers.

I attended one such incident myself in this locality while on temporary detached duty to Chi' on detached day duty. It involved an abandoned suspect car parked half on the footpath and half on the roadway in Alfred Street. The car was thought to contain a device. We positioned our appliances in Franklin Street which ran across at right angles to Alfred Street. The A.T.O. set up shop with his men and equipment not far from us, so we could see what he was up to. He unloaded his tracked robot, colloquially known as a wheel barrow, from its carrying vehicle and prepared an explosive charge to blow the car's boot lid open. The explosive charge was secured to a metal frame which in turn was mounted on the front of the robot. This method of placing a charge proved, through experience, to be imprecise in directing the placement of the charge accurately, so later it was decided to fit a remote controlled closed circuit camera to the robot and a shotgun type firing mechanism that fired a high pressure water pellet at the lock of a vehicle. This method also had the advantage of being less likely to accidentally trigger a bomb.

The A.T.O. started the robot off moving slowly forward to the rear of the car, its control cable paying out behind. Because of the awkward angle the car was sitting at on the pavement and with an intervening lamp standard immediately behind it, the A.T.O. had difficulty positioning the robot in close proximity to the boot locking mechanism. However, eventually, after much toing and froing it was positioned to his satisfaction. That was difficulty number one out of the way, but when trying to disengage the robot from the charge it was seen, that because of the awkward angle between road surface and the carrying frame, the charge would not release. The A.T.O. was then left with the dilemma of either approaching the vehicle on foot to manually disengage his robot or firing the charge with it still mounted on the wheel barrow. He chose the latter course of action. When ready, he called out the obligatory warning of the impending firing by count-down and shouted 'firing' simultaneously pressing the firing button. There was a small explosion-the car boot flew open-and his robot flew across the road leaving a trail of its innards as it went, landing unceremoniously on its side some yards away.

Still not knowing if there was a device contained in the car or not, there was no other course of action left to him but to approach it. He got into a crouched position as if ready to start a sprint race-took a few deep breaths and shot off-when he got to the lamp standard and while still running at the double-he grabbed the lamp standard in the crook of his arm managed to take a quick glance into the boot- and without loosing momentum-propelled himself like a slingshot around the lamp standard and headed hell for leather back towards his control point. There was indeed a bomb in the boot but it had failed to detonate. These are the type of risks these chaps on occasions were obliged to take and I thought it was rough being a Firefighter.

Belfast Co-operative... The Belfast Co-Operative had stood on its site in York Street from the early 1900's. It was one of the City's most popular general stores and was an institution for shoppers from all over Ireland. As well being one of the biggest stores in the city, massive ·is probably not an overstatement of its size, it was reputed to be the largest Co-Op in the U.K. This four floor building was some 100ft high by 255ft long and 320ft deep and was divided into two parts by an interconnecting bridge at second and third floor level. I remember my own Mother taking me there to shop or for a wee treat, especially at the end of the 'Co-Quarter' when share holders would flock to have their 'divy'-dividend-entered in their share books.

When I was attached to the Brigade's Fire Prevention Department in 1970 I remember that the building was being rebuilt and refurbished. Great debate had taken place in the Department between senior F.P. Officers about whether or not the external cladding of glass reinforced plastic-fibre glass-should be permitted in such a large four storey building. This cladding had the effect of not permitting any natural light into the building, which allied with the failure of the emergency lighting in the eventuality the premises had to be evacuated in an emergency, would have had caused substantial difficulties for the evacuees as the exit routes were equipped with a combination of escalators and stairways. In any event the argument for the cladding won the day, it was allowed to be installed, presumably for architectural effect.

The poor old Co-Op building was a target for terrorist attack on several occasions. It served all sections of the community, created employment, and did harm to no one. Was it considered by the terrorists that an imbalance in Roman Catholic/Protestant employee ratios existed? I think not. I dismissed that argument on the basis that a large number of other similar commercial targets had been, and were, being fired and bombed in Belfast every week around this time. Or perhaps it became a cause celebre with the terrorist factions involved. Maybe they did not like a snook being cocked at them, in that their will to destroy it was being thwarted and they were not going to be allowed to prevail, who knows. The fact remains that the Co-Op had been rebuilt after the previous firebombings and had risen Phoenix like from the ashes.

On the 7th March 1972 prior to the major conflagrations of the 10th and 23rd May there was an explosion and fire in the Co-Op building. I have related the events of that particular incident elsewhere in my narrative.

So it came to pass on the 10th May 1972 that 'they' decided to have yet another go. This time with near disastrous consequences for the Brigade's personnel. A bomb had exploded on the third floor pushing out portions of the exterior walls and in the process severing sprinkler lines and fuel service pipes to the boiler-room on the roof. Smoke was seen billowing from the area of the roof and the Brigade was summoned at 1655hrs and responded with fire appliances from Whitla Street and Chichester Street Stations.

SERIOUS FIRE AT THE
Co-OP : MAY 10 1972

240

While jets were being run out to tackle the now well established major fire, Divisional Officer Leslie Johnston accompanied by Sub Officer Jack Warden entered the building to investigate a report that persons were still trapped inside on the roof. It had been thought that the building had been fully evac-uated without incident-the citizens of Belfast are the best trained evacuees in the world-so the two Officers began to climb the stairways, even though they were aware of reports that a secondary device had been planted within the building to look for the missing civilians. At second floor level they observed several civilians in the adjoining Orpheus building which is joined to the main building by an overhead pedestrian walkway. They were not in any immediate danger but were told to leave the scene immediately.

Leslie and Jack continued up towards the roof. Whenever they emerged into the smoke on the roof they did not realise that the boiler fuel pipes sup-plying the roof top daily tanks to the boilerhouse had been ruptured by the explosion at third floor level-thus feeding the fire with an indeterminate quan-tity of fuel-a fire which was by now rapidly gaining hold. By the time they realised this they had both become disorientated due to the fact that their line of vision to the roof exit-from whence they had entered- had been lost by the rapidly increasing thick black smoke.

When I asked both men separately about the incident during my research, each told me, one second the other was there, and then had disappeared from view into the thick black smoke. As Jack Warden continued to try to find an exit route he caught a glimpse of Leslie Johnston through the swirling smoke standing on the parapet as if ready to jump and quickly made his way over to join him. Johnty had obviously been the first of the two to realise their predica-ment and had managed to locate the parapet where he was able to attract the attention of Chi's Turntable Ladder operator Alan Brown by waving his hel-met-in fact, in desperation, at one point he considered throwing his helmet down at him to gain his attention. Alan was positioning his appliance at the front of the building, ready for use. When Alan saw Johnty waving he knew immediately it was not a casual wave but more a gesture of desperation and a summons for help.

Time was of the essence and it was not on his side if he was to success-fully rescue his two colleagues from the roof of the building. Such was his cal-culated haste-without deploying the turntable's ground jacks, which is critical to the safe operation of the ladder-he elevated, trained, aimed, and finally extended the head of the Merryweather ladder upwards towards his human quarry on the parapet of the Co-op. Protesting at these unacceptable ladder loadings the automatic safety systems on the ladder started to sound alarms. They rang loud in Alan's ears. He continued regardless, but he could not quite get the ladder head depressed beyond its limits close enough to Johnty for him to safely climb aboard. With great skill and ingenuity he began to flex the ladder by alternatively depressing and then quickly elevating it, as an angler would whip a fly rod back and forth. As the ladder was extended fully beyond its safe limits of operation automatic alarms continued to sound off ...

This technique worked and at one point in its downward whip the ladder head came almost within reach of the two men. At the next whip at its lowest point Johnty timed it right and jumped, he managed to grab a round on the underside of the ladder and then heave himself around onto the topside. He was at least was safe. Meanwhile Jack had also managed to get up onto the parapet where he balanced while Johnty's self rescue was taking place. When Johnty had settled himself he motioned to Jack to jump, which at the next whip he did. He managed to land a grip also but found himself hanging full length from the underside of the ladder just as Johnty had previously. Leslie was able to give him some support and helped keep him from falling the 80 feet to the ground.

Plucked from the Jaws of Death

Alan rotated the ladder away from the building the alarm bells and all the safety indicators having by this time gone off the scales. It was out of the question to attempt any slick ladder operation given this loading Alan's thought was that if the ladder was going to collapse the men at the head stood some sort of a fighting chance if the ladder was to collapse onto the roof of the building on the other side of the street opposite to the Co-Op building. So continuing to train delicately round Alan finally dropped his 'fish' on the roof opposite amidst much wiping of fevered brows. Fears for the safety of customers escaping due to this external cladding were not realised, but there can be little doubt that the cladding contributed to serious smoke logging of the building. Some good news television footage of this dramatic incident exists. I am sure both Officers cringe when they reflect on the incident for a variety of reasons. I know my flesh creeps whenever I see the pictures, how lucky they were.

The fire burned for five hours before it could be brought under control. Seven hundred and fifty employees lost their jobs and the bill for the building and contents was some ten million pounds sterling. On the 18th May 1972, PIRA issued a written statement admitting responsibility for the incident and justifying it by adding that the store was British owned. Each of the three personnel involved in the rescue were later given a Chief Officer's Commendation.

Brigade Circular No:63/72 Fire at Belfast Co-Operative Society Wednesday 10th May 1972.

"... Did you hear a sound ... like a belt snapping ... just then??"

Chief Officers Commendation.

Whilst carrying out a search for persons trapped on the roof of the Belfast Co-Operative Society, Divisional Officer L. Johnston and Sub-Officer J.Warden found themselves trapped by heat and smoke and only with the greatest difficulty were they rescued by the use of a

Turntable ladder operated by Fireman A. Brown. Divisional Officer Johnston and Sub-Officer Warden showed initiative and courage in a tense situation complemented by the coolness and skill of Fireman Brown in effecting their rescue.

It gives me great pleasure in commending them on a successful operation. Chief Officer.

Divisional Officer Johnston was later awarded the M.B.E.-Member of the British Empire-an award of the Sovereign.

There was a further incident in the Co-Op building on the 23rd May, 1972 involving a fire on the fourth floor. This seemed to have been the floor favoured for attacks. The time of call was 2344hrs. The stop message was originated 0415hrs 24th May 1972. There had been a device placed on this floor which had exploded causing a serious fire, it was extinguished with the use of eight jets and three breathing apparatus. The Co-Op is still there.

...fun's over, nearly time to go home.

Multi-Storey Story... Throughout my period of service, of all the selfless acts of raw courage and heroism that were undertaken, I have not been aware of, nor witnessed, one that was more fraught with potential danger to life and which received so little official recognition as the one that I am about to relate.

Day duty at Chi', morning drills completed, personnel had been detailed to carry out their Station chores. Some personnel had been detailed to the hose store, others to the B.A. house for repair and maintenance of equipment, drivers to the engine room for maintenance of appliances and equipment. The Chief who was not familiar with the topography of the City had a daily driver assigned, his duties also involved bringing him, his Polo mints and paper in the morning, tidying up his office at lunch times and taking him on frequent visits to the City Hall for Police Committee meetings. I had been detailed for this duty many times as a rookie, in the sixties, things were still the same now in the seventies. I felt by this time his topography of the City should have improved, If he had been an appliance driver, fresh in from the country he would not have lasted that long. I suspect he felt his rank entitled him to this little perk and he enjoyed the status of being chauffeured about.

On this day in May 1972 just before lunch time a call was received by Blue Watch to an activated '77' at a multi-storey car silo in Franklin Street, not far from the city centre. A full attendance of four appliances with Station Officer Schofield in charge was sent from Chi'. Enroute as the machines snaked their way through the lunchtime traffic-personnel were getting dressed in their fire gear-B.A. wearers were donning their sets-and the Officer-in-Charge was trying to pre-plan tactics in his mind's eye, all were apprehensive of what was going to greet them. On arrival thick plumes of smoke could be seen billowing from the basement of the building, with little or no sign of actual fire. Jets were ordered to run be out in readiness. There is little to burn in a car park except cars naturally but because of their high content of rubber, plastics and petroleum they can and do produce large impressive quantities of suffocating impenetrable black smoke. B.A. entry procedure was set up, the Entry Control Officer taking the wearer's tallies from them-each with the wearer's name and pressure of air in cylinder recorded on them. He recorded these and slotted them into his board, telling the men when and what pressure they were due out at. Guide lines are were used whenever deep penetration entry was made into the building by the B.A. teams so they could retrace their steps. Several cars were found to be alight, fire was not the impeding or danger factor in locating and tackling the blaze, smoke was. However the fire was located and knocked down relatively quickly, it was all over bar the shouting, as they say, or so they thought. Men had been withdrawn and were having a breather after the initial flow of adrenaline which had fed the excitement and expenditure of energy.

Divisional Officer Tommy Douglas who was in charge by now was informed that the sound of a car horn could be heard coming from within the still smoke logged building. By this time in the duration of the 'Troubles', operational practice, dictated by bitter experience -after some crew members were buried alive in an electrical shop in College Square North while they were within the building when a bomb had detonated inside-that it had become official sensible fireground practice that a building was not to be entered until it had been declared safe by the A.T.O. This was not always carried out in practice. Sometimes it was taken for granted that conditions were safe because there had been a detonation-which was the case in College Square North-before the Ammunitions Technical Officer had arrived or 'cleared' the premises even though it was difficult for an Officer-in-Charge to resist the challenge of tackling the incipient fire before it go out of control occasioning more damage.

The sound of the car horn indicated that someone was still inside the building trapped in their vehicle and unable to escape because of the still dense smoke, which was penetrable only by those wearing B.A. Another entry had therefore to be expedited and effected for the purposes of search and rescue. Dick McKee and Lloyd Brown, both experienced, long serving Firefighters were not ordered to go into the building for search and rescue-the, by now, on scene A.T.O. had said there was a report of another device-but these two Firefighters considered it their duty to have a go at locating the trapped person or persons.

Groping their way into the building they set off guided only by the sound of the repeated honking of the car horn, the sound getting louder as they gradually headed in the general direction of the trapped person, all the while conscious of the threat of this other explosive device in their path. As they progressed further into the building the paid out their guideline behind them, one keeping physically in touch with the other at all times and linked by their short personal lines to the main guideline. Because of the tortuous route and having to clamber over and weave in and out of parked cars the rate of deployment of their guideline increased until the point was reached some 180 feet in when the guide line came up short in its pack running out before they reached their intended destination. Guessing by the volume of the car horn that that they were close to their quarry, the safety critical decision had to be made, do we detach from our line-proceed-or turn back? Conversing as best they could to each other, through the speech diaphragms of their B.A's, they decided, this was a shit or bust operation so they decided to go on. Apart from being linked to the main guideline they also had personal B.A. lines which were attached to the main line from their B.A's. giving them an additional working radius of some fifteen feet, paying out this umbilical they scribed a circle trying to locate the car with the trapped person in it, no luck. They knew they were close but did not know how close. It was decided between them that Lloyd should detach, he was to make the last physical push on into the unknown to try and locate those trapped. This is quite simply the high risk strategy of desperation.

Lloyd detached his safety line and set off in the famous searching shuffle taught the world around to Firefighters-back of the hand out in front to guard against live cables testing the floor-the leading foot testing the safety of the floor-both sweeping rhythmically from side to side to locate the casualty. After what seemed like a life time still guided by the car horn he located the car in question-he opened the door-grabbed the semi-conscious male occupant-who muttered something to the effect that Lloyd took to mean that he was glad to see him-the casualty losing consciousness in the process.

After dragging the man some considerable distance in what he guessed should be the correct direction back to towards Dick, Lloyd's air cylinder low pressure warning whistle started to sound off, indicating he had less ten minutes of air left -normally this whistle should only ever operate when the wearer is well clear of the building or hazardous atmosphere-time was distinctly running out-Lloyd turned off the whistle. The realisation was setting in that by this time he might not be going to make it out to fresh air with his casualty.

Dick, meanwhile, had begun to flash his torch at floor level to give Lloyd something to home onto. Lloyd at one point lay the casualty on the ground while he paused for breath, as yet he had not seen the light from Dick's torch. By this time circumstances were getting pretty desperate. Lloyd considered his options-should he stay where he was and share the last of his air with his casualty with the hope that his colleagues would come for him-or should he press on until he ran out of air. He just felt it was best not to quit nor to give up. Remembering an old trick from his early training days he held his own breath and kept still and quiet. In the distance almost miraculously he was able to hear the clicking of Dick's B.A. air demand valve opening and closing. Again half carrying, half dragging the man Lloyd set off in this new direction eventually seeing the flashing light of his colleague's torch in the gloom. Finally he managed to relocate Dick and together they all struggled along making a safe egress from the building to fresh air as Lloyd's set ran out. Greater love hath no man....

The next day the Army discovered a forty pound bomb in one of the other cars that was left in the car silo.

The two men received no accolade of recognition from the Brigade for their courageous actions. However, three months after this event they both were contacted through the Brigade by the gentleman, whose life they had been instrumental in saving. They had not met since the incident. Mr. W.W.Torrens from Greenisland a suburb of Belfast on the shores of Belfast Lough wanted to show in some tangible way his gratitude to the two men for saving his life. How can you put a price on such acts? Nevertheless the only way he thought to do so was by taking them out for a thank you meal to the then Chester Park Hotel-this Hotel was to eventually succumb to terrorist attack-a gesture which was much appreciated by those involved. No matter how many people you rescue or help very few if any ever return to say a simple thank you. Perhaps that is society for you.

... *Lloyd* ...

Another little incident-unconnected to the rescue-occurred which involved Lloyd. One day while making his way on duty he came upon a collapsed girl in North Street, who had taken a drug overdose. He made her vomit, an Ambulance was called, and he accompanied her to hospital. This action inevitably made him late coming on duty, for which he had to write a report explaining his reason for being late. He later received a letter of thanks on the girl's behalf from the Chief as a footnote it also mentioned no action would be taken against for him being late on duty. It soured the gallant obligation somewhat. Noblesse Oblige. The world gets funnier by the minute doesn't it.

Buried Alive by a Sucker Punch... Different feelings of apprehension and foreboding always travelled with personnel on their way to a call, each thinking of what might lie ahead. The crew sit deep in uneasy silent thought, some have time for a final mental prayer to their God. These feelings were never so prevalent than when responding to a civil disturbance incident, regardless of the nature. It might have been a standby at a suspect car bomb, with the accompanying tensions, wondering, when or indeed if, the device would explode.

The oft repeated scene. The suspect vehicle in the distance. The unnatural silence in the concrete forest. The silent 'hunters' watching their quarry intently. By day the cloud shadows constantly changing the shadows and moving the spotlights, by night the moon sprinkling will o' the wisps in and out of the malevolent shadows cast by the street lamps. The casual observers muttering behind their security tapes. The arrogant care less pigeons striding inquisitively about unmoved by neither man nor machine's evil intent. The shuffling Firefighters absentmindedly drifting off to the 'normality' of the favourite trout pool or the weekend garden. The absolute contradiction of silence rising to a crescendoing aria broken by the command... 'FIRING'!

Every survival instinct straining nervously, as much as tiredness would permit, at its apogee of awareness. Ready for the flight or fight. Whenever it did it explode the relief valve of the tensions that had been waiting to escape would blow off like so much mental steam in concert with the receding echoes bounding off the surrounding buildings. The eye, Olympic like, picking out the largest, highest, climbing, piece of gear box or engine. The avalanche of deadly metal and glass, the zinging in the ears, the hot blast in the face, the acrid smell in the nostrils and the acidic taste in the mouth, and of course the all pervasive, eternal, dust.

An instant, followed by the residual questioning fear-had you deployed the appliances and crews at a safe distance-to avoid the subsequent fallout of debris from the vehicle, or the shards of lethal glass that cascaded down from the surrounding buildings. Was everyone ok? Was there another sympathetic detonation to come. Were 'they' waiting along a command wire somewhere to deliver the 'sucker punch'?

Yet more tension when searching a building for fire bombs in the early days of the fire bombing campaign in the Belfast City centre-before a policy was agreed not to enter premises until they were cleared by the A.T.O. When with every step one anticipated the thud of the device going off and you hoped it was not close by. Then there was the persistent dilemma when a bomb had already actuated in a building, was the Officer-in-Charge going to commit personnel before it was cleared by the A.T.O., in order to save the property? It was a deliberate policy of the Provos to place secondary devices to 'dissuade' those responding to the incident from interfering with the purpose of the bombing.

In the street language of the times for obvious reasons this was known as the 'Sucker Punch'.

The moment of worst fear and deep foreboding was whenever those first faltering steps were taken inside to tackle an ensuing fire. This was to be one of those near disasters.

A dull Friday in November, 1972 a full attendance of four appliances was dispatched from Chi' with Station Officer Victor Mc Allister riding in charge, to a '77' in Electrical Supplies, College Square North. When the device had actuated, fire had broken out but the Army said to stay out. Acting Divisional Officer Graham who had arrived by this time, decided to take the gamble and commit personnel to tackling the fire. Firefighters Lloyd

"... or on the other hand ... it may not be a hoax??"

Brown, Billy Harris, Ivor Madeley and Bobby Pollock entered the building with Station Officer Mc Allister and Firefighter Ken McClune in close attendance. As they moved forward there was a bright blue flash somewhere in the ground floor area. Bobby Pollock related afterwards that he had not really heard any explosion he just felt the blast. The front portion of the building was

immediately blown out into the street and the first floor collapsed, trapping two of the men. Firefighter Madeley was blown over a washing machine, Bobby Pollock through the door, and Firefighter McClune across the street. Firefighter Ron Harris was trapped underneath Lloyd Brown, who was in turn was trapped by debris with his head firmly wedged inside his fire helmet, unable to move. Ron

A startled young Pollock (front)

Harris because of the pressure on his chest struggled to breath and was screaming because of the pain in his chest.

Meanwhile Bobby Pollock was stunned and disorientated and could not see. When he partially gathered his thoughts he switched on his hand torch but could still see nothing other than the dust that hung in the air and reflected back his torchlight beam. As the dust settled and the atmosphere began to clear he located his heavy leather fire belt which he had been wearing when he entered the building. It was lying on the floor still fully buckled as it was when he had been wearing it. The blast must have caused his diaphragm to momentarily collapse his abdominal muscles thus allowing the belt to drop from his waist to encircle his feet. This was not the first time in the Brigade that personnel were to witness the quirky and unpredictable behaviour of bomb blasts.

Due to the over commitment of the Brigade's other appliances that day and the urgency of the situation within the collapsed building, a call went out from the scene to Controls instructing that they mobilise personnel from both the Brigade Training School and Fire Prevention Departments, which were both based within the Chichester Street complex, to assist in the search and rescue of their colleagues. All available men and equipment were sent to the scene. The work of removing the debris from around the trapped men had to be executed very gingerly for fear of further collapse, Lloyd Brown and Ron Harris were the most difficult to extricate but eventually the job was completed successfully without any further injury to any of the men. Thankfully the injuries sustained were minor in nature and ranged from shock and cuts to legs, to the effects of blast on eardrums. All those involved, not just those trapped , got off comparatively lightly considering the proximity of the bomb. The direction of blast can usually be predicted with some degree of certainty, although it had the affect of bringing the building down, thankfully in this instance it didn't wreak the sort of injuries on the casualties that we had become used to witnessing on others in recent years in Belfast.

Anyone who has undergone such a traumatic experience whether it be mental or physical has to cope with the subtle and sometimes stark residual psychological damage that such an event deposit on the individual. Lloyd Brown and Billy Harris were on sick leave for seven and eleven weeks respectively, they recovered well, however Firefighter Harris after attending other incidents where bombings were involved resigned from the Brigade within a year.

A **Spectre Out of the Darkness...** Strange how it is, that most of us can recall, exactly where we were and what we were doing at specific times in our lives, when matters of importance have happened, be they of world importance or simply personal. In my case, these events would be the assassination of President Kennedy-his brother Bobby-Martin Luther King-the first manned moon landing-and the cosmic moving event for Sandra my wife the birth of my two children.

This recollection also applies to that day, on 6th February 1973, when a young Belfast Firefighter called Brian Douglas was murdered on duty. I did not know him personally, save to say, that I had asked on the Station when I had first seen him who the new face was. I was told that he was an only son-single-who lived in the Shore Road area of the city-where he looked after his widowed blind father and that he had joined the Brigade on 18th May 1970.

He was a quiet, willing lad, keen and amenable to the disciplines of the job and was liked and respected by his colleagues. It was not casual nosiness that prompted my questions. It was always prudent to obtain a little background information on every Firefighter, for you never could tell when that particular person might arrive on your Watch on detached duty. It is much better to be in a position to have some brief knowledge of the Firefighters likely to be riding in the rear of your appliance for your very life may be dependent upon it. Sadly his length of service was to be short lived.

The morning of the 6th February 1973 began quietly enough in the Brigade. I was on day duty with my Watch, Blue Watch, Ardoyne. This was a special day in Loyalist community. A General Strike had been called to protest against the Sunningdale Conference which in Loyalist minds had only one item on the agenda, the re-unification of Ireland. In the event the strike was not a success but another strike day was to follow later with more death and destruction.

During the course of the morning the Brigade's daily routine was punctuated with a number of hoax car bomb calls throughout the city. These hoaxes-as intended-snarled up the city traffic and a tense atmosphere prevailed. No one really knew what this terrorist activity presaged. We wondered if these incidents were the prelude to something really sinister and if any of them were going to be the real thing as eventually 'they' worked themselves into the usual killing frenzy. The calls on this occasion, were not instigated by P.I.R.A., but were from 'Loyalist' sources.

That day I was as usual in charge of the Pump Escape and Sub Officer Sammy Hill in charge of the Pump. We had attended a standby at a '77' at a Maxol garage on the Crumlin Road at the corner of Tennent Street, while the A.T.O. checked it out. It proved an elaborate hoax. We were also redirected to a number of other suspect cars which had been abandoned in the favoured manner which denotes a car bomb, that is askew in the middle of the roadway, with all the lights on and the doors open. These also proved to be false alarms. Not good for the old nerves. We were aware that the U.D.A. were mustering their companies throughout the city, in a show of strength, and that marches were planned. Due to the unrest and congestion in the vicinity of the Station I decided to stay out on radio watch and not return to Station, until things settled down, in case we could not get out in the event of a call.

On the early afternoon of this day I recall being in Cambrai Street which runs between the Shankill and the Crumlin seeing the U.D.A. parading thousands of its men from that area. All dressed in para-military uniforms-some wearing sun-glasses-others with scarves covering their faces-in an attempt to disguise their identities. It was a spine chilling feeling, as we sat there in our appliances waiting for the next call, watching them march past, not knowing if there would be any hostility displayed towards us. They marched quietly but with solemn dignity with determined looks on their faces of those we could see. These legions of marching men were not to be confused, at that time, with what we now know as hardened terrorists. Doubtless there were, however, those amongst them who were perpetrators of such terrorist acts. No, in the main, these were just ordinary working class men, fearful of what future British Governments and Republican terrorist policies held in store for them and their families.

Apart from another hoax call we were able to return to Station by mid afternoon without any further ado. I was thankful to get off duty and home safely that evening.

Meanwhile by late afternoon of the 6th February, elsewhere in the city, the unrest and Loyalist political frustration of that particular day had carried on over into the late afternoon for it was becoming clear by then that the Strike call was a failure. Lavery's public house-in Bradbury Place, not far from the city centre-was one of a chain of old established family run pubs in the city which had been firebombed that afternoon. A short time previously one of the Lavery brothers had been blown to pieces while foolishly attempting to remove a bomb from outside one of his pubs on the Lisburn Road. Donegall

Pass and Willowfield Road Police Stations had also been attacked by Loyalist crowds and it had been strongly rumoured that gunmen were active in the Sandy Row area-'Loyalist' gunmen.

Later that evening I went out to visit a cousin and her husband who lived not too far away from my home. While there, it came over the television news in a news flash that a Firefighter had been shot in Belfast. I was shocked and appalled but not surprised, tears welled up in my eyes and after the initial shock had worn off I rang Brigade Controls to enquire who it was. I was told it was Brian Douglas, but they did not know at that time, what his condition was. Later on that evening, another news bulletin stated the name of the Firefighter and that he had been shot dead. Like most of the other personnel in the Brigade I was shocked, but not totally surprised. The odds of this type of tragedy happening since we had become involved in civil disturbance incidents, had been shortening all the time. Now the worst possible scenario that the Brigade's personnel could envisage had happened.

Apparently that evening Major's flower shop just around the corner from Lavery's Pub in Bradbury Place was fire bombed. This shop stood on the corner of Sandy Row/Lisburn Road at its busy junction with Bradbury Place and the Malone Road. The apex of the junction between the Malone and Lisburn Road was occupied by a small triangular park known as Prince William Park. A park frequented by the elderly from the neighbourhood who used to watch the world go by whilst feeding the pigeons.

The Brigade attended the incident with two appliances and Station Officer Jack Fell was the Officer-in-Charge that evening. Several of the personnel who attended the incident at which Brian met his death that night have independently related to me the simple chain of events which led to his tragic death.

When the two fire crews from Cadogan Station further up the Lisburn Road drew up at the incident they parked close to the junction of the Lisburn Road with Sandy Row. Several personnel who attended the incident that night have independently told me that the fire crews were advised by the Army not to cross the road at the Sandy Row/Lisburn Road junction. One wonders in the urgency and emergency of the moment if these words in fact reached the ears of the Station Officer Fell?

Station Officer Fell ordered hose lines to be run out towards the burning shop. Brian was running one of these out across the roadway, at the top of Sandy Road when a gunman stepped out of the shadows of a side street,

Moores Place, just opposite Sandy Row District Orange Hall a short distance down Sandy Row-and opened fire with a sub machine gun. Brian was hit almost immediately and fell onto the roadway, just opposite a little green patch of the park. As his young life ebbed away, he was cradled in the arms of one of his colleagues until his crew were able to get him in to the Ambulance and away to hospital. He had no last words to say to his crewmates. Firefighter Brian Douglas was pronounced dead on arrival at the hospital.

Brian's post-mortem disclosed that he had been hit low in the trunk the bullet having deflected upwards causing serious damage to a number of major organs. Thus ensuring his rapid, untimely, and needless death.

Brian's Father gave permission for a full ceremonial Fire Brigade funeral. The penultimate journey for Brian took place from his family church on the Shore Road, to Carnmoney Cemetery in the North of the City overlooking Belfast Lough.

...'Whether on the scaffold high or in the battles van...the noblest place for a Man to die is where he dies for Man'...

Firefighter Reg.No 557 B.H.Douglas's coffin was carried on a flower bedecked turntable ladder as is customary in a Service funeral, draped with the Union Flag. Thousands of our Public-those for whom we were demonstrably prepared to pay the final price- attended the funeral. Family, friends, nearly every Brigade in the United Kingdom was represented. As we marched along silently behind the turntable ladder that bore Brian's coffin I reflected inwardly, as I'm sure my other colleagues such as Billy Whyte and Dickie Sefton did who also had suffered near misses, there but for the grace of God go I. The cortege must have stretched for a quarter of a mile.

I had never seen a blind man cry before. I hope it is the last time. It was so sad to see a blind man cry.

Messages of condolence flowed in from all over the world, from Fire Brigades and civilians alike. The Fire Service is a global brotherhood, and when one of our number falls we all mourn, and so it was with Brian Douglas...

'While the innocent sleep my soul stands guardian by their gate...'

There was never any official internal Brigade inquiry into Brian's death. Why not?

Was the Brigade afraid that if its findings were made public it would be seen to have had prior knowledge of gunfire in the area that evening and continuing knowledge of insurrection by the para militaries in Sandy Row which was further compounded by their knowledge of events that had taken place in that particular Loyalist area during the course of that day. If that was so, and logic would seem to dictate that that was so, then the Brigade should quite properly have been put in the Public Dock, but it never was.

The events of that day and into the evening had shown that serious Loyalist unrest was prevalent in Belfast. Petrol bombings had already occurred in the immediate vicinity, in fact Brian was helping to extinguish another one when he was shot. Had not Senior Officers or at the very least Controls not instructed Station Officer Fell to proceed with caution on this evening? This was after all by now normal practice whenever civil unrest situations arose? In any event whether Controls did or did not so inform this Officer-in-Charge ordinary experienced prudence should have dictated that a very cautious approach was called for in this area when responding to calls that day? Given that the crew had been clearly warned of gunfire by the Army when they first arrived in attendance at the scene.

It is foreign to a Firefighter's nature and training to stand idly by and watch a building burn. However I thought we had really learned the harsh lessons of the past four years, but evidently not. Property, no matter what value is placed on it, is not worth the risk of injury or death. Buildings can be rebuilt bigger, and better-which they have and will continue to be, in this Province-but no warm living human being can be replaced. Just one more victim's name to be added to Ulster's mounting death toll.

Officers-in-Charge of any emergency service who have been entrusted with the lives of personnel, are entitled to be in receipt of the most up to date fireground information that is available at the time. When they choose to proceed they then do so in the light of that knowledge and will, of course, bear the legal and more importantly the moral consequences of their decisions. The Fire Service has great latent potential for creating widows and orphans. Lives should not be put at risk for expediency or appearances sake nor should they be hazarded unnecessarily for the exigencies of the Service or some mistakenly perceived machismo image. The working maxim in these types of situations should always be to 'make haste slowly'. On this tragic occasion the Watch lost a respected colleague and friend, the Brigade lost a Firefighter, and appallingly, a needy father lost a caring and devoted son.

The murder of Brian Douglas stands as a salutary and stark testimonial to the misapplication of the above sensible pragmatic philosophies. Other public services-themselves equally unwilling participants in this struggle of good over evil-who continued to put human life at unnecessary risk were to take longer to learn from this murderous lesson-but learn it they did, eventually, and always the hard way.

I am on record after being shot in April 1972, when filling in a Fire Brigades Union questionnaire-which asked if I thought any blame could be attributed to my employer-when because I felt there was a strong likelihood of such an incident recurring, I had answered in the affirmative. Of course no one could have foreseen the tragic consequences of what had been just another hectic day for the Brigade and Belfast, but because the Brigade and its personnel worked in such close proximity to the Security Forces the Brigade's senior management simply could not have been unaware of the risks we were exposed to out in the city streets and the Spectre of threat this portentous relationship had for us all. Several self evident warning incidents, including my own, had occurred. All was required was to read the writing on the walls in every literal sense of that expression. Clearly no one could be bothered. Maybe their view was that it was just another case of 'Wright always being right' again.

In Northern Ireland it is not necessarily the trigger finger of the gunman alone that kills. This action was the last act in the chain of circumstances which came together to bring about this dastardly deed. If caution is abandoned the lives of personnel are put at risk. Firefighters during this period played a continuous game of Russian roulette at many similar such incidents. Most walked away to tell their tale-some did not-others have been left to tell their sad tale for them. The whole truth may never be told, just as it so seldom is in so many other similar events, only those who may have something to hide will ever know the stark truth and what part events and decisions may have played in Brian's demise.

When one of us gets kicked we all limp. Travel the world and present yourself at any Fire Station in any country for whatever reason-whether it is for assistance-natural curiosity how the other half operate-or as an unofficial ambassador for your Brigade-and you will never be turned away but made welcome with open arms and feted, even if it is only as a curiosity or as another crazy Firefighter.

When the new Station at Whitla Street opened in 1975, Brian's colleagues were permitted to name a room after him. He was Stationed in Whitla and had been on out duty to Cadogan whenever he was murdered. His father was invited to an official function at Belfast's City Hall to commemorate the Station's opening, which he attended. During his visit he was escorted by several of the senior Fire Brigades Union officials, including Jock Hall who asked him if he would like to visit the building's beautifully appointed Council Chamber with its handsomely carved wooden seating and decor. Joe recalls Brian's blind dad-himself an expert woodworker, who was employed at Stormont Government Buildings-caressing the smooth hardwood with his hands, admiring the detail and skills of the craftsmen who had fashioned it. One would not have thought that this simple man was still mourning the recent loss of a much a beloved only son, such was his courage on that day.

A Firefighter friend wrote this very poignant poetic panegyric in memory of Brian.

> *So you are from Ulster, say what have you done?*
> *You shot a young Fireman, an old blind man's son.*
> *So you are from Ulster, so proud and so true.*
> *Well, he was from Ulster and so proud of it too.*
> *And when on your death bed, you one day must lie.*
> *I hope you remember, you made an old blind man cry.*
> *And when on your death bed, when your life has run done.*
> *I hope you remember, you murdered his son.*
> *But one day in heaven, where there is no blind.*
> *He will meet with his father, if heaven be kind.*
> *And there at that moment, as that father sees his son.*
> *I wonder where you'll be, you man with a gun.*

Firefighter George.W.Johnston. 1973

Brian's Father met with his Son a short few years later.

God, alone, knows where the man with the gun is…

Fireman Reg: No 557.
B. H. Douglas.
Requiem Aeternam Dona Eis.

CHAPTER 9

The Wanderer Returns ....

A **Return to Roots...** Returning to White Watch Knock from Cadogan in August '73 following the Amalgamation was reminiscent of coming home after being away for four years. I had seen and done a lot in those intervening years within the Brigade and I was certainly older and wiser. The wheel had now turned full circle. This had been my first posting as a Temporary Station Officer in 1969 and I was even lucky enough to be given my old Watch back. It was pleasing for me to see a few of the old faces still there whom I had served with in 1969. A few more wrinkles and bit of hair less here and there, I felt just like a big Cheshire cat! Although self evidently the transfer from Cadogan did not displease me, it would have been very easy for me to fall into the stagnation trap.

Knock Station had been opened in 1968, and though a reasonably quiet Station at that time, it still retained its relatively fresh and new appearance and was a pleasure to serve in. Its three Watches had seen their fair share of action during the early days of the 'Troubles', especially in and around the lower end of the Newtownards Road, Short Strand area. It was here in the narrow back streets that the Protestant and Roman Catholic communities abutted one another and where history had pre-ordained that the tribal battle lines in the East of the City would be drawn.

It is well known throughout the Fire Service world that a busy Station is a happy Station. There is no time to be bored and thus no opportunity to allow all those little petty idiosyncrasies, irritations, and squabbling, between idle personnel, to creep in. Personnel who, of necessity, have to live at close quarters with one another. A placid, tolerant attitude is what is demanded from personnel. Some have it, some not. Pettiness can sometimes bedevil a Watch affecting performance on the fireground as well as making life on Station irksome at times. It usually falls to the Station Officer to arbitrate in such matters. Common complaints can include, accusations that certain duties on Station have not been allocated fairly by the duty officer, or then again, trying to accommodate requests for leave changes. Even arguments about who has the first choice of which T.V. programme to watch can be fraught with problems. Sounds just like home, does it not! Fire Stations are a home away from home for Firefighters when on duty. For a few the Station is preferable to the homes from whence they come. So keep them happy at all costs, well nearly.

Knock's Station ground covers East Belfast which included the old housing stock situated in the Newtownards, Albertbridge, Mountpottinger Roads, and Short Strand areas. This patchwork of streets of nineteenth century houses nestled in the shadow of the world famous Harland and Wolff's shipyard. It is still conspicuously dominated by its two giant one thousand ton cranes, Hercules and Goliath, which can be seen from miles around.

The 'Yard' has given employment to the local population for over one hundred years and has seen ships such as the Titanic and Canberra slide down its now redundant slipways. Shipbuilding is not only in everyone's backyard it is also in their heritage and bloodstream. My cousin sailed on the Canberra and my grandfather helped to build the Titanic. It was hardly the 'yard's fault' that the latter hit an iceberg on her maiden voyage and sank, but I bet they still rue the day when someone painted the words 'Even God can't sink this ship' on her bottom thus tempting the Gods. The slipway where the Titanic was built and launched still exists today but is now relegated to the less glamorous and more mundane duty as an open air storage area.

Canberra was the last passenger liner to be built in the 'Yard' she had the distinction of being the first ever ship to be designed with a bulbous bow under her waterline, the brain child of a university student at Queens University. Supertankers have dominated the shipyard skyline of East Belfast ever since the Canberra she slipped her moorings in 1967 to circumnavigate the world in luxurious style. She has now come to the end of her active life and is presently is being cut up for scrap, with difficulty, as the shipyard workers who built her might proudly expect, on a beach in India. The shipyard itself has gone into a long slow state of decline, but its day will come again.

Knock's entire Station area contained a mixture of working, middle, and upper class housing, extending out to Dundonald in the South East and Holywood in the East. The Harbour Estate was the industrial hub of East Belfast with industries as diverse as the Harland and Wolff's shipyard, Short Brothers and Harland the aircraft manufacturers, Shell Oil refinery, and the City's gas plant, which manufactured domestic gas from petroleum naphtha, a by-product of the refinery. This by-product was then pumped to the storage and distribution tanks in the city's old gasworks in the Ormeau Rd district, near the city centre, and thence for distribution to the consumer. Various other oil tank storage facilities also existed on the Station's patch.

A number of schools, which were dotted throughout residential neigh-bourhoods, also served the educational needs of the children of the area. Each and every fire risk was as varied as they were interesting and challenging. They all had to be frequently and regularly re-appraised in the potential risks they presented for fire-fighting purposes in particular those presenting a sleep-ing risk were given an extra coat of looking at.

It was the Harbour Estate that held the fascination for me and whetted my appetite with its numerous industrial hazards. I looked forward to the topogra-phy visits, especially to the shipyard with its ever changing throughput of ship-ping tonnage. I never failed to be amazed at the yard's capability to produce mammoth vessels, seemingly, out of thin air. One day you would be within the precincts of the shipyard and taken a mental note that the giant building dock had nothing being assembled in it. Then, perhaps a month or so later we would be visiting again and there sitting in it, dominating the skyline, would be a quarter million ton tanker ready to be floated out. It is an old Belfast joke that you never saw anyone actually working in the yard but still they turned out magnificently built ships.

The question that I would regularly ask of a newcomer to the Watch dur-ing lecture periods, in relation to the Station topography, would be, to name a sleeping risk in the Station area. The enthusiastic rookie would usually rhyme off a list of hospitals and old peoples homes. It would elicit a laugh from the rest of the boys when I would say, much to his embarrassment, 'you forgot about the shipyard on night shift'. Although having said that there could be strong competition for that description from Stormont Parliament and the politicians just up the road from the Station.

Yes, I relished being back at Knock.

Since shortly after the onset of the present 'Troubles' Belfast's old housing stock, which was some of the worst in Europe, had been undergoing a metamorphosis. A rebuilding programme undertaken by the Northern Ireland Housing Executive was underway at the time. Large areas of slum housing were earmarked for demolition and were being replaced with new developments. Some of these were models of good planning. Yet others were new slums for old, storing up for the future the same problems that the present ghettos had helped to spawn in the past.

East Belfast, like Ardoyne, New Barnsley, Crumlin, the Markets, had seen the greatest population movement in Europe in the late sixties and early seventies since the Second World War. Families from what were previously, reasonably well integrated communities had left their homes, lock, stock and barrel. They had fled to seek a safe haven amongst their own kind, not always of their own volition, having been driven out by either fear or intimidation. From August 1969 to 1974 it was estimated that 60,000 people had moved from the City and resettled elsewhere. Today the polite euphemism for this movement is called 'ethnic cleansing'.

The original strategy of the rebuild programme was to be one of integration. To this date, and I fear for the foreseeable future, it is doomed to failure. While mistrust and terrorist groups are still functioning how can it succeed? The physical enclaves that were there previously are still there, but with perhaps a new glossy facade. The dormitory towns of Antrim, Carrickfergus, Bangor, Lisburn and Newtownards took the majority of the overspill from Belfast. Those who chose to stay in the City, in their previous environs, were temporarily re-housed close to their old homes whilst new ones were built for them. There is an old Belfast saying, 'You can take a man out of the Markets, but you cannot take the Markets out of the man'. The implication of this being that those who left, brought their inherited cultures and beliefs, both good and bad, with them to their new locations. How do you rebuild the enclaves of the mind that house bigotry and hatred?

It was the fire-raising brought about by the continuing programme of demolition, during this ten years or so of rebuilding, that contributed to the biggest percentage of the fire calls attended by Knock's crews. No sooner would houses be vacated by their occupants, and before the Housing Executive's building squads had time to secure them by bricking up the doors and windows than the vandals, scavengers and professional thieves would move in. They would search for and ransack any personal belongings that were left. Strip out lead and copper piping, remove roof slates for resale, and on occasions allow gas to escape from supply pipes which in turn they would maliciously ignite. Sometimes derelict houses would be used, coming up to the eleventh of July bonfire night, for storage of bonfire materials. Whenever this was set alight, it not only compounded our problems but also presented a hazard to adjoining occupied property and the children who stood guard over their haul of prized materials. I would not like to have been given the job of trying to compile the number of man hours spent dealing with these needless fires.

I reached the stage whenever a row of houses was seen to be 'going well'- rather than tie up valuable men and resources for hours in extinguishing properties that were already clearly earmarked for destruction and would only be re-ignited anyway after our departure-I would let it burn until the roofs collapsed and destruction was nearly complete and then deploy a high pressure water monitor from the aerial hydraulic platform pump and simply flood the fire out. As might be expected by using this technique I did not always happen to ingratiate myself to visiting Senior Officers as it is foreign to a Firefighter's training and instinct not to extinguish fire expeditiously. However at heart all Firefighters are pyromaniacs and everyone loves to watch a good fire. It was lovely to indulge ourselves for a time, to stand back and watch it burn, this being a small bonus for our efforts. At night I used to excuse myself by saying we needed to let it get going so we could see what we were doing!

However any personnel such as myself who served in various Stations within Belfast from the onset of the current period of civil unrest will have experienced the different phases and nature of terrorist acts and violence that each Station had to cope with. There were times of intense activity when all Stations were under pressure or other periods when events rotated around the city and each Station seemed to be lumbered in turn with the high work load. If however you were on the transfer merry-go-round you might be unlucky enough to land at each Station just as it turn for the 'highlights' became due. The strain could be quite intolerable but I suppose that is all part and parcel of the job.

Knock had its share just as Ardoyne did. Although East Belfast housed a large Protestant majority, there existed at the city end of the Newtownards

Road where the Short Strand interfaces with the Protestant Newtownards Road a small Roman Catholic community. This area has seen on numerous occasions violence no less vicious than that which occurred in other such regions of the city.

I recall-immediately following *'Internment Day'* 9th August '71- being sent on relief and damping down duties following the aftermath of fires that had been raised in the Mountpottinger Road adjacent to the Short Strand, by those who had actively objected to their friends and relatives being whisked away by the security forces in the early hours of that particular morning. The Wellington Tank Co-manufacturers and galvanisers of the said product-Harkness the Carriers-and MacNaughton and Blair the city's largest plumbing and hardware warehouse all of which received the visitations of the fire raisers in the venting of their anger at internment without trial.

It reminded me of those early days in '69 on the 'Falls' when I thought World War III had broken out. All these premises in which decent people had previously earned a living now lying in depressing smoking ruins.

From that point forward Brigade activities in East Belfast had been relatively quiet, quiet that is, if you discount Knock personnel attending a fire aboard the old World War II submarine depot ship 'Maidstone' which was currently being used as a prison ship to house Republican prisoners. The vessel was moored alongside Airport Wharf within the Belfast Harbour Estate. Bedding was set on fire by some of her Republican guests who did not like the accommodation nor the hospitality shown to them by their hosts, the Army. It was soon after this incident that seven of the inmates took leave of absence from the vessel, escaped through a porthole, and swam to freedom across the shipyard's Musgrave Channel. They commandeered a Belfast Corporation bus into the city-very public spirited of them to support public transport-but I don't think the conductor lifted any fares from his rowdy passengers.

Many an enjoyable visit was made by Knock personnel on 'topography and familiarisation visits' to the 'Maidstone's very hospitable Petty Officers' Mess where one could sample a cheap tot of rum and delicious cuisine, the recipes for which had been gleaned through the ages from all over the world. Our principal contact on board the 'Maidstone' was Petty Officer Bob Stafford who was a physical training instructor known in navy parlance as 'Clubs' and the Mess entertainment Officer. Two amusing incidents associated with this period come to mind.

Personnel from the Station were invited to attend a 'Beating of the Retreat' to be played by the band of the Irish Guards. It was a beautiful still April evening as in the company of the rest of the invited dignitaries, we took our seats in the temporarily erected open stand on Airport Wharf alongside this World War II old maritime Warhorse. The band-some of whose members also looked as if they were World War II veterans themselves-lead by the Regimental Irish Wolfhound-played and the guards marched and counter marched up and down in front of us to their rousing tunes. This magnificent Irish Wolfhound was taller than some of the guards. Just as the sun was setting with the last of its horizontal rays painting the scene with a golden hue the band commenced playing 'Sunset'. A naval rating was slowly lowering the White Ensign on the Quarter Deck and we were looking forward to getting into the P.O.'s Mess. As the band fell silent the serenity and dignity of the moment was almost palpable. A head suddenly popped through one of the portholes in the after end of the vessel and a voice rang out loud and clear through the still air with a term of endearment directed at the Army which is the name I believe of an African ape 'You Pongo Bastards'. Silence still reigned supreme but by now you could have cut it with a knife. The Royal Navy shore patrol broke ranks and immediately raced up the gangway. We never did find out who the offender was-almost certainly a naval rating-who if caught would no doubt have his daily tot of grog stopped for a while. It certainly was not one of the P.I.R.A. 'guests' as they had long since vacated the ship for the happy shores of the Long Kesh former wartime bomber air base an establishment which was later to be renamed Her Majesty's Prison 'The Maze'.

On another occasion an Army patrol had come on board-it was being used by them for temporary accommodation-at the end of one of their long patrols on the streets of Belfast. It was standard practice to check their weapons were clear of live rounds 'up the spout' before going below decks. One tired squaddie was commencing this operation when he got the safety sequence wrong. Instead of having the safety catch on and clearing the breach he pulled the trigger. There was a burst of automatic fire as bodies dived every where for cover. Thankfully-but only for some-the weapon was pointing shore-side towards British Petroleum's nearby Tank Storage Farm. There did not initially appear to be any harm done.

Then we began to notice a commotion in the vicinity of one of the tanks. On closer inspection it was discovered that the squaddie's accidental discharge had stitched a neat line of bullet holes in a tank containing molten tar which could be seen cascading out and forming an ever growing pool at the base of the tank. No workers from the site were prepared to tackle the problem of stopping the flow from the bullet wounded tank until one of the management appeared, a Mr. Head, who indeed did have a cool head. He requested that several wooden spigots be sharpened and an extension ladder be placed close to one side of the holes. Dressed in his pin-stripe business suit he climbed the ladder to the top hole first and delicately inserted the spigot from a sideways angle into the hole and hammered it home. This was repeated successfully with all the other holes. When he came down there was only a few spots of tar on his suit. This molten tar was kept viscous and steam heated to a temperature of 250 degrees Fahrenheit. If any had gotten onto his skin it would simply have burned clean through to the bone. Oh the responsibilities of management!

In May '72 Knock personnel also had the onerous and gruesome task of picking up the pieces of eight people, four of them I.R.A. members, when they blew themselves up in the Short Strand. Apparently another own goal. The I.R.A. members had been handling the device when it went off prematurely.

I suppose I could say with conviction that within the context of what was going on in the remainder of Northern Ireland, Knock had been pretty quiet since 'Internment' was initiated, quiet as the grave that is, until the Ulster Worker's Council strike of May 1974.

Ulster Workers Council Strike... The government had been trying to re-establish an agreed administration for Northern Ireland since Stormont was prorogued in 1972. The way forward was seen by them as a joint power sharing Assembly sitting at Stormont. The proposed Assembly was set-up with Brian Faulkner Leader of the Unionist Party as its Chief Minister-he had been the Prime Minister in office when Stormont had been dismissed-with Gerry Fitt-the Leader of Nationalist Social Democratic and Labour Party-holding the post of his deputy. The forums constituent members were to be Nationalist and Loyalist politicians.

This Northern Ireland Assembly was to be the elected product of the tri-partite agreement thrashed out at the Sunningdale Conference in Berkshire, England. The most contentious of the Sunningdale Agreements-as it was to become known-was that which related to the setting up of a Council of Ireland which would have harmonising and executive functions in matters such as the environment, agriculture, and tourism, as well as a general consultative role. It had yet to be ratified by all parties to the provisional agreement. The electorate of Northern Ireland had not been consulted on any of the decisions reached at the Sunningdale Conference which were contained in this proposed Agreement and the Loyalist population viewed, with particular suspicion, that section pertaining to the establishment of a Council of Ireland, perceiving it as a staging post to a United Ireland.

This non-democratic Agreement foisted on Ulster by Westminster was to be the catalyst which was to trigger off a stoppage in the Province that lasted for fourteen days in May 1974 and was to bring the last vestiges of 'normal life' it to a virtual standstill. It was known as the Ulster Workers Council Strike-something of a misnomer then-as it still is today. Support for the 'strike' was neither immediate nor spontaneous. Its ultimate 'success' was ably assisted by those who did not belong to the U.W.C. at all. Before it came to a conclusion it was to become a popular, passive rebellion of the Protestant people who were prepared to suffer hardship to achieve the destruction of what they per-ceived to be this pernicious Sunningdale Agreement.

From a slow beginning, resistance to the Agreement became self perpetu-ating and grew in momentum the longer political discussions on the Agreement continued. A siege mentality and community spirit rapidly devel-oped amongst a large proportion of the Protestant populace in response to the intransigent attitude of Merlyn Rees, the supremo at the Northern Ireland Office. Neither The Northern Ireland Office, the Executive, nor Trade Union leaders were capable of either averting or calling off a general strike once it gained its own momentum. This momentum was fuelled by the perception that the Secretary of State could through 'persuasion' be eventually made to listen to 'reason' from partial sources and to the will of the majority of the Province's people.

What after all was the point in a democratic society of imposing by dictat an Agreement on people the majority of whom clearly did not wish to have it imposed on them and most certainly not without their electoral consent. No democratic referendum was to be made available to them to register their views and so it was Protestant grass roots opinion which took up the cudgels of resistance and in doing so forced the entire community into deprivation and potentially the ultimate disaster, civil war.

The strike had humble beginnings. It was Harry Murray a Belfast shipyard worker who announced on 14th May to journalists, following a debate in the Northern Ireland Assembly, that there would be a General Strike the following day. It was to be called by the Ulster Workers Council an obscure organisation that existed only on paper with its twenty one strong executive drawn from the six counties. This public statement was duly reported in the Press the following day. Those of us who read about it recalled the failed Ulster Loyalist Council strike of 1973 lead by Bill Craig which received little or no popular support largely due to the intimidation that was visited on Protestants by other Protestants in keeping them away or chasing them from the workplace.

The strike began the next day but had no impetus, not until the legions of the paramilitary Ulster Defence Association were ordered to offer 'encouragement' to the populace to refrain from attending their places of work. It was only by lunch time that day when news began to spread amongst work forces that this strike was 'for real' that numbers began to leave work. Although a list of emergency services and people who would be exempt was drawn up by the U.W.C. Co-ordinating Committee most of the strike strategy was simply 'made up on the hoof' and implemented as it progressed. The main strategy was to deny electricity power supplies to industry. This screw was slowly turned with great success.

We in the Fire Service wondered how it would affect us in either getting to or from work or in discharging our duties on the street. On the very first day of the strike, in my capacity as a civilian, I was to experience the shape of things to come in the ensuing fortnight.

Along with a Fire Service colleague, Jimmy Millar, I had hired a van to move my elderly parents from their home in Belfast. Our family home off Donegall Pass had been shaken in recent times by the shock waves of several nearby explosions and my parents' quality of life was being affected so we decided to move them down to a little bungalow close to where I lived on the County Down coast some twenty miles distant from Belfast. We had driven through Newtownards with only six miles to go to our destination with our load of furniture when we were stopped by a group of hooded figures at a road block outside the town. We were asked to identify ourselves and state our business which we did. I invited them to inspect my load but they refused saying 'how do we know what your carrying'. Look and see I told them but no one moved to take up my invitation. We were refused free passage unless we back-tracked into Newtownards and obtained a pass from the Orange Hall. So that is what we did. Take it from me in Northern Ireland you don't argue with a band of hooded men.

This was to be the pattern of events for travellers right across the Province for the next two weeks no matter what their business. The Brigade did not and could not issue any specific instructions to personnel about travel to or from duty. No-one could forecast from day to day how events would unfold, circumstances dictated a course of action and the remainder had to be played by ear on a daily basis. As for myself and other Watch Commanders at Knock we joined similarly minded people in the lengthy queues at the U.W.C. co-ordinating headquarters in Hawthornden Road which was only half a mile from the Station, seeking official passes for our personnel. Petrol supplies began to run down which became another problem for getting on duty, barricades also sprung up and had to be negotiated through pass or no pass. The whole society was teetering on the brink of civil war.

Electricity was rationed throughout the Province on a rota basis Belfast's Fire Stations did not have any problems with this as they had their own stand-by generators which gave us power to operate emergency equipment on Station. For domestic properties if you did not have a portable gas cooker you cooked on an open coal fire. As the strike began to really bite and power Stations reduced output fear began to grow that hospital equipment which needed high voltage would become unusable, thus putting lives at risk. It was also feared that the power Station generators if permitted to run down below a certain output would sustain permanent irreparable damage but apparently those operating them knew just how far they could go. At least we hoped so.

Hi-jackings of vehicles became very commonplace, they became a handy addition to a barricade, and many were set on fire. We usually only attended those well alight which were threatening property. Police and Army did little to prevent the hi-jackings or remove the obstructions. Whenever a barricade was removed by them another would magically appear close by.

Fire calls during this period were really quite run-of-the-mill. Perhaps due to the fact that no incursions were made into foreign territory by either faction. Each looking after their own security.

There was another more serious and fundamental problem . Pubs closed early or did not open because of lack of supplies caused by the strike. However the private illegal drinking clubs seldom ran short and were used by the chosen few. Private deals were entered into between some para militaries and the breweries to keep them supplied. Other, never-say-die-hards who did not belong to these inner sanctums and wanted or needed a drink went into Catholic areas. Where, believe it or, the drink flowed freely and the pubs were packed to the doors. Poor old working class Prod drinkers like myself had to suffer. Felt physically better for it though.

Initially some local politicians secretly opposed the strike but later when it became evident that success was imminent in bringing down the Power Sharing Executive, they tried to hi-jack the movement claiming it as their own brainchild. Ever the opportunists.

The Power Sharing Executive was bound to fail even after strenuous efforts were made by Gerry Fitt the Leader of the participating Nationalist Social Democratic and Labour Party and Stanley Orme a Northern Ireland Office Minister to persuade the S.D.L.P. to agree to the phasing in of the Council of Ireland. These entreaties were to no avail-the Power Sharing Executive fell within a 14 days of the commencement of the strike-culminating in the resignation of the much respected Chief Minister Brian Faulkner who was forced to resign as a consequence of the failure to agree by parties involved in this patently unworkable proposal.

The Power Sharing Executive for all its unworkability was nevertheless seen, at that time by many moderates, as the only real hope for political stability in the Province. The efforts of those who assisted in its demise could not have foreseen that although they had been instrumental in the demise of this Agreement the concept of power sharing was simply not going to go away. The government having had its 'beard singed' once was determined not to be thwarted twice. Clearly there are always two ways to skin a cat and the British government is more adept than most of doing just that. The issue of power sharing had really went never gone away nor would it. An amicable and workable agreement had to be reached by peace minded moderates from both sides communities if there was to be any movement forward to bring to an end this self destruction.

The British Government bided its time. Eleven years were to elapse before it was able to have another bite at the burning issue of power sharing, but what is that time span in the matter of Irish politics. In 1985 the government under the leadership of Margaret Thatcher took another gamble when they by-passed Northern Ireland's politicians completely and entered into the Anglo-Irish Agreement with the Republic of Ireland. This agreement embodies many of those principles that were abhorrent to the Protestant strikers of 1974. At the time of this new Agreement Loyalist opposition was vociferous, demonstrations and marches were held-the Loyalist slogan of 'Ulster Says No' was displayed on the facade of those council offices held by a Loyalist dominated majority-many of these offices twelve years later still displayed the banner and although Ulster's majority may still say 'No' the Anglo-Irish Agreement is still in place.

Following the announcement of the Agreement the R.U.C. became the handy whipping boys of extreme Protestant opinion who decided that the time was fast approaching when the survival of the Province was going to be fought out in civil war on the streets of the six counties and that the Loyalists were going to need every son of Ulster on their side. Well someone had to found 'guilty' of this unwelcome development didn't they? Sir John Herman the R.U.C. Chief Constable countered this Loyalist strategy by publicly stating that the Force was neutral and was there to serve all of the community. He gave a lie to the naive assertion by some extreme Loyalists that the R.U.C. should and would come out on the side of the majority if called upon to do so. This extremist Loyalist stance turned into an exercise to test where the loyalty of each member of the Force lay with Protestant Loyalism or with earning their daily bread in support of their families. It was a cruel and reprehensible dilemma for anyone to place Policemen in that unenviable position. In the unlikely event the members of the Force did not supported this sentiment-though given the title 'Royal' in their name by Royal Charter and thus being entrusted with the duty to uphold the Sovereign's Law they were effectively being invited to mutiny by the Loyalists and you can only take loyalty so far. Cynics however could be forgiven for repeating the old saying 'Loyal to the Crown and the half-crown'. If this mutiny had transpired even to a limited extent it would have played directly into the hands of Republican propagandists who have always accused the R.U.C. of being a Loyalist Police force for a Loyalist people. Policemen like the Army having once been thought of as being the saviours of one community or the other were now, once again, the Enemy. As they say 'between a rock and a hard place'. Individual Policemen and their families became the target for attack from some Loyalist extremists because Sir John Herman, himself an Ulsterman had unequivocally held the line in, as he saw it, bi-partisanship.

The Brigade attended a number of fire bombings of Policemen's homes in Loyalist areas. I attended one in East Belfast where a petrol bomb had been smashed through the front ground floor window of a little terrace house of London Road, causing little fire damage but unnerving the constable's young wife who was alone with their baby at the time. Policemen had gravitated to Loyalist neighbourhoods believing them to be a safe place to reside amongst 'their own' when they could not find peace of mind and physical safety in Republican areas for themselves and families. Ironically the situation became so potentially dangerous for some officers at this time in these 'safe' areas that the R.U.C. made arrangements to have those families under serious threat to be accommodated in housing across the water in England.

Although objection to the Anglo Irish Agreement was widespread the strike card had been played once already and was not to be used again. It was now Westminster's turn to cock-a-snook. One wonders today if the power sharing assembly had stood would Northern Ireland have had to endure what it has endured since that time? I doubt it, though that I suppose is a question best answered by the paramilitaries.

Democratic passive resistance practised by Gandhi won the day in the struggle for independence in India- democratic passive resistance was good enough for black majority rule and Nelson Mandela's view of democracy in South Africa-but this self same democratic principle was not to be 'encouraged' a second time by a democratic British government sitting at Westminster who did not wish to gamble on nor accept the will of a majority. What next for Northern Ireland?

Malicious Calls... Malicious calls had been a bee in my bonnet for a number of years during my Service. I was determined to see at least one successful prosecution before I retired from the Brigade, for what is after all, not only a jailing offence but a heinous threat to the safety of all the public due to the absence of emergency cover whilst the appliance rush hither and thither to fruitless hoaxes. I had been very close on a number of occasions to apprehending the persons whom I new to be the culprits, and whose modus operandii was always the same. To do so required the active assistance of the Police but no urgency, motivation, or intent ever seemed to exist on their part. The only written reply I ever received to any of my communications to Chief Fire Officer Morrision in relation to my plea to him to have something positive done to bring someone to book was that this was to be attempted with the assistance of the Police and British Telecom. His negative reply was partly due to the fact that the technical expertise did not exist at that time whereby calls could be traced quickly and these malefactors apprehended. Notwithstanding this, however, a declaration of intent and information imparted to the public would have been helpful by making them aware of the hazards malicious calls can present, not only to ourselves but to the public at large in depleting vital resources which might be required for a genuine call. It might also at least have had the effect of creating awareness and enlisting their assistance in bringing some perpetrators to justice.

It always made me sick to see how some weak minded individuals got their kicks by torturing innocent victims in their pernicious use of hoax calls. I have witnessed only too often not only us arriving at a house but a whole cavalcade of vehicles converging on the poor unfortunate's home. Everything from the Police, Ambulance, Fire Brigade, taxis, Chinese takeaway deliveries, emergency gas and electricity squads. Some type of grudge or feud seemed to be the motivating force in many cases such as this, it simply had the effect of driving some recipients of this 'bounty' to near distraction.

The saddest manifestation of this senseless and dangerous practice that I had the misfortune to encounter occurred while serving at Knock. It is a 'bonus' to some of the cretins who suffer from this malaise that as well as getting kicks from this sick practice if their actions can in some warped way be directly linked during this unwholesome practice to the 'Troubles', then so much the better.

One winter's evening on the way to attend night duty with a colleague-he was driving-we were approaching the Station. We were about three hundred yards from the road junction where Knock Station is located and the traffic had come to a halt. We were getting anxious about the time as it was fast approaching the 'witching hour' of 1800 hrs. Up ahead there appeared to be some sort of hold up at the Knock junction traffic lights. Suddenly as we waited we saw the flashing blue lights of two fire appliances turning out of Knock Station. They overtook the congestion at the lights that seemed to be causing our delay and then roared on up the main road past us in full flight. 'No need to hurry on duty now' I said to Bobby, 'We've no fire engines to play with when we get there'. 'That looks like an R.T.A. up ahead, our machines must have turned out to something else' so I decided to approach on foot and see if I could render assistance. Bobby would follow as and when the traffic would permit. As I drew closer only then did the actual scene begin to unfold before my eyes, but it was not until much later that evening that we were to learn the full implications of what had actually happened.

A crowd of people-including some of my own lads who had rushed out of the Station to help-were gathered around two vehicles which were locked together in a death embrace. One was a Volkswagen Golf, the other, an Army Saracen armoured vehicle with a Felix the Cat logo emblazoned on its side. This was the insignia of the A.T.O. teams operating in the Province (Ammunition Technical Officers) in other words bomb disposal. The Golf was facing up the Upper Newntownards Road-out of town direction-resting half on the footpath, and had obviously just passed through the traffic lights. The Saracen had been turning right from the North Road into the Upper Newtownards Road and the Golf was travelling straight up the main road. Some one of the two drivers had clearly gone through a red traffic light.

The Saracen had impacted on the drivers side stoving it in. The armoured car's huge bulk dwarfed the little car which looked like a kiddie's toy beside it. The driver of the car appeared to be unconscious and was still trapped in his seat with one of the Saracen's huge wheels resting against him. I vividly recall seeing something clinging to the rubber treads of the armoured vehicles wheel. It was such a bizarre sight that it took a few moments to register in my brain what it was. It was the knap which had been removed by the friction of the wheel's rotation from the duffle coat of the driver of the Golf which he was wearing when the wheel struck him.

An Ambulance was present and two of the other occupants of the car were inside receiving treatment having been removed from the Golf without any difficulty. One was the pregnant wife of the driver the other his little two year old daughter and in the meantime they were both taken off to hospital. I was the Senior Officer in attendance so it was up to me to initiate the removal of the driver, but first the Saracen had to be disentangled from the car. The Saracen's driver did not appear to be available and know one knew of his whereabouts and in any event he would be probably be too shocked to be much use to the situation anyway.

One of my lad's Bob Chrysler who was there and was ex-Royal Navy volunteered to reverse the Saracen off the Golf. A delicate kind of manoeuvre. For my part I had been able to climb into the back seat via the passenger side to try and assess the condition of the unconscious driver. All that I was able to ascertain was that he had a pulse and that he was still breathing. We all held our breaths as Bob gingerly reversed the twenty ton vehicle away from the car. Good lad I thought to myself, as a gap opened between the two vehicles. A doctor who had stopped at the scene, then joined me in the car, he took the man's vital functions saying that his pulse was strong at the moment but we needed to get him out in a hurry.

At this point the Emergency Salvage Tender and a Pump arrived on the scene from Chi'. I called for the jammed driver's door to be levered open. This was accomplished with some difficulty after several 'lifetime' minutes accompanied by a lot of quiet swearing, brute force, and ignorance, from the struggling Firefighters. Closer inspection revealed that the driver was pinned to his seat by the steering wheel which had been driven back onto the casualty. I was able to release his seat belt and the reclining lever and gently lower him back to a near horizontal position. We were nearly ready to extricate him. I said to the attending doctor, 'He is going to come out by hook or by crook and there isn't going to be any finesse about this. How's he doing? 'O.K., go ahead, but hurry.' The driver's legs were swung clear, and as gently as we could the casualty was man handled from the car and onto an Ambulance stretcher. I personally didn't give to much for the poor soul's chances but he was in the lap of the gods now.

When walking the few yards back to the Station I recalled how similar this accident was to the one in which Knock's P.E. was involved several years before, with me sitting in the suicide seat. This was another Firefighter's nightmare in which while rushing to help someone else an innocent life-or in this case-two were lost. It took place in the early hours of the morning about four hundred yards down the road from the Station at the Albertbridge Road/Upper Newtownards Road 'Y' junction. We had turned out to a call in the shipyard. In a near head on collision with a civilian car, my crew and myself were able to walk away, but the collision left the two occupants, a Police officer and a lady passenger, dead. My driver that night was subsequently charged and found guilty of having gone through a red stop light.

While on night duty that fateful night we been entertaining some guests on the Station in what up until then had been a pleasant relaxed social evening which was drawing to close. Our guests were beginning to leave and we were battening down the Station hatches for the night. The inter-station Tannoy clicked into life with a 'Full Attendance Fire Call to the Harland and Wolff shipyard'. I jumped into the suicide seat of the Pump Escape which was the lead appliance and turned out on the first leg of the downhill journey which took us down towards the 'Y' junction of the Newtownards and Albertbridge Roads.

As the cavalcade approached the intersection with our blue flashers and two tone horns piercing the stillness of the early hours. I became aware of the lights of an oncoming vehicle to my front left. The world seemed to slow down at this point and go into slow motion. It seemed to me at the time that there was ample time to take avoiding action but in reality there was clearly none for either driver. As the approaching car momentarily partially disappeared from my view under my side of the windscreen I caught a glimpse of the look of horror and realisation on the faces of the two front seat occupants. We did not feel the impact as both vehicles collided in a three quarters head on posi- tion-we just heard the sickening crunch of metal on metal-and then I saw the car bounce off and go spinning crazily in our wake.

Real time-in my mind's eye-quickly resumed as Colin my driver wrestled in vain to control the direction of our appliance and I braced myself for the sec- ond impact as we careered across the entrance to the Lower Newtownards Road mounting the off side pavement and 'taking out' the traffic light control box that we thought had given us the green light right-of-way to proceed straight down the Newtownards Road. We eventually came to a grinding halt within a few inches of a newsagent's shop window. In the following few sec- onds the scene became eerily silent. I looked across the cab to see Colin trans- fixed still clutching the steering wheel. A quick glance into the crew's cabin told me that they were all 'ok' in the back. The other appliances had halted and I gesticulated to their Officers-in-Charge to carry on to the incident whilst I radioed Controls to inform them of our predicament and requesting that another Pump Escape to be dispatched to the incident at Harland and Wolff shipyard. This only took a matter of seconds. We were not going anywhere.

I steeled myself for the next ghoulish task that I knew almost certainly awaited me. Along with the crew I dismounted and looked back towards the other vehicle. The mangled Morris '1100' lay some twenty yards behind the appliance facing in our direction of travel. When I looked into the driver's side there were two slumped and motionless bodies inside. There was no sign of movement from either the male driver or the female passenger. I knew imme- diately from experience that they were both dead. A hand gun was visible wedged in the pedals near the driver's feet. It did not matter any longer if he was a policeman, soldier, or terrorist, he was never going to fire it again. The Ambulance and Police quickly arrived on the scene and my crew helped extri- cate the casualties while I walked back to the appliance to check on Colin's whereabouts. He was no longer there. Someone said they saw him walk off towards the maze of side streets that made up the Lower Newtownards Road. I began my search by walking into the nearest street which was Connswater Street and quickly located him wandering aimlessly about the road in an obvi- ous state of shock. I was able to lead him quietly back to the scene of the acci- dent.

By this time Divisional Officer Jack Smyth had arrived and the Police allowed him to take Colin away in his staff car. He was in no fit condition to be interviewed. A Brigade personnel carrier soon followed which transported us back to Knock in numbed silence. My messages from the scene had been heard on the Station and all there were aware of the tragedy that had overtaken all of those involved within seconds of us leaving the station. Naturally Divisional Commander Douglas along with D.O. Smyth were soon on my tail, enquiring about my version of events. I felt they were more interested about whether alcohol had been consumed by my driver or not but I reassured them that he was a non-drinker.

Knowing that a Court case was inevitable and in order to try and establish what went wrong that sad night I attempted with the crew to recreate the sequence of events of our approach to the traffic lights. Colin had taken the routine middle-of-the-road line when nearing them and had taken the off side traffic light as his guide. We were able to determine that this particular traffic light-coming from the direction of the Station-when illuminated with the green filter light-which indicated left into the Albertbridge Road was illuminated in combination with the red stop light to its right In this combination the red stop light stopped traffic from our position from proceeding straight ahead down the Newtownards Road. However this red light at a particular angle was obscured as the appliance moved towards the junction by a lamp standard which was placed in front of the traffic light assembly. We could therefore only assume that he had observed the green filter in his haste and had not seen the red stop light due to the obstruction.

Colin was subsequently charged with 'Dangerous Driving'-found guilty-awarded a heavy fine-and six months disqualification from driving a Heavy Goods Vehicles. A light punishment one might feel. If he had been charged with 'Causing Death by Dangerous Driving' he may been jailed. It was with the assistance of a Road Traffic Engineer that the pre-crash scene evidence was presented to the Court and this must have been taken into account as mitigating evidence in the case as it cast a serious doubt on the allegation that Colin had been driving with premeditated recklessness.

During the hearing pathological blood samples taken from the deceased driver were not admitted in evidence because apparently samples ought to have been taken by the Police from the Brigade driver at the time of the accident but they were not. The Fatal Accident Inquiry that eventually took place disclosed that the car driver had alcohol in his bloodstream and it was stated that this may have impaired his driving judgement. Funny old thing British justice.

The British Fire Service 'National Joint Conditions of Service' permit the Fire Authority at their discretion to reimburse the employee for any driving fines incurred. Subsequently after the findings of the Fatal Accident Inquiry as a test of the Brigade's loyalty Colin at my behest decided to put their charitable instincts to the test. They chose not to exercise their discretion on this occasion. Another anomaly which surfaced following this case was the fact that although Fire Service personnel shoulder the unpaid added responsibility of driving they are not indemnified by their employers for their private car insurance should a claim be made against them while driving for the Service. This came to light when Colin went to renew his personal policy. The Fire Brigades Union were informed but by this time they did not want to know. The driver takes the pain and the strain and the Fire Authority get the job done on the cheap.

Colin did not want to return to being a driver on his resumption to duty-the trauma and pain was so indelibly inscribed on his soul-but like the vocational person that all good professionals are he did. This was not the only fatal incident of this nature around this period of time. The Brigade seemed to be taking more lives through road accidents than they were saving from the ravages of fire. Incidentally the original call I was despatched to was a 'false alarm good intent'.

As well as the appallingly tragic loss to those two victims' families this whole tragedy left a tremendous legacy of guilt with all those involved even though we had all been trying to do our best. Fortunate are those who can say 'there but for the Grace of God go I'....

In the meantime when we had helped clear the Saracen and the Golf from the scene we all walked back to the Station to book on duty. It was only then that I learned where the Station's two appliances had been turning out to when they had passed us on the road. They had gone to a suspect '77' call at Robinson's garage in Dundonald on the outskirts of our Station area. The Army bomb disposal team in their Saracen were also responding to the same call when it was involved in this unfortunate accident. The two crews which had attended Dundonald now had to be relieved with a change of Watch. A personnel carrier was dispatched from Chi' and we were transported to the incident. I knew that the garage was situated in a Loyalist trouble free area and I suspected it would turn out to be a hoax. This was duly confirmed to be the case at approximately 2100hrs by the A.T.O. and we then returned to the Station.

With accidents such as those that we had attended that evening, especially if a family are involved, personnel like to keep track of how treatment is progressing for the casualties. This incident being no exception I rang the Ulster Hospital at Dundonald where the family had been taken to inquire how they were. Normally this information is not given out to strangers, but when I told the Sister who we were and our personal involvement she informed me that the little girl had died and the father had multiple fractures although his wife was not seriously injured. We were all stunned when we learned the fate of the little girl. Perhaps if the appliances had not been mobilised to the hoax call we might have been in a position to provide this child with succour a lot more rapidly. Who knows? One of my Watch said he knew the family-they lived near to him in East Belfast-the father apparently was a school teacher. Sad and furious are a strange combination of emotions to experience at the same time so I spent a bit of time that evening giving to vent my feelings in particular about those malignant imbeciles involved in malicious calls.

I sat down that night and penned a letter describing the events of the evening which had lead to the decimation of this little family. I targeted it at the B.B.C. Radio Ulster news programme that was broadcast each morning and at that time was presented by a lady called Helen Madden. I wanted the public to know of yet another senseless loss of a young life-but more importantly on this occasion-I wanted to let the bastard-who had initiated the malicious call-know the carnage he had wrought on a young family. I had my letter hand delivered to the B.B.C. that night. Helen Madden rang me later and asked if I would come on the programme the next morning. I told her I would have to get permission from my Senior Officer. I contacted the duty Divisional Officer and explained this to him, permission was refused, and I told her this. The next morning when news of the accident was broadcast no mention was made of the circumstances which had actually caused the fatality and injuries. The story was not to end there. This family were to suffer more. The child that the expectant wife eventually delivered was a Downs Syndrome baby. I have often thought God must have a difficult job, but in the case of this hoaxer I trust that His judgement was straightforward, slow, and painful.

Hollywood Comes to Town... Allegations of exploitation of the Troubles were often made by politicians, local press, and self styled public representatives, against certain individual journalists from the world's visiting press. Over the years these journalist were always sure of either a good news or picture story from Ulster to relay to their respective readerships. They were always 'sure' of a good story by fair means or sometimes foul, that is. The substance of these allegations was that when the supply of the horrific dried up for that reason or this then these unscrupulous 'reporter pot-boilers' when it best suited their needs-would contrive, usually by paying youths sums of money-to set up a seemingly realistic situation which they could then reported on to their avid consumers.

Conversely in the interest of impartiality, it must also be said, that local paramilitary elements, on occasions took advantage of the media's presence, to further their own dubious ends. Because of the unwarranted bad images of Ulster that these 'doctored' and 'normal' scenes portrayed to the world I always felt that there was indeed a good case for press censorship in situations such as we were experiencing in the Province. Democratic government uses it own more subtle 'machinery' in these circumstances when it suits the agenda. The reader by now might be thinking, is this another political statement in what is supposed to be a book on the BFB? Well not exactly, but it is a personal burning issue and it is necessary to illustrate my point over the next few passages.

I had never before at first hand witnessed any of these 'arranged' Hollywood Extravaganzas, but one evening in the summer of '83 I was about to. As I have dwelt on at some length elsewhere in the tome the population exodus from homes in Belfast had begun in the late 1960s. It was still continuing right into the mid eighties. One area of houses in the Lower Newtownards Road, in and around Bryson Street and Madrid Street, would in the sixties, have been considered when compared to some other streets in the district as a middle working class area. These two streets were long and wide compared to other narrow mean back streets. The houses stood tall and proud having attics and parlours, unlike their neighbours who didn't have anything so grand. The frenzy of people moving house during this early period of the pogroms had by now dwindled to a trickle, being reduced to a few old die hard residents, who had hung on through thick and thin, but who now had to move due to the enforced rebuilding programme. What the petrol bomb and intimidation could not do the Housing Executive were able to do with a Vesting Order. It was to semi derelict streets such as this that we had responded hundreds of times over the years to clear up other people's messes.

When we got the call this night it was treated as casually as we would have any other to the area. Out of the Station and turn right down the Upper Newtownards Road through the Albertbridge junction-no matter how many times we went through it my flesh always crept with dread and anticipation when we passed over the spot where we had our accident-On down the road and left into Bryson Street. Madrid Street lay at right angles to it and was at the far end. As we approached the area we could see dense smoke wafting from round the corner of Madrid Street. As we neared the junction I thought I could see or sense flashes up ahead but I had no time or inclination to pay any attention to what was causing it. My first thought was that it was probably an electric meter intake in the house on fire shorting out. This often happens in derelict property when fire has reached the electric box. Wrong Allan, there they were waiting our arrival, two photo journalists, male and female, festooned with all their regalia of cameras and photographic equipment. Popping away at us they were, with their flashes, as we approached, with a crowd of youngsters there, gaily playing around them. I immediately grasped the scenario that was being enacted. Apparently we were to be the unpaid, but invited floor show, for the delectation of these two and ultimately, any media audience to which they would profitably sell their wares to.

The ground floor of the house was alight as we made our entry with a jet. I followed the branch men up the smoke filled hallway-note leading from the rear. The flashes seemed to pursue us even then. I turned around and there this male photographer was, behind me virtually on top of my shoulder. At this time I told him as politely as I could under the circumstances, to withdraw-as the fire was not yet under control-and I could not guarantee his safety-but I didn't say from what. He was not to be dissuaded but continued to advance along with us into the building. I turned around again and let out a couple of expletives, just in case he didn't understand English. The international language of the big boot. This verbal tirade along with a strategically placed accidental elbow in the guts, had the desired effect of hastening his exit from the premises.

Whenever the fire situation had settled down I took the opportunity of engaging both these journalists in conversation in an attempt to ascertain their credentials and to identify the nation from whence these creative individual came. It transpired they hailed from Boston in the good old U.S. of A. I asked if they had arranged this little fiasco? No more information was proffered on this particular topic other than where they came from. Now I would never presume to deny anyone the right to earn their daily bread, but I do object to a crime being committed in the process when in pursuance of that commendable and necessary task. A lot of Firefighters get needlessly injured on stupid incidents like derelict buildings as it is without doing the unpaid John Wayne bit as well.

In an effort to establish whether this was in fact the case when I returned to the Station I rang the Station sergeant at Mountpottinger R.U.C. Station, in whose area the incident had occurred. I fully described the circumstances surrounding the incident and my own misgivings. He was actually able to tell me that he was aware of the presence of these two in his Station area and that they were staying in accommodation in the Mountpottinger Road. Subsequent follow up calls from myself failed to elicit any formation as to whether or not investigations had taken place. I finished up as I had done on other occasions, going round in ever decreasing circles, we all know where they lead to. Another example of the apparent official apathy that existed in relation to trying to diminish the number of malicious calls being perpetrated.

Not until some years later when I got to know a chap who is a sound /cameraman and who had been employed by the B.B.C. for a number of years was I able to gain more insight into these regular Hollywood specials. This guy had filmed all over the world during his career, from Vietnam to Northern Ireland. In fact he was a member of one of the last film crews to evacuate Saigon before it fell to the Viet Cong. On one occasion we were chewing the fat about our collective experiences which were derived from being caught up in terrorist and civil disturbance situations. Amongst those that we happened to touch upon were the set up, or contrived incidents similar to the minor one I have just related.

He was reminiscing about several of the news stories which he covered in the Province and told of at least one occasion whenever he came into conflict with his producer/presenter who had arranged in company with himself to film a so called joy riding incident in West Belfast. This kind of incident had proliferated and snowballed particularly in West and North Belfast since the Seventies and had resulted in the deaths of 'joy' riders by Army gunfire. Because the filming was prearranged it appeared obvious to my friend that it was a set up and he made his feelings known to his producer/presenter. The response which he received was to the effect that his contract did not give him editorial control over anything that he was asked to record and he was therefore not permitted to exercise any control over the matter. Boxing clever-in order to counter this reposte-he then asked to be given certain guarantees to cover him in the event of injury or threat of legal action being taken if it was considered by the authorities that what they were participating in was an illegal act. He subsequently requested further confirmation on the nature of the insurance cover that he and his equipment were protected under and without further ado his employers simply cancelled the filming of the incident.

This incident and other unsatisfactory strictures on his work over which he had little control made him decided to go freelance at a later date. At that point in time he now enjoying this new independent status within which he could pick and choose the subject matter that he wishes to cover. His work no longer includes news coverage. His revelations only served to endorse my own experience and give credit to the protestations that had come from other official quarters in the past in that that news stories in Ulster are regularly obtained by fair means or foul. It would be naive to think that this has practice has changed today either. These acts are but another facet of human nature and the only point to be made in their defence would be that they among the more gentlemanly of practices to be foisted on the people of Ulster and as such are well down the list of priorities that require to be investigated and dealt with by the representatives of law and order. I doubt that they ever shall though.

Vent-A-Car... Every Firefighter looks forward with anticipation as the day of their twentieth year of service approaches. It is the milestone that Her Majesty the Queen has decreed by Royal Charter be marked with the presentation of Her medal for 'Long Service and Good Conduct' and for 'Exemplary Fire Service'. Mind you it is worth mentioning that one has have had to blot one's copy-book in a most serious manner not to be the recipient of the award. So it was in 1984 one year past the appointed date, in the company of some of my colleagues that my turn came to receive my reward. As they say, medals are a bit like haemorrhoids every so often every bum gets one.

I decided to make the presentation day a family day out. My watch was on duty at Knock so I took leave to attend the medal presentation ceremony at the rural location of Portadown Fire Station in County Armagh which is the apple orchard of Ireland.

En route from home with Sandra, Julie and Christopher I broke our journey and called into Knock to drop of my own car, having arranged to borrow a spare Fire Safety car to make the trip in semi-official style. So off the little family group went in the 'firms' Fire Car for a fun day to have the Queen's blessing and gratitude bestowed on me and enjoy the Brigade's hospitality free gratis, financed out of the Fire Authority Chairman's entertainment fund, courtesy of the British taxpayer. If only for a day I was to join the ranks and rub shoulders with the illustrious.

The day went swingingly enough the niceties and protocols of an official gathering were observed, caps were doffed and forelocks were knuckled and pleasantries were exchanged with the attending freeloaders from the Fire

Authority. My fellow recruit Archie Culbert Northern Ireland Executive Council Member for the Fire Brigades Union, in keeping with consistent Trade Union anti-establishment views, failed to attend to receive his 'gong'. During the course of the afternoon the amiable Chief Fire Officer Billy Beggs seemed to have taken a shine to my wife Sandra, as he kept plying her with the obligatory vol-a-vents and refilling her glass to overflowing with copious quantities of wine. They also serve who stand wait and occasionally pray for us.

So it was with regret that a very convivial and pleasant afternoon eventually staggered to a finale with the taking of obligatory photographs for the family album and the local rag. My family group having said our goodbyes to friends and foes extricated ourselves from the few die-hards who were still imbibing and bundled into the little pure white Vauxhall Nova for the return journey to Knock.

Tootling along at a leisurely fifty miles an hour on the M1 motorway towards Belfast and about fifteen minutes into the journey, I heard Sandra, who was looking decidedly pale, mumble something that sounded like, 'I'm going to be sick'. My reactions did not keep pace with her involuntary actions. As her hand floundered in vain to reach the passenger window handle nature overtook her and took its course. With an almighty splat the day's diet of vol-a-vents and wine decorated the inside of the passenger window, just as she managed to wind the offending obstruction down. By this time I had pulled up on the hard shoulder where it was necessary to wind all the windows down. An emergency mopping up operation on the inside of the car was carried out. Unfortunately that which had disappeared inside the door along with the lowered window was gone forever.

When I arrived at Knock I drove the car to the far end of the Station yard well out of view from the peering, inquisitive eyes of my Watch members who had lined the first floor window of the recreation room to see their boss bedecked with his new ceremonial ribbon. Having transferred a very limp Sandra and two nauseous children to my own vehicle I drove the foul smelling Service car to the wash bay, keeping the bouqueted side as close to the wall and out of sight from the by now somewhat curious onlookers. The boys must have thought it strange why I only gave their welcoming cheers a half hearted wave of acknowledgement as I played the hose on the inside of the door in an attempt to wash out the offending glutinous mess but without a lot of success.

In the weeks that followed this unfortunate incident I couldn't help but feel sorry for those unfortunate Fire Safety Officers who had occasion to drive the ill fated car on their duties. Even in the street as it passed I could always tell 'Sandra's car' the occupants always seemed to drive it with the windows down even in rain, hail, or storm. I wonder why?

Bob Finklestein... Finklestein, now there is a name to roll around the tongue probably the family were originally from Ireland! I laugh to myself each time I think of the name Bob Finklestein and Bob if this book ever makes it to the States I hope when you read this you may laugh too, although your role in the short anecdote which I am about to relate was possibly of a slightly more serious nature.

Back in 1985 during a lunch break at Knock I received a call over the Station loudspeaker system to take a phone call in my office. When passing the watchroom the Dutyman said to me that the gentleman wanted in fact to speak to Station Officer King but as Tony was not on duty that day, he said that I might be able to help him. When I lifted the phone a voice with a rich American accent said ' Hello Mr. Wright, my name's Bob Finklestein'. Having been taken by surprise my reply-as any Ulsterman who thinks he's about to have the mickey taken out of him, would be-was ' Oh yea! in as laconic and as an American drawl as I could immediately muster. 'I'm with the Department of Justice in Baltimore'-he went on-' I wonder could you help me with some inquiries about a Lee Montgomery who used to be with the Belfast Brigade'. At that point I began to take matters seriously, so I replied-' If I can, what's the nature of your inquiry'-though still somewhat suspicious.

Lee had served on my Watch at Whitla Station some years before. He was well liked by his colleagues, a good Firefighter, something of a gregarious character and a brilliant mimic. He was also a talented musician and played in the Brigade's group. His last posting prior to him leaving the job had been on Blue Watch Knock where his Watch Commander had been Station Officer Tony King. I knew that Lee had gone to the U.S.A. with his wife but there had been no feed back about him since he departed .

Bob continued-you can see I immediately took him to my heart-'Mr. Montgomery has applied to the United States for political asylum'. Shock/horror-leaps back in amazement-you know the scene-'What the hell's going to come next I thought? 'He and his wife have split and he has taken up with a United States national and would like to reside with her in this country. He has stated on his application that he had been hounded out of the Brigade because of his political beliefs, thus implementing his move to the States. According to

Mr.Finklestein, Lee when he was on duty and attending bomb incidents had been required on occasions to defuse these devices-he had reached a point where he simply could not take anymore and that is why he resigned from the Brigade and left the country'!

As I lay on the floor in hysterics digesting these statements it took me a moment or two to compose myself. My first thought was 'I cannot be hallucinating and the sun is not yet over the yard arm so I couldn't have forgotten the pleasure of getting drunk so early in the day'-could I? Obviously for the reasons stated my emotions were a mixture of incredulity mixed with a trace of anger at what Lee was reported as having said on his application form. I said to Bob-by this time as is the American way we were on first name terms-'Bob, Lee was well liked and a good mixer. I was never aware that he had any serious political leanings. He is a Protestant in a predominantly Protestant Brigade, he lived in a Protestant area. Last but by

"... honest to God.
It came apart in my hands!!"

no means least no Firefighters were ever required as part of their duty to defuse explosive devices. Although the my Best Man Walter Wilson nearly defused a bomb the hard way. Walter was crawling around on his mouth and nose in thick smoke trying to locate the fire at a warehouse in Corporation Street. He crawled over an object but did not know what it was, until the place had been ventilated. Guess what?

That having been said I did tell Bob that personnel have from time to time been caught up in actual explosions and been injured and I myself had been shot but there has never been any deliberate official attempt or intent to kill or maim Firefighters by either terrorist faction from both sides of the religious and political divide in the Province. Except on one occasion.

I went on to say that as a Brigade we have guarded our impartial role jealously and on occasions have battled with officialdom to this end. We believed that if we did not preserve our impartiality then we would not be able to carry out our duties and be accepted by both sides of the community. I ended by saying that 'Lee's talking nonsense'. We finished our conversation with a few pleasantries and he thanked me for my time. When I put the phone down I was somewhat bemused about what had been discussed. Well, well, well, I thought to myself, you never know what a day in the Fire Service is going to bring. This is probably one of the attractions of the profession.

Much later I heard that Lee had indeed been granted asylum. Surprise! Surprise! Unfortunately had suffered some form of stroke and is presently living somewhere in Welsh Wales after returning from the U.S.

I saw Bob Finklestein recently on television following the death of Frank Sinatra. He was being interviewed with Nancy Sinatra on CNN's Larry King Live. Apparently he now represents the relatives and estate of old 'Blue Eyes'.

Dun's Gun... Bob Dunsmore was a Firefighter driver with me at Knock, he was also a member of the Reverend Ian Paisley's Democratic Unionist Party and as such was a Democratic Unionist Party Councillor on Lisburn District Council. He was a quiet unassuming person and bore no resemblance as far as I could see to his political leader in that he was quietly spoken and didn't have the booming voice of Mr. Paisley. He was an active and caring Councillor and took his responsibilities seriously both in his Fire Service profession and his constituency work. This was self evident when he was engaged in debate from time to time by either myself or his colleagues.

One evening while on night duty Bob came to my office and asked if he could have word, I wasn't ready for what he was about to tell me. Most Councillors and Member of Parliament in the Province are aware that they are possible targets for political assassination. This was painfully obvious following the murder of the Unionist M.P. Reverend Robert Bradford, Bob was in a similarly invidious position. He told me that he felt I should know that he had been granted a Firearms Certificate by the Royal Ulster Constabulary to carry a pistol-I knew he wasn't talking about a water pistol-and that it was his intention to carry the weapon even when he was on duty.

Here was another first that needed some thought. A number of questions ran through my mind such as-who in authority in the Brigade should be informed-do I inform the rest of the Watch-do I tell him not to carry it while out on calls? It certainly put me and his colleagues in a difficult and potentially lethal position. The implications were legion not the least of which would be should an attack on Bob be unsuccessful because of his ability to defend himself would it call into question the total impartiality with which all the para-militaries regarded and treated the Brigade.

Setting aside the fact that Bob might be under threat, if the Police thought him to be at risk sufficient for them to justify the issue of a Firearms Certificate then it implied to me that his colleagues could also be at risk either on the Station or out on a call while in Bob's presence. No one knew the word collateral damage in those days but by heavens it did not need a dictionary to figure out what would happen if a malicious call was received with the express intent of getting Bob out onto the street as a target. He and we would all have been at risk either way whether Bob carried a weapon or not. In the dark all Firefighters looked alike and the envisaged scenario was blood curdling to say the least.

The Station was secured during the hours of darkness but was not impenetrable What if security was breached and someone came to have a shot at him while he was asleep? Mistakes of identity were a regular occurrence in such matters. It did not bear thinking about and I did not have any answers. In any event the only thing I could think to say to him having taken these factors into account that I would tell no-one else and that he should inform the new Chief Fire Officer, who was the recently appointed Clive Halliday, about it. Let him decide what was to be done and whether or not he should be posted to a less vulnerable posting within the Brigade. It is called passing the buck, which I did not like doing, but this one was bigger than the both of us and was a unique situation for any Watch Commander to find himself in, never mind the Firefighters.

Shortly after this the three Watch system in the U.K. Fire Service was changed to that of a four Watch cycle due to the introduction of a shorter working week. Bob was transferred to the newly established Green Watch-hardly in keeping with his particular political colour-but I can assure you I did not raise any objection to his being moved. Much as I had appreciated his services while with me I was quite frankly relieved when he was transferred. In any event his new Watch Commander did not have cause to worry for Bob is still around today and what he didn't know didn't seem to do him any harm but it certainly made me quite nervous for a while.

Kincora Conundrum... When the Terrorist Genie popped out of the bottle around about this time it was not the only evil Genie to plop out. Paedophilia slimed and wriggled its way out also. The word 'Kincora' might not summon up any particular memories to anyone outside Northern Ireland and even if it did it would only be by those of us of a particular generation old enough to remember the distasteful episodes which took place within the precincts of this boys hostel during the mid to late seventies.

Today paedophilia is like its repugnant practice a much abused word. If you have not been 'abused' in your childhood then the chances are that you are unlikely to make it as a success in the media these days but true paedophiles and paedophilia do nevertheless exist. Prostitutes are paragons of virtue by comparison with these characters.

The Genie of Terrorism provided a wonderful stony shadow under which abhorrent 'trades' including drugs and paedophilia could exist and flourish. Of course these 'trades' have always existed and no doubt always will but the hostilities were a Devil sent opportunity for them to expand and almost brazenly display their 'favoured' pastimes in a city whose collective focus was elsewhere for the moment.

In addition to the general public not having been told the whole truth about Kincora-which if it had been it would have undoubtedly destroyed more lives and careers that it has hitherto-this scandal remains unresolved to the entire dissatisfaction of the public interest in Ulster to this very day. Until this resolution occurs the circumstances surrounding the vortex of abuse-that of the whirling cesspools of political chicanery-will remain a stain on the integrity and conscience all those who albeit unwillingly contributed to what the intelligent populace of the Province perceived, rightly in my opinion, as a bare faced 'establishment' and security cover up. This could be the only natural conclusion to draw based on the political posturing over the disclosures of events at Kincora. At that time it did not take a genius to work out that the tentacles of these nefarious activities extended all the way up into the very bosom of the power politic.

What, the reader might wonder, has a boys home scandal got to do with what are essentially writings about the Belfast Fire Brigade? Let me explain. I had been puzzled for many years regarding a small event which took place at Knock Fire Station during this shameful period and which has never been fully explained to my satisfaction. I can only conclude in the light of subsequent hearings-after the story broke-that this minor incident, in which I was a fleeting player, was part of the sinister affair which until then had not surfaced.

Kincora was a boys hostel on the Upper Newtownards Road Belfast less than fifty yards from Knock Station and was effectively or 'neighbour'. Station personnel regularly inspected this adapted Victoria house for fire safety and fire precautions on behalf of the Eastern Health and Social Services Board. Kincora was a non custodial, temporary refuge for boys between the ages of fifteen and eighteen, from various unstable domestic backgrounds. It was not a home for boys with criminal backgrounds. These poor unfortunates were there to be looked after by a supposedly caring staff in a safe environment, until they were capable of making their own way in life. However it was brought to light that the Warden was involved with other parties and members of staff in procuring boys from the home for sexual exploitation by adult males. It was assumed that the cover up ensued because some of these 'adult' degenerates were known to be either part of the security forces, civil service, the political scene, or of all three.

On more than one occasion- even before the story broke-in my routine inspection work I met one of the two Assistant Wardens a gentleman called Raymond Semple. He seemed to me to be dressed rather flamboyantly for a middle aged man-rather like a 'child of the sixties'-with his flower-power tie and his suit with flared trousers. Really not the usual type one would expect to see in charge of a children's hostel. Some things did not quite ring true in my mind. He looked rather out of place in a boys home, I thought. A snap judgement maybe, but, then I was used to meeting all sorts in my work and it paid for health reasons sometimes to get it right first time.

My thoughts were later to be proven right in court when the Chief Warden William McGrath, Semple's boss, was arraigned in the Dock charged with various lewd offences with the boys of the home. McGrath, who was known to be involved with an evangelical group, was a founder member of an Orange Lodge-'Ireland's Heritage'-Loyal Orange Lodge Number 303. He also had para-military involvement with a group known as 'Tara'-called after an historical site north of Dublin, location of the seat of the High Kings of Ireland. Tara was a Loyalist organisation that was not proscribed and none of whose members had convictions for any sectarian or political crimes. It also transpired that McGrath was a homosexual and like his sorcerer's apprentice had little of sartorial elegance about him either.

McGrath was born in Belfast during the Great War in 1916. Much later in his youth he married an Englishwoman called Kathleen and they set-up home in the Antrim Road area of Belfast, with, in the fullness of time, their three children. Religion being ever in abundance in Belfast they eventually established and set up the Christian Fellowship and Irish Emancipation Centre across the city in another district known as Finaghy, in a large house they named 'Faith House', where they set about, in kindred spirit with many other of the time, 'saving' the wayward youth of the city from themselves and showing them the way to eternal life.

McGrath, who was originally a Methodist, developed his own bizarre version of the 'Truth' which he vigorously peddled to those crazy or desperate enough to listen. His 'Irish political ' views hardly merit comment in that they were a woeful amalgam of the disingenuous right across the across the idiosyncratic spectrum to the just plain daft.

It is not clear when McGrath became a homosexual nor pederast but he was most certainly that. He rose to infamy with the rise in the political tension in the Province of the early 60's where he developed his political dimension, mostly in the shadowy fringes of the Loyalist communities of Belfast.

About this time in the wider world the Cold War was still in full swing and McGrath became one of many, who continue to this very day, to attempt to proselytise the peoples of the then Soviet Republics. The sincere, though misguided attempts, of many of these religious fanatics translated in to the direct actions of attempting to smuggle Bible tracts and other such media in to the potential 'believers' of the Soviet Union.

Then, as now, these groups attract much attention from western intelligence agencies who not unnaturally regard them as a useful conduits for two way traffic, in and out, of such regions. These religious sects are readily penetrated by these agents and thus it was the McGrath came to the attention of MI6 who of course referred his activities to MI5 who were and continue to be deeply involved in the manipulations of politics within the Province.

McGrath made ideal material for a potential agent in that he had, for those 'unenlightened' days, when homosexuality was a criminal offence, the ideal Achilles heel which could be used at the appropriate time as leverage against McGrath when his controller wished him to pursue this or that particular tactical direction of his paymasters.

The basic thrust of MI5's work at that time, or so McGrath was led to believe, was the task of forming a shadowy group called Tara the function of which was ultimately to penetrate Loyalism at all levels and to provide 'government' in the event that the British abandoned the Province and went home. However, there was another more sinister agenda.

Around this time the Northern Ireland Prime Minister was opening a dialogue with the Republic's government and a spirit of realistic pragmatism was beginning to gain ground. Clearly this was not in the strategic interests of the UK government which still needed bases on the Atlantic sea board for NATO reasons. So it became imperative that these political developments should be thwarted and destabilised and into the shadows slid the bold McGrath. His tasks were to engage in limited gun running which would establish his credibility with the Loyalist paramilitaries and to foment and distribute misinformation in a manner that an unthinking dupe can only do so well.

McGrath's sexual predilections opened some very 'heavy' political, and most certainly many bedroom doors for him in local, provincial, and London's circles so his warning of impending doom were well listened to. Unfortunately for him two significant developments were to lead to his ultimate downfall.. Aircraft were made to fly further and faster; Governments and politicians along with their sexual appetites changed; and consequentially with them military strategic policies.

Along the way McGrath arrived 'mysteriously' and without any form of qualification at Kincora to tend to the boys. Additionally it was physically convenient to the then seat of power at Stormont Government buildings and quite clearly provided suitable cover for his covert activities. Unfortunately his sexual appetite simply ran riot and that allied with the changing political and strategic times eventually led to his demise as an MI5 agent . His usefulness having been compromised or exhausted he was simply thrown to the lions of the judicial system but even then it is clear his downfall was somewhat cushioned by friends in high places, he served a limited amount of 'time' for his criminal activities, latterly, passing his remaining days quite literally at the seaside and subsequently passed away in 1995. A case of from nowhere to obscurity in one exhausting swoop.

One evening while on night duty at Knock the Dutyman tannoyed me to the engine room. When I arrived he said that there was an armed plain clothes Policeman on the Station. He told the Dutyman that he was searching for an escaped boy from Kincora whom he had been escorting. I called the Duty Officer and together we began a search of the Station not just for the Policeman but for the boy also. Eventually we bumped into this so-called Policeman in the Station yard who was waving a revolver about-in somewhat of an agitated state-quite obviously he had not yet located his prey. I told him quite forcefully that he had no right to be on the Station without my permission and certainly not with an exposed firearm. He repeated the tale to me that I had already been told by the Dutyman and without further ado he quickly pocketed his weapon and left the Station. That was the end of the brief episode.

It was only whenever the scandal came to light later in 1980 that I reflected on this peculiar incident. Why was an armed 'Policeman' escorting a boy, either to or from Kincora. It was not a penal institution and most certainly no criminality could have been involved? Why had that boy absconded from his custody or perhaps he was on the run with a lot of dangerous information in his possession? The further question arises of just how many boys disappeared from Kincora around this period. Perhaps some of them are still propping up motorway bridges in way or another who knows? I leave you to draw your own conclusions, I have long since drawn mine.

To embark on any further comment would I feel only go into the realms of what was a very complex story of paedophilia and the ensuing cover up at a very high level. Westminster politicians, Police and even MI5 were reported as being involved in the scandal. Six enquiries failed to establish the whole truth.

I believe Chris. Moore's investigative study 'The Kincora Scandal' gets quite close to the overall truth.

Prohibition… Contact with the Police is part and parcel of everyday life during attendance at incidents. However, sometimes circumstances occur which are not quite the run of the mill involvement that one has come to expect in this working relationship. Illicit, surreptitious drinking by certain individuals, usually on night duty, has occurred on Stations as far back as I can remember. These individuals on most Watches and Stations-including Brigade Headquarters on occasions-had devised and adopted their own method of dispensing and the concealment of this forbidden nectar from 'official' prying eyes-be that an overzealous nocturnal prowling Station Commander-or a snap inspection by a Divisional level Supervisory Officers. I have little doubt that in respect of some personnel this weakness may well have been one of the by-products of the some of the scenes they may have witnessed or experienced during their Service but it is a rather vacuous excuse when the general public are depending on us for their very lives.

These 'prohibition' incursions occasionally met with success but the Station grapevine was usually so well tuned and such a high emphasis was placed on Station security-especially on night duties-that the 'Untouchables' success rate was very low. However if a find was made-like the days of prohibition in the States-the game was moved to another location until the 'heat' came off. It was when the Station Commander-the Trojan horse inside the fortress-decided to have a personal kit locker inspection that the 'cat really was amongst the pigeons' and the most disruption of the relative tranquillity of Station life occurred.

At the first hint of a raid barrels and tinned goods of the liquid variety would have to be spirited away. I truly dreaded if I happened to be caught on duty when one of these snap raids was to take place and when, as happened, I was ordered by the Station Commander to accompany him on his rounds. The favoured method at Knock was to commandeer a spare kit locker or two in the locker room where tins of beer and kegs would be secreted away with the dispensing pump neatly secured to the inside of the door. Usually a trusty member of the Watch would look after the financial and dispensing end of matters in the Shebeen. In fact we had a chap on the Watch who [his real name has been changed from Jim to James to protect his identity] used to commercially install the pumps for Scottish and Newcastle Breweries and this was how James was first introduced to the Brigade and came to hanker after a career in it during his 'unofficial' pump servicing calls to the Station.

During the rounds the accompanying Duty Officer would use the spare keys to open the lockers. When a locker was opened belonging to another Watch not on duty I cringed at what might be revealed whenever that particular door swung open. It was a very stressful business.

Determined efforts were taken by the Brigade from time to time to stamp out these practices but they were to meet with little success. This was one reason why I was an advocate for 'wet' canteens-which were a common feature throughout the Service, probably because of the long hours of duty-where drinking could be permitted under supervision and whence it could be strictly controlled. It was a tiresome issue which has now been completely resolved and eliminated I am glad to say by the advent of drink/driving legislation and a substantial reduction in duty hours.

It would appear however that the Brigade was not the only civilian service where problems of this nature arose and as it happens I stumbled on this fact by chance of circumstances one evening at Knock. My office work complete, I had gone to bed hoping for a quiet night when I heard the front door bell ring. As my office/bedroom was closest to the front of the Station I got up to answer. Standing at the door was a uniformed Policeman and parked nearby an armoured Landrover. He could not have known my rank as I was only clad in vest and trousers. I greeted him and asked if I could help assuming that he had called on official business. His first words nearly floored me, he asked if he could have a 'carryout'. I was temporarily taken aback, when I came to my senses I told him that 'we don't do carry-outs here', 'but we got some here before' was his reply. 'Not here you didn't mate'. By this time I think both he and I realised a gaffe had been committed, he having obviously got his previous 'take-aways' from another Watch. Is it any bit of wonder my furrowed brow has stretched up to the crown of my head by now. As they are prone to say in the House of Lords 'One never ceases to be amazed by the working class, does one'.

Chinese Take-Away... Humour is always part of the job. Here is another short light-hearted romp into that sandpit. Just across the road from Knock Station stood the long established Girton Lodge Hotel. This Victorian building had been at one time, a sumptuous family residence. It had been tastefully converted and extended to become a small hotel with some ten bedrooms, a bar, dining and function room with the usual facilities. Its clientele mainly consisted of transient business men. No doubt the twice weekly disco nights helped to boost the takings. Occasionally when on night duty we would hear the music and the comings and goings of the revellers into the early hours. The premises had changed ownership on numerous occasions and at the time in question was being run by a Hong Kong Chinese gentleman.

Early one bright summer's morning shortly after first light I was awakened by the 2 to 8 watchroom Dutyman. He said that he had gone outside to stretch his legs and 'take the airs'. While outside the front of the Station his attention was attracted to a gentleman perched on the roof of the vestibule entrance hallway of the Girton. According to the Dutyman he seemed to be in need of assistance to reach terra-firma. So up wearily I got and had a look, sure-enough there he was. I told the Dutyman to go and quietly fetch a few of the lads-there was no need to waken the whole Station-so off he went to do as he was bid. Equipped with a short wooden extension ladder my little rescue party trudged off across the road to the aid of this seemingly poor unfortunate, pondering all the while as the troops grumbled along what was he trying to escape from, maybe he had been caught in flagrento delectii by a passing husband-perhaps his room was on fire-had he smelt smoke in the corridors-perhaps he was attempting to commit suicide?

The answer to my ponderings were soon to become all too obvious. If we had not arrived at the scene when we did I think physical injury of some description would undoubtedly have taken place. Only thing was this suicider's attempts would have been more than capably assisted by a Chinese gentleman standing at the foot of the hallway wielding a meat cleaver in his hand and urging the chap to come down with the other. Not until we arrived did he take up the Chinaman's offer to descend. As soon as he reached the ground the Oriental gentleman let out a tirade of what must have been Mandarin and by the sound of his tone he wasn't exactly asking him what number on the menu he wanted to order. Yes, our friend had been attempting to do 'a runner'. By the look of him he obviously had enjoyed a good night and had stayed over-he may have booked for bed-but certainly he had no intention of staying for breakfast. Before things really got out of hand the friendly local constabulary arrived which I think was only marginally preferable to his potential fate. The 'boys' duly whisked him off in their paddy wagon, only this time he wouldn't be asked him to pay for his lodgings in the meagre guest house he was bound for. So off we all dandered back to the Station-all in a night's, or by this time, morning's work.

Dessie's Daughter... It was around about the same time the Watch attended another R.T.A. This time, however, with extremely sad and gloomy implications for the Brigade as a whole and for one individual in particular.

Knock's Pump and Pump Ladder along with Chi's Emergency Salvage Tender were mobilised late one evening to an R.T.A. on the Knock road at the junction with Kensington Road just beyond the Royal Ulster Constabulary H.Q. On arrival I found that three cars had been involved in a collision. Each lay a few yards apart having sustained various degrees of damage. An Ambulance paramedic informed me that they had one confirmed dead in one vehicle but that there was an unconscious young girl in another which he had just examined. I stepped over and scrutinised this particular car. In it, lying in the front passenger seat was a young girl-no injuries were immediately apparent to me but she was trapped by her left foot-her ankle being jammed between the engine bulkhead and the nearside front wing which had been crushed in by the side-on impact of one the other vehicles. She was wearing an evening dress and it appeared that the occupants of this particular car had been on an evening out. Harry Williamson the attending Sub Officer on the Emergency Salvage Tender produced a penknife and quickly and efficiently cut away the heel of her shoe immediately releasing her trapped foot. She was rapidly and carefully extricated from the seat and put onto a stretcher and then taken away by the Ambulance personnel. During these brief few moments of our work she did not exhibit any signs of life.

No sooner had she been taken off to hospital than Divisional Officer Dessie Graham arrived in his staff car. He was partially dressed in uniform and civilian garb so I thought that obviously he had been at home on standby duty. I immediately thought he had been mobilised to the incident as the nearest Supervisory Officer to attend but not necessarily for his particular rank. Before I could take the opportunity to appraise him of the situation he immediately asked me 'Where is Sharon?' 'Who's Sharon, Dessie?' I replied, 'My daughter'. He went on to tell me that one of the other passengers had contacted him by phone from the scene and informed him that she was one of the passengers injured. I was dumbstruck. This is every Firefighter's frightful fear-the ultimate in nightmare scenarios-the bad dream that every parent with a teenage child dreads-the terror of the knock at the door, receiving word that your child may have been involved in a road traffic accident. Trying to think fast and not to cause too much distress, I told him we had just released her and that she was on her way to hospital. I then made the mistake of asking him if he would like me to supply a driver for him to take him to the Ulster Hospital nearby. He snapped at me 'Why would I need a driver?'. We both knew then that I had let the cat out of the bag. He got into his car and drove off at speed. It was an unusually thoughtful and quiet crew that tidied up the scene and returned to Station that evening.

When I returned to Knock I thought it only prudent to inform the Chief Fire Officer of what I imagined was going to transpire shortly. I got his home number from Controls and rang him, making my apologies for disturbing him so late. I informed him of what had happened and my forebodings about the outcome. He thanked me for my consideration and courtesy, and our conversation concluded. There really was not much else either of us could say until it was definitely established if in fact Sharon was a victim. That, sadly, transpired to be the case.

Her subsequent funeral cortege included, as might be expected, a large contingent of Brigade personnel from all ranks. I recall the poignancy of the moment when I saw her young boyfriend on crutches, himself a victim of the accident, amongst the many ranks of the mourners. Dessie told me later that it was her first formal evening function and that she had made her own dress for it. It was difficult for all of us who heard this and who had been involved at the scene of the accident to hold back the tears. I did not have the effrontery at that time to ask him what were the extent of Sharon's injuries and it was not until a year or so later when he and I were alone during a visit by him to Knock

Station that I posed the question. His words were 'Allan there wasn't a bone that wasn't broken in her body.'

Divisional Officer Dessie Graham retired from the Brigade several years later when his Service was completed. He went to work as a Fire Prevention Officer in Belfast City Council. Sadly he died a few years into his retirement unfortunately not living long enough to enjoy the fruits of his labours. Heartbreak is still a condition not to be found in any of the medical dictionaries.

CHAPTER 10

Reflections and Ruminations ....

Casualties-Mind over Matter?... Pre and post traumatic stress disorder-PTSD-have often been described by those in authority as all a question of mind over matter. In the perspective of the Fire Service 'we' don't mind and you don't matter. 'Pull yourself together' is another sterling piece of advice freely handed out from the Ivory Tower as though we are all Toby jugs with handles all over us which we pull on when we are trying to determine whether to change our underwear or find holes to put our fingers in as the bits of metal whizz by with that peculiarly evil thrumming noise.

I have often been asked by interested parties, both during and after my service, how do you cope with the Spectre of fatalities, mutilation, and dismemberment? My immediate response would usually be, 'with difficulty.' But to give the questioner an honest considered and serious answer it might involve wandering off down the tortuous highways and by-ways of my mind. In my case seeking usually entails large measures of golden nectar. I am glad to say I have never come out the other side of the emotional and mental maze yet. So I have had to

"... here, take this asprin".

repeat this exercise regularly and assiduously. I offer no magic solutions nor potions. If you have lived life at the sharp end you will empathise, I hope, with my views. I am dribbling off again.

I am not one of the 'old school' who subscribes to the belief that Post Traumatic Stress Syndrome does not exist. I argued the case with Senior Officers for years to get the Brigade to recognise that there was in fact two types of illness, physical and emotional. Even on one occasion when being medicalled by one of the Brigade's Doctors I could not resist the temptation of bringing the subject up for his opinion. His retort was that he was being well paid for what he did and had no interest in bringing an argument of this nature to the attention of the Brigade. So much for that caring professional.

So the fundamental question arises does this emotional condition exists. The simple answer is, yes of course it does. Unfortunately the condition is as usual exploited by cynical opportunists which of course throws the shadow of deceit across genuine sufferers. These opportunists, an ever increasing number of whom seem to come from the stage, screen, and television, tend to regard this curse as some kind of accolade on the basis you are not a dramatic success these days unless you have been abused as a child, been counselled over the death of your cat, and suffered an expose on the Oprah Show. Where, pray, did I go wrong? There is, nevertheless, a truly serious side to this affliction.

The experts are simply going to foam at the mouth at my simplistic approach to what is undoubtedly a complex subject. I am not offering a trea- tise on the subject just a good old Firefighter's practical opinion based on expe- rience, so you can take it or leave it as you choose.

Unlike the rest of us mere mortals few, if any, psychological experts, or if you are that far gone, psychiatrists, will ever have lived life at the sharp end away from their secluded couches with their ambience of tranquillity and money. It is never a good notion either to destroy the mythology which is cur- rently building up around this topic in Fire Service circles, it does however, need a little gentle debunking and a fresh pragmatic look at the topic.

I have always addressed the subject of PTSD using, I hope, a particular sensitivity of language. I do not regard anyone afflicted with this trauma as being either mentally deficient or unstable. I prefer to come at the issue on the basis of an emotional injury analogous with a physical injury. So is psycho- logical and emotional fitness a prerequisite for this type of work ? It most cer- tainly is, if my experience in my daily work with personnel and indeed the heightened experience while working in Belfast during the Troubles is any- thing to judge by.

In keeping with many another Firefighter I have suffered the effects of this unusual phenomena myself from time to time. It is my considered view that PTSD should simply be recognised and considered as physical and emotion- al exhaustion which by a quirky set of circumstances inevitably leads to emotional injury. I have seen it affect different personalities in different ways over indeterminate time spans during my service. The effects are not necessarily seen immediately-they may be latent for life-and a limited recovery and recognition by the affected individual of the recurring symptoms-and the reactions, look to be about the best that can be achieved by the individual sufferer in the long term.

The condition is best regarded as just another form of injury. We expect and do not find it surprising that when we receive a physical injury it will take time for the bruises to appear, to recover, and for the pain to ebb away, with the resultant physical scars left behind. Why then does it come as such a surprise-and do we have such apparent difficulty in coming to grips with an emotional injury- which is no more, nor no less, the same as a physical injury only this time it is to the emotional system.

Perhaps it is just the failure by the individual to recognise that it is possible to receive this of type of injury that leads to an extended recovery time. The vulnerability of the emotional system to injury seems to parallel the vulnerability of the physiological system to injury. In other words, accidents excluded, if the physiological system is unfit or the emotional system is tired from daily stress or generally unfit due to personal circumstances then the vulnerability to sustaining such injury seems to be greater. The old expression 'my batteries need recharging' is probably unwittingly a truism of that particular individual's emotional state.

Practical experience dictates that there are three essential principal factors which need to be present to create the atmosphere wherein emotional injury can occur. The current physiological fitness of the individual and the emotional robustness of the rescuer-the proximity to, and direct contact with, an entrapped or mutilated victim whether alive or dead-in other words quite literally the face to face or hand to hand contact-and finally, most critical of all, the time span over which this contact is maintained. To sum up therefore, if a rescuer is physically and emotionally exhausted through 'normal' circumstances and is exposed in close physical proximity to a victim or victims, or to the victims relatives or friends, in a highly charged emotional atmosphere, for an extended period of time, then there is the high probability that an emotional injury will occur. The converse seems also to hold true the, 'quick in do it- and out again' leaves less of a legacy.

Immediate post-event counselling after such a scenario, even if available, is of dubious value. Recent research reflects that to relive the events immediately afterwards during so called 'defusing' sessions does more harm than good. In effect the diffusion session is an almost immediate re-run in the mind of the rescuer of the living nightmare that caused the harm in the first place with the associated risk of a hamfisted counsellor pushing the victim over the emotional edge. I might also question the voyeuristic tendencies of some so called 'counsellors' who quite rightly used to be described as 'Nosey old Parkers' or 'kitchen sink gossips' in my childhood.

The emotional 'bruises' acquired may take some considerable time to surface and then be treated. In its own complex way this 'surfacing' may be a healing process in itself. I have know sufferers to appear perfectly well for years after the principal event only for the condition to surface due to a completely unrelated accident or other stressful occurrence. It most certainly helps to talk to someone who was there and shared the horror of this or that experience. How could anyone understand who had not been there at the time?

Half the battle, by the individual concerned, is the recognition and private admission to concerned family or friends that some form of emotional injury has indeed been sustained. Misplaced machismo image, pride, and self respect are stumbling blocks to this process. The essential recognition that this injury is producing unusual behavioural and sometimes physical side effects and that these symptoms are a perfectly normal healthy reaction to the abnormal and nothing to be frightened or ashamed of. That the symptoms will-given either the correct treatment or simply time/rest to suit that individual-heal to an almost apparently complete recovery. This developed understanding either by the individual thinking it through on their own or with assistance of those who truly understand the working circumstances that will occasion such an injury can be especially reassuring to the injured at a delicate point in their recovery phase.

It is after all completely normal to be upset and hurt inside by some of the situations we have all had to deal with from time to time. Repetition and repeated exposure to harrowing events can and do have, in the longer term, a dehumanising effect which is the eternal legacy of this type of work. We would be less than human if we did not recognise what is happening. The recollections we have of such moments will never entirely leave the mind. Unfortunately they are simply stored away in a form of Pandora's Box to be re-triggered some time in the future when time and distance have dimmed a little the awful memory of events. The mind is a weird and wonderful contraption.

It is clear therefore that an individual rescuer with an emotionally unstable family back ground, which may be a temporary phase of any normal family life, or indeed an emotional burden of any description, works less well and is prone to earlier emotional exhaustion than others without such burdens. It is therefore a serious error to commit an emotionally burdened and tired person to the scene of a disaster to work in stressful conditions where they are likely to meet large numbers of traumatised victims. Such individuals usually end up using the remainder of the crew as an emotional life-raft. There is quite enough to cope with without bringing your own problems with you. I have no doubt that those who have worked in an environment with personnel like this will immediately identify with these circumstances that I have outlined and will know only too well the troublesome Watch management problems I have referred to.

So how does the current recruitment system into the Service, in terms of pre rather than post trauma syndrome conditioning, work. Well the fact is no such system of pre-recruitment psychological assessment, during training, nor pre-posting, exists at all. Brigades like other emergency services, until recently, and especially since the introduction health and safety legislation into the workplace, only engaged medical occupational health consultants to carry out physical examinations and assessments. Never psychological. The potential psychological maladies which could inhibit or dictate a recruit's physical capabilities, were always well known, but the potential problems of personnel, who have physical responsibilities not only for the safety of Public, their colleagues, or themselves, have never been adequately addressed.

However there appears to be a developing contrary national trend, which needs to be looked at closely by interested parties, including the medical and legal professions, into job related legal damage claims for Post Traumatic Stress Syndrome resulting from incidents attended. I first noticed this trend develop following incidents like King's Cross Disaster in London which is the obvious incident that springs to mind. Once the financial claims bandwagon starts rolling its going to be hard to turn around. Just look at the upsurge in industrial injury claims there has been since the introduction of the 1974 Health and Safety at Work Act. I do not necessarily blame the individual litigants, of course there are genuine cases, but there are also those out for personal financial gain who now milk the system.

The search for potential sufferers of PTSD should start when vetting takes place during the recruitment process. The job, particularly due to the type of incidents that have to be dealt with, carries a high stress risk factor. Aversion therapy might be a good idea, send them to Northern Ireland for their probationary induction period. So how does it work in reality. Well it still is very much a do-it-yourself self imposed conditioning course.

Personnel from their induction into the Service know that they are likely to have to cope severe injuries and fatalities, including perhaps their own, at some stage of their career. They would be wise therefore to mentally prepare themselves for this eventuality in order to be able to cope with it if ever it occurs. Most do, each in their own informal way. Everyone no matter who, or of whatever rank, length of service, or experience, handles this kind of emotional challenge differently. Like having to deal with other unnatural situations such as heights and claustrophobic conditions some people never really become acclimatised to any of the above and it would be the exception, rather than the rule, for any one person, to be able to avoid facing down the fears experienced by all of us.

This topic is something of a standing joke on a Fire Station whenever a rookie recruit arrives on his first Watch, fresh from training school, full of enthusiasm, anticipation and expectation. Sometimes the individual themselves may timidly or with an air of bravado eventually raise the subject. They are always eyed with suspicion by the 'old hands' wondering how they will shape up to the job. Past fatal or gory shouts may be relived aloud and deeds recounted, when in their presence, in an attempt to solicit and gauge a reaction. It is psychological warfare, Firefighters as well as being kind and considerate, can on occasions be a cruel and callous bunch, but the real purpose of the exercise is to try and determine if the rookie will be an asset or liability to themselves and others. How will they cope with their first fatal?

To answer this question fully, one must by necessity go into some little detail and elaborate on the various types of injury and fatality one is likely to encounter and how the mind is preconditioned to deal with the more shocking aspects of the job. To venture down this path would simply be to venture down the path of the voyeurs serving little useful purpose. However even in this ghoulish matter there are perverse 'rules' and in the exceptional matter of bomb victims perversion is the order of the day. Victims will be mutilated or dismembered beyond recognition. Others blown to smithereens, completely unrecognisable as a former living breathing human being. The latter sickening as it is, however does have the perverse compensating factor of lessening the effect, as you no longer identify the remnants as human beings, sometimes.

This does have the effect of disguising the reality of the situation to a degree as long as one does not dwell on it. So we all deal with this type of exceptional problem in our own way. Some fail to deal with it entirely and become a liability to us all.

On one occasion I had a chap who had requested a transfer to my Station, not necessarily to my Watch I would hasten to mention, as he apparently was having colleague problems at his former Station. This transfer was eventually granted. He was not long on Station before he asked to speak to me. During the informal discussion in my office he disclosed that he was not happy with his new Watch and wished to return to his previous posting. He actually broke down in front of me into tears. I was somewhat taken aback at this request as I considered that I was running a happy ship. I encouraged him to give it a longer trial and settling-in period with his Watch and he reluctantly agreed.

Following this interview I requested my Watch officers to keep an eye on him both on Station and on the fireground. I felt during our talk that I detected a domestic problem. It appeared to me that he had a domineering wife who forced him into making repeated house moves-who did not like him on night duty-and when off duty he had to mind the kids, etc,. Hardly an extraordinary state of affairs. He was obviously under considerable pressure. Reports came back that he had panicked on several jobs while wearing breathing apparatus and had had to leave the building in a hurry. This was serious and I felt that I had no choice but to bring it to the attention of my Divisional Commander, which I did. He concurred with my analysis of the man and the dangers presented to others by his peculiar actions. In my presence he rang the Deputy Chief Officer and outlined the situation and asked, at my prompting, that this Firefighter receive a psychological examination. The Deputy's reply was that the Brigade did not have facility for this type of examination and he suggested that he be referred to his own Doctor.

My Divisional Commander actually rang this chap's Doctor and went over the scenario with him. The Doctor's attitude was predictable. His reaction was one of indignity and incredulity that we as 'non-medical' types should presume to have any perception of psychiatry or psychology and how dare we attempt to meddle in what he snootily considered to be matters confidential between him and his patient. No account was taken by him of the dangers presented by his patient not only to himself but members of the Public. Nor that our opinion in this case of occupational medicine based on considered purely pragmatic experience might be far more relevant than any clinical opinion he might express in his comfortable surgery. I often wondered what this medic's opinion might have been if it was his ass that this Firefighter abandoned on a working job. Bet he would have changed his tune rather rapidly then. When you rear is getting warm it really does focus the mind!

Pressure was eventually brought to bear on this Doctor by the Brigade to refer the man to a National Health Service psychologist, which reluctantly he did. The sting in the tale was that Tommy did not attend for his appointments. The anomaly of the situation was that although contained in the Brigades 'Conditions of Service' was a section whereby personnel in order to attract the benefits of sick leave and sick pay must subject themselves to medical examination by the Service's doctor, when required to do so. As there was no occupational psychologist employed by the Brigade there was a loophole in the Regulations which could be exploited and he did. Tommy was eventually sent on a Breathing Apparatus refresher course which he failed, to hardly anyone's surprise. After intensive on Station training with help from myself, Watch Officers, and colleagues he passed the next course but there was always doubt in the back of everyone's mind whether he was going to be a future weak link in the chain on the fireground, a doubt that will always remain.

Do people of a nervous disposition belong in the Fire Service or any other emergency service for that matter? Certainly not. Did these applicants not have the wit to realise, or did no one tell them when considering joining, that it was not the Boy Scouts they were getting into? We all have become depressed or frightened from time to time because of the dirty jobs we have had to do, that is only natural. Currently personnel just have to pick themselves up, being the professional they are, dust themselves off, sometimes with help of those around them, a start all over again. Much however remains to be done in this field of Fire Service Medicine.

Hero or Harlequin?... This book could not and would not have been countenanced if it had not been for the fact that there has been an continuing terrorist campaign in the Province of Northern Ireland for what is, at the time of writing, in excess of twenty seven years, nearly three generations. This mighty tome was planned and commenced life as a simple tribute to Belfast's Firefighters but has evolved and expanded to encompass some of those issues and events that have been inextricably linked with both the old Belfast Fire Brigade, the Northern Ireland Fire Authority and includes the founding of the Fire Authority for Northern Ireland in 1973.

It has meandered from the intended mainstream stories into the streams, gutters, and sometimes the sewers, of contentious major and minor political issues that needed to be resolved by politicians both local, national, and international and by Elected Members of the various Brigade Authorities and not least by uniformed and civilian administrators who on occasions have been in conflict with a Fire Brigades Union doing its best to represent the perceived best interests of their members and the Public at large. I cannot help concluding, having been a serving Firefighter for what was the best twenty six years of my life, that the Brigade would undoubtedly still have functioned despite their combined efforts, in that the 'Ordinary' Firefighter, would still have accomplished the aim of the Fire Service and would have continued to extinguish the fires and clear up society's mess on the streets of Ulster.

Here, seen through the eyes of an Ulsterman, were some considered and, I hope, thoughtful opinions. The truth as they say will always surely, always out.

Everyone in the world over loves a Firefighter, with the exception, of course, of those countries where the political masters have used them for political purposes in civil disturbances. This could so easily have been the case in Belfast. Thank goodness for the wisdom at that time of our senior Fire Brigade Union leaders, who resisted the dictates and ill conceived thinking of some of the City Fathers and indeed some senior officers in the Brigade who in the early days of the present 'Troubles'; before amalgamation took place in 1973, would, at the instigation of the Security Forces, have had us turn our hoses on street protestors.

Yes, everyone loves a Firefighter, or do they? The Fire Service is generally perceived by the public at large through rose tinted glasses as the heroes of the emergency services. Because they more than any other civilian public service are seen to put their lives at risk in times of crisis in order to save the lives and property of others. They are the only body in the U.K. adequately equipped to respond immediately to a cry for help, no matter where or when that cry comes. Try getting a Doctor at 3 o'clock in the morning on a snowy Christmas Eve? However, the public only sees and hears what the media, government, and officialdom wants it to hear, until that is, somebody blows the whistle. The media has generally been kind to the Fire Service because of their role in society and their heroic deeds-deservedly so-but it would not take a good investigative journalist to have to dig too deep, to unearth some of the sad 'unsavouries' present in this and other public services, some of which I have already related. However it is neither clever, nor fair, to destroy all the mythology.

Human nature, as diverse as it is, therefore displays the good, the bad, the righteous, and the evil in all of us. Firefighters like any other fallible earthling possess all of these traits and are therefore no different than anyone else. Save that they are trained and charged to display the best attributes of human nature, which they do, with a large measure of success. Long may it continue so.

Crises bring out the good and bad in all of us, every Firefighter isn't a hero, no more than every criminal is all bad. There are moral and physical cowards as well as moral and physical heroes in the Service. I believe that people generally gravitate to their own level and to a large degree when they take on the mantle of a particular profession, they also adopt the persona of that profession, or is it visa versa, does the personality of the individuals dictate how the profession is perceived? Go ahead be my guest, test the theory. Try and identify any friends or acquaintances and make a mental comparison of how they reflect the image of their job. Isn't human nature just wonderful?

Freedom's Flickering Candle... By the light of freedom's flickering candle I try to read the smudgy prescription of hopes and aspirations for my children's future. Thirty years of terrorism and civil unrest have seen both communities and politicians squander the opportunity for peace and reconciliation between the factions in Ulster. The now well worn phrase *'Parity of Esteem'* that I first heard coined in August 1994 following the P.I.R.A. ceasefire now rings hollow. As equally, does the understanding and respect for one another's cultural heritage and traditions. Did they ever really exist? Those were heady days in November '95 with President Clinton's well intentioned, courageous, and all conquering visit. Hope was reborn then. In his case William Shakespeare said it all the good that some people do 'is oft interred with their bones'.

I have often pondered in recent times and asked the question of friends- something that ten years ago would have been thought of as heresy if openly raised in debate in either community- what is today's definition of a *'Loyalist'* or a *'Nationalist'*. Does today's Loyalist owe his allegiance to a British government that is perceived by Loyal citizens as championing their cause for a permanent and secure place within the United Kingdom, I think not? Do they still have respect and have loyalty for the Monarchy? Is the National Anthem still played in Northern Ireland and if so, do Loyalists stand out of respect for the Crown? Is the Union flag any longer acceptable? I have yet to hear answers to these questions that are compatible with the old ideals held prior 1968. What does this mean?

So why do Nationalists still cling to this historical and mythical dream in the island of Ireland that it *must* be United? England, Scotland, and Wales are one geographical land mass but I do not hear any crisis to unite and make them as one. In fact the reverse is happening. Do the Nationalists really think that Dublin wants them? Where was the heroic Dublin government when the pogroms of '69 were being committed against the minority? Is the way forward within a developing Europe? Is there an overwhelming case for a new flag, a new tune, a new identity? I think so.

Have the extremists not realised by now that violence will not unite this island's people. The beliefs, minds, and wills of people cannot be subjugated by violence. Neither will a lasting settlement be reached in the Province by governments from afar talking on behalf of two different factions, it is the real people, the so called 'Ordinary' people, who must come together. In the circumstances that prevail in Ulster, the legacy of history, fate, and their politically duped parents have segregated them. It is my belief that *'Loyalist'* and *'Nationalist'* alike should be united in a common cause, that of securing peace and wealth for their children and their childrens' children and their respective loyalties should now transcend the old hatreds that have been manipulated for far too long. It is to this common cause of humanity that the two communities owe their loyalties not to any other institution or body.

I may have fallen, in this book, into a trap that I have often accused the media of during all these troubled years, that of, misrepresenting to the world what is happening in Ulster. The religious terms of Protestant and Roman Catholic have been too loosely used when describing events. It is expedient for the media to pigeon-hole people into a religious category, it saves news-print and column inches. The violence perpetrated here under the guise of religion has no authority nor moral charter from these respective faiths. We do not have control over our place of birth. Neither do we have control over which side of the religious divide we are born into. The United Kingdom as a whole likes to think of itself and to be seen as a Christian country. So does Northern Ireland, but this thinking has little reality in fact, especially when attaching a religious tag to acts of violence. The violent activists within both communities, although having been christened into their respective churches have probably never actively followed that faith since Communion or from the time when they were able to reason for themselves. They would have been given little choice whether or not they would attend worship at church or Sunday school, and would, not unlike myself, be frog-marched to the holy ground by their parents. No, it is an insult to all those people in the Province of Ulster for their religion to be linked with this anguish-even if unintentionally-by a world that has viewed events here through the various media organisations that have exploited and prospered on Ulster's miserable corpse. Yet another issue that needs to be redressed.

Intolerance is the symptom and cause of the Province's malaise and needs radical surgery to excise this malignancy before the case becomes terminal. We have now seen three generations spawned and reach maturity who have never known peace.

When it comes time for the negotiators to walk into the conference room, like the House of Commons, when the Division Bells ring, and the House divides for a vote and the Members trip into their respective voting chambers, two rooms should be made available for our politicians. Each with a sign over the door that reads instead of the 'Ayes' to the right and the 'Nays' to the left *'Intolerance'* and *'Tolerance'*. Those who choose to enter the room of *'Intolerance'* should have the room locked after them and the key thrown away. Those who enter *'Tolerance'* should be locked in and not released until permanent agreement is reached. There are, to date, only two colours in Ulster's visual spectrum Orange and Green. When these are mixed Brown is created, I would settle for this, even if it does remind one of the waste product that has been spoken and created by those who claim to represent the electorate for all these years. How relevant is this to *'Burning Issues!'*.

You may well ask?

Until a negotiated and meaningful settlement is reached-not by two governments who each have their own different agendas and vested interests in seeking a settlement and which are not necessarily those shared by the citizens-but by the people of Ulster and Ireland as whole, Ulster's Firefighters, along with the other emergency services, will continue to shovel up the jetsam and flotsam of human debris from the streets of this Province for another thirty years. For all their dedication, vocation, and expertise there is only one rescue a Firefighter can never carry out that is to save someone or a peoples from themselves.

The Dying Embers of Youth... The year of big changes both from a Brigade standpoint and domestically was 1973. The newly formed Brigade was created by Amalgamation. It was a difficult uneasy time for us all. This was 'future unknown' time.

In 1973 the newly formed administration needed the enthusiastic commitment of all of us in management. Like it or not the die was cast we all simply had to move with the times with the hope of influencing and shaping the new Brigade. It was immediately apparent that this new entity clearly needed all the informed advice it could get its hands on. However it was not long before it was plain to see that this new administration was an omnipotent autocracy which did not encourage nor invite debate from its Officers-in-Charge of Stations. An unhealthy philosophical condition for any new command structure to seek corporate success from. Particularly when it depended on the engine drivers at the bottom end to implement their 'new speak'. This nihilism generated frustration and led to the break down of dialogue in respect of controversial issues. This is the continuing genesis of the Province's problems yet we seemed not to be able to learn this lesson in-house so those issues that needed to be discussed in an open forum by all those who were involved with and who would be affected by policy decisions reached were not to be allowed to make a contribution. Nevertheless I believed I should continue to make the effort.

Any criticism or advice I subsequently tendered was-as far as I had been concerned-always offered with a constructive demeanour, certainly not destructive. I fear though that it was not always perceived this way by those in authority. My constructive advice came from grass roots level. From the school of hard knocks, where a better grasp and understanding of feelings and events is often more readily available and decidedly more accurate. Surely this view is preferable to the insular and detached view often taken by those in senior rank in the administration who by the very nature of their work-through no fault of their own-were isolated in their ivory towers and who were as a consequence inclined to think they knew best. No one seemed to think that it is an incumbent duty upon those in higher office to stay in touch with the rank and file. Those who regularly lay their lives on the line. I felt sadly, that the sound advice proffered was seldom construed as such.

Since my gunshot wound in April 1972, when I had been due that weekend to go to the Fire Service College in England, for a course-which by now was conditional for promotion, but not mandatory-I was not been offered another course until 1983. Was I being deliberately shunned by the establishment because of the position I had often taken on these current management issues and on past issues such as 'Danger Money'?

When Sandra and I got married in 1967 we moved into our new home in Sydenham which was on the suburbs of East Belfast. We lived there for the first five years of our marriage until 1973 in sight of 'trains and boats and planes' as a popular tune of the times so aptly put it. Sandra was eight months pregnant at that time with what was to prove to be her first successful delivery from four pregnancies. By this time in the pregnancy she was feeling, and I was observing, the acrobatic contortions, thumps and bumps of our unborn child. It was either going to be a ballet dancer or a boxer. This particular morning we heard in the distance the unmistakable thud of an explosion going off somewhere in the city. I remember thinking how much longer is this insanity in Ulster going to continue? It was there and then that we decided it was time to move away from the city-if only for the sake of our child-a city we still loved, where we had been born and raised.

I considered it was no longer a suitable place for us to bring up the most precious thing that we were ever likely to have. Enough of life's risks already existed in bringing an infant into this world without the additional travails of trying to rear the baby in a strife torn city with all the physical, mental and moral dangers, that now prevailed in Belfast. I felt it was enough for me to continue working within its precincts, but no way were we going to attempt to raise our child in it. The first of our two children Julie was duly successfully delivered in February in the Ulster Hospital, Dundonald. She weighed in at a thumping 9lb 3ozs. her arrival at this weight certainly helped to make up for 'the might have beens' of lost time and those many unborn babies that we had lost. Christopher, my son, and second born was to come along later in 1976.

In September, we moved into our new home in the little County Down seaside village that we both knew and loved. Sandra had spent a lot of her childhood there and it was where we had spent a lot of our courting time in the early sixties. I never really seriously contemplated a move or promotion from Knock, within the Brigade, from that time onwards. I was in my element and enjoyed Watch life and dealing with the Public too much to give it serious consideration. I had often accused others of their self interest putting domestic contentment before the exigencies of the job, perhaps staying at Knock, was mine. There was the odd time when a seemingly plum job would come up, which I would tease Sandra about simply to gauge her reaction to a move, knowing there was really no way either she or I wanted to leave our now well established residence and circle of friends. Not for us the upheaval, upset, and break in continuity of education for my children. What little success I had had within the job came early, others got their accolades later. I had capitalised on it and had planned domestically and financially for the future, it seemed to me that it would not be long now before I could reap my retirement rewards such was the speed that time flew by.

Too often I have witnessed men prepared to uproot their families and move to the other end of the Province in search of promotion, not once but numerous times. Climbing the ladder of promotion was how some measured success in their lives. Many lived to regret their decisions and admitted openly to this error later in their more mature years. The poor souls, as often as not, when they made the Brigade aware of the difficulties that they had brought on themselves, by moving home-difficulties sometimes imaginary-or as often as not those experienced by their wives-were eventually taken by the hand, and resettled in a more amenable post that suited them and their spouses. One chap on promotion and amalgamation of the two Northern Ireland Brigades chose on promotion to accept a move for him and his young family to 'Derry from Belfast for fear he would be passed over for promotion if he refused the move. It was years later-to his eternal regret-before he was able to return.

By July 1987 nearly fourteen years had passed since amalgamation in 1973 the year in which I had transferred back to White Watch, Knock as an operational Station Officer. My God, fourteen years I thought, have come and gone. It just seemed just like yesterday when I stepped back onto Knock Station. I had loved this job, for fourteen years now and I had nailed my own particular flag of convenience to the mast. Had I overstayed my time and welcome? This was now the question that I needed to address and for which an answer was required. From being the blue eyed boy of the Brigade and a rising star in 1969, I was by now the longest serving Station Officer Watch Commander in Belfast. Was this to be considered as a plaudit or an embarrassment. Was I becoming a Dinosaur? Was fourteen years at Knock too long? Was I losing my operational touch? Was I as mentally fast on the fireground as I used to be-I doubted it.

A series of minor back injuries I had sustained over the years were now dogging me and giving me hell. I had been diagnosed as having several damaged discs and was on occasions having extreme difficulty turning out of my bed on Station, at night, to calls. My legs were deciding to go 'walkabout' on their own at unpredictable times, due to attacks of sudden and unexpected pain. I was becoming a safety hazard and liability to myself and others. No one in the Brigade knew officially of this-remember self preservation-this was another facet of it. To disclose my condition would have meant being medically discharged by the Brigade Doctor. Too soon, I thought, to be discharged.

I felt I had a positive contribution to make to the Brigade yet and in any case I had insufficient pension time in service-I had not yet reached the magic twenty six years service, when going out on medical grounds attracts full pension rights. Why throw this away, something which I had worked for and contributed to financially, all these years. This was my dilemma, what to do?

Then I thought why not have some of the luxury of a 'normal' life that others, less deserving were getting. I had nothing left to prove either to myself or the Brigade. Was this sour grapes creeping in on my part, or was it the necessity of survival? A sideways move or promotion to a less physically demanding post was certainly attractive and became more desirable with every passing tour of duty. A horse shoe can only hold so much operational luck and by now mine must be nearly empty.

This was one bone of contention that the membership had with the local committee of the Fire Brigades Union over the years. Personnel who could have been placed in less rigorous jobs, due to health conditions, were disqualified from them because of the Fire Brigades' Union's stance. No matter what job one holds down within the Brigade one must be operationally fit for firefighting. The policy which they adopted was contrary to that of other Union committees on the mainland and was often counter to the interests of the individual members they represented. There were cases when personnel could have moved into non operational posts, but because of this policy, they were forced into early retirement on medical grounds, this suited some but not others.

I believe the Regional Committee feared if they allowed posts to be filled by invalids, that this could lead to an elitist position being created, within the Brigade, where specialist jobs such as Fire Prevention, would eventually, no longer be open to the rank and file. Operational personnel, when they move into an F.P. post, either temporarily or supposedly permanently, as often as not, most come back out, eventually, to operational duties. The experience and knowledge gained undoubtedly has a beneficial effect on their operational duties. This was something that I knew at first hand, as the Fire Prevention Department in my early formative few years as a rising star was something of a transit camp for me between operational posts. The spin off benefits and experience gained would be lost if Fire Prevention departments were not open to operational staff. However when I pondered on it for sometime it became clear that no one was going to come along and hand me a job on a plate. So a change of job would have to be competed for, something which I had not done for a long time.

My affections had always lain out on the fireground with the Public I served and the men I had been responsible for. By contemplating a move would I be betraying the loyalties and principals that I had adhered to all these years, when others had simply cast theirs aside? My last thoughts on the matter-in conjunction with Sandra-before making a decision on what course of action to follow was that not only does charity begin at home, it also ends there.

My decision to try for a move was not only coloured by the above criteria, but by the fact that a strained relationship had existed for some time, between myself and my Divisional Commander. There was very high sickness record within the Brigade, I was considered by him to be one of the offenders, this having been contributed to not least by a number of minor injuries caused over the years in the service of the Brigade.

By August I had applied for two posts. One was District Officer in charge of Newtownards and Portaferry Stations. Both lay within the Ards Peninsula, and were manned by part time retained personnel. I had this post on a temporary basis for a year in 1983 as a Temporary Assistant Divisional Officer. It was a pleasant change. I got to know and like the Retained personnel in the four Stations-as they were then-that were under my care. Working with them over the period of a year had largely dispelled many of my misgivings-probably attributable to their stance in the Firefighters Strike and my own limited contact with them in the big smoke-about the character of their makeup and the value of their contribution to the Brigade. Retained Stations were dotted about the Province as they are in any County Brigade. By their very nature they are often isolated from the main stream of Brigade affairs and are therefore dependant on the links established between themselves and their District Officer in keeping them supplied with up to date and reliable information, which in turn dispels rumour.

By serving with them I was able to appreciate more fully their views and contribution to the job. Retained personnel are seen by their community as something of the local heroes, as indeed they are, a certain clannishness still exists within their ranks, outsiders are treated with suspicion, and it was I who had to gain their trust. I virtually worked on my own and was domiciled at the Station during working office hours, giving fire cover with the use of a staff car from home. The only drawback for someone like myself was that it was a solitary and lonely post after being used to the camaraderie, hustle and bustle of a whole time Station. This would have been a nice job to land permanently, no moving house involved. It would have been nice to finish my time at 'Ards Station. Unfortunately this was not to be. Brigade personalities disguised as politics will out.

The second post advertised was for a Personnel and Welfare Officer in the Staff Department at Brigade H.Q.'s. Lisburn. It was a new and permanent post which had been filled on a temporary basis by a number of Station Officers over a period of time. The feed back of information on the appointment was that it was a bitch of a job. Some of the responsibilities that the post holder was responsible for was the efficient operation of the temporary promotion procedures and the compilation of the Brigade's fire reports for onward transmission to the Fire Research Establishment Department of the Home Office for subsequent statistical analysis. Drudgery, and boredom were my first thoughts, but I did not care or thought I did not. It is a job and it needs is a great master, beggars cannot be choosers.

I was fortunate enough to be short listed for both appointments. The interviews fell on the same day, fortunately for me I happened to be on duty at Knock. In the morning I booked of duty and attended the first interview for the position of District Officer 'Ards. This was held in the Committee room of the newly opened Phase I of the new H.Q.'s. building. The panel consisted of the C.F.O. and eight civilian members of the Fire Authority. They were there to see that justice was done and that no fear or favour was shown to any applicants. I had a reasonable interview but nothing spectacular. My knowledge of the personalities that go to making up the Fire Authority was limited to what I had been told by some of my F.B.U. colleagues. Some were considered to be well intentioned do gooders, others, some of whom had served on the old B.F.B. Police Committee, seemed to make a habit of being appointed to public committees and in my opinion were only there for the attendance money and expenses.

I did not even impress myself at the first interview, usually a sure sign that you did not impress anyone else either. This proved to be the case, shortly after my return to Knock, at lunchtime, the Chief rang and informed me that I had been unsuccessful. At least he had the courtesy to put me out of my misery quickly and not leave me living in hope and dying in despair. A prodigy of mine who had been a Leading Firefighter on my Watch at Knock had gotten the job. Davy Dickson, a good common-sense bloke and well qualified, better so than me, but with less operational experience. It was now the younger man's turn to leave the old hand floundering in his wake, just as it once had been mine. I had no regrets. The Chief wished me good luck for the afternoon interview.

After lunch, into the car and up to H.Qs. again. The Lord loves a trier I thought to myself as I drove the eight miles along the back road to Lisburn from Knock. When I was summoned in for the second time, before I entered the lion's den, the Chief came out and told me to 'go in there fighting'. I did not know if this was a good omen or that I was well down the list of favourites. A deep breath and in I went, here goes I thought, shit or bust. The questions posed, surrounded what I thought the role of a Personnel and Welfare officer should be. As I always had a commitment to my men it was easy to expound my theories. Answers came naturally I rabbited on merrily and shut up before I talked myself into trouble. Yes, I felt a little happier about this one. On arrival back at Station the phone bell tolled for me again. This time the Chief gave me his congratulations. Near panic set in immediately, I did not know whether to laugh or cry. What have I done I thought? Now I have to tell my boys, but the Brigade tom-toms did the job for me. This was to be a step into the unknown. I was about to breath in the rarefied air of the heavens and to walk with the Gods.

My appointment was to take effect from the 1st November 1987. My Watch organised a farewell dinner on Station for me on the evening of the 28th October. I was delighted to see previous Watch members take the trouble to attend. White Watch Knock for some of them had been their first taste of operational life within the Brigade and I had been their first Watch Commandeer. It had been my first command back in 1969 as a Temporary Station Officer so the Watch had fond memories for us all. Most had been transferred on promotion. I liked to think of myself as having been their mentor in that my influence, teachings, and guidance, had inspired and assisted them in climbing up the ladder of promotion and success in their chosen profession.

A few of my old colleagues and Watch Officers chose not to attend. This move of mine, to them I suppose seemed like a betrayal on my part, this was their unspoken way of letting me know their feelings. Knowing what I knew of my own physical condition I could not tell them that it was no such thing, but was simply an exercise in survival and self preservation for me and my family's future standard of living. After having been presented with a handsome, inscribed plaque-with my Christian name wrongly spelt on it-Alan as opposed to Allan-I always take pleasure out of telling someone who commits this sin that there is an 'L' of a lot of difference. I gave my farewell speech-it was delivered not so much as a simple goodbye to the Watch but more of a valedictory address to the operational side of my Fire Service career. For one who had been used to addressing my Watch from a lecture plinth it took me all my time to get through it without choking up. After twenty four years of Watch shift duty, that night duty was to be the last time I slept on a Fire Station.

The next morning I awoke early and went into Tom Fleming's room he was the current Sub Officer on the Watch. I told him that I was slipping away early before the rising call and asked him to take charge. I knew what the boys would have planned for me. A 'tying up' and a good soaking with a jet, if I was lucky. At worst, tied to a lamp post outside the Station for the early morning public to view as they passed on their way to work.. It was not the indignity of it that I was running away from, more the mental pain of this kind of final goodbye. So I got offside without any hassle. As I drove home that morning to Donaghadee alone with my past thoughts and memories of the last twenty four years, little did I realise that I was closer than I knew-not only to the end of my operational service- but also to my Fire Service career, full stop.

The new Headquarters building in Lisburn had been under the planning for years. When I arrived to take up my new post Phase I of the building had been completed. It was an impressive building. with its nearly completed new mobilising Control-room with its state of the art computer technology.

In my mind the ensuing months would determine whether or not I would continue in the Service. This was dependant on a number of factors. Firstly, if I liked the job and could cope with the changes that were inevitable. Secondly, if I liked the working environment and if some of my long held convictions and forebodings about the administration, both uniformed and civilian were not realised. In the eventuality I found that I could cope with the duties of the post, but did not like it. One of the principal reasons was that it was far too iso-lated from the Brigade that I knew and understood. I was smothered by my new high flyer of a boss who was at one time a rookie Firefighter under my command in Ardoyne. I was unable to any large degree to develop the post as freely as I thought it should be in keeping with the role as a Personnel and Welfare Officer for the Brigade. I felt totally frustrated and treated as a menial, in fact as a glorified office boy, having been used previously for twenty odd years, to being in charge of and looking after the well being of men.

Perhaps it was only to be expected that I might take this jaundiced view after being my own boss for so long but the whole atmosphere of Headquarters did not help dispel these views either. To my disappointment, my suspicions and fears were soon realised. I found that there was a power struggle under way, empire building was in progress, between civilian and uniformed staff for administrative control. Some job references carried out by uniformed personnel might indeed have been more suitably discharged by the civilian administrators and vice-versa. It was often a case of who could get their face imprinted on the memories of visiting Fire Authority members. Yes, Headquarters was the place to be if you wanted to create an impression, get noticed, and seek further promotion, but not to get on with doing a sensible job with a sensible purpose.

At times hypocrisy seemed to reign. The messing arrangements in the new Headquarters building was such that uniformed ranks of Station officer and above, plus senior administrative staff were segregated from the lower ranks both uniformed and civilian, at meal times. This was in a mess where a removable partition had been installed during the construction phase of the building, between the Officers dining area and the 'other ranks'. Much debate had gone on as to whether or not the Union would allow this class distinction to take place when the building was commissioned. The two areas were in fact divided but were opened on those social occasions when it suited, to allow the 'workers' to mingle with the 'bosses'. This simple physical structure was, for me, indicative of attitudes that existed in Headquarters, it was a 'them and us' scenario. Something that had been foreign to me on a Fire Station. I would sit in the mess on occasions, during tea breaks and witness the posturing and pontifications of some Senior Officers, it sounded sometimes like a mutual admiration society. I had always felt that it was the Firefighter on the Fire Station who was in fact the Fire Brigade and still believed this to be the case. At BHQ I found a number of people who had lost touch with their roots and the reality of the job and thought that they were in fact the Fire Brigade. No, I didn't like the atmosphere here one little bit.

An typical example of the hypocrisy was that personnel on Station were never officially permitted to have a supervised and controlled wet canteen as was the case in a number of English Brigades. However it was not the first time nor the last that I was ordered as a staff driver to take one of the female civilian staff to a nearby off licence outlet to purchase alcohol with £200 from the Fire Authority Chairman's entertainment fund, public money I may add. It is not for me to pass judgement on the efficacy of a Chairman's entertainment allowance, however I do feel justified in castigating the practice of the consumption of alcohol by on duty Senior Officers whilst self righteously condemning the rank and file for such surreptitious practises on the Stations.

Entertaining in the Staff Department usually took place behind closed doors whether it was for a visiting dignitary such as Her Majesty's Inspector of Fire Services or on the appointment and promotion of a Senior Officer. Doors to the first floor Staff Department corridors would be closed and only those directly involved with the function were permitted in the vicinity. Eating and embibement of alcoholic beverages would then ensue to the point when, on numerous occasions some senior officers, who were on duty and bound to respond to fire calls, had to be driven home by subordinate senior officers. These were the law makers of the Brigade, how does this Square in their language with no drink on Fire Stations? Double standards were the order of the day I always knew this Spectre would someday come back to haunt the perpetrators.

One of the more interesting aspects of my post as Personnel Officer was my role of Conducting Officer in Disciplinary cases. This involved setting out the old Headquarter's Boardroom for hearings, seeing that the Chief was given all the written evidence and conducting witnesses in and out. One particular case I recall being involved in was that being heard against a young Station Officer from the Fire Prevention Department at Knock. He had been charged with misappropriating a Brigade staff car in that he got a driver to chauffeur him to the Larne ferry terminal in order that he could commute to Stranraer in Scotland to have a clandestine liaison with a female friend whom he had met whilst on a course at the Fire Service College in Gloucestershire. They say that love will always find a way, the poor chap was caught with his pants down, in every sense of the word.

The case was heard and the accused was found guilty, the Chief awarding him a Reprimand for his trouble. This would stay on his record for several years before being expunged. It must not have done him much harm for on my retirement he got my job in Headquarters, on second thoughts, perhaps that was an additional punishment.

Ask not for whom the Watch Bell tolls... I stuck the post until June 1988, and no, I did not feel inclined to join the rat race and go for further promotion. On the 16th June I cleared my desk in preparation for going on summer leave, I knew I would never be back. Off I went with my family to France and on my return went on indefinite sick leave. I was told by a surgeon that I was to undergo another abdominal operation. Following this in January I had decided in my own mind it was time to call it a day. With a little bit of help from a sympathetic Brigade medical advisor we mutually agreed that because of my abdominal and back conditions I was a liability to the Brigade. So twenty six years of service came to an abrupt end. So perhaps I had been rather prescient when I had said my farewell to the boys of White Watch Knock on my transfer to Brigade Headquarters in October '87. That had been my final farewell, for I never received one from anyone in Headquarters. In September of '89 I wrote and asked the Chief, Mr. Ken Mc Neill, for a reference of my Service, this is what I received.

'TO WHOM IT MAY CONCERN'

'This is to confirm that the above named was employed in the Fire Service on 29th July 1963. During his service he rose to the rank of Station Officer.

On 1st October 1987, Mr. Wright was transferred to the Personnel Department at Brigade Headquarters, and following several bouts of illness he retired from the Brigade on 2nd September 1989 for medical reasons'.

I did not know when I received this cold and impersonal note whether to laugh or cry. I mostly felt rage. In ten cryptic lines this 'reference' summed up twenty six long arduous years of service. A large slice of my life. The lack of human spirit in this missive typifies the cynical value that most employers attach to loyal service and its sterility of spirit is counter-productive in the long run. These, of great rhetoric and much pompous hypocritical flourish, are mean spirited and their paucity of vision and compassion only serves to elevate further the blinding torch of inspiration that Firefighters untiringly hold aloft above their 'bosses' corporate, dispassionate, intellectual darkness. Firefighters are worthy of far better.

From time to time everyone reaches a milestone in their life. Clearly I had reached one of my own. It seemed singularly appropriate for me to rest on that metaphorical milestone to spare a few moments to ruminate on all that has transpired during this hectic Fire Service life. I was and continue to be a daytime dreamer. As it says in the Seven Pillars of Wisdom these are the people to be wary of. We can all dream dreams in the twilight hours, that blissful period between sleep and harsh reality, but those who dream by daylight have a habit of fulfilling their dreams. I hope I have fulfilled just a part of mine.

I have now completed my Honours degree in life. Now, I needs must, gracefully surrender the idealism of my youth. I have retired from the Fire

Service, I am sad to say. What of my sunset impressions as I sit on my milestone ?

The terse emotionless statements in my 'reference' can never erase nor tarnish the glorious golden memories of the camaraderie-the excitement-the fear-the challenge-the joys-the failures-the blood, sweat, and most of all the tears. Bombs-carnage-human misery-despair-extremism-and, regrettably, only occasionally, heroism, were no strangers on my pathway of life.

I am proud to have been a Fire-fighter. It is a vocation you either have or you do not. It is a noble calling. There can be no half measures nor half way houses. You commit your life to the service of others or you do not. It is as simple a matter as that. I chose to do so. J'ai regret rien.

I did not set out to acquire trophies but to lend a hand. The peoples on this Emerald Isle know all about conquest, war, poverty, Great Hunger, the four Horsemen of the Apocalypse, and, standing there, in the shadows of the sinister Horses and their Riders-second class citizenship. If you have been there to witness you understand.

The final abiding and reassuring impression I am left with at the end of this great adventure of life is the vision of awe-inspiring compassion that continues to be displayed by the vast majority of ordinary men, women, and children of goodwill of all Ireland's communities when motivated by the abject despair of others. It is indeed the noblest of spirits. I am privileged to have been a mere teardrop in this vast river of collective compassion. Long may it flow on. With all its sham, drudgery and broken dreams it is still a beautiful world full of virtue-you simply have to seek diligently .

Finally, I hope that my many impressions may well inspire, encourage, stimulate and refresh the next generation of Firefighters and hopefully progress, in a pragmatic way, the gift of ultimate compassion available to some strangers who stumbles with their tragic burden somewhere along life's highway.

Until the end of my Service, and even now, I continue to be inspired by the raw personal courage I daily see demonstrated in the streets by the Firefighters of many far off lands to their Public by a new generation of young Firefighters both male and, intriguingly, after all these years, female. Courage is indivisible and genderless. Their valiancy and audacity is nothing less than breath taking. They pause not to question the race, colour, nor creed, of their supplicants. Their courage is not some false spur of the minute bravado rather it is a cold and calculating professional approach to the salvation of their fellow men, women, and children. In spite of knowing on many occasions that all the odds are stacked against them, they still advance ardently into the incident, ready to do battle or pay the price.

'Greater love hath no man ………'

Vade in pace.

(Go in peace)

A. Allan Wright.

1999.

Bibliography ....

Other events that occurred in the outside world in 1968.

January-	U.S. spacecraft surveyor soft landed on the moon.
February-	U.S. planes bombed outskirts of Saigon.
March-	Six Africans hanged in Rhodesia despite Queen's reprieve.
April-	Martin Luther King assassinated at Memphis, Tennessee.
May-	Violent clashes in Paris between students and Police. French workers occupy factories.
June-	Senator Robert Kennedy shot dead in Los Angeles.
July-	Courve de Murville replaces Pompidou as French Prime Minister. Pope issued encyclical condemning all forms of birth control.
August-	Chicago riots at National Democratic Convention.
September-	Departure of Soviet troops from Prague. France again vetos British entry into Common Market.
October-	Olympic Games open in Mexico City. Treaty signed providing for stationing of Soviet troops in Czechoslovakia. Pres. Johnson orders halt to bombing of North Vietnam.
November-	Richard Nixon wins U.S. presidential election.
December-	Apollo 8, makes first lunar orbits, aboard are Borman, Lovell and Anders. China tests thermonuclear weapon.

Other events that occurred in the outside world in 1969.

January-	Soviets launch Venus probe. First docking in orbit of Soyus 4 & 5.
February-	Arab attack on Israeli airliner at Zurich.
March-	Golda Meir chosen as Israeli Prime Minister. Maiden flight of French built Concorde.
April-	General de Gaulle resigns as French President after referendum defeat. Maiden flight of British built Concorde.
May-	Landing of Soviet spacecraft on Venus. Queen Elizabeth II maiden voyage began.
June-	President Nixon and Thieu announce withdrawal of 25,000 troops from Viet Nam. Spain closes frontier with Gibraltar.
July-	Armstrong and Aldrin first men to land on moon. Investiture of Prince Charles at Caernarvon castle as 21st Prince of Wales.

August-	Hurricane Camille sweeps across Mississippi Gulf.
September-	Death of Ho Chi Minh President of North Vietnam.
October-	Peaceful demonstrations of Americans against Vietnam war. Talks in Peking on China-Russia border dispute.
November-	Soviet Union and United States ratify Nuclear non-proliferation Treaty.U.S. renounce use of biological warfare.
December-	E.E.C. Hague summit agree on negotiations for British entry.

Other events that occurred in the outside world in 1970.

January-	Federal Nigerian troops Capture Owerri in Biafra.
February-	Pope reaffirms celibacy as basic law of Latin church. Israeli bound Swiss airliner explodes killing 47.
March-	Queen Elizabeth II begins tour of Australiasia. Nuclear Non-proliferation Treaty in force. U.K. House of Commons rejects Bill to impose sentences of 30 years for murders of Policemen.
April-	Israel bombs Nile delta. Splashdown of Apollo13 after near disaster and complex space rescue, aboard Lovell, Halse and Swigert.
May-	Four students shot dead during demonstration at Kent State University U.S.A. South Africa expelled from International Olympic Committee. French carry out nuclear test in Pacific.
July-	Division of West Pakistan into 4 Provinces. Damages awarded to 28 deformed thalidomide children and their parents.
August-	Cease fire in force along Suez Canal. German-Soviet non-aggression signed between Mr.Kosygin and Herr Brandt.
September-	President Nasser of Egypt dies. World Council of Churches proposes financial aid to African guerrillas.
October-	Dr.Salvadore Allende, Marxist Socialist, elected President of Chile. China and Canada establish diplomatic relations.
November-	President Charles de Gaulle of France dies. United Nations votes to admit China without necessary two thirds majority. U.S. resumes bombing of North Vietnam after two year halt.
December-	Elections in Pakistan. Divorce becomes legal in Italy. General Franco commutes death sentences on six Basque Nationalists.

This small cross section of world events from 1968-1970, which generally reflects mans continuing inhumanity to man, simply raises the question has the world progressed, regressed, or simply learned nothing at all?

A.A.W.

****

CONDOLENCES.

BELFAST FIRE BRIGADE-BRIGADE CIRCULAR No 11/73
Death of Fm. B.H.Douglas Reg.No: 557
Some of the messages, letters, and telegrams of condolence received:
The Officers, Northern Command, H.Q., N.I.F.A.
Londonderry,
Northern Ireland.
Red, White, Blue, Watches Londonderry, N.I.F.A.
Northern Ireland.
Athlone Fire Brigade, Republic of Ireland.
Birmingham Fire & Ambulance Service, England.
Cork City Fire Brigade, Republic of Ireland.
Firemaster & Members Glasgow Fire Brigade, Scotland.
Officers & Men Monaghan Fire Brigade, Republic of Ireland.
Lisburn Branch Fire Brigades Union, N.I.F.A., Northern
Ireland.
Central Citizens Defence Committee, Northern Ireland.
Harry Jackson, Monsanto Chemicals, Northern Ireland.
Fire Force Commander, Northern Ireland Fire Authority.
Angus Area Fire Brigade, Scotland.
Bury Fire Brigade, England
Clones Fire Brigade, Station Officer McGorman, Republic
of Ireland.
Dewsbury Fire Brigade, England.
City of Liverpool Fire Brigade, Liverpool.
Northern Command, N.I.F.A. Divisional Officer Harvey.
Ballycastle Fire Station, Section Leader Elliot, N.I.F.A.
Northern Ireland Fire Authority.
Chief Fire Officers' Association, England.

Chief Constable Royal Ulster Constabulary, Northern Ireland.
Hospital Service Reserve, W Ryan, Northern Ireland.
Red Cross Society, F.Talbot, Northern Ireland.
Belfast Ambulance Service, G.Magill, Northern Ireland.
Moderator of Non-subscribing Presbyterian Churches of Ireland.
Administrator, St. Peter's Presbytery, Milford Street, Belfast, Northern Ireland.
Fire Surveyors Section Ministry of Finance(N.I.) Northern Ireland.
Chief Engineer Belfast & District Water Commissioners, Northern Ireland.
Staff of Fire Magazine, London, England.
Pye Telecommunications, Cambridgeshire, England.
Lancashire County Fire Brigade Ffr. Ellerton, England.
Mr. A.I.Hunter, Dundonald, Belfast, Northern Ireland.
Handful of senior citizens per Mrs. G.K.Oliver, Northern Ireland.
Miss E.M. Perkin, Cardiff,Wales.
R.E. Follows, Hove, England.
Mrs. K. Burrows, West Wimbledon, London.
Miss D. Cobain Sheffield, England.
Mr.W. Channell, Chester, England.
Mr. R.A. Beech, Grays, Essex, England.
Mary & Paul McCormick, Cadogan Park, Belfast.

United Kingdom Fire Service Rank Structure.

Ffr.	Firefighter.
L.Ffr.	Leading Firefighter.
Sub.O.	Sub Officer.
S.O.	Station Officer.
A.D.O.	Assistant Divisional Officer.
D.O.	Divisional Officer Fire.
S.D.O.	Senior Divisional Officer.
A.C.O.	Chief Assistant Officer.
D.C.F.O	Deputy Chief Fire Officer.
C.F.O.	Chief Fire Officer.

ACKNOWLEDGEMENT

Thank you to Denis Waring and Belfast City Council for use of Belfast Coat of Arms on Fire Brigade Badge.

OTHER SOURCES.

Leslie Johnston , Divisional Officer (Retired).
Bobby Pollock , Divisional Officer (Retired).
Archie Culbert, Assist. Div. Officer, (Retired).
Richard Sefton, (Assist. Div. Officer (Retired).
Lloyd Brown, (Ex. Sub Officer).
Jock Hall, Northern Ireland Chairman, Fire Brigades Union, (Retired).
Mrs. Isobel Huddleson and son Ronnie, La Mon House Hotel.
Belfast Telegraph Photograph Library.
Linda Greenwood and staff of Belfast Educational and
Library Board, Central Library. Humanities and Newspapers
Departments.
Yvonne Murphy and staff, Northern Ireland Political Section,
Linenhall Library, Belfast.
Noel Henry, Community Education Officer, U.T.V. Film
Library and Graphics Dept., Ulster Television.
Belfast Newsletter.
Ashleigh Wallace, Journalist, Bangor Spectator, Co. Down
Ulster Hospital, Dundonald, Belfast.
Ulster Museum, Stranmillis, Belfast.

PUBLICATIONS.

Nineteenth Century Ireland-The Search for Stability by D.George Boyce Published by Gill & MacMillan, Dublin, Republic of Ireland.

Chronology of the 'Troubles' 1969-1974, by Richard Deutsch and Vivien Magowan. Published by Blackstaff Press, N.Ireland. 1984.

A Chronology of the 'Troubles' 1969-1993 by Paul Bew and Gordon Gillespie. Published by Gill and Macmillan, Dublin, Ireland.

Forged in Fire, Edited by Victor Bailey, History of the Fire Brigades Union. Published by Lawrence and Wishart, London. 1992.

20 Years, by Michael Hall. A Concise Chronology of events in Northern Ireland 1968-1988. Island Publications, N.Ireland. 1988.

The Kincora Scandal by Chris Moore. Marino Books, Dublin 1996.

Blood on the Flag, by Patrick J Twohig. Published by Tower Books, Ballincollig Co. Cork. 1996.

14 May Days, by Don Anderson. Gill & MacMillan. Ireland 1994.

****

A very special thank you is due to my old colleague and friend Paul Burns, whose creative literary talents for outshine mine. He spent countless devoted hours over a six month period providing additional material during the completion of the final edit of this work. Without his determination, expertise and tweaking, as he would say, accompanied by the cajoling required to squeeze the last ounce of energy from my exhausted brain it would never have come to fruition. All this when we were both sick to death of looking at my efforts on screen, if not one another on occasions. The co-operation shown on the project by two persons from both sides of the Irish religious and political divide exemplifies that which is best in any society and demonstrates what can be achieved by people of goodwill and tolerance. This should serve as a simple lesson to those who inherited intransigence or bigotry dictates otherwise.

Thank you Paul.

****